Sustainable Financial Innovations

Editor
Karen Wendt

External Lecturer
Modul University, Vienna, Austria
Munich, Germany

CRC Press
Taylor & Francis Group
Boca Raton London New York

CRC Press is an imprint of the
Taylor & Francis Group, an **informa** business

A SCIENCE PUBLISHERS BOOK

CRC Press
Taylor & Francis Group
6000 Broken Sound Parkway NW, Suite 300
Boca Raton, FL 33487-2742

First issued in paperback 2020

© 2019 by Taylor & Francis Group, LLC
CRC Press is an imprint of Taylor & Francis Group, an Informa business

No claim to original U.S. Government works

ISBN-13: 978-1-4987-9673-6 (hbk)
ISBN-13: 978-0-367-78047-0 (pbk)

Library of Congress Cataloging-in-Publication Data

Names: Wendt, Karen, editor.
Title: Sustainable financial innovations / editor, Karen Wendt, External
    Lecturer, Modul University, Vienna, Austria, Munich, Germany.
Description: First Edition. | Boca Raton, FL : Taylor & Francis, [2018] |
    Includes bibliographical references and index.
Identifiers: LCCN 2018002461 | ISBN 9781498796736 (hardback)
Subjects: LCSH: Financial engineering. | Sustainable development. | Risk
    management. | Capitalism--Social aspects.
Classification: LCC HG176.7 .S87 2018 | DDC 332--dc23
LC record available at https://lccn.loc.gov/2018002461

Visit the Taylor & Francis Web site at
http://www.taylorandfrancis.com

and the CRC Press Web site at
http://www.crcpress.com

Preface

It was a formidable task to assemble such an authoritative set of contributors' for this publication. It could also be seen as the coming of age of *Innovation and Impact Investing*. Many volumes have concentrated on global and professional perspectives of sustainable investing using concepts like the UN Principles for Responsible Investment or Socially Responsible Investing. This book focuses on investment and finance reinvention with new concepts, new products and emphasises on innovation, which is now in the eye of the storm.

The book as should be recommended reading for all business leaders, investment bankers, intermediaries, pension fund managers and Phd students and for all who are preparing for careers in financial services, technology or social science. All service professionals should be required to reflect on the issues and cases presented herein and to respond in writing, describing their own practice against such a background.

While the social welfare state has been the answer of the 20th century to aforementioned problems, sustainable financial innovation and impact investing using an integral approach may prove helpful in delivering the answers to the challenges of the 21st century. Sustainable Financial Innovation has a potential to create value for humanity. Following the financial crisis of 2008, corporates, banks and national governments have come to realized that they need to increase financial stability, reduce systemic risk, strengthen governance and reinvent the industry in a sustainable cooperative manner inviting innovation for social and environmental good while addressing social and environmental challenges in business through a new approach in investment and finance. Social entrepreneurs and civil action is growing all over the planet. These new entrepreneurs, however, need structured business models and access to capital. The World Bank and the United Nations have estimated that the investment gap is as large as 7 trillion US Dollars. What investors have to create through clever structures is access to capital for those entrepreneurs who are in a nascent stage and need support and capital to grow and become stars of the future—the share companies of the future. This gap will not be solved by socially responsible investing or any tool or filtering approach like governance and ESG. This gap will not be addressed by just investing in the existing vessels, be it on the stock market or the debt market. This gap can only be addressed through new products, new entrepreneurs and newly structured vessels that allow these new entrepreneurs access to the capital market, that emerge in co-creation between disciplines that have been apart before and that now join and create new markets. Green Bonds, Social Impact Bonds, Impact Investing and Social Entrepreneurship are good examples of this. First, however, one has to get the foundation right, otherwise the new marriage will crack and collapse. The foundation is the inner attitude of the investor, the manager, the entrepreneur, the intermediary and the investee and the integral approach to investment and finance include the internal and cultural dimensions of humanity. Integral investment is able to work like an alchemist and turn social capital into financial capital. All authors in this anthology have approached their topic in an integral manner while drawing and integrating different disciplines.

This book will enable readers to gain insights into the current debates, step away from myths that for long have adversely influenced the investment and finance approach and be enabled to move on from simple stereotypes.

I hope this anthology will start off a fruitful discussion and I and all the authors, that contributed to this volume with a lot of passion, professionalism and purpose, are looking forward to making this discussion take some concrete shape and form.

Karen Wendt

Content

1

The Purpose of Doing Business is not Business—It is Flourishing

Why an Intelligent Sustainable Impact Investment Dedicates Resources to the Cultivation of the Mind and the Heart

Diego Hangartner

- -

Introduction

> *Most people are about as happy as they make up their minds to be.*
> Abraham Lincoln

We all strive for flourishing and be happy. Some of us look at economic means to give us a sense of prosperity, while others find pleasure in society, organisation or family as a source of purpose and success. Without question, these aspects of success are important.

But when the basic requirements of our biological survival are fulfilled and there still remains an unfulfilled longing, it seems that something more important is missing. It is alarming to see that in the midst of our society of plenty, many apparently successful people still feel empty. When things

diegohangartner@icloud.com, The Wheel of Mental Balance.
Email: www.diegohangartner.org.

are 'fine' and our biological survival is secure, the question that arises: is why do our feelings of unrest, dissatisfaction and depression continue?

This leads us to ask more profound questions: What do we mean by success and prosperity? What is life's purpose? What brings real well-being?

When thinking about these questions sincerely, it becomes obvious that the pivot where we can find answers to these questions is at the mental level, in the deeper domains of our mind. Answers to these large and central questions are not limited to societal, economic, environmental or organisational well-being; they require involvement of the personal dimension. If we want to lead a fulfilled and truly happy life, we need to understand how our actions and behaviours are formed, what they result in, and ultimately, we need to concentrate on the reasons that can truly lead to well-being.

Business, society and individuals share one commonality—they all aim to prosper. In the modern context, these aspects are highly interrelated and interdependent. Unfortunately, most discussions on economic changes, environmental degradation, social well-being and individual prosperity look at these domains in a very compartmentalised and incomplete manner. Most approaches assume that these domains are independent and that the challenges can be resolved outside of the larger context of complexity and human nature.

Fundamentally, people aspire to prosper in order to lead a good and happy life. Accordingly, their well-being depends on multiple aspects of health—physical and mental health of individuals, a healthy society, business and environment.

However, largely due to human activities including the running of business, the world is facing many critical challenges—the cities have become inhospitable and threaten health, cause environmental degradation, loss of species, water shortage, acidification of oceans and climate change. Only through a pooling in of resources and in particular, a dedicated will and determination of politicians, governments, the NGO sector and, foremost, businesses and individuals can collectively address these issues.

It is evident that we cannot economically ignore the global climate change and financial market challenges because pursuance of economic growth has led us to them in the first place.

It is increasingly clear that the current challenges cannot be solved with the present mind-set and values. These questions cannot be addressed without including the human mind, inner values and their expression in the form of corresponding actions.

The present-day mode of doing business, such as governmental regulations, monetary incentives, tapping into new markets, more (or less) spending will not help to deal with the current challenges. We are expected to consider our inner resources and what defines us as humans—our heart, our courage, our dreams, and our hopes.

In the context of business, most initiatives look at improving the performance of leaders and teams, aim at developing better management tools and practices, help envisioning and implementing strategies and support adaptive change management. Many of these initiatives fail as leaders and workers tend to fall into the same old traps and mental habits. The tools and programmes that leaders learn are rarely directed at the human being who is placed in the midst of such initiatives. As a consequence, individuals often show decrease in resilience, exhaustion, burnout, fears, even depression and suicide, thus making businesses, communities, leaders and co-workers suffer unnecessarily.

If we aspire for a fulfilled life, we cannot disregard the current insights of science, the mental dimensions and the need to balance our minds. A similar sentiment is expressed by the leading business thinker, Gary Hamel, who says,

> "The biggest barrier to the transformation of capitalism cannot be found within the observable realm of org charts, strategic plans and quarterly reports, but rather within the human mind itself. … The true enemy of our times is a matrix of deeply held beliefs about what business is actually for, who it serves and how it creates value."[1]

In the following pages I will address many of these questions. I will begin by exploring the current situation, what this means within the context of business and look at the complexities involved. Then I will look at some of the recent scientific explanations about some of the assumptions and values we hold dear, particularly in view of our motivation/incentive system, values and money, and how to transform them. By drawing on an ever-increasing body of research around cultivation of positive qualities for flourishing, it will become evident how important positive qualities of the mind, like happiness and compassion, are and how these aspects can be trained. Next I will explore some of the consequences for leadership training. A section will follow on different aspects of sustainability (inner vs. outer), the need for identifying and changing mind-sets and the importance of teaching and educating inner values. The exploration will finish with a focus on the connections between organisations, purpose and values, and conclude with an appeal to take interdependence seriously for personal and social well-being.

Where are We Now?

No society can surely be flourishing and happy
of which the far greater part of the members are poor and miserable.
Adam Smith

Over the past 100 years, the standard of living has improved greatly. However, global economic development has also led to a widening of the gap between the rich and the poor besides contributing to environmental changes. The damage done by these 'accomplishments' is not foreseeable and it becomes evident that scarcity of water, oceanic acidification, challenges to the food chain and other domains will only increase and ultimately be felt by all.

Unfortunately, the dominant economic model overlooks the fact that we cannot have unlimited growth depending on unlimited resources, after all, we only have one planet. We cannot outgrow the current condition with established models that have caused the problem in the first place. The emerging situation is increasingly challenging us in our established worldview, particularly because the issues are extremely complex, interdependent; they will not be resolved with one single approach nor with the current mind-set.

The present prevailing mode of business is established on competition, market forces and winning at all costs. It might be argued that these are the rules of the game and that it will be impossible to change them. But if we learn something from history, then it is that changes have always happened. Research in many domains clearly shows that patterns of behaviour are not biological traits but results of conditioning, overarching systems and entrenched habits. Surrendering to our assumed beliefs will not save the society we care for, the businesses we depend on for food and survival and to protect the planet we live on.

Besides taking care of the external limitations and environmental constraints, we need to learn to take care of our internal resources. Concepts and practices of sustainability need to be expanded and applied both to the external world (environment, business, society) and to the inner dimensions of our minds and hearts.

Context of Business

We have always known that heedless self-interest was bad morals.
Now we know that it is bad economics.
FD Roosevelt

Most business activities invest with the aim to turn investment into profit, but the question remains: What is considered profit? Is it just financial, or are there other forms of profit?

It is often said that business works independent of persons and that values, attitudes, society and environment do not matter. But ask any leader or employee, and it will be clear that the person, her character, his kindness and the style of interaction with others highly matter. In the current landscape of business, the major challenge is to align personal values with external circumstances and in order to align inner purpose with external requirements, we are nothing short of a deep personal and institutional transformation.

If we look closely, the majority of reasons why we work and how we spend our earned income are not purely for economic or for survival reasons, but largely due to emotional motives—the car model we buy, the types of food we eat, the surroundings we live in.

If the purpose of business is to increase one's well-being and not only to maximise profit, then business leaders, employees, shareholders and organisations at large will need to learn new ways of thinking about the effects of their actions—not only the societal, environmental and monetary impact—but also their impact on the mental flourishing of all involved.

The financial crisis in 2008 showed clearly that markets are not a neutral mechanism that result in collective well-being. The theory of market equilibrium needs to be replaced by the view of a market as a dynamic, interdependent relationship that is both shaped by our mind-sets and choices, and at the same time reciprocally shapes our mind-sets and choices. This requires a deep understanding of interdependence and how the mind works.

Another flaw in mainstream economic thinking is the real price and profit of a product or business. Many so-called *externalities* are excluded or ignored in the process of determining the price and the profit. Inclusion of externalities can be regarded as a shift from the *growth-transactional model* of economics toward a more *sustainable-relational economic model*. The new economic theory goes beyond linear supply/demand exchange models to more sophisticated models of co-creation. Of equal importance is understanding how to serve the real human needs with renewable resources and capturing the value created through this. These needs go beyond merely material 'economic needs; they have to include emotional, social, and ecological needs.[2]

Unfortunately, most businesses and leaders are stuck—the existing paradigms keep them locked in a reactive mind-set, focused on their own needs and those of the stakeholders and top management. When an adverse situation develops, they just hang on and hope for improvement the next time around. It takes all their energy to keep the current business going, avoid losses and pay employees' salaries. Yet, some companies plan for the future—they embrace a proactive mind-set. They have the mind-sets, resources and foresight to weather the storm and create shared value.[3] They include multiple levels of value and complexities and represent reality more accurately.

Complexity and Interdependence

> *As the world becomes increasingly interdependent and fragile,*
> *the future at once holds great peril and great promise. … We must join together*
> *to bring forth a sustainable global society founded on respect for Nature,*
> *universal human rights, economic justice and a culture of peace.*
> UN Earth Charter

Successful global companies are becoming increasingly aware of the complexities of interdependence and interconnectivity—and their successful leaders integrate these qualities not only in the company, but foremost in themselves.

Individuals are not independent; neither are companies, societies, nations, or any system. Due to globalisation, economic, environmental and migration challenges, the current world is realising how true the concept of interdependence is. If we remain stuck with the view and value that individuals and businesses are independent, then we are prone to get into more problems because reality will reveal its nature of interdependence. It is therefore, critical to look at issues from a more interdependent and, in the words of the Dalai Lama, holistic perspective.

The concept of interdependence has been central to the Buddhist notion of the world, humans and of consciousness. Since the Buddhist tradition has an over 2500 year-long history of looking at reality as an interdependent phenomenon, it is to this tradition that I will look as a guide in the coming arguments.

In order to be able to face the highly complex challenges, Buddhist world-view suggests that it is critical to develop both *wisdom* (the understanding of how interdependent various phenomena manifest) and *compassion* (the courageous concern for the well-being of others based on the understanding that everything depends on something else).

Since the nature of reality is interconnectedness, people can only be effective to the extent that they understand and operate according to the reality of interconnectedness. From this it follows that, for any model of business or leadership to be relevant today, it needs to be rooted in the principle of interconnectedness.

Everything exists as a temporary phenomenon dependent on causes and conditions. Since we are fundamentally interconnected and interdependent with everyone on this planet, the key lies in the recognition that by developing a broader, altruistic, responsible mind-set, such inclusion is actually in accordance with one's own interest. Furthermore, one's attitude and way of perception determine a large part of how we experience a situation.

In many dialogues, the Dalai Lama has identified various levels of complexities, which are features of today's business reality. With regard to successful leaders, they need to think holistically and accordingly need to consider their actions at the following multiple levels of complexity:

- Responsibility and care for oneself
- Responsibility and care for others
- Responsibility and care for all

In today's complex and interdependent world, it is the third dimension that is becoming more relevant, which in turn poses an additional challenge.

As business is progressively using the language of science as theirs, I will explore a few key findings of recent research. These insights stem from multiple dialogues between contemplatives (representing the wisdom tradition) and sciences, and need to be considered by the business world to understand and find solutions to the above challenges.

Science

> *Science without religion is lame, religion without science is blind.*
> Albert Einstein

Over the last 20 years, neuroscience, psychology, clinical science, physics, economics and other branches of science have become increasingly interested in exploring the dimensions of personal and societal flourishing. They are progressively translating and confirming insights stemming from the wisdom traditions, as they are looking at the following questions— What is reality? What role does consciousness play to articulate, or maybe even create, that reality? Can the mind have an impact on reality? What does it mean to be happy and well?

Many of the business models, advocated by the grand economic thinkers like Milton Friedman (The Business of Business is Business) or John Maynard Keynes, are in principle, beliefs or ideology only but do not represent the scientific facts.

A few years ago, in my role as the COO of the Mind and Life Institute,[4] I had the privilege to organise a large conference in Zürich, together with Tania Singer and Matthieu Ricard, who are two leading experts in the fields of neuroscience and contemplative practice.[5]

Whilst the three of us were more familiar with the workings of the mind, we were aware that systems and contexts play a role in the formation of a particular mind-set: culture, childhood/adulthood, environment.

We were particularly interested in the question whether an economic system could, in principle, be altruistic instead of 'serving the fittest'. We wondered whether our innate values were truly egoistically motivated (the classical *homo economicus*), or whether there could be something like an economy of happiness. Of special interest was the question if our current incentive system (where egoistic behaviour seems to fetch big rewards) is appropriate to cultivate well-being, or if we have fallen victim to an immediate, but not so healthy reward habit that, in the long run, could be detrimental to our happiness and prosperity.

For this purpose, we brought experts from a wide variety of scientific fields, like Neuroscience, Psychology, Anthropology, Economics, Business and Leadership, together with His Holiness the Dalai Lama to explore the above questions. The dialogues gave insights into the nature of economic systems, thereby profoundly challenging the belief of a rational and self-centered *homo economicus*.

Current neuroscientific, clinical and contemplative research points towards the fact that with appropriate cultivation and mind training, attitudes, mental qualities and behaviours can be changed. Every thought, every action has a corresponding brain area that is involved in a task. With training, these brain areas can change connectivity with other areas, and alter their own density and functionality. This is true not only for the young and developing brain, but also for the adult brain. Scientists speak of brain plasticity, i.e., the brain changes shape, both by voluntary and involuntary activities, throughout life. Not only are the changes evident in behaviour, but also research has repeatedly confirmed that these changes can also be found in the underlying brain areas. This has huge implications for what is learnable and possible.

The findings illustrate how biology and experience shape our empathic and altruistic behaviour in significant ways. Among experts, compassion and meditation dramatically affect the brain's degree of reactivity to stimuli that depict suffering. It also confirmed that only two weeks of training can change the brain and increase altruistic behaviour. As the neural circuits are plastic, levels of altruism and compassion are not fixed but through proper training, and a corresponding supportive environment, it is possible that a large segment of the population could become more (or less) compassionate.

Furthermore, research confirms the beneficial effects of compassion. When asked about the insights that the Dalai Lama gained from the dialogues between Buddhist science and Western science, he answered: "One of the most important outcomes is a common understanding that love and compassion have profound effects on health, including the immune system, and obviously human relations. Hatred and anger have deeply destructive effects on one's own body, as well as alienating and harming others."[6]

Motivation Systems

Economic theory has long proposed that people are fundamentally self-interested, yet recent research tells a different story. It suggests that each of us possesses a great capacity—maybe even a biological proclivity—for compassion, cooperation and altruism. The Zurich gathering reaffirmed the new model of humans as fundamentally pro-social beings, relegating the myth of *homo economicus* to what it was in the first place—an illusion.

Psychologists and neuroscientists agree that we have several underlying motivational and reward systems in our brain.[7] While the brain is obviously very complex and many differentiations need to be made, the human brain has basically three types of motivational systems:

- Reward or wanting system
- Threat or fear system
- Affiliation or caring system

The *reward* system (also called incentive, wanting or seeking system) is fundamentally related to wanting, pursuing, achieving, consuming and impatience. It is driven by excitement. While it is important for survival, it can get out of balance and overtake other functions. Since this system can evoke euphoria, it also triggers the wish to want more. Forms of this can be witnessed in compulsive behaviours and addictions (to drugs, money, greed, power, sex). When such patterns manifest, they are signs that the reward system has lost balance and has taken over.

The *fear* system alerts us to dangers and is vital for survival but, up to a point. When we see real danger, it is this system that responds promptly. It is implicated in producing feelings of anger, aversion, stress, anxiety and panic. When this system works normally, it signals when we need to act or change our route, moving us to self-protection and safety. But when it is in a constant state of activation, for example, during prolonged stress or threat, it can create serious health issues by increasing our *cortisol* levels.

While the first two systems are critical for our basic survival, it has been proven that for mental well-being it is the *caring* system that is most important. The affiliation system is critical for mother-child bonding, for love, feeling connected and contented, and for our feeling of being wanted or useful. When the caring system is activated and this system's main hormone, oxytocin, is released, one ends up feeling relaxed, calm and soothed.

Although these three systems are at the basis of our emotions and central to our experience, it is probably only humans who can consciously access, activate and train these motivational systems, if we so care. If not, we remain stuck under the influence of these systems and they control us. The system that produces the best and longest effect of trusting, mental health, purpose in life and pro-social behaviour is the caring system.

The Marshmallow Test—Delayed Gratification and the Benefits

A 'now famous' experiment was conducted in the 1960s and it became known as the Marshmallow test. The experiment began by bringing a child into a private room, sitting her down on a chair and placing a marshmallow on the table in front of her.

Then the researcher offered a deal to the child: he told the child that he was going to leave the room and that if the child did not eat the marshmallow while he was away, she would be rewarded with a second marshmallow. However, if the child decided to eat the first one before the researcher came back, then she would not get a second marshmallow. So the choice was simple: one treat right now, or two treats later.

After the researcher left the room, the child was on her own for 15 minutes. The footage of the waiting child (available on YouTube) is rather entertaining. On conducting the same experiment on other childrens, some jumped up and ate the first marshmallow as soon as the researcher closed the door, others wiggled, bounced and scooted in their chairs as they tried to restrain themselves, but eventually gave in to the temptation a few minutes later. A few children managed to wait the entire time.

The surprise finding was only revealed 40 years later. Children who were willing to delay gratification and waited to receive the second marshmallow ended up having higher college acceptance scores (SAT), lower levels of substance abuse, lower likelihood of obesity, better responses to stress, better social skills as reported by their parents, and generally better scores in a range of other measures. In other words, this series of experiments proved that the ability to delay gratification was critical for success in life.

The capacity to postpone instant gratification is now considered to be one of the most important characteristics for success in health, work, and life.

On the other side, the issue of why people act selflessly has long puzzled evolutionary psychologists. If our behavior is truly driven by Richard Dawkins' famous 'selfish gene', why do we waste time and resources on helping strangers? New research provides a plausible answer: Altruists do indeed get rewarded—with better sex lives.[8] Why is selflessness sexy? Arnocky and his colleagues argue that altruistic behaviour is what biologists call a 'costly signal'—an activity that requires some exertion, but also advertises one's attractive qualities to potential mates. Who doesn't want a partner who is kind and giving? So even from an evolutionary standpoint, our 'selfish genes' need a well-functioning society if they are to survive and thrive. It makes sense that over the course of natural selection, a behaviour that helps sustain this positive social environment would be rewarded.

Values

In any exploration related to business and our personal activities, values play a central role. What value do we attribute to success, what is considered success (money, fame, reputation) and what ideologies and values do we abhor (slavery, racism, child labour)?

Values can be defined as a personal regard that something is held to deserve. It also contains the idea of the importance, the worth, or usefulness of something. There are economic dimensions to value (a measure of the benefit that may be gained from goods or service), but also an ethical understanding of value (principles or the degree of importance).[9] These dimensions are not necessarily the same: while health has a high degree of importance and the measure of its cost might prove difficult.

The World Business Council for Sustainable Development (WBSCD) states in its WBCSD Vision 2050 Road Map that there is a need for new values: "Strategic planning towards sustainability requires engaging people in profound change. An inner shift in people's values, aspirations and behaviours guided by their mental models, leads to an outer shift in processes, strategies and practices."[10]

At this point it might be appropriate to investigate values from a particular angle—which values and causes give rise to real mental peace and happiness? Do they depend on inner qualities or outer accomplishments?

Values are obviously culturally defined. Even within a single culture, values change as individuals grow older. However, the current world seems to strongly converge on concepts of success around materialistic or external values. The bigger the house and the more we own, the happier we are.

Research by psychologist Tim Kasser has shown that people with materialistic values often lack empathy; they have fewer friends; they are unhappier, and they are unhealthier than those who consider inner values more important.[11]

If we analyse the dominant economic system, we see that its values are based on material growth, profit maximisation, efficiency, short termism, individualism and linear thinking. But in today's complex and interdependent setting, it has become irrefutably clear that in order to achieve long-term sustainability and personal well-being, we need to look at environmental, economic, societal, psychological and even, spiritual dimensions.

Current research correlates mental states, attitudes and outlook to happiness and well-being. In today's world of distraction and competition, focus, mental balance and clarity of mind are a precious and valuable resource. The new luxury goods are not mere physical things; they are security, an intact ecosystem, friendship, time, happiness, and a meaningful life. Limiting our outlook to values of material growth will neither lead to the well-being of the civil society, nor to that of investors, consumers, and individuals. What we need is a holistic view of the economic, societal and ecological dimension of a single product.[12]

Money

Many people assume that money and happiness are losely interlinked—the more money one has, the more happiness there is. As proven repeatedly, this is only partially true. Financial freedom does give a certain degree of happiness, but only to a point. People who have escaped poverty indeed show a greater degree of happiness than those who are struggling to meet their basic needs. But the more the income increases, the more one tends to socially compare with others. As Nobel laureate in Economics, Daniel Kahneman, writes:[13] There is a strong difference between one's own evaluation of life and one's emotional well-being and that emotional well-being does not increase after a certain income. High income does not buy happiness, but rather creates a *desire* for more money—the next car, the bigger house, the next salary increase. This cycle can produce greed, grasping and sometimes even a wish to harm others.

If there is a relationship between money and happiness, it is that the correlation is opposite to what people think: money does not bring happiness, but it appears that happiness can result in more money. A review by Lyubomirsky, King and Diener[14] of all the available literature revealed that happiness does undeniably have numerous positive by-products, which appear to benefit not only individuals, but families, communities and the society at large. The benefits of happiness, however, include higher incomes and superior work outcomes (greater productivity and higher quality of work), larger social rewards (more satisfying and longer marriages, more friends, stronger social support and richer social interactions), more activity, energy and flow and better physical health (a bolstered immune system, lowered stress levels, and less pain) and even longer life. They found that happy individuals are more creative, helpful, charitable and self-confident, have better self-control and show greater self-regulatory and coping abilities.

Through her current research, Lyubomirsky suggests that there are five cognitive and behavioural strategies that are central to happiness:

- Regularly setting aside time to recall moments of gratitude, i.e., keeping a journal in which one counts one's blessings, or writing gratitude letters
- Engaging in self-regulatory and positive thinking about oneself, i.e., reflecting, writing and talking about one's happiest and unhappiest life events or one's goals for the future

- Practicing altruism and kindness, i.e., routinely committing acts of kindness, or trying to make a loved one happy
- Affirming one's most important values
- Savouring positive experiences, e.g., using one's five senses to relish daily moments, or living this month like it's the last one in a particular location.[15]

Notice that none of these factors for happiness refer to money, but rather speak of building intrinsic goals, instead of aiming for extrinsic ones.

While past research examined the effects of income on happiness (how much more income is supposed to create more happiness), current research suggests that it is equally important to see *how* people *spend* their money. Rather than how much money we earn, spending money on others has a more positive impact on happiness. Research participants who spent money on others experienced greater happiness than people assigned to spend money on themselves.

Every act of exchange, be it monetary or personal, is driven by motivations, circumstances and certain practices. The key therefore is to understand how our mind works, what the drivers in us are and to become aware of the consequences of our actions—not just for ourselves, but also for others.

"Time and money serve as people's two most precious resources", write University of Pennsylvania's Cassie Mogilner and Harvard Business School's Michael Norton in a research review.[16] "Both are scarce (sometimes painfully so), and both can be saved, budgeted, wasted, or spent in the pursuit of life's necessities and joys." They found that people who valued time more than money, who indicated that they would sacrifice money to save time and that they would prefer to work fewer hours, and earn less—tended to have higher well-being, greater life satisfaction, higher positive emotion and lower negative emotion. Why? Previous research found that inducing people to focus on time, rather than money, leads them to spend more time socialising and less time working and be more willing to give to charity—activities that have been associated with well-being.

Scientific research by E. Dunn and M. Norton[17] found that an abundance of desirable life experiences undermines people's ability to savour simpler pleasures. This results in people often feeling disconnected, isolated and lacking joys in the present. This lack, unfortunately, develops into a vicious cycle, which can lead to compensating by becoming busy, competing to match others' possessions and accumulating additional objects of prestige; diverting us even more from the present.

Evidence abounds that one of the most powerful ways to counteract inner emptiness is by stilling the inner voices, investigate the working of the mind and cultivate mindfulness, compassion and introspection.

Cultivation

Education is the most powerful weapon which you can use to change the world.
Nelson Mandela

Research points to the fact that there are fundamentally two principles of approaching life: a basic, more reactive strategy to experience (hunter and gatherer) and a more developed proactive strategy of cultivation. This can be applied to all domains of life, even on the mental level.

Human beings differ in a critical way from animals—they can plan, project outcomes into the future and cultivate results. Anthropologists agree that a tremendous shift in evolution occurred when humans began to cultivate. About 10,000 years ago, humans moved from a culture of hunters and gatherers to a civilisation of agri-cultivation; this went in hand with a shift in mind-sets. Our civilisation is based on the capacity to plan for the future and forego immediate rewards—not eating the seeds for planting, family planning, education systems and smart investments in the hope they will bring a good result in the future.

While I trained and worked as a pharmacist, I always questioned the strong focus on sickness, particularly in the domain of mental illness and psychopharmacology, where there was a lot of talk about disease and ailments, such as fears, psychosis, anger, depression, but I never encountered a discussion about what a healthy mind consists of, even less on how a thriving and happy mind is cultivated.

In a way we could say that all these conditions are below a baseline (below zero), but in no way did we explore what 'above zero' would entail. Early on I mistrusted the assumptions that happiness means the absence of ailments and that it was just a chance occurrence. It was a personal relief to discover a whole discipline that was centred on the exploration of a healthy mind and its cultivation: that tradition is Buddhism.

It was only later, in the 1990s, that Dr Martin Seligman led the emergence of the new field of Positive Psychology. Reflecting my own thinking, Seligman was not so much interested in the negative traits of people, but more in the positive qualities, with a special focus on happiness and well-being. For some strange reason, psychology did not have much interest in that question over most of the discipline's existence.

Seligman is attributed with coining the term "a meaningful life", and he cites several factors and elements that define such a life—positive emotions, engagement, relationships, meaning/purpose and accomplishments (summarised in the acronym: PERMA).

The PERMA model represents a helpful summation of the ground-breaking findings of positive psychology. [P] stands for the study of positive emotions and articulates the following positive emotions to be beneficial: hope, inspiration and joy. [E] signifies 'the engaged life', a life where our unique human strengths are engaged and how this pillar of well-being and growth is actively applied to life and work. [R] underscores how flourishing depends on high-quality relationships, and the centrality of the other being with regard to flourishing. [M] is all about meaning and how, without a life of meaning and purpose, there can be no deep sense of flourishing. Finally [A] stands for accomplishment and that part of well-being that is not fleeting, but enduring.

Through this work in psychology it is now firmly established that these factors play a very important role in personal flourishing—to a large extent independent of the economic position one has. The findings have a deep impact on how we look at life and happiness and have wide repercussions on the understanding of flourishing and well-being. It turns out positive mental experiences are a consequence of how we lead our life, both privately and at work.

Unfortunately, the cultivation approach to our lives can be highjacked by our response-activating mechanisms (the fear and reward systems) in the brain. When those brain areas are triggered, we might respond strongly and immediately, but that need not be. Humans learn by experience *and* by reasoning. Once we have understood the shortcomings of certain behaviours, through insight we can change the perceived value that we attribute to an object. Since values are not inherent, by developing a different relationship we can cultivate a more appropriate response.

Compared to biological functions, cultures and habits shift rather quickly. About 50 years ago, people did not consider physical exercise important. I remember running in the forest when training for my sport; we were considered a bit eccentric, if not crazy. Shortly afterwards, clinical science began to research and correlate the dramatic increase of cardio-vascular diseases, such as heart attacks, with its causes. It quickly became clear that lack of exercise and unhealthy nutrition were the main reasons. This resulted in a change of values and ideas with physical exercise (like running in the forest) being considered healthy, and many people have understood the value of regular physical exercise. They have built a corresponding routine into their lives because physical exercise is considered important and healthy. The cultural shift has happened by accepting and applying the scientific fact that we need to exercise *regularly* to develop physical well-being. This does not imply exercising just once intensively and then it's enough for the rest of the year, or our lives.

But what about the mind? When do we take care of this inner dimension and how do we develop the healthy qualities of the mind? It is a fact that each thought, our daily routines and habits, cultivate and develop our mind and the brain structures related to these functions. Unfortunately, we rarely cultivate our positive qualities intentionally.

Flourishing/Well-being

> *For every minute you are angry you lose sixty seconds of happiness.*
> Ralph Waldo Emerson

Contemplative practices have been around for millennia and their prime aim has been to develop mental flourishing or well-being. These traditions have been advocating the fact that investing in a healthy mind is possible and that the benefits of well-being can be boundless. In a highly interdependent environment for one to thrive, the following aspects of human nature need to be cultivated—compassion, long-term thinking, creativity and mental balance.

As we can witness from the increasing number of research and publications, even science has begun to take this issue seriously. Accordingly, there has been a growth in happiness research, and there is now a large body of research that tells us what is important to acquire happiness. It is no longer mere speculation.

Happiness

What is happiness, and what makes us happy? Researchers describe happiness as "the experience of joy, contentment, or positive well-being, combined with a sense that one's life is good, meaningful and worthwhile."[18]

We know that in developed, and also in developing economies, a major source of happiness comes from good relations with one's spouse, with friends, and with colleagues. Maintaining good social relations is the key. Furthermore, scientific evidence hints that behaving altruistically may make us happier. Alas, the current economic system does not put enough value on this.

One major obstacle to human happiness is envy—people suffer if others with whom they compare themselves earn more. Envy is a very destructive emotion and that raises the important question of how we can overcome it. In the Buddhist view there are mental factors, such as compassion and rejoicing, that can help decrease envy. Buddhist scholar, John Dunne, speaks of Buddhist economics, or more specifically, of holistic economics, that is both internal and external. The highest good we seek is happiness. Empirical research shows that those resources are primarily internal and thus these internal resources of happiness are of the highest value. Accordingly, the resources that lead to this goal are considered most valuable.

We often misunderstand the nature of happiness and the true cause of happiness. One major confusion is the misconcept that sensual pleasures are identical to happiness. We are unclear about the causes of happiness. Buddhist thinking about that confusion poses a challenge to the West because of the life led of distraction and involvement in external economics. There is no time to observe the internal economics as the Westerners often end up chasing after external resources, instead of cultivating the internal resources that are necessary for happiness, for flourishing, for well-being. This is not to say that external resources are not necessary, but by themselves they do not constitute the causes for happiness.[19]

When a cost-benefit calculation is done on the basis of such an understanding, it becomes clear that some actions, i.e., those that lead to mental imbalance and frustration, should be avoided. Many external gains often come at an internal cost (for example, working long hours and passing sleepless nights; anger and aggression in order to gain profit). By taking internal resources into account, the cost-benefit calculation will change.

This does not mean that external exchanges do not matter; they do. Nonetheless, the key is that a change in perspective can be very helpful as it can lead to the cultivation of inner riches. A truly holistic economy takes both internal and external resources into account. This thinking correlates with the earlier mentioned research on *how* to spend one's money.

In the Buddhist context, the fundamental axiom that drives people is the search for happiness. It is this fact that makes all humans equal, but, due to delusions, most of us end up focusing on ourselves only. Our understanding of the world and the reality of interdependence is very limited. Although we aim for happiness, our distorted views and cognitions are driven by self-centredness and this ends up frustrating our search for happiness. Compassion and altruism serve as a way out, directing us from limited and short-term perspectives to inclusive and long-term benefits and goals.

In 2012, the General Assembly of the UN recognised the importance of happiness as a purpose and accepted a resolution by Bhutan to make the conscious pursuit of happiness a fundamental human goal.[20]

Compassion

What is compassion good for? Why should we train compassion? Compassion is the felt wish of all beings to be free from suffering. There are different degrees of compassion–compassion for members of one's own group; an extended form of compassion that includes outsiders of the group; and boundless compassion that does not differentiate, is not biased to any being, including difficult people and even enemies. The shift from smaller compassion to larger, all-inclusive compassion requires intelligence and cognitive training based on reasoning and wisdom. This involves a deeper acceptance that all beings suffer and that they do not want to suffer and is directly aimed at the fundamental cause of suffering.

In a series of intriguing experiments, it was shown that human children as young as 18 months of age (pre-linguistic or just-linguistic) quite readily help others to achieve their goals in a variety of different situations. This required both an understanding of others' goals and an altruistic motivation to help.[21]

Ernst Fehr, a world-renowned professor of microeconomics at the University of Zürich, uses in his research insights from economics, social psychology, sociology, biology and neuroscience to shed light on sociological and psychological aspects of modern economics. To explore co-operative economic exchanges, he developed the *trust game* experiment (also called the social dilemma experiment). By pairing two complete strangers with each other and engaging them in a financial transaction, he was able to measure the degree of trust and the altruistic behaviour of the participants, disproving the long-held belief that humans are innately self-interested.[22] As he explained, "Altruism provides social insurance; altruists help if help is needed. That's very important. Altruism also increases the volume of mutually beneficial economic exchanges. Why? Because we are more willing to keep obligations if there are people in a society who behave altruistically, or who punish altruistically. Altruism helps enforce the cooperative norms that are at the very basis of human culture, of modern democracy and individual liberties."[23]

From the above it becomes clear that pro-social and altruistic behaviour is, to a large extent, built into our system because it is relevant to our survival and well-being. Depending on culture and circumstances, however, much of these innate qualities for personal benefit seem to be lost.

With regard to personal happiness and well-being, cultivating compassion is the most impactful and beneficial mental training possible. Research shows that we are psychologically best regulated when we feel loved, connected, valued (rather than unloved or alone), **and** when we are loving (rather than indifferent, disliking or hating).

It has been proven that compassion has many benefits—it builds trust, strengthens mental health, gives purpose in life and encourages care and pro-social behaviour.[24] What we call the self does not exist independently of others. Compassion is not naïve but realistic because it moves one's misunderstanding of an independent self toward a more correct view that we, and our happiness, depend on the welfare of others. As the Dalai Lama said: "We live in a highly connected world. Therefore, the entire world is part of me; whether we like it or not. An altruistic attitude considers the whole rest of humanity as part of me." By moving away from self-centredness to other-centredness, we begin to see the world more clearly.

In practice, in both religious and non-religious forms of cultivating compassion, there is first an understanding that oneself **and** the others are dear and are worthy of one's concern. On that basis, the practitioner then begins to recognise that the other is in need and cultivates the motivation to help. Tradition recognises three steps of compassion training: First, sharing the feeling of suffering; second, the wish to help relieve that suffering and third, courage, determination and self-confidence.[25]

Why do we need compassion? When asked, the Dalai Lama responded without hesitation: "Our wisdom or intelligence tells us that it brings inner strength, inner peace. It also brings benefits to others. (It's precisely) due to the lack of (compassion and care) that we face many unnecessary problems. By using intelligence, we have to develop a holistic way of seeing the bigger picture. Such a holistic vision brings conviction and peace of mind. A more calm, compassionate mind brings inner strength and self-confidence. It reduces stress, tension, anxiety, fear."[26]

Positive emotions, like empathy, have their limitations—they need the help of intelligence, because intelligence brings purpose and goal. Generally speaking, when we see the possibility of overcoming suffering, our concern for that suffering becomes stronger and more realistic. Without that possibility, what we have is a feeling of concern, some wishful thinking, a lack of enthusiasm and a sense of difficulty. As a result, we may feel helpless, discouraged or demoralised. To train our mind properly, the combination of wisdom and compassion methods are essential.

Mental Training

My friend...care for your psyche...know thyself, for once we know ourselves, we may learn how to care for ourselves.
Socrates

Cultivating positive mental qualities is at the forefront of contemplative practice. The Dalai Lama points out that the purpose of meditation practice is to help develop compassion, mental clarity and other positive mental qualities, such as wisdom, altruism, responsibility, an open mind, with purpose and courage. If our mind is inclusive, compassionate, open to the other, we will be in a much better position to deal with any situation. Accordingly, meditation means to train the mind by cultivating positive values and training pro-social qualities, which lead to a positive, responsible and proactive attitude in life.[27]

Any activity is considered beneficial if it ultimately leads to happiness, undermines negative habits and selfish attitudes. Because it benefits both the receiver as well as the giver, the motivation to help others is considered a positive and healthy mental state. Cutting edge science is increasingly pointing in the direction that positive, wholesome mental qualities like compassion, care, joy, focus and resilience are trainable traits, that have significant benefits for society, business, as well as—where it matters most—at a personal level.

The purpose of mental training practices, such as, for example, mindfulness and compassion meditation, is to reduce the dependency on our automatic responses. As mental power increases, the mind becomes less dependent on physical elements, or biochemical processes.

Some practices (such as mindfulness) work on the premise that by analysing the working of the mind and by developing specific skills and mental patterns, we can overcome negative aspects of our mind and cultivate wholesome qualities.

Recent research confirms these ideas. Neuroscientists have observed that people can learn to shift out of preoccupation with oneself. When concerned about oneself, the self-referencing network is activated and it more or less automatically controls the minds of untrained people. Through mindfulness, the default network can shortcut into the state of mind that is more open to concerns for others and the larger environment. This openness corresponds to an open loop of our brain activities that result in a state of presence, or heightened awareness.[28] It has been shown that compassion training up-regulates experienced positive affect and associated neuronal networks,[29] resulting in more positive experiences in life.

Renowned neuroscientist, Dan Siegel, describes this process as 'integration', which is considered the prime function of a healthy mind.[30] Integration, as Siegel defines it, is not merely an internally oriented process within the brain; it is both embodied and interpersonal (which means that it is shared through relationship with others and the world). The process of integration in fact entails the process of recognising one's natural interconnectedness with the world.

Meditation can help gain clarity about complex issues, as it triggers creative thought. Meditation is crucial to build the resilience to cope with the complex and multitude of stresses in life.[31]

Applying these traditional methods in combination with the current scientific understanding can therefore contribute, and eventually lead to the much-desired mental balance by uprooting the hindrances and cultivate the flourishing of the mind, and by extension, in businesses, society and the world at large.

"It is important to remember that some things have their limitations," says the Dalai Lama. "When material development is concerned, there are always limitations; so in that field it's better to practice contentment. With mental development, for which there is no limitation; it's better not to have contentment there and instead try to further develop it. But usually we do just the opposite. Few pay much attention to mental development. But on the material side, even if there are limitations, all our hope is put into seeing if we can go past the limit."[32]

In the context of business and economics, transparency, truthfulness and a clear and stable mind are vital. If the mind is full of greed, with too much attachment, or with too much hatred, one cannot see reality objectively. Strong emotions distort reality; they cause a mental projection to happen. According to psychologist, Paul Ekman, when a person is angry or full of desire, one's perception changes the object by some 90 per cent. This means that only 10 per cent of one's perception is correct; the rest is imagined.[33]

Due to the nature of the business world there arises an additional challenge. When the mind is full of desire, hatred, jealousy and competitiveness, it is difficult to be calm and the risk of making bad decisions increases. That is why compassion is important. As explained earlier, limited compassion depends on how others react to you and what they can give you. Unbiased compassion is orientated towards genuine well-being of others, regardless of what they can give. Compassion is profoundly helpful to maintain one's peace of mind.

This is also true for the business world: Leaders who have empathy, clarity and altruistic motivation as their source of action simply make better decisions. Leaders who are more mindful and compassionate, who are using these deep transformative practices in their own lives, have more calmness of mind, act differently and can carry more responsibility because they tend to see the larger picture.

Compassionate Leadership

According to Bill George, former CEO of Medtronic and Professor for Leadership at Harvard Business School, the 2008 economic crisis was partially a failure of economics, but in a deeper sense it was a spiritual failure.

Many people believed that, in essence, they could find happiness through material wealth and that the more material wealth they accumulated, the happier they would be. But they found that the opposite was true: they were not happy and were causing great harm to others. He calls for the need to get back to the fact that true meaning can only come from serving other people. For that we need compassion and an altruistic approach that benefit all of society. The leader's role has a deep responsibility to the people they serve: responsibility to organisations and the public. Hence compassionate, authentic leadership is essential. Leaders need to have a positive impact on individuals, on organisations, and on society.[34]

The role of the leader in this century is different from that in the past: it is to bring people together around to the sense of meaning, purpose and values. In the past, it was often the case that the dominant prevalence of motivation was extrinsic (fame, money as a reward, acclaim, adulation and power) instead of the intrinsic satisfaction of helping other people, of engaging in a deeper relationship with people and creating good for the world and for society.

One of the many challenges for leaders is not to get lost on the way because these external gratifications—money, power, titles, status, and prestige—are very appealing. In all that rush, leaders of many failed corporations never developed an inner life; they failed to cultivate their hearts. It is therefore important to secure and enable a lifelong development that is parallel to the development of their inner life and the cultivation of their hearts. Each day, leaders have to practise their values in their lives and lead with their hearts; not just state them.

The ultimate role of compassionate leaders is to create organisations that are altruistic, that serve society. It is the only way to sustain an organisation. The question that arises is: can an organisation create value for everyone it serves—for its customers, its employees, and its investors? Does it create that kind of lasting value? This is an essential requirement for a superior performance in the long term.[35] Such a broad-minded perspective, coupled with a more holistic view, which can see reality in its totality and understand the long-term effects, is essential in leaders today. And for that, they need to train their inner values. The Dalai Lama says: "Now the time has come when ability or vision or intelligence or education alone is not sufficient (for a leader); we need a compassionate heart to be seen as a quality of leadership."[36]

Looking at these deep issues, it is apparent that a new leadership model in business is required. Modern leaders need to be able to effect a sustainable system change at three interrelated levels—the individual, the organisational, and the collective—spanning both inner and outer dimensions.

The most effective executives display moods and behaviours that match the situation at hand, with a healthy dose of optimism mixed in it. They respect other people's feelings—even when feeling sad or defeated—but they also model what it looks like to move forward with hope and humour. Based on the insights from their research into emotional intelligence, Goleman, Boyatzis, and McKee describe in *Primal Leadership*[37] that for all intents and purposes, four components of emotional intelligence need to be in action:

- **Self-awareness** is the most essential competence. It is the capacity to read your own emotions and moods and to realise how you affect others
- **Self-management** is the ability to control your emotions and act with honesty and integrity in reliable and adaptable ways
- **Social awareness** includes the key capabilities of empathy and organisational intuition by showing that you care for others and you can decipher the office climate
- **Relationship management** includes the abilities to communicate clearly and convincingly, disarm conflicts and build strong personal bonds

These four components are critical to develop and maintain inner sustainability.

Sustainability

> *Ours is a world of looming challenges and increasingly limited resources.*
> *Sustainable development offers the best chance to adjust our course.*
> Ban Ki-moon, Secretary-General UN

Sustainable could be understood as supporting a long-term perspective in combination with a careful handling of resources, but what resources are they—inner or outer, physical or mental? What is meant by long-term—physical thriving or mental flourishing and well-being?

In the context of this exploration, I draw the attention to inner mental resources. We rarely take them into account; we only do so when we experience a disappointment, a mental crisis, or even a burnout. We do not know how to take care of our inner resources. Once we know which resources we value—outer, inner, or a balance of both—we will understand much better how we use and deplete them, as well as how we can restore them.

With regard to a business operating in the context of its environment, any impact and corporate sustainability ideas need to be seen alongside four broad groups of stakeholders:

- The person and the inner landscape
- The value chain (customers, suppliers, investors, regulators [primary stakeholders], including the sectors, industry and competitors)
- Society (secondary stakeholders, including communities and civil society)
- Ecosystems (nature, environment, biodiversity and the next generation)

When we think about the relative roles of competition and cooperation in creating successful economic systems, we need to distinguish between individuals and organisations. Many believe that among organisations, particularly business enterprises, the best kind of relationship is competition, where each organisation tries to do as well as it can and, if possible, better than its competitors. While such an attitude is presented to the outside world, the demands inside a company are for cooperation. Spanning *cooperation vs. competition* is often a difficult stretch because these are two fundamentally different types of relationships. Even the founder of modern economic theory, Adam Smith, stressed the importance of both. Unfortunately, subsequent economic theories have tended to overemphasise the importance of competition, not only between organisations, but between individuals as well.

The shift towards sustainable business implies a departure from the linear three-pronged production process—consumption-financing model in which money is abundantly made available by banks, to a more holistic life-based model in which constraints in financial, natural and ecological resources are recognised as normal and consumers are recognised as citizens. It is a shift from the speculative debt/growth economy to the real economy, not only in a macroeconomic sense but also in terms of understanding the *real* drives of economical value and sustainable business performance. The rules of the new economic game are no longer only to maximise returns on invested capital, but also to create optimum resilience of the system by enhancing well-being, value creation, and performance of the participants within the system.[38]

We need to understand how to act and invest wisely—the motivations, circumstances and practices that will make our giving and our impact as effective as possible. It will not be easy, but research shows us that there is reason for hope. To realise this hope, we need to understand our behaviour, train accordingly our positive qualities of the mind, such as altruism and compassion and gradually change systems and policies that have been built by humans. It is only by doing so that we will be able to sustainably develop and protect our environment and material prosperity, thus ensuring a meaningful and flourishing life.

Mind Set

The world as we have created it is a process of our thinking. It cannot be changed without changing our thinking.
Albert Einstein

The current problems and solutions can be traced back to the concepts, paradigms, beliefs and values that we hold in our minds, i.e., in our mind-sets. Scholars use several terms interchangeably when referring to mind-sets, including worldview and mental models. Mind-set refers to the interior patterns of the mind or frames of reference. Our mind-set determines how we see the world, how we reason and how we make meaning and behave in response to our experiences in the world.[39] According to psychologist Carol Dweck,[40] there are broadly two mind-sets and they characterise a whole world of difference—fixed mind-sets and growth mind-sets. While a fixed mind-set provides short-term security, in the longer term it causes a lot of problems because reality tends to outgrow a particular mind-set. Growth mind-set, on the other hand, provides flexibility and the opportunity to learn. As we have seen in our discussion about neuroscience and brain structure, people can shift and transform their mind-sets. But how?

These questions are researched in several academic disciplines. *Motivational psychology* studies how motivation manifests in an individual's orientation to his or her life or work. *Constructive-developmental theory* is another new field of the study of purpose and meaning-making in leadership. *Leadership psychology* intersects with various other fields, including neuroscience and branches of social psychology, organisational dynamics and sustainability. Here, the concept of shared purpose is recognised as an important leadership attribute. This is particularly the case in the field of *transformational leadership*, a concept that is contrasted with *transactional leadership*. While the latter defines leadership as skills and knowledge aimed at making people work effectively *within the current status quo*, transformational leadership helps others advance to a stronger motivation and higher purpose. Transformational leadership leads to clarity and direction for oneself and for others, who recognise themselves in the purpose.[41]

In reviewing the literature, Tideman identifies the following six mindsets that are relevant to leaders in the future (called 6Cs):

- Holistic thinking, expressed by *Contextual Awareness*
- Compassion, where *Connectedness* to all stakeholders is the basis of action
- Responsibility, driving from a *Centred* and calm self-perspective
- Creativity, in the service of a *Collective Vision*
- Collective effort, which creates value through *Creative Competence*
- Education of mind and heart, developing *Consciousness*, values, and clear mind[42]

Since there are many mental aspects that are considered helpful and beneficial to develop, the foundation for developing a stable and malleable mind can be summarised as the three dimensions of focus—inner, other and outer focus.[43] Those contemplative traditions that have a mind-training component begin with the cultivation of attention, since there is an intrinsic connection between inner, other and outer perception and transformation.

Teaching and Education

The problem is that the entirety of humanity needs altruism or empathy, not necessarily as part of their religious faith, but to reduce certain problems we are facing today due to their absence. We must find a way to promote those values within a secular, non-religious and inclusive perspective.

Dalai Lama

Leaders and their views are not born or made, but cultivated and developed. Successful leaders train the regulatory process of their minds, thus expanding their mind-sets and worldviews. How can these mind-sets and inner values be developed?

It is important to consider the conditionality of altruism and mental states. As Ernst Fehr pointed out, altruism can only flourish when the setting allows it. For example, research shows that when more illegal activities and criminality are observed, it is likely for other individuals, on an average, to be willing to engage in criminal acts themselves. This conditionality is hugely important as it implies that a task for policy-makers, for CEOs, and for everybody in society is to contribute to the expectation that all cooperate, because that in itself generates cooperation. Such an expectation breaks down if you do not have supporting institutions that somehow constrain free riding. Historically humans did this by sanctioning non-cooperation—

criminals are sanctioned, people who do not pay taxes or contribute to the public good are sanctioned, and so on.[44]

Change the Individual or the System?

When asked the question whether changing the individual would lead to this outcome, or whether changing the institutions, laws and regulations would support the flourishing of altruism, the Dalai Lama answered, "Both are equally important. Unless people change their way of life, their way of thinking—unless that takes place, no matter how beautiful the laws are, the beautiful resolutions on paper, etc., there will be corruption and it will not be implemented. But you cannot blame the people alone, because they come from a society where there is a lack of altruism and concern about the welfare of others."[45]

In order to enable such a shift we must nurture the positive things. Positive emotions like warm-heartedness and a sense of responsibility are of benefit to oneself and others. Society as a whole considers compassion and love to be important. Technology, on the other hand, brings immediate results, so naturally people are very excited about that. I think this has led to forgetting our inner values. Material and matter have nothing to do with compassion. But for the last few centuries, we have been very excited about them because of their immense usefulness. "Now the time has come in which we are experiencing the limitation of material values. And we are facing many unnecessary problems. So gradually we are returning to our basic human values with a new appreciation. We are still human beings. We have the experience of pleasure and pain. Material values and technology cannot change these things, and they cannot bring inner peace."[46]

In business terms, a wrong perception of reality is likely to lead to a wrong strategy, missed opportunities for the organisation and to a poor reputation. Worst of all, this prevents an effective approach to address key global challenges.[47]

An increasing number of pupils, students and graduates find themselves rather ill-equipped to face the pressures of modern life, let alone be able to generate creative solutions to increasing social and ecological challenges. These challenges are systematically linked to current knowledge generation and education. For over four centuries we have refined and developed our way of understanding the world, based on the desire for objective and value-free (scientific) knowledge. The school system, which was built to support this understanding, concentrates on developing (disciplinary) brain and rational thinking.

The prime aim of current education is to develop objective, rational and value-free knowledge. We think we 'master' and manage our relationships, the world and ourselves. These cognitive skills may be needed to get a degree and get a job. But these skills have proven insufficient for people to develop to their full capacity as they do not enable people to understand the complexities of today's society, its opportunities and its systemic challenges. We have created an artificial barrier between mind, heart, body, other human beings and our natural surroundings. This creates an artificial schism between schooling, life and work, even though it is in the integration of these domains that we find the sources of health and happiness.[48]

The Head vs. the Heart

As explained above, knowledge of neuroscience and psychology, as well as examples from top athletes and high-performance teams, provide many insights. A subjective and relational experience is an essential element in learning: however, what we call rational or cognitive learning (the 'head') represents only a fraction of human capacity. But it is the subjective experience, including emotions, social skills and motivation (the 'heart') that represents the much-needed ability to adapt to, and overcome, the challenges of today.[49]

According to science, our mind turns out to be more than our physical brain: the neural networks spread all over the body. As Daniel Siegel asserts, the clusters located at the heart ['and the gut'] are not only an integral part of the neural circuitry including the brain. They also serve as a conduit for the activation of feelings, such as empathy, a sense of ethics and justice, an orientation to social relationships and they generate feelings of well-being and contentment.[50]

The heart is not only relevant as a metaphor for the 'soft' or emotional aspect, but is also the foundation of emotional resilience, well-being and happiness, as well as of our relationships with others. Moreover, experiments at the intersection between neuroscience, psychology and mindfulness show that this subjective 'heart' dimension can be cultivated and trained. Besides being a central part of who we are, subjective experience is a largely untapped potential. It is a missing link in our understanding and forms an essential part of how we can upgrade education, business and society at large. To an increasing number of people these inner values provide a new perspective on unlocking human potential for tackling the challenges of today and they do not necessarily come from religion, but come from the inside of oneself.

How can we unlock the heart? Firstly, by empowering the individual to look inwardly and to connect with a feeling of inspiration or passion within. Meditation can help profoundly, but it is not necessarily the only way. Secondly, by encouraging the individual to be compassionate so that it becomes a natural response and to reach out to others. Thirdly, by stepping outside of the usual learning process and perceiving what is really going on.

Organisations

In order for us to develop humanity in a secular world, we need to integrate compassion into our economy and business.
(Ruud Lubbers, former Prime Minister of the Netherlands)

Management researchers Rajendra Sisodia, David Wolfe and Jadish Sheth write in their 2007 bestseller, *Firms of Endearment*:

Today's greatest companies are fuelled by passion and purpose, not cash. They earn large profits by helping all their stakeholders thrive: customers, investors, employees, partners, communities and society. These rare, authentic firms of endearment act in powerfully positive ways that stakeholders recognize, value, admire and even love.[51]

Organisational transformation involves two elements—leadership and every person in the organisation. Both these elements need to be aligned and the leaders need to set the tone so as to be able to inspire every individual. Increasingly, the key is a common mission, when people come together around with a common sense of purpose. It cannot be a set of words but needs to be lived and embodied. If not, people will not develop the necessary trust, but rather become cynical.

The leadership of a healthy organisation has to be fully committed, knowing there will be times when it will be difficult to stay true to the values. They need to go through the whole process themselves because only that can inspire trust in the others. It cannot be a mission statement in a report; it has to be something that goes on inside people and it means a transformation of consciousness. Without that transformation, it cannot work. People need to believe that their leaders really care about them coming together for a common purpose, a set of beliefs and a set of values.

When companies focus on creating value for all their stakeholders, beyond merely shareholders to include employees, suppliers, customers, Nature and society, they perform better in financial terms, especially in the long term. Key challenges for sustainability goals seem to be the notion that the 'incentives are simply not there'. While awareness of social and environmental impacts is present, the implementation of these goals is lacking. In many companies, much of this activity is superficial and largely in the interests of maintaining their reputation. While some shareholders may tacitly recognise some 'value' in a sustainable company, the investment industry has not given strong value to social and environmental impacts in the market. The 'system' simply does not permit it.[52]

The crisis of 2008 resulted in most economic and political authorities amending the system through structural adjustments: bailing out banks, setting higher reserve ratios, creating stricter monetary controls, cutting costs, establishing monetary easing, stimulating consumer spending and so on. Thanks to the crisis, it became obvious that business as usual was no longer an option. By focusing on financial structures alone (such as monetary reform, debt restructuring and austerity), we are avoiding the exploration of the deeper causes of the on-going crisis: a crisis of values, worldviews and vision. We are invited to look at the question of what creates a sustainable economy or resilient society. Specifically, we have been ignoring the human capacity for resilience, initiative, optimism, responsibility and creativity—the human aspect of change.[53]

Over the past 15 years, research increasingly indicates that companies implementing sustainable business practices (not only in words) outperform those that do not.[54] These are public-traded companies that use sustainable models and environmental, societal and governmental (ESG) practices. It is safe to say that a common and shared purpose on the basis of compassion is the best gauge for personal, economic and societal success.

There is a caveat: many businesses are focussing on leveraging human and social capital, but this gives rise to the unhealthy and unfortunately widespread picture of overworked employees. As Harvard University Business scholars, Michael Porter and Mark Kramer, describe:

> "In recent years, business increasingly has been viewed as a major cause of social, environmental and economic problems. Companies are widely perceived to be prospering at the expense of the broader community... a big part of the problem lies with companies themselves, which remain trapped in an out-dated approach to value creation. ... Companies must take the lead in bringing business and society back together. Yet we still lack an overall framework for guiding these efforts and most companies remain stuck in a 'social responsibility' mind-set in which societal issues are at the periphery; not the core. The solution lies in creating economic value in a way that also creates value for society by addressing its needs and challenges: business must reconnect company success with social progress."[55]

Purpose

> *The meaning of life is to find your gift.*
> *The purpose of life is to give it away.*
> Pablo Picasso

It is increasingly evident that the hidden driver of long-term business success is a 'shared purpose' between business, society and individuals. However, most people and companies do not subscribe to the idea that organisations can be transformed into a force for societal good. Although financial needs of business and clients are seen, any constituency beyond that is considered as an *externality*.

Traditional managers are trained in the delivery of quarterly or yearly financial performance, while many do not look further into the future. Many feel trapped in a rat race of performing for the bottom line. When asked about their purpose, many do not have a clear idea—or they have lost it—and experience some sort of *purpose gap*. The result of such a purpose gap is a sense of disempowerment. When the purpose is lost, the only thing that matters becomes survival, the next deal, the next pay-check, the next report to the boss, the next salary review.

How can this vicious cycle of disempowerment and blaming the system be transformed? By helping managers to see that such a purpose-based approach is not a luxury, but a necessity in the face of their increasing dependence on external stakeholders.[56] In 2009, the Dalai Lama recognised this question when he said: "The financial crisis teaches us to look beyond material values and unrealistic expectation of limitless growth. When things go seriously wrong, it is often because a new reality is still being viewed with out-dated concepts, and this is certainly the case with the economy today."[57]

When people can link their work to a higher purpose, they are more motivated to present the best of themselves at work. For that, purpose, compassion, mental stability and responsibility are the core issues.

Triple Value

> *When we are no longer able to change a situation, we are challenged to change*
> *ourselves.*
> Viktor Frankl

In view of the complex and multiple levels of purpose, a corresponding structure and map of care and values needs to be developed. Sander Tideman proposes a conceptual model that contains three levels of considerations:

- *The larger system* (including globalisation, macroeconomics and economic policy, society, ecosystems)—called the **'all'** dimension
- The business *organisation*, and its products and services that are offered in the market—called the **'Org'** dimension
- Leadership, *individual* mind-sets, view, intention, responsibility, ethics, and efforts—called the **'I'** dimension

By studying the changes at these levels, he concluded that at each level we are witnessing a similar shift in paradigm. This is a shift from the *growth-transactional* to the *sustainable-relational* paradigm, which entails an expansion of value creation from purely singular financial value for the benefit of the shareholders to **multiple value creation**, including societal, ecological and economic value for the benefit of all stakeholders. He calls this 'Triple Value'.[58]

Triple Concerns–Triple Values

The current challenges are too complex for any single individual, organisation or nation to solve. When people learn to let go of restrictive mind-sets and adopt more expansive and holistic frames of reference, they often discover new inner resources that empower them to make life-changing decisions. By developing these qualities of the heart, the people become more capable of building sustainable relationships and this enables them to collaborate and collectively find new solutions. Education of the heart therefore should underpin business and management education in particular, as businesses have the means to scale up and reach many people and communities across the world. By extending individual actions into collective systems, personal well-being, societal health, sustainability and ecological resilience will be included.

Based on Nestlé's concept of transforming the value chain, Porter and Kramer describe the concept of 'creating shared value' (CSV), which differs from the traditional redistribution approach underlying the notions of classical economics, corporate philanthropy and corporate social responsibility (CSR). This is not about *sharing* the value already created by firms; instead, CSV is about *expanding* the pool of economic and societal value.

This speaks to the three levels of complexity previously identified as the concept of **Triple Value**:

- Personal ('I') addresses the development of all human capacities. It is not limited to cognitive ability, but includes the physical-emotional-social-societal dimension of human beings (*the whole being*)

- Organisational ('Org') emphasises the need for interactive valuable relationships between employers and employees, between companies and their clients, between students and teachers, and between school, parents, family, community, business, and society (*the relational dimension*)
- Systemic ('All') is concerned with an attitude of taking responsibility for the happiness and well-being of all: oneself, one's relationships, one's organisation, and one's community, society and ecosystems[59]

Performance Indicators

By cultivating the three dimensions of focus (inner, outer, other) and a proper understanding of interdependence and compassion, every individual has the potential to cultivate their mind-sets and align their inner world with the outer world, thus contributing to solving today's problems. In the context of business, it means that by placing leadership and their mind-sets at the foundation of the triple value creation process, it creates a new perspective on the potential role of leadership and personal transformation in solving today's complex challenges.

Conclusion

> *I fear the day that technology will surpass our human interaction.*
> *The world will have a generation of idiots.*
> Albert Einstein

The above explanations aim at tackling the problems of modernity. It brings many disciplines together to explore the operational environment, the societal context of business, the models of human decision-making processes and the challenges for leadership.

The insights can be summarised as follows:

- Genuine well-being and smart sustainable impact investment need to be considered at many levels, including the cultivation of inner resources
- Inner resources depend on mind-set—mind-sets can be trained
- The twenty-first century requires a different type of thinking from that of the previous century. We do not pay enough attention to inner values
- The most important mind-set that ensures the flourishing of internal and external dimensions is intelligent and well-informed compassion
- Our world is highly interdependent and complex and hence the global and social responsibility of business is shifting

- Many problems we face today arise because we lack a profound understanding of interdependence. By acknowledging this interdependent reality, we need to develop awareness and new mental models expanding the 'in group' and shrinking the 'out group', and transforming our mind-sets

- We need to note seriously the new view of the human being. Human nature is not fundamentally driven by greed, materialism, extrinsic motivations and egoism only; of equal importance are the principles of cooperation, moral fairness, altruism, intrinsic motivation and psychological well-being

- The average person is guided by an innate sense of fairness and care, but their environment and surroundings highly condition their behaviour and values

- Creating sustainable economic systems requires us to shift the objective of economic activity away from maximising transactions for economic value, to balancing economical, social and ecological value and well-being

- It is an unavoidable fact that all changes (not only technical or structural) ultimately force the leadership to work with their own emotions (working with the inner self/mind, and the heart) and to identify and develop positive mental qualities beyond cognitive skills. Compassion and wisdom are the most important skills and mental qualities. It requires leaders to cultivate and embody these inner assets in order to unlock a person's full potential—within and in others

- Our own mental dimensions play a central role both for leaders and employees. These qualities can be developed and trained: the brain and our emotions are adaptable and can be cultivated

- Compassion is not just a warm feeling of empathy, but a practice that involves critical thinking and the courage to act

- A mind trained in compassion will have inner strength and self-confidence, which in turn will help to overcome the stress and anxiety that is part of the modern world. It is especially needed for those engaged in leadership

- Leaders need to include personal purpose and develop new ways of engaging with the world

- Teaching inner values, such as warm-heartedness and care, is even more important for managers and business people. People with this attitude will be better equipped in a transparent and highly interdependent world than those who are not

In his many dialogues with scientists, educators, economists and business people, the Dalai Lama repeatedly emphasises the following points. His wisdom may serve as an appropriate conclusion to the above exploration:

"The changes that are needed to bring about a more compassionate society are not coming from the government or companies, or from the UN or the EU, but from individuals. You should create a compassionate atmosphere, first for yourself, then for your own family, and then you can influence others.

"It is no use waiting for the building of a more compassionate society in any other way than each of us applying these ideas first in our own minds, then in a family context and in a business context, and then in wider and wider circles, like ripples on a pond. No one, I believe, should feel they cannot contribute."

"I believe that every individual has the potential to make at least some contribution to the happiness and welfare of humanity. You see, positive things do not come by nature. For positive things we have to make an effort. We must make the effort. Nobody, no one else, can do that. The present generation must make every effort; it is our responsibility." [60]

For more information: www.diegohangartner.org

References

1   Hamel, G. and Breen, B. (2007). The Future of Management, Cambridge, MA Harvard Business School Publishing.
2   Tideman, S. (2016). Business as an Instrument for Societal Change, Greenleaf Publishing, p. 211ff.
3   Tideman, S. (2016). Business as an Instrument for Societal Change, Greenleaf Publishing, p. 217.
4   Mind and Life Institute: www.mindandlife.org/ www.mindandlife-europe.org.
5   Proceedings of the conference published as: Caring Economics, Conversations on Altruism and Compassion, Between Scientists, Economists, and the Dalai Lama, 2015, Picador.
6   Tideman, S. (2016). Business as an Instrument for Societal Change, Greenleaf Publishing, p. 156.
7   Singer, T. and Ricard, M. (2015). Caring Economics, Conversations on Altruism and Compassion, Between Scientists, Economists, and the Dalai Lama, Picador.
8   Steven Arnocky, Tina Piché, Graham Albert, Danielle Ouellette and Pat Barclay (2016). Altruism predicts mating success in humans. British Journal of Psychology.
9   Wikipedia.org; December 2016; there are many more meanings to the noun value (colour, music, linguistics), but for the current discussion the two understandings mentioned should suffice.

10   SBCSD Vision 2050, A Roadmap for Vision 2050, p.10f; www.wbcsd.org/Overview/
      About-us/Vision2050/Resources/Vision-2050-The-new-agenda-for-business,
      downloaded Feb.2017.
11   Kasser, Tim. (2003). The High Price of Materialism, Cambridge: MIT Press.
12   Singer, T. and Ricard, M. (2015). Caring Economics, Conversations on Altruism and
      Compassion, Between Scientists, Economists, and the Dalai Lama, Picador, p. 144.
13   Kahneman, D. and Deaton, A. (2010). High income improves evaluation of life but not
      emotional well-being. PNAS, 107(38): 16489–16493 (in the USA about US$ 75,000).
14   Lyubomirki, King, Diener. (2005). The benefits of frequent positive affect: Does
      happiness lead to success? Psychological Bulletin, 131(6): 803–855.
15   http://sonjalyubomirsky.com/ retrieved Dec. 2016.
16   Ashley V. Whillans, Aaron C. Weidman and Elizabeth W. Dunn. (2016). Valuing time
      over money is associated with greater happiness. Social Psychological and Personality
      Science, 7(3): 213–222.
17   Dunn, Elisabeth and Norton, Michael. (2014). Happy Money: The Science of Happier
      Spending, Simon & Schuster, NY.
18   Lyubomirski, S. (2008). The How of Happiness, Penguin.
19   Singer, T. and Ricard, M. (2015). Caring Economics, Conversations on Altruism and
      Compassion, Between Scientists, Economists, and the Dalai Lama, Picador, p. 91.
20   United Nations (12 July, 2012) Resolution 66/281 on Happiness, Happiness: Towards a
      Holistic Approach to Development. New York, NY: UN General Assembly.
21   Warneken, F. and Tomasello, M. (2006). Altruistic helping in Human infants and young
      chimpansees. Science, 311(5765): 1301–1303.
22   Singer, T. and RIcard, M. (2015). Caring Economics, Conversations on Altruism and
      Compassion, Between Scientists, Economists, and the Dalai Lama, Picador, p. 82.
23   Singer, T. and Ricard, M. (2015). Caring Economics, Conversations on Altruism and
      Compassion, Between Scientists, Economists, and the Dalai Lama, Picador, p. 84.
24   Jinpa, T. (2015). A Fearless Heart, How the Courage to be Compassionate can Transform
      our Lives, Hudson Street Press.
25   Singer, T. and Ricard, M. (2015). Caring Economics, Conversations on Altruism and
      Compassion, Between Scientists, Economists, and the Dalai Lama, Picador, p. 22.
26   ibid.
27   Tideman, S. (2016). Business as an Instrument for Societal Change, Greenleaf Publishing,
      p. 238.
28   Lutz, A., Slagter, H., Rawlings, N., Francis, A., Greischar, L. and Davidson, R. (2009).
      Mental training enhances attentional stability: neural and behavioral evidence. The
      Journal of Neuroscience, 29(42): 12418–13427.
29   Engen, H. and Singer, T. (2015). Compassion-based emotion regulation up-regulates
      experienced positive affect and associated neural networks. Social Cognitive and
      Affective Neruoscience.
30   Siegel, D. (2009). Mindsight: The New Science of Personal Transformation, New York,
      NY, Random House.
31   Singer, T. and Ricard, M. (2015). Caring Economics, Conversations on Altruism and
      Compassion, Between Scientists, Economists, and the Dalai Lama, Picador, p. 181.
32   Singer, T. and Ricard, M. (2015). Caring Economics, Conversations on Altruism and
      Compassion, Between Scientists, Economists, and the Dalai Lama, Picador, p. 144.
33   Ekman, P. (2008). Emotional Awareness: Overcoming the Obstacles to Psychological
      Balance and Compassion, Holt Paperback, NY.
34   Singer, T. and Ricard, M. (2015). Caring Economics, Conversations on Altruism and
      Compassion, Between Scientists, Economists, and the Dalai Lama, Picador, p. 176.
35   Tideman, S. (2016). Business as an Instrument for Societal Change, Greenleaf Publishing,
      p. 109.
36   Singer, T. and Ricard, M. (2015). Caring Economics, Conversations on Altruism and
      Compassion, Between Scientists, Economists, and the Dalai Lama, Picador, p. 181.

37 Goleman, Boyatzis and McKee. (2010). Primal Leadership: The Hidden Driver of Great Performance, Harvard Business Review, p. 179.
38 Tideman S. (2016). Business as an Instrument for Societal Change, Greenleaf Publishing, p. 207.
39 Tideman, S. (2016). Business as an Instrument for Societal Change, Greenleaf Publishing, p. 225.
40 Dweck, C. (2006). Mindset: The New Psychology of Success, Random House, NY.
41 Tideman, S. (2016). Business as an Instrument for Societal Change, Greenleaf Publishing, p. 230ff.
42 Tideman, S. (2016). Business as an Instrument for Societal Change, Greenleaf Publishing, p. 229.
43 Goleman, D. (2013). Focus—The Hidden Driver of Excellence, Harper, NY.
44 Singer, T. and Ricard, M. (2015). Caring Economics, Conversations on Altruism and Compassion, Between Scientists, Economists, and the Dalai Lama, Picador, p. 131.
45 Singer, T. and Ricard, M. (2015). Caring Economics, Conversations on Altruism and Compassion, Between Scientists, Economists, and the Dalai Lama, Picador, p. 95.
46 Singer, T. and Ricard, M. (2015). Caring Economics, Conversations on Altruism and Compassion, Between Scientists, Economists, and the Dalai Lama, Picador, p. 181.
47 Tideman, S. (2016). Business as an Instrument for Societal Change, Greenleaf Publishing, p. 147.
48 Tideman, S. (2016). Business as an Instrument for Societal Change, Greenleaf Publishing, p. 176.
49 Tideman, S. (2016). Business as an Instrument for Societal Change, Greenleaf Publishing, p. 177.
50 Siegel, D. (2013). The Developing Mind: How Relationships and the Brain Interact to Shape Who We are, New York, Random House.
51 Sisodia, R., Wolfe, D. and Sheth, J. Firms of Endearment: How World-Class Companies Profit from Passion and Purpose. New York, NY, Prentice Hall.
52 Tideman, S. (2016). Business as an Instrument for Societal Change, Greenleaf Publishing, p. 129.
53 Tideman, S. (2016). Business as an Instrument for Societal Change, Greenleaf Publishing, p. 164.
54 Tideman, S. (2016). Business as an Instrument for Societal Change, Greenleaf Publishing.
55 Porter, M. and Kramer, M. (2016). The big idea: creating shared value, Harvard Business Review, 1 January–February) 64–77. *In*: Tideman, S. Business as an Instrument for Societal Change, Greenleaf Publishing, p. 168.
56 Tideman, S. (2016). Business as an Instrument for Societal Change, Greenleaf Publishing, p. 129.
57 Tideman, S. (2016). Business as an Instrument for Societal Change, Greenleaf Publishing, p. 164.
58 Tideman, S. (2016). Business as an Instrument for Societal Change, Greenleaf Publishing, p. 167.
59 Tideman, S. (2016). Business as an Instrument for Societal Change, Greenleaf Publishing, p. 178.
60 Singer, T. and Ricard, M. (2015). Caring Economics, Conversations on Altruism and Compassion, Between Scientists, Economists, and the Dalai Lama, Picador.

Part 1
Environmental Impact Finance

2

Investment Turnaround
A New Way of Investing Based on SDGs
Karen Wendt

- -

Investment Reinvented—Sustainable Financial Innovation in the Context of Adam Smith

Behavioural finance, social entrepreneurship, impact investing, zero carbon, Paris Agreement, COP 21 and UN Sustainable Development Goals, green bonds and Social Impact Bonds are merged in Integral Investing.

No society can surely be flourishing and happy
of which the far greater part of the members are poor and miserable.
Adam Smith

    Adam Smith can be seen as the first behavioural economist. He is the author of the invisible hand, the *'Wealth of Nations'*[1] and most importantly, *'The Theory of Moral Sentiment'*.[2] It provided the ethical, philosophical, psychological, and methodological underpinnings to Smith's later works, including The Wealth of Nations (1776) and Essays on Philosophical Subjects (1795). It is interesting to see that this publication appears to be undersupplied in the world of MBAs. The shift to total rationality came with the Nobel Prize-winner Vilfredo Pareto (1897),[3] who banned psychology from economy: "It is an empirical fact that the natural sciences have progressed only when they have taken secondary principles as their point of departure, instead of trying to discover the essence of things. ...

Modul University, Vienna; karen.wendt@modul.ac.at
karen@responsible-investmentbanking.com

Pure political economy has, therefore, a great interest in relying as little as possible on the domain of psychology." And he followed through and described his position thus in a letter to the mathematician, Herman Laurent: "I am not interested in the reasons why man is indifferent between one thing and another. I notice the pure and naked fact. Every psychological analysis is eliminated from economics (retrieved from Bruni/Sudgen 2007)." Pareto introduced the concept of Pareto efficiency and helped develop the field of microeconomics. It took another Nobel Prize–winner, Milton Friedman, to state 50 years later in Methodology of Positive Economics (1953):

"The abstract methodological issues we have been discussing have a direct bearing on the perennial criticism of orthodox economic theory as unrealistic as well as on the attempts that have been made to reformulate theory to meet this charge. Economics is a dismal science because it assumes man to be selfish and money-grubbing, a lightning calculator of pleasures and pains, who oscillates like a homogeneous globule of desire of happiness under the impulse of stimuli that shift him about the area, but leave him intact; it rests on outmoded psychology and must be reconstructed in line with each new development in psychology. ..."[4] According to Friedman, the "business of business is business" and it is not so important whether the assumptions of the underlying model are right, but that the calculated outcomes are workable.[5] Among some more recent Nobel Pize–winners, is Kahnemann, who succeeded in proving that assumptions in the standard economic model are outrightly wrong. A psychology professor at Princeton's Woodrow Wilson School of Public and International Affairs, Kahneman won the Nobel Prize in economics in 2002 for his work—much of it done with the late Amos Tversky—on decision-making under uncertainty. The Royal Swedish Academy of Sciences cited the professor for "demonstrat[ing] how human decisions may systematically depart from those predicted by standard economic theory." In reality, people often act irrationally. In order to be rational one has to assume that the decisions are made in a consistent and coherent manner and that important mathematical principles, like the ranking principle, are not violated. In the 1990s, James Buchanan and Bruno S. Frey were among the pioneers in recognising and empirically proving that not only profit but also ethical considerations, such as fairness or avoiding conflicts, influenced market participants' decisions (Buchanan 1994, p. 132; Frey 1992, p. 139).[6] Recent results from behavioural finance research identify several decisive elements for market participants' actions. In the context of investments, fairness, both in terms of substantial values and procedures, seems particularly relevant (for an overview, see Singer 2012, p. 440, and for risk behaviour, Baisch and Weber 2015, p. 163–167).[7] Accordingly, an important role is attributed to so-called internal constraints motivated—among others—by ethical principles (Stringham 2011, pp. 101–102). With regard to investment banking, new research results indicate that the archetype of a profit-driven rationally acting investor does not exist in reality (Kaufmann 2015)." As Diego Hanartner points out in the introduction to this anthology:

> *"Over the past 100 years, the standards of living have improved greatly. However, the global economic development has also led to a widening of the gap between rich and poor, and it has contributed to environmental changes. The damage done by these 'accomplishments' is not foreseeable, and it becomes evident that scarcity of water, oceanic acidification, challenges to the food-chain and other domains will only increase and ultimately be felt by all."*

The Inconvenient Truth about Investing—You cannot not Invest—Call for an Integrated Model of Innovation

Is the present-day mode of doing business, such as governmental regulations, monetary incentives and tapping into new markets working well enough to deal with the current challenges? It becomes more and more evident that this is not the case. Paul Watzlawick coined the term "One cannot not communicate—Every behaviour is a form of communication" according to Watzlawick's Five Axioms of Communication (1996, 53).[8] The second axiom, states that there are both "content and relationship levels of communication". In extension to Watzlawick we can conclude, "One cannot not invest". Every behaviour is an investment and touches the content and relationship level. The fathers of the Harvard Negotiation Model, Fisher and Ury[9] acknowledge that fact. In Getting to Yes— Principled Negotiations,[10] they balance the content and relationship level without "giving in". Likewise investment is nothing we can just consider from the external domains. We are invited to consider our inner resources and what defines us and our investments as humans, i.e., our heart, our courage, our dreams and our promises.

From the perspective of integral theory (Wilber's 2000). In order to fulfil the promise of parity between people, planet and profit with passion and purpose, we need an integral model that goes beyond the neoclassical theory and takes into account the internal dimensions that express themselves through external actions and behaviours.

> *You cannot create the future using the old strategy tools. ... The big challenge in creating the future is not predicting the future; instead the goal is to try to imagine a future that is plausible, that you can create.*
> Charles Handy

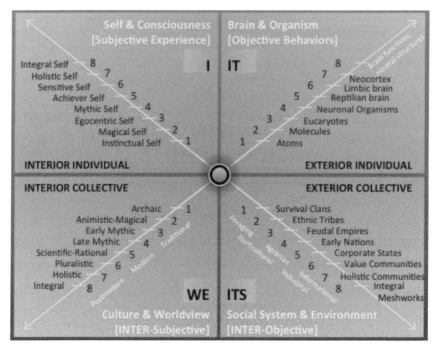

Ken Wilber: A Theory of Everything in Dr. M. Bozesan (2015).[12]

In A *Theory of Everything*, Wilber links his explanatory schemata to real-world problems and situations and in doing so, presents a convincing case that only an integral approach to personal and societal development will get humanity through the difficult times ahead. He distinguishes four quadrants that interact in any decision-making process. The 'I', the individual internal subjective level, the 'WE', the internal collective level which expresses our interests and needs, which we then reveal through choices, behaviour and action on the external level.

In order to address the challenges we will need to leverage on all four quadrants: understanding our internal needs and interests, the collectively shared needs and interests (our cultural framework), the individual artefacts and manifestations of those needs and interests in form of behaviour, products, investments and materials as well as the compound effects we create together when fulfilling our needs and interests with our 'investments'. According to Diego Hangartner, "Businesses, society and individuals share one commonality—they all aim to thrive. In the modern context, these domains are highly interrelated and interdependent. Unfortunately, most discussions around economic changes, environmental degradation, societal well-being and individual thriving look at these domains in a very compartmentalised and incomplete manner. Most approaches assume that these domains are independent and that the challenges can be resolved outside of the larger context of complexity and human nature." In other words we do not integrate the four quadrants that push and pull our decisions.

Integral investors have operationalised Ken Wilber's *Theory of Everything* for use in investment and finance and created an integral investment model which is able to map the push and pull factors that are important for any investment decision.

> *"The application of Wilber's integral model provided us with a very powerful de-risking tool. It gave us a differentiated view of our investees depending upon the vertical altitude in each quadrant (Fig. 1) but also on how well the horizontal integration across the quadrants has occurred. It opened our eyes to a reality that is made of a complex web of interrelated and intra-connected ecological structures, social systems and cultural determinants, all of which are subject to evolution from simple structures to more complex ones."*

Mariana Bozesan AQAL Foundation[13]

The reason why, within the parameters of neo-classical economics, the two territories of felt experience and culture—individual and collective interior—have apparently been excluded, is because it erroneously seemed difficult to prove in a scientific manner (Camerer and Loewenstein 2004). This separation occurred because neither behavioural economics (Kahneman and Tversky 1982) nor scientific psychology existed as academic disciplines at that time. According to Bozesan (2015), "As a result, the interior dimensions were dropped all together and neo-classical economics was reduced to profit and utility maximisation. Based on the prevalent collective centre of gravity at that time, the notion of the self-interested homo economicus (Aspromourgos 1986) was born.

The World Business Council for Sustainable Development (WBSCD) states in its *WBCSD Vision 2050 Road Map* that there is a need for new values: "Strategic planning towards sustainability requires engaging people in profound change. An inner shift in people's values, aspirations and behaviours guided by their mental models, leads to an outer shift in processes, strategies and practices."[14]

The world as we have created it is a process of our thinking. It cannot be changed without changing our thinking.
Albert Einstein

Shared Values

The Harvard Strategy professor, Michael Porter and his colleague Marc Kramer, state in *Shared Values*:

> *"A big part of the problem lies with companies themselves, which remain trapped in an outdated, narrow approach to value creation. Focused on optimising short-term financial performance, they overlook the greatest unmet needs in the market as well as broader influences on their long-term success. Why else would companies ignore the well-being of their customers, the depletion of natural resources vital to their businesses, the viability of suppliers, and the economic distress of the communities in which they produce and sell?"*[15]

Social Entrepreneurship: From Incubation to Innovation

A movement known as collective impact[16] has facilitated successful collaborations in the social sector and it can guide companies' efforts to bring together the various actors in their ecosystems to catalyse change. Incubators have emerged worldwide on a large scale. A business incubator is a company that helps new and startup companies to develop. The U.S.-based International Business Innovation Association estimates that there are about 7,000 incubators worldwide.[17] Europe's European Business and Innovation Centre Network (EBN)[18] association federates more than 250 European Business and Innovation Centres (EU I BICs) throughout Europe.[19] Impact Hubs are opening their doors around the world together with movements inside and outside the impact investing industry. Tanya Woods from KindVillage asks in this anthology: How would you react to the following pitch of a social entrepreneur?

> *"We have some big problems and they have been around a long time. Hunger, poverty, unequal access to education and health care, pollution and climate change, conflict and human rights violations persist globally. These challenges are increasingly complex and the status quo approach is too slow. We can do better and we must do better. With your support, our team will apply some of the most intelligent technology solutions available today—big data, artificial intelligence, blockchain—in a globally accessible and gamified online product offering that not only tackles these issues but also makes you a better person, neighbour and citizen in the process. Our team will exponentially increase the value of every dollar you invest as we reach two billion people, making them better humans too. Invest in us, because we will achieve our mission to create sustainable positive changes everyone can benefit from."*

So would you invest? Her answer to this question is the following: "Five years ago, I would have been sceptical and wondered how many episodes of Silicon Valley this dreamer has watched in the last week on Netflix. Today, I would be more likely to invest not just money, but my time, knowledge, goods and abundant enthusiasm to keep this person going, and to help them focus on creating an excellent solution. Today, I know that if this entrepreneur's pitch is properly executed, what she is proposing is possible in the next three to five years. The UN and its 193 member states and stakeholders have identified 17 Sustainable Development Goals (SDGs) that require priority level attention from all country leaders, businesses and citizens.[20] The 17 SDGs provide implicit insight into what the issues are and what the end goals should be when taking action to address them. Also the World Economic Forum is an ally in social entrepreneurship and Impact Investing. The WEF has stated, that 'reducing inequality and accelerating real, meaningful and widespread inclusive [economic] growth are the most urgent challenges of our age.'[21] In order to make implementation happen, we have to investigate the root causes for poverty and other challenges not only from the eagle's, but also from the duck's perspective, learning from the meta level, the macro, meno and micro level, where entrepreneurs are active in making a difference. The Kind Village team is building social impact technology solutions with a holistic view of the big issues when considering how technology tools could support the achievement of well-being for others. The process of constant self-evaluation is native to technology start-ups and entrepreneurs that succeed. Asking the hard questions and being open to all of the feedback—good, bad, or otherwise because it is essential to developing a great solution that people like, trust and will adopt. Exponential Tech and Sustainable Development goals therefore are no antagonism, they go very well together as allies."

From Intuition to Institution or From Office to the HUB the Learning Organisation

Anais Saegesser from STRIDE, the Un-school for Entrepreneurs Leadership in Switzerland also addresses the large gap between doing well and doing good. *"This relates to the fact that our economic systems take money as the matrix of everything which is seen in the GDP, growth (and not development) units used to govern ourselves and the difficulty to integrate the 'good' in these systems: the good remains an externality, i.e., is not captured by our usual matrix and hence is not used to drive what we do,"* she writes. Whether or not a social business is scalable and how fast it has to scale—a so-called Six Sigma for Social Entrepreneurs—has been an often discussed question in entrepreneurship. It, however, depends on the definition of social entrepreneurship itself and of the context in which it operates. After an evaluation of social entrepreneurship definitions and comparison of social entrepreneurship to other forms, one can argue both ways. One can either argue that further research should concentrate on social entrepreneurship as a context in which established types of entrepreneurs operate or allow for a wider definition as some social entrepreneurs are only able to scale when they have set a new context or a new ecosystem and when they have unlearned paradigms and replaced them with others. Anais Saegesser explains the context factors in her contribution: "Setting the preliminaries to sustainable financial ecosystems: from doing well to doing good." Social or impact-driven entrepreneurship may be part of implementing the Sustainable Development Goals, but do not ask these new entrepreneurs to work with the same tools and within the same boundaries and limited mind sets of the old system that caused the problem in the first place. This may very well imply going beyond six sigma in social entrepreneurship.

Many feel that capitalism itself is at a tipping point. Its reputation has never been so low. This being said, even social entrepreneurs must make a surplus, which they can reinvest in the business to make it financially sustainable and to escape the problems of the 'grant scheme' that finally burns money, as they are not putting in place an effective scheme that allows to redeem the investment.

What about State-of-the-Art Tools—Ready for Mainstream?

The following building blocks of Innovative Impact Mainstream Investments can be recognised as of today. Sometimes they are underpinned with the sustainable development goals or ecosocial standards that were applied before for long by eco-social rating agencies. The topic of integrated ratings and reporting is beyond this anthology, but those interested may have a look at CSR and Financial Ratings.[22]

The anthology will focus on the most advanced concepts and innovative investment tools in Social Entrepreneurship and Impact Investing like social impact bonds, green bonds, proven energy efficiency initiatives—like the Investors Confidence Programme and Social Impact Incentive Schemes for social Entrepreneurs. It will also discuss fiduciary duties in context of climate change and put a special focus with a broader CSR lense on the very important Chinese market.

The following sectors have been identified by investors as being SDG aligned thus far:

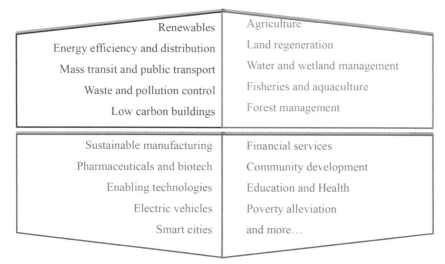

Fig. 2: Taken from EccoScience.www.eccoscience.io.

In **Social Impact Incentives (SIINC),** roots of impact demonstrate in various case studies how social enterprises improve profitability and reach scale around the world, using the SIINC approach. Premium payments for real impact achieved can systematically close the gap between financing demand and supply. Social Impact Incentives (SIINC) empower social enterprises to raise large amounts of investment and to grow sustainably while creating positive social impact at scale.

Roots of impact and the Swiss Agency for Development and Cooperation co-developed Social Impact Incentives (SIINC)—an innovative blended finance model enabling high-impact social enterprises to improve profitability and reach scale. With SIINC, social enterprises are rewarded for the real impact achieved. They monetise on externalities that in the Standard Economic Model are regarded as 'cost' or unwanted externalities. An outcome payer, usually a public funder or philanthropic organisation, agrees to act as a key customer to the enterprise, paying premiums for its social contribution. Thus, impact is incentivised very directly: It becomes linked to the social enterprise's levels of profitability and automatically raises its attractiveness for investors. SIINC launched in 2015 a pilot project in Latin America and the Caribbean and can be seen as an extension or consequent evolution of Social Impact Bonds.

In **Social Impact Bonds (SIB)**, beyond financial innovation, Rosella Care describes the implication of SIBs on the real economy and the public and private sectors and deals with impact matrix and standards.

Defined as financial assets, their objective is to attract investors to fund social programmes by providing them an incentive if the project meets its predefined targets, Social Impact Bonds (SIBs) have become rapidly the most talked-about instruments within the social finance landscape. Considered as the next step in marketisation of public sector delivery (Joy and Shields 2013; Dowling and Harvie 2014; Cooper, Graham and Himick 2016), this particular financial innovation monetises the benefits of social interventions and can be used to enhance the transparency and evaluation of expenditures made by the government (Schinkus 2015). As with the concept of social entrepreneurship, there is a wealth of different definitions of impact investing. One could argue that impact investing currently is in search of a definition. Rosella revisits the definitions and selects the one used by Canadian Task Force on Social Finance (2010, p.5) as:

> *"The active investment of capital in businesses and funds that generate positive social and/or environmental impacts, as well as financial returns (from principal to above market rate) to the investor."*

This definition underlines the simultaneous presence of two different kinds of returns, in which, the first is related to a social or environmental dimension and the second refers to a financial dimension and reflects the pro-active intention to actively place capital in business activities by expecting something that goes beyond a mere financial return. The Global Impact Investing Initiative GIIN emphasises the importance of a theory of change in impact investing stressing that an impact investment should influence the market and its players. Rosella examines this viewpoint from a scientific perspective and provides a case study analysis of prominent cases. According to the Social Finance's database,[23] 74 SIBs have been launched and more than 70 are in a development phase with a total amount of raised capital of $ 278 million. SIBs are actually available in Australia (3), Austria (1), Belgium (1), Canada (3), Germany (1), Finland (1), France (2), India (1), Israel (2), Netherland (7), New Zealand (1), Peru (1), Portugal (1), South Corea (1), Sweden (1), Switzerland (1), UK (32) and US (14). An interesting part of her research is the risk analysis, the value for money analysis and the conclusion that during the last years many instruments have been developed by academics and practitioners in order to measure and compare social value creations (Kroeger and Weber 2016), such as the Impact Reporting and Investment Standards (IRIS) and the Global Impact Investing Rating System (GIIRS), but there is still not yet any universal standard for measuring impact. IRIS is a catalogue of publicly available standardised performance matrix (more than 550) that cover the social, environmental and financial performance of companies, organisations, or funds while GIIRS is a rating methodology that grants up to five social impact stars to rated companies and funds (Kroeger and Weber 2016). However, the SDGs may provide the level playing field for chaning the game and provide the framework for a universal measuring system.

Based on the consideration that using exclusively, the financial parameters are not able to measure the full impact of activities, Social Return On Investment (SROI) is a methodological framework for measuring and accounting for changes in a much broader concept of value (Brandstatter and Lehner 2016), which, according to Rosella, is a mainstream concept as it constitutes mainly a cost benefit analysis. The rest of her contribution deals with the question how banks can be part of the Social Impact Bonds (SIB) market and the implications for scaling this asset class, should the big banks join.

From Social Bonds to Green Bonds

What still is to be investigated and considered for Social Impact Bonds has become a reality for Green Investment, where banks have created a new market standard and instrument: the green bonds and the green bonds principles. In recent years, green bonds have become the rising stars of the global bond markets not only for those who are interested in sustainable finance. Despite the fact that the market share of green bonds is still well beyond one per cent, the public showed strong interest in this kind of financial instrument which is supposed to be the answer of the financial industry to the global ecological challenges, especially to climate change. The kind of innovation linked to the green bonds is remarkable, however nobody should take it for granted that green bonds will end up as an established part of the financial world. The authors undertake a critical analysis of the existing green bond principles and the Climate Bonds Initiative alongside and analysis of the green impact of those bonds. They state, "Given that the volume of green bonds with positive sustainability impact may significantly be less than the quoted 150 billion USD." Then again, the Climate Bonds Initiative claims that the multiple, a whopping 700 billion USD of climate-aligned bonds have already been issued, detecting a 'universe of bonds financing climate-aligned assets that do not carry a green label' (Climate Bonds Initiative 2016a).

For sure, green bonds are at the centre of redirecting capital to a green economy and financing of a rapid transition to a low-carbon and climate resilient economy. Green bonds are in the centre of the strategy to redirect huge financial resources into climate projects which will be crucial in order to reach the two degree target agreed upon in Paris. The Global Information Infrastructure Commission (GIIC)[24] expects green bonds to be the key for tapping the capital at low costs (GIIC 2015). Differentiating between the investors and the issuers view, Klotz and Pex conclude that it is surprising that labelled bonds do not carry a market premium over labelled bonds, although the costs of green labelling are quite significant. They put this finding into context with its implication for market stability and market growth.

Innovation in the Financing of Energy Efficiency

Steven Fawkes, Senior Advisor to the Investor Confidence Project Europe (IPC) introduces us to the world of energy efficiency. IPC is a project of the Environmental Defence Fund, working with a wide array of stakeholders to develop standard methodologies and protocols for energy-efficient project development and documentation. These protocols are designed to reduce transaction costs associated with energy efficiency investment and develop actuarial data to unlock capital markets.

It explores the potential of energy efficiency. In this view, the 'energy efficiency gap' that is often discussed separates the economic potential according to the investor's criteria from what is actually invested in and implemented. The level of implementation is driven by factors, such as the degree of attention paid to the issue by management and the quality of energy management programmes. In organisations with good energy management programmes, we would expect the energy efficiency gap to be small because all, or nearly all, economic opportunities are exploited as they occur.

In reality, all potentials are dynamic and affected by shifting technological, economic and management factors. Energy efficiency needs to be thought of as more like other energy resources. Energy efficiency potentials are in a very real sense, only there when you look for them, in the same way that an oil field, or a shale gas field, only becomes visible when you search for it. Then it has to be developed and exploited. The International Energy Agency (IEA) estimates that in 2015, the total global investment into demand-side energy efficiency was USD 221 billion,[25] USD 118 billion in buildings, USD 39 billion in industry and USD 64 billion in transport. Investment in energy efficiency was less than 14 per cent of total energy sector investment but increased by 6 per cent in 2015, whereas investment in energy supply fell. The US, EU and China represent nearly 70 per cent of the total investment in efficiency. Over the last few years, a number of innovations in energy-efficiency financing products as well as innovations in energy services contracts, market infrastructure and energy markets occurred which are described and evaluated in his contribution.

Steves undertakes a cost benefit analysis, discussing why and how we should use the potential of energy efficiency measures, and he continues with the innovations and presents the Energy Efficiency Financial Institutions Group (EEFIG) and their toolkit. In continuation of the EEFIG

2015 Report findings, the De-risking Energy Efficiency Project Consortium, consisting of COWI,[26] BPIE,[27] EnergyPro,[28] NTUA,[29] Fraunhofer ISI[30] and Climate Strategy & Partners,[31] was formed to support EEFIG during 2016–2017 in its work addressing the fundamentals of energy efficiency investments in the buildings and corporate sectors through two main work streams: the creation of an open source database for energy efficiency investments providing performance monitoring and benchmarking, and the development of common, accepted and standardised underwriting and investment framework for energy efficiency investing.

In November 2016, the EEFIG's De-risking Energy Efficiency Platform (DEEP)[32] was launched with over 7,800 projects in an open-source, pan-EU database to improve the sharing and transparent analysis of existing energy efficiency projects in Buildings and industry. The DEEP now holds data on more than 10,000 projects and in 2017 the present EEFIG Underwriting Toolkit[33] was launched.

Is the Take Up of Zero Carbon Opportunities by Investors sufficient?

For green bonds and the 100 per cent Divest Invest Movement[34] the answer appears to be yes. Important investors like Swiss Re or Deutsche Bank have announced to build up green bond portfolios for at least 1 billion USD. For such investors the green bond labelling is important because it allows them to prove the fulfilment of their announcement.

From a slightly different point of view, rational investors can be expected to optimise the risk-return-properties of the portfolios they manage. As several studies have shown, bonds associated with the above average ESG scores tend to exhibit less risk for a given return expectation, everything else being equal. This is even true after controlling the financial rating (For a comprehensive presentation of corresponding papers, see Friede, Busch and Bassen 2015; or oekom research and Klotz 2014).

However, looking at the biggest financial fund industry, the pension fund industry, the picture is less rosy. The pension sector's response to climate change is disappointingly slow and inconsistent, especially in light of the long-term horizons of this industry. One frequently given reason for this is the alleged barrier posed by fiduciary duty. This article authored by Bethan Levesey from ShareAction explains why this excuse has been exposed as invalid and considers what the real barriers to action are. Although recent data from MSCI show a strong correlation between corporate performance and strong ESG related risk management, the uptake of this message by pension funds is slow: The MSCI EM ESG Leaders Index,[35] consists of 417 companies scoring highly on ESG factors and have consistently outstripped the MSCI EM benchmark since 2008 (Kynge 2017), which can be regarded as a long enough time to conclude that taking into account climate change and environmental factors makes dollars. So why do pension funds not react, although they arguably have a ficuciary duty to do so, in particular when they are not giving up return in exchange for climate change defence? The important report into fiduciary duty and ESG undertaken by the Asset Management Working Group of the UNEP Finance Initiative explains that the position is based on the application of the modern prudent investor rule (UNEP Finance Initiative 2005). Like fiduciary duty, this incorporates a duty of care and a duty of loyalty. Climate change has serious financial implications for pension funds (and other asset owners). There are physical risks to assets from extreme weather events (including infrastructure, agriculture, timberland and property) as well as risks associated with the transition to a low carbon economy. Growing regulation could cause high carbon companies to lose value given the financial implications for business models built on risky or non-exploitable resources (Economist Intelligence Unit 2015). The global asset management firm, Schroders, has issued warnings about climate change risks, particularly in relation to policy and regulatory changes and the risks posed by the physical effects of climate change. It estimates that, on an average, 15 to 20 per cent of company cash flows are at risk (Mooney 2017). So it is astonishing that this large investment industry has not yet integrated climate change measures sufficiently although the MSCI EM ESG benchmark yields better than the conventional MSCI EM. Bethan Livesey from ShareAction is providing insight and explanation of these phenomena. It can be argued that a regulation may be required to redirect the pension capital.

Water, the Life Source of Mankind

Robert C. Brears, Founder of Mitidaption and Urban Water Security Center, examines how water utilities around the world are implementing innovative management practices and technologies to meet their increasing demands while enhancing the environment and lowering emissions. As the century progresses, water utilities managing public water systems are facing increasing pressure from a wide range of social, technological, economic, environmental and political trends that challenge their ability to provide a sustainable, reliable and affordable water service that meet the customers' expectations in the future. Therefore, the examination of innovative management practices and technologies is the key. There are two types of innovation: inputs and outputs. Innovation inputs consist of all the resources dedicated to promoting innovation and includes new strategies, knowledge, capital and human resources and environmental public policy components such as water and wastewater fees and charges, new technologies, for example, energy recovery from wastewater, as well as innovative infrastructure, like providing of alternative water supplies. Innovative outputs include customer value and efficiency measures, better customer service as well as information, images and ideas that increase the efficiency of the existing water supply system (London Economics 2009).

Much more than Micro–MicroFinance and Investment for Development

Switzerland plays a key role in impact investing due to the strong involvement of specialised asset managers in relevant areas, microfinance being the first and currently largest field while other topics are expected to catch up. 'Investments for development' is identifying itself as a subcategory of impact investing. Results show that institutions in Switzerland, with 10 billion USD assets under management, represent one-third of the global market of investments for development. Given the growing need for investments to finance development, the role of the financial sector has gained public attention, both on an international and national level. Projects such as the UNEP Inquiry, looking into how the financial system can contribute to a green and sustainable economy, have led to intense discussions on the role of financial players in contributing to sustainable development. At the same time, financial service providers increasingly recognise the opportunities resulting from such investments. Julia Meyer and Kelly Hess investigate this question in their article: Swiss Investments for Development.

What about China?

Last but not least, Shidi Dong, Lei Xu, Ron Mc Iver and Shiao–Lan Chou and Harjap Bassan from the University of South Australia, Adelaide introduce to us the progress made in China with regard to CSR disclosure, political connections and their impact on ownership structures and performance and make some policy suggestions. These two articles are complemented by research on corporate tax sustainability by Guodong Yuan, Ron Mc Iver, Lei Xu and Sang Hong Kang.

I personally hope that this anthology both widens the investment and social innovation horizon, is fun reading and a great learning experience.

References

1 Smith, Adam (1776). An inquiry into the Nature and Causes of the Wealth of Nations. 1 (First Ed.). London: W. Strahan. Retrieved 2012-12-07., vol. 2 via Google Books.

2 Smith, Adam (1761). Theory of Moral Sentiments (second Ed.). Strand & Edinburgh: A. Millar; A. Kincaid & J. Bell. Retrieved 26 May 2014. Smith, Adam (1790). Theory of Moral Sentiments, or An Essay towards An Analysis of the Principles by which Men naturally judge concerning the conduct and character, first of their neighbours, and afterwards of themselves, to which is added a Dissertation on the Origin of Languages. II (Sixth Ed.). London: A. Strahan; and T. Cadell in the Strand; and T. Creech and J. Bell & Co. at Edinburgh. Retrieved 18 June 2015, via Google Books.

3 Bruni, L. and Sudgen, R. (2007). The Road Not Taken: How Psychology was Removed from Economics, and how it might be brought back. The Economic Journal 117: 146–173.

4 *In*: Patrick Minford, Milton Friedman's Methodology, Macroeconomics and the Great Recession, http://www.oxfordscholarship.com/view/10.1093/acprof:oso/9780198704324.001.0001/acprof-9780198704324, Chapter 30.

5 ZBW Leibnitz Information Centre https://www.econstor.eu/bitstream/10419/29863/1/506389952.PDF.

6 Christine Kaufmann. *In*: Karen Wendt (ed.). Responsible Investment Banking, https://link.springer.com/chapter/10.1007/978-3-319-10311-2_34/fulltext.html.

7 ibid.

8 Paul Watzlawick: Pragmatics of Human Communication, MRI Palo Alto.

9 Fisher, Roger, Bruce Patton and William Rury. (2011). Getting to Yes: Negotiating Agreement Without Giving. New York: Cambridge University Press.

10 ibid.

11 Dr Mariana Bozesan in Routledge Handbook of Social and Sustainable Finance. O.M. Lehner (ed.). https://publikationen.bibliothek.kit.edu/1000072284.

12 Dr Mariana Bozesan in Routledge Handbook of Social and Sustainable Finance. O.M. Lehner (ed.). https://publikationen.bibliothek.kit.edu/1000072284.

13 Dr Mariana Bozesan in Routledge Handbook of Social and Sustainable Finance. O.M. Lehner (ed.). https://publikationen.bibliothek.kit.edu/1000072284.

14 SBCSD Vision 2050, A Roadmap for Vision 2050, p.10f; www.wbcsd.org/Overview/About-us/Vision2050/Resources/Vision-2050-The-new-agenda-for-business.

15 Porter, M.E. and Kramer, M.R. (2011). Creating Shared Value. Harvard Business Review.

16 Kathryn Worstman, Investment Director, MaRS Catalyst Fund cited in "MaRS Catalyst Fund focuses on the 'double bottom line'—social impact and returns", March 16, 2016, Financial Post: http://business.financialpost.com/investing/investing-pro/mars-catalyst-fund-focuses-on-the-double-bottom-line-social-impact-and-returns/wcm/17c706eb-3897-42d7-8463-f5d4734b1c1d.

17 http://ssir.org/articles/entry/collective_impact</note>(introduced in 2011 by John Kania and Mark Kramer in the Stanford Social Innovation Review).

18 Centre for Strategy and Evaluation Services. Benchmarking of Business Incubators. Brussels: European Commission Enterprise Directorate General, 2002.

19 EBN—Innovation Network

20 United Nations, Sustainable Development Goals at: https://sustainabledevelopment.un.org/?menu=1300 (last visited June 4, 2017).

21 World Economic Forum. Social Innovation: A Guide to Achieving Corporate and Societal Value (25 February 2016) at 1. 'To be transparent, as a social impact entrepreneur and global citizen'—I agree whole-heartedly with this statement.

22 https://www.g-casa.com/conferences/berlin17/ppt%20pdf/Wendt.pdf https://www.researchgate.net/publication/309773930_Nachhaltiger_investieren_durch_integrierte_Ratings_-_Konigsweg_oder_Utopie.

23 http://www.socialfinance.org.uk/database/.

24   Global Information Infrastructure Commission http://giic.org.
25   Preliminary numbers show this increased to USD 231 billion in 2016, USD 133 billion in buildings.
26   COWI consultants http://www.cowi.com.
27   Buildings Performance Institute Europe http://bpie.eu.
28   https://www.emd.dk/energypro.
29   National Technical University of Athens https://www.ntua.gr/en/.
30   Fraunhofer Institute http://www.isi.fraunhofer.de/isi-de/.
31   http://www.climatestrategy.es.
32   https://deep.eefig.eu.
33   https://valueandrisk.eefig.eu.
34   http://divestinvest.org/wp-content/uploads/2015/06/PRESS-RELEASE-Divest-Invest-June-Announcement.pdf- Divest Invest campaign on track to achieve target 200 signatories by COP 21 in Paris in December.
35   https://www.etfstrategy.co.uk/msci-launches-new-environmental-social-and-governance-esg-indices-for-emerging-markets-and-acwi-21457/.

Other Readings

Aspromourgos (1986). Political economy and the social division of labour: The economics of Sir William Petty. Scottish Journal of Political Economy, 1986 – Wiley.

Baisch, R.H. and Weber, R. (2015). Investment suitability requirements in the light of behavioural findings. European Perspectives on Behavioural Law and Economics, Springer p. 163–167.

Bozesan, M. (2015). De-Risking VC Investing for Outstanding Returns: A Family Office's Sustainable Approach toward the Integration of People, Planet and Profit available at https://investmentwende.com/wp-content/uploads/2017/11/AQAL-AG-White-Paper-copy.pdf accessed May7,2018.

Brandstetter, L. and Lehner, O.M. (2016). Opening the market for impact investments: The need for adapted portfolio tools. Entrepreneurship Research Journal, degruyter.com.

Bruni, L. and Sudgen, R. (2007). The road not taken: How psychology was removed from economics, and how it might be brought back. The Economic Journal 117: 146–173.

Buchanan, J. (1990). The domain of constitutional economics. Constitutional Political Economy 1(1): 1–18.

Bugg-Levine, A. and Emerson, J. (2011). Impact investing: Transforming how we make money while making a difference. Innovations: Technology, Governance, MIT Press. Note Many of their other writings may be found at www.blendedvalue.org.

Canadian Task Force on Social Finance. (2010). Mobilizing private capital for public good. MaRS Report on social finance. Availabe at https://www.marsdd.com/wp-content/uploads/2011/02/MaRSReport-socialfinance-taskforce.pdf.

Climate Bonds Initiative. (2016). Bonds and Climate Change: State of the Market 2016. Available at https://www.climatebonds.net/resources/publications/bonds-climate-change-2016.

Camerer, C. and Loewenstein, G. (2004). Behavioral economics: past, present, future. pp. 3–51. In: Camerer, C., Loewenstein, G. and Rabin, M. (eds.). Advances in Behavioural Economics. Princeton: Princeton University Press.

Cooper, C. et al. (2016). Social impact bonds: The securitization of the homeless. Accounting, Organizations and Society, Elsevier.

Dowling, E. and Harvie, D. (2014). Harnessing the social: State, crisis and (big) society. Sociology, Annual Special Issue: 'Sociology and the Global Economics Crisis', Guest Editors: Ana C Dinerstein, Gregory Schwartz and Graham.

Frey, B.S. (1992). Tertium Datur: Pricing, Regulating and Intrinsic Motivation. Kyklos 45: 161–185.

Frey, B.S. and Stutzer, A. (2002). What can economists learn from happiness research? Journal of Economic Literature 40(2): 402–435.

Frey, B.S. and Neckermann, S. (2008). Awards—A view from psychological economics. Journal of Psychology 216: 198–208.

Friede et al. (2015). ESG and financial performance: aggregated evidence from more than 2000 empirical studies. Journal of Sustainable Finance and Investment. Taylor & Francis.

Friedman, M. (1953). Choice, chance, and the personal distribution of income. Journal of Political Economy, journals.uchicago.edu.

Joy, M. and Shields, J. (2013). Social impact bonds: the next phase of third sector marketization? Canadian Journal of Nonprofit and Social Economy Research 4(2): 39–55.

Kahneman and Tversky. (1982). The psychology of preferences. Scientific American, JSTOR.

Kaufmann, C. (2015). Respecting Human Rights in Investment Banking: A Change in Paradigm. Responsible Investment Banking, Springer.

Moore, M.L. et al. (2012). The social finance and social innovation Nexus. Journal of Social Entrepreneurship 3(2): 115–132. Routledge.

Porter, M.E. and Kramer, MR. (2011). The big idea. Creating shared value-Harvard business review, philosophie-management.com.

Schinkus, C. (2015). Positivism in finance and its implication for the diversification finance research: Diversifying finance research: From financialization to sustainability. International Review of Financial Analysis, Elsevier.

Singer, T. (2012). The past, present and future of social neuroscience: a European perspective. Neuroimage, Elsevier.

Stringham, E.P. (2011). Embracing morals in economics: The role of internal moral constraints in a market economy. Journal of Economic Behavior & Organization, pp. 101–102 Elsevier.

UN PRI. (2013). Overcoming strategic barriers to a sustainable nancial system: A consultation with signatories on a new PRI work programme. Authors were requested to participate via Email on January 21, 2013, by the United Nations Principle for Responsible Investing (UN PRI).

UN Sustainable Development Goals (SDGs): http://www.un.org/sustainabledevelopment/sustainable-development-goals/.

Wilber, K. (1998). Marriage of Sense and Soul. New York: Random House.

Wilber, K. (2000). Sex, Ecology, Spirituality: The Spirit of Evolution. Boston: Shambhala.

Wilber, K. (2000a). Integral Psychology: Consciousness, Spirit, Psychology, Therapy. Boston: Shambhala.

Wilber, K. (2000b). A theory of everything: An integral vision for business, politics, science, and spirituality. Boston: Shambhala.

Wilber, K. (2006). Integral spirituality: A Startling New Role for Religion in the Modern and Postmodern World. Boston: Integral Books.

Wong, L.W. (2005). Venture Capital Fund Management: A Comprehensive Approach to Investment Practices & the Entire Operations of a VC Firm. Aspartore Books. pp. 160.

World Commission on Environment and Development. (2009). Our Common Future. Oxford: Oxford University Press (original work published 1987).

3

Innovations in the Financing of Energy Efficiency

Steven Fawkes

Introduction

The industrial revolution brought with it large-scale economic growth but of course was built on the foundation of fossil fuels, coal to start with and then increasingly oil and gas, with the well-known local and global environmental impacts or air pollution and climate change that we are now working to overcome. We are currently in the middle of the latest in a series of energy transitions, one that is leading to a new energy system that is cleaner, more distributed and more flexible. The highest profile aspect of that transition is renewable energy but improving energy efficiency, reducing the energy input for a given level of output, is also a vitally important component of the shift to a new energy system—probably the most important aspect—and one that has been relatively ignored until recent years. Transitioning to a new, cleaner, more flexible energy system and making the positive environmental impacts we need and want will require maximising the use of the energy efficiency resource—the resource which is the cleanest and cheapest source of energy services we have available. We need to maximise the efficiency of every building, industrial process and transportation system. This will entail rapidly scaling up both the level of investment into energy efficiency and the financing of energy efficiency. This chapter looks at the current status of the energy efficiency financing market and some innovations within it that offer the prospect for achieving that scale-up.

BSc, DipTechEcon, PhD, CEng, FEI, FBIS; steven.fawkes@energyproltd.com

Defining Energy Efficiency

Technically energy efficiency means the ratio of energy in to energy but this only makes sense for machines that convert one form of energy to another ('conversion systems'), such as power stations, internal combustion engines and light bulbs, for example. It does not make sense for 'passive systems' such as buildings where the useful energy used for space conditioning, lighting, etc., is finally 'lost' by degrading to low-grade heat in exchange for providing us with useful services. When we talk about energy efficiency of a system like a passive system, we are really talking about energy performance or productivity. We are familiar with some everyday measurements of energy performance, such as miles per gallon or litres of fuel per 100 kilometre for car fuel efficiency; and less familiar examples include energy input to a building per square metre to produce a certain temperature for a certain period of time; energy use per passenger mile for aircraft; or energy per one thousand tins of beans produced in a factory.

Fundamentally we need to improve energy productivity, i.e., get more units of economic output out of every unit of energy (Stern 2012). Reduction in absolute energy use requires growing energy productivity faster than economic growth—so-called decoupling (Stern 2003) and in parts of Europe and the US, this has been happening. The challenge now is to accelerate and spread that trend.

The energy efficiency of all technologies tends to improve over time. As well as constant incremental technological changes, there are major paradigm-busting changes, such as completely new processes that work to improve energy efficiency over time. The process of improving energy efficiency or reducing energy input for a given output is a process of technical and/or behavioural change that is driven by technological, financial, management, social and political drivers and restrained by constraints of the same type. When we talk about 'energy efficiency' we often really mean 'the process of improving energy performance or productivity'. What we need to do to achieve our climate goals is to accelerate the rate of improvement.

Examples of energy efficiency in practice include reducing energy usage in a building from 300 kWh/m² to 200 kWh/m² per annum assuming constant comfort conditions and building usage, or reducing energy use from 5,000 kWh/tonne to 3,500 kWh/tonne of steel produced.[1] A familiar example is given by LED lighting, a 16-watt LED that replaces a 34-watt fluorescent light produces the same light at roughly one half of the energy usage (Electricity and Fuel, accessed Nov 17, 2017).

Distributed generation technologies such as solar and biomass boilers or combined heat and power, are often described as 'energy efficiency'. Although they can reduce on-site energy costs, they do not in themselves reduce the amount of energy demand by the ultimate use, be it a building or a process and therefore, should not be called energy efficiency. They may improve the energy efficiency of the energy supply system beyond the boundaries of the end-user by reducing peak loads, thus reducing the need to run less efficient generation plants, but those benefits fall to the supply system operator and not the project host.

Similarly, demand response, the short-term time shifting of electrical load, does not in itself improve end-use efficiency. Like distributed generation, demand response can improve the overall efficiency of the power system by reducing the need to operate inefficient stand-by power generation assets and in some jurisdictions, as with distributed generation technologies, there are incentive payments to encourage demand response to assist the grid system operator.

Although in a pure sense on-site generation and demand response are not energy efficiency technologies, in the real world many 'energy-efficiency' projects will increasingly include elements of demand response and/or local generation, and energy storage, as they can create value. In fact as we move towards a more decentralised energy system buildings and industrial facilities of all types are likely to become more tightly integrated into the electricity supply system and move from being simply consumers of energy towards being both energy consumers and producers—prosumers. In this emerging energy system, flexibility of demand in itself is likely to have value.

There are many diverse energy-efficiency technologies. They include technologies in space heating and cooling, building fabric, mechanical and electrical environmental systems, controls technologies, lighting, electric motors and drives, on-site energy generation and distribution systems (including steam and hot water systems), industrial process heating and heat recovery. They are mature and well proven. With a very few exceptions, which should always be made explicitly and with full understanding of the risks, energy-efficiency projects utilise proven, well-understood, commercially available technologies and do not involve technology-development risks.

The Economics of Energy Efficiency

Energy-efficiency projects can bring many types of benefits beyond just energy savings and the benefits appear at three levels—the project host (individual or organisation), the energy supply system, and at the national level.

Benefits to the Host

Energy-efficiency projects often have rapid paybacks resulting from energy cost savings alone. Experience and anecdotal evidence shows that most energy-efficiency projects in industry and commerce have payback periods below three years (a typical investment criteria). In EEFIG's DEEP (Derisking Energy Efficiency Platform)[2] database (described in more detail later), which includes over 10,000 projects, the average reported paybacks are five years for buildings and two years for industrial projects. The average for buildings can be misleading as there are two very different types of projects being considered, relatively simple single-technology projects with rapid payback periods and more complex, multi-technology, whole-building retrofits which achieve deep energy savings. The latter typically have long, but compared to infrastructure investments, still attractive returns. The DEEP also shows that the avoided cost of energy across some 10,000 projects is 0.012/kWh for industry and 0.025/kWh for buildings, well below the end-user prices of energy. This evidence supports the view that energy efficiency is our cheapest source of energy services.

As well as energy cost savings, there are two other types of energy benefits that can occur which pass to the project host—firstly, reduced vulnerability to energy price volatility and secondly, reduced need to invest in on-site energy supply infrastructure, such as larger boilers or upgraded input cables bringing electricity into a site.

Apart from these energy benefits, it has recently become more recognised that energy-efficiency projects can also bring a wide range of non-energy benefits. Non-energy benefits are situation-specific and can be hard to measure and value, but they are very real and can often be seen by decision makers as much more strategic and therefore, interesting to decision makers. Non-energy benefits that fall to the project host, and have been demonstrated, can include (amongst others):

- Increased building value
- Reduced rental voids/faster rentals or sales
- Improved productivity
- Reduced employee absenteeism
- Reduced staff turn-over
- Better learning outcomes
- Better health outcomes

Benefits to the Energy System

The benefits of end-users improving their energy efficiency on the energy supply system is particularly clear in the electricity supply system, but also applies to fuel supply. Improved energy efficiency can contribute to system reliability, particularly in sections of the grid that are overloaded. It can also reduce or defer the need for capital expenditure on new energy supply infrastructure, in generation, transmission and distribution. In addition, energy efficiency can also reduce the need for hot standby power plants that consume fuel without being connected to the system.

Benefits at National Level

At the national level, energy efficiency can also bring multiple benefits including reduced need to import fuel, reduced need to invest in new generation capacity, reduced level of energy subsidy payment, job creation and more competitive industries. To properly assess the economics of energy efficiency, all benefits at all levels should be identified and valued.

The Potential for Energy Efficiency

When discussing the potential for reducing energy consumption through improved energy efficiency, it is important to distinguish between technical potential and economic potential.

The ultimate potential for energy efficiency in any particular process is the difference between what is being achieved now and what is theoretically possible as defined by the laws of physics. This potential is beyond our current technical abilities to achieve. The technical potential is the difference between what is being achieved now and what can be achieved utilising existing, available and real technologies. The economic potential is the difference between what is being achieved now and what can be achieved utilising all existing, available, real technologies that are economic. This raises the question, 'What is economic?'. The only sensible way to measure what is 'economic' in the micro-case of an individual firm or organisation is to use the investor's own criterion. In macro-studies however, it is necessary to take some fixed criterion, such as a payback period or an Internal Rate of Return as it is not possible in any large sample to measure everyone's definition of economic.

The 'energy efficiency gap' that is often discussed separates the economic potential according to the investor's criteria from what is actually invested in and implemented. The level of implementation is driven by factors, such as the degree of attention paid to the issue by management and the quality of energy management programmes. In organisations with good energy management programmes, we would expect the gap to be small because all, or nearly all, economic opportunities are exploited as they occur.

In reality all potentials are dynamic and affected by shifting technological, economic and management factors. Energy efficiency needs to be thought of as more like other energy resources, which are, only there when you look for them, in the same way that an oilfield, or a shale gas field, only becomes visible when you search for it. Then it has to be developed and exploited. The potential at any time is driven by energy prices and the cost of energy-efficiency technologies. If energy prices increase, the potential increases; if energy prices fall, the potential falls. If the price of an energy-efficiency technology falls, the potential increases and if it increases, the potential falls. Therefore, any quantification of potential is only an estimate of a quantity at a fixed point in time under certain prices and a particular stage of technology development.

Since the 1970s, some energy analysts, such as Lovins[3] and Leach[4] have argued that energy efficiency was a cost-effective resource with massive potential that due to a number of factors was not being fully exploited and that utilisation of that resource would result in a future with much higher levels of efficiency and lower overall energy consumption. When both Lovins and Leach published their 'low energy' scenarios, they were widely attacked and denounced by the energy industry and energy policy makers. They were considered to be impossible to achieve although history has shown that the reality has turned out closer to these low-energy scenarios than the official, high-energy growth scenarios of governments and the energy supply industry of the time.

Since the early studies of Lovins, Leach and others, many researchers have shown that across all sectors of the economy there remains a massive and cost-effective potential to improve energy efficiency. There have been studies of the technical and economic potential covering the world, various regions and most countries, all sectors of the economy as well as specific sectors, all technologies as well a selection of technologies, as well as technical potential or economic potentials. The results of only a few such studies can be briefly summarised here.

The 2007 study by McKinsey & Co.: *"Curbing global energy demand growth: The energy productivity opportunity,"* helped to kick off renewed interest in energy efficiency. It estimated that improved energy efficiency could reduce growth in global energy demand from 2.2 per cent p.a. to 0.6 per cent p.a., reducing demand by 2020 by 64 million barrels of oil equivalent per day.

In its 2011 study, *'Reinventing Fire'*, Amory Lovins and Rocky Mountain Institute estimate that the US could reduce the 2050 energy demand by 40 per cent compared to Business As Usual and reduce CO_2 emissions by 82 to 86 Per cent.

In 2012, the International Energy Agency *'Efficient World'* scenario would boost cumulative economic output through 2035 by $18 trillion—equivalent to the size of the economies of the US, Canada, Mexico and Chile combined. This would require additional investment of $11.8 trillion, reducing fuel expenditures of $17.5 trillion and supply side investment by $5.9 trillion. In this scenario, the growth in primary energy demand is halved and oil demand and CO_2 emissions peak by 2002.

In 2011, Cullen, Allwood and Borgstein looked at the technical potential for energy efficiency and estimated 73 per cent savings potential. Although this is not only the economic potential, it does illustrate the gross inefficiency of our existing buildings, industrial, transport and energy production systems.

Apart from macro studies there are many, many case studies covering all kinds of sectors of the economy that show energy savings have been achieved and also the financial returns resulting from those investments.

Current Investment Levels and the Investment Need

The IEA estimate that in 2015 the total global investment into demand-side energy efficiency was USD 221 billion,[5] USD 118 billion in buildings, USD 39 billion in industry and USD 64 billion in transport. Investment into energy efficiency was less than 14 per cent of total energy sector investment but increased by 6 per cent in 2015 whereas investment in energy supply fell. The US, EU and China represent nearly 70 per cent of the total investment into efficiency.

To date about 85 per cent, of all energy-efficiency investment has been financed with existing sources of finance or self-financing rather than specific energy-efficiency products or programmes. The global market for Energy Performance Contracts, which are most often associated with external financing, was USD 24 billion in 2015 and of this, USD 2.7 billion was in Europe. In addition, about USD 8.2 billion of green bonds were used to finance energy efficiency.

In order to achieve climate targets, the level of investment in energy efficiency and the level of energy-efficiency financing, will need to increase substantially. The IEA and IRENA estimate that to achieve their '*66 per cent 2°C*' scenario cumulative, global investment in energy efficiency between 2016 and 2050 will need to reach USD 39 trillion of which USD 30 trillion would be in the G20 economies, implying a global level of c.USD 1 trillion a year—a five-fold increase on current levels, as estimated by the IEA.

Why has Energy Efficiency been Neglected?

Energy efficiency has always been, and still remains, relatively neglected and under-valued by policy makers and market actors. Given that there is this large, under-exploited resource of economic energy efficiency, it is proper to ask why. Efficiency has a number of characteristics that help to explain this neglect, some of which we explore here.

First of all, of course energy efficiency is 'invisible'; it is a counter-factual. It cannot be metered in the way that electricity and fuel can, although with Measurement and Verification (M&V) techniques this has become easier. Secondly, it is by its nature made up of many small projects using a diverse range of technologies from a diverse range of companies. Most of the companies in the energy-efficiency industry are small (although there are also giants like Siemens and Schneider Electric). The energy supply industry is very large with very large units and in all countries, since the start of large-scale electrification, there has been a very close link between electrical power and political power. Over the last few years, much attention has been focussed on renewables and the returns to be made in renewables, particularly when these are under-pinned by government subsidies through mechanisms like Feed-in Tariffs, have prevented investors looking at efficiency. Within organisations energy efficiency is usually not considered to be strategic and management attention and investment resource are focused on strategic issues, such as production quantity and quality. This characteristic is often reinforced by the way that energy-efficiency business cases are prepared. The business case is usually centred on savings and payback from reduced energy costs and often ignores other benefits, such as increased asset value, improved quality or improved comfort. These non-energy benefits are often more strategic and more valuable than the pure energy cost savings.

Why should Financial Institutions be Active in Energy Efficiency?

Multi-lateral development and policy banks have all had a long interest in energy efficiency but till the last few years it has largely been ignored by private sector financial institutions. Those institutions that have implemented-efficiency financing products and programmes can be considered pioneering or early adopters. Despite growing interest in energy efficiency, aided and supported by the activities of institutions such as the Energy Efficiency Financial Institution Group (EEFIG) and the G20 Energy Efficiency Finance Task Force, the levels of investment to date fall short of both what is possible and what is needed to meet energy and climate targets. Financial institutions, both lenders and investors, can take positive action to accelerate the flow of capital into this important area which can be both profitable and address key areas of corporate and systemic risk and are starting to innovate in this important area.

There are four reasons why financial institutions should consider deploying capital into energy efficiency which are considered in more detail below.

A Large Potential Market

As described above, in order to achieve our environmental targets, we need to increase investment into energy efficiency by a factor of five. Although only 15 per cent of current investment is financed by specific energy-efficiency related instruments growing the availability of finance for efficiency will help grow the total investment. This represents a large business opportunity for financial institutions which can be divided into two categories:

- creating new business lines for specific energy efficiency projects, e.g., specific energy-efficiency loans, mortgages or funds
- ensuring normal lending and investing which is being used to finance projects where energy efficiency is not the primary objective, e.g., building refurbishments or production facility upgrades, is leveraged to ensure funded projects achieve the optimum cost-effective levels of energy efficiency which are usually higher than 'business as usual' levels

Risk Reduction

Energy-efficiency investments can reduce risks for financial institutions in two ways:

- Assisting individual clients, whether they be businesses or individuals, to reduce their energy costs improves their cash flow and profitability, as well as increasing their resilience to energy price rises. Reduced expenditure on energy translates directly to improved cash flow which improves the affordability of loans or mortgages, thus lowering risks to the lender
- Tightening regulations around energy efficiency, particularly buildings, such as Minimum Energy Efficiency Standards, mean that it will become impossible to rent or sell energy inefficient buildings. This is a stranded asset risk for the owner and lender

Increasing levels of energy efficiency is a central part of energy policy in most jurisdictions around the world.

Some EU member states, notably the UK and the Netherlands, have implemented Minimum Energy Efficiency Standards (MEES) which mean that after a certain date, buildings with an energy efficiency below a set level cannot be sold or rented. These regulations mean that significant proportions of existing real estate portfolios could lose their income and asset value if they are not upgraded to a higher level of energy efficiency, a significant risk for owners of large property portfolios, as well as funds and banks lending to property. Research in the UK, in 2016, suggested that one in five commercial properties were at risk of devaluing and that the fall in value of the UK commercial property portfolio could be as much as £16.5 billion.[6]

Corporate Social Responsibility

For many years advocates of energy efficiency have argued that it is the lowest cost source of energy services and a low-cost route to achieving significant reductions in greenhouse gas emissions, something that is increasingly recognised, both by policy makers and by many financial institutions. Energy efficiency has been described as *'the linchpin that can keep the door open to a 2°C future'*. The IEA estimates that in achieving a 2°C scenario energy efficiency must account for 38 per cent of the total cumulative emission reduction through 2050, while renewable energy only needs to account for 32 Per cent. For financial institutions looking to make a positive impact on resolving environmental problems as part of corporate social responsibility programmes supporting energy efficiency should be a high priority. Besides reducing emissions of carbon dioxide that drive global climate change, reducing energy consumption can also have a positive effect on combatting local air pollution.

Pressure from Financial Regulators

Financial regulators are taking increasing interest in systemic risks, including climate change. There is also a growing interest from regulators and governments in encouraging the growth of 'green finance'. The European Systemic Risk Board in its *Scientific Advisory Committee Report* of February 2016, *'Too little, too sudden'*, warned of the risks of 'contagion' and stranded assets if moves to a low carbon economy happened too late or too abruptly. The report's policy recommendations including increased reporting and disclosure of climate-related risks and incorporating climate-related prudential risks into stress testing.

In December 2016, the Financial Stability Board (FSB) Task Force on Climate-related Financial Disclosures (TCFD) published its recommendations, which included disclosure of organisations' forward-looking climate-related risks.

In July 2015, France strengthened mandatory climate disclosure requirements for listed companies and introduced the first mandatory requirements for institutional investors as part of Article 173 of the *Law for the Energy Transition and Green Growth*. These provisions require listed companies to disclose, in the annual report, *"The financial risks related to the effects of climate change and the measures adopted by the company to reduce them, by implementing a low-carbon strategy in every component of its activities."* Institutional investors will also be required to *"mention in their annual report, and make available to their beneficiaries, information on how their investment decision-making process takes social, environmental and governance criteria into consideration, and the means implemented to contribute to the energy and ecological transition."* The law also requires the government to implement stress testing, reflecting the risks associated with climate change.

This trend towards greater disclosure and open assessment of climate-related risks for financial institutions is likely to continue, putting pressure on them to take more action in respect of green finance and energy efficiency in particular.

Categories of Energy-Efficiency Investment

There are three categories of projects that improve energy efficiency:

- *Energy-efficiency-driven retrofits*. This category includes retrofitting existing buildings, industrial processes, transport systems or energy systems with the primary purpose of improving energy efficiency. The expenditure in these cases is mainly on energy-efficiency equipment and systems. Examples include installing LED lighting or adding heat recovery to an industrial oven

- *Modernisation of existing assets*. This category includes refurbishing existing buildings, industrial processes, transport systems or energy systems where the primary purpose is not energy efficiency, but other factors, such as the need to bring an old building up to modern standards or improve reliability. In these cases, opportunities to maximise energy efficiency should be exploited to avoid locking in high-energy use for the life of the project. Examples include installing a new heating system or adding insulation during the refurbishment of a building

Table 1: An energy productivity investment typology.

		Buildings & the Built Environment	Transport	Industry	Utilities
Energy Efficiency Investments	**Energy Efficiency Driven Retrofit**	Retrofit building structure, systems and controls. Retrofit street lights to LED lamps.	Retrofit vehicles (e.g., aerodynamics, drive train).	Retrofit processes & buildings for energy efficiency reasons, e.g., variable speed drives.	Retrofit power plant, transmission & distribution systems for energy efficiency reasons.
	Modernisation of Existing Assets	Refurbishment of a building to make it fit for modern working environment.	Refurbishment of existing vehicles for non-energy reasons, e.g., refurbishment of buses or trains.	Retrofit/ refurbishment of industrial processes for non-energy efficiency reasons, e.g., quality, production output (incorporating some efficiency improvement).	Retrofit/ refurbishment of power plant, transmission & distribution systems for non-energy efficiency reasons, e.g., reliability (incorporating some efficiency improvement).
Mainstream Investments	**New Assets within Existing Industrial Structure**	New high-efficiency buildings, Near Zero Energy Buildings or Net Energy Positive buildings. New street lighting installations.	New high-efficiency vehicles.	New high-efficiency production plant using same process. New plant using new process for existing industries.	New high-efficiency generation, transmission & distribution plant.

Source: KAPSARC

- *New assets*. This category includes investments in new buildings, industrial processes, transport systems or energy systems for the existing structure of the economy. In this case the primary purpose is not energy efficiency, but the value or outputs that come from the new building, process or system. New buildings or processes are typically more efficient than older ones, but there are still opportunities to maximise efficiency and financial institutions can play a role to maximise the take-up of these opportunities

The Risks of Energy-Efficiency Investments

We saw above that energy-efficiency projects can result in multiple energy and non-energy benefits, many of which can be valued.

Besides value creation, of course, all investment projects carry risks and energy-efficiency projects are no different in this regard. The main types of risk with energy-efficiency projects are:

- *Performance risk*: the risk that the project under-delivers
- *Construction risks*: the risk that the project is late and/or over-budget
- *Counter-party risks*: the normal credit risks

The performance of an energy-efficiency project can be driven by intrinsic and extrinsic factors. Intrinsic factors include things like poor design and modelling, equipment failure (relative or absolute); whereas extrinsic factors include the weather and patterns of use which can differ from those assumed in the investment case. Energy efficiency projects can suffer from a 'performance gap', with savings being different from the projections.

The energy-efficiency industry needs to consider ways of reducing performance risk and banks and investors contemplating scaling up capital deployment into efficiency need to understand the issue. This does not mean don't invest in efficiency; it just means understand and where possible, mitigate the risks.

Most energy-efficiency financing at the moment is straightforward consumer or commercial lending just and just like any other loan, the borrower is responsible for repayments howsoever the project performs. The next largest area of efficiency financing is funding investments made under an Energy Performance Contract (EPC) where an Energy Service Company (ESCO) provides a guarantee that the predicted level of savings will be achieved and if they are not, pays the difference. So assuming the ESCO is experienced and credit worthy all is well for the bank, the project fails to deliver, the ESCO pays the client and the client pays back the bank. This has led banks to practically ignore the performance risk.

Even when financial institutions are not explicitly and contractually taking the performance risk, they should be concerned about it for six reasons:

- Depending on jurisdiction consumer credit law may make a lender responsible for equipment performance over its lifetime
- Under-performance can lead to customer dis-satisfaction, which leads to disputes, which put repayment at risk. They also consume time and energy on both sides and create a negative customer experience which

these days can be quickly communicated and can cause reputational damage

- Some financial institutions count the improved cash flow resulting from the projected energy savings in their credit risk assessment. Even though they do not contractually take credit risk, this means that they are implicitly taking performance risk; if the savings are not delivered the customer's credit risk is higher than the assessed number

- Failures of project performance at scale in residential financed projects may lead to mis-selling scandals. In the US and UK, there has been negative press about the performance of energy-efficiency retrofits. Imagine if a bank financed millions of retrofits on the promise of savings being greater than repayments and they were not delivered, the reputational risks and the cost to rectify would be huge

- A better understanding of performance risk will allow development of new products which take some performance risk for higher returns. This has started to happen in wind power, for instance where lenders who previously would take no performance risk are now taking some higher returns. Done right, energy efficiency can be highly profitable and secure so there is an opportunity for a funder who really understands the risks

- Re-financing markets, specifically the green-bond market, will require assurance that underlying projects are performing and having a genuine environmental impact. The green-bond market is imposing more stringent standards on what qualifies as green. In order to attract the most investors at the best rates, it is important to be able to prove that the underlying projects are actually performing as they were supposed to

Innovation in Energy-Efficiency Financing Products

Over the last few years, a number of innovations in energy-efficiency financing products have occurred and here we describe some of them. There have been also been innovations in energy services contracts, market infrastructure and energy markets which are described in later sections.

Types of Energy Efficiency Finance Products

Before considering innovation, it is useful to review the different ways in which energy efficiency can be financed, the choice of which is dependent on the type and size of the investment, the risk preferences of lenders/investors and market acceptability. Possible types of energy-efficiency financing include:

- Loans/mortgages specifically for energy-efficiency upgrades in residential and commercial buildings, industry and commerce
- Loans/mortgages specifically for the purchase of energy-efficient buildings
- Leasing for energy-efficiency products
- Ensuring normal lending/investment for everyday building refurbishments or upgrades incorporate the optimum level of cost-effective energy-efficiency measures and achieve levels of performance beyond business as usual
- Specialised energy-efficiency funds offering equity or debt for projects
- Property funds specifically for energy efficient/green buildings
- Financing of specialised energy service contracts, such as Energy Performance Contracts (EPCs)
- Secondary financing can be achieved through forfaiting funds-purchasing receivables from energy service contracts, securitisation or bonds

Here we describe a few examples of innovations occurring in various categories of energy-efficiency financing products.

Consumer and Commercial Lending

Most energy-efficiency financing is simply through normal lending, either to the residential or commercial sectors. In most cases this activity is not specifically identified as energy-efficiency lending as the detailed purpose of the loan is not usually known in sufficient detail, whether energy efficiency is the main purpose or it is embedded into a larger project. In the residential sector, for example, the loan may only be identified as being for 'home improvements'.

Most consumer and commercial loans for energy efficiency are recovered from the borrower in the normal way but there are specialised means of loan recovery in the global energy-efficiency financing market which have considerable potential for growth in Europe, namely On-Bill Recovery and Property Assessed Clean Energy. These are described below.

On Bill Recovery

On-Bill Recovery—also known as On-Financing (OBF)—allows customers to repay loans made for energy-efficiency improvements on their electricity bills. Typically a customer will apply for a loan for an energy-efficiency project, usually one of a defined set of projects that qualify for OBR, and the repayments are then added to the customer's electricity bills. OBR has a number of advantages for customers and financial institutions. For customers, OBR:

- Means there is only one bill to pay
- Is simple to understand
- The tariff can be set such as the OBR component is less than the energy cost savings, giving positive cash flow
- Is transferable as it is tied to the property meter and not the individual householder
- Can be long-term debt
- It can reduce the credit barrier as electricity bill default rates are well known

  For financial institutions, OBR:

- Allows use of existing electricity invoicing system to recover the loan which reduces overheads
- Gives access to large customer base
- More reliable repayment. Non-payment rates for electricity bills are rare and well known
- Is transferable as it is tied to the property

OBR is used in several states across the US for residential energy-efficiency loans and in some states for commercial and industrial loans. The most widely known example of OBR in the Europe was the UK's Green Deal which was a failure but generated some useful lessons. The Green Deal was established by the UK government in 2013 but was cancelled in late 2015. An analysis of the failure of the Green Deal in 2016 by the National Audit Office highlighted a number of reasons for its failure, including failure to test the mechanism before a full launch, exclusion of popular measures such as double glazing, and the marketing focus on financial benefits whereas consumers are more driven by benefits, such as a warmer home. High interest rates and bureaucratic process also contributed to the outcome.

Property Assessed Clean Energy (PACE)

Property Assessed Clean Energy (PACE) is a financing mechanism that enables low-cost, long-term funding for energy efficiency, renewable energy and water-conservation projects that is widely used in the USA. PACE loans are repaid as an additional payment on a property's regular local property tax. This method has been used for many decades to finance infrastructure upgrades, such as sewers and was first applied to clean energy in Berkeley, California, in 2008. PACE legislation is active in 33 states plus the District of Columbia (DC) and there are active programmes in 19 states plus DC. Since 2010 PACE has been used to finance USD 3.7 billion of residential home improvements (148,000 projects) and over 1,000 projects in commercial buildings with a total capital of USD 400 million, with the largest project being USD 40 million. To date, USD 3.4 billion of PACE funded projects have been securitised. These securitisations are the first examples of a secondary market for energy-efficiency loans.

PACE needs to be enabled by local legislation at state and municipal levels. It can be used to cover 100 per cent of a project's hard and soft costs and repayments can be spread over up to 20 years. Non-payment of the PACE element is treated the same way as non-payment of property tax, which can lead to seizure of the property. In Europe there is interest in adopting a PACE-like mechanism although of course, the way that local property taxes are calculated and charged varies from country to country.

Green Mortgages

A green or energy-efficiency mortgage is one that is used to finance purchase of an energy-efficient building or refurbish a building to a higher standard of efficiency. Lower energy bills resulting from high levels of energy efficiency improve the building owner's cash flow and improve the building's value and therefore should reduce risk of default and potentially allow lenders to offer higher levels of borrowing and Loan to Value and/or lower interest rates.

Energy efficiency mortgages have been available in the USA since the 1990s through a programme supported by the Federal Housing Administration, which provides mortgage insurance for qualifying loans. Borrowers must obtain a home energy assessment and financed measures must pass a cost-effectiveness test. When the home being purchased meets minimum energy-efficiency standards, the borrowers' qualifying debt to income ratio can be stretched two percentage points above standard limits.

At present there is no clear definition of a green mortgage as different lenders are offering consumers different options. To address this issue and help grow the market for green mortgages, the European Mortgage Federation and European Covered Bonds Council (EMF-ECBC) have started a project known as the Energy Efficient Mortgages Action Plan (EEMAP).

The aim of this project, co-funded by the European Commission, is to create a standardised energy-efficient mortgage in which building owners are incentivised to improve the energy efficiency of their property, or acquire an already energy-efficient property, by way of preferential financing conditions linked to the mortgage. The project will identify and summarise best market practices, define energy performance, identify the pre-requisites for the assessment of 'green value', substantiate the correlation between energy-efficiency and the probability of default and define and design an energy-efficient mortgage based on preferential financial conditions.

Ensuring Normal Lending and Investing Encourages Energy Efficiency

Every working-day loans, mortgages, leases and investments are made into new buildings, building refurbishments and modernisation as well as upgradation and replacement of industrial processes and production plants. In nearly all cases, energy efficiency is not the primary purpose of the investment being financed but the future levels of energy efficiency are effectively being decided and 'locked into', in some cases because of the long life of major assets for many decades. Although new buildings, refurbishments or new production plants generally achieve higher levels of efficiency than the units that they replace due to (a) improved technologies and (b) tighter regulations and codes of practice, many cost-effective opportunities to improve energy efficiency are missed. This occurs due to a number of reasons, including lack of knowledge on the part of project hosts, time pressure, the conservative nature of engineering design and treating regulations as a target that have to be achieved rather than a minimum level of performance. Banks and financial institutions can play an active role in ensuring financed projects of all types achieve optimum levels of efficiency over and above business as usual by adjusting the lending/investing process to include queries about energy efficiency and the provision of assistance to identify viable projects. By doing this, they can both reduce risks by financing measures that improve customers' cash flows, and potentially increase lending.

The EBRD has long been a pioneer in exploiting the opportunities provided by manstream lending. The EBRD was established in 1991 to finance reconstruction and development in the former Soviet Union. Due to the extremely low-energy productivity of the former Soviet Union, typically one-quarter of that of Western Europe at the time, improving energy efficiency and productivity was always a major driver within the EBRD. Having established a specialised energy efficiency unit early on, it has financed energy-efficiency projects in the power and gas sectors (including reduction of gas flaring), as well as in industry, building and transport. In 2012, more than 26 per cent of the EUR 8.8 billion lent was for energy efficiency and renewable energy projects or energy efficiency and renewable energy components of larger projects. Besides specialised efficiency projects, the EBRD checks *all* industrial or commercial loan applications to assess the potential for energy-efficiency improvements. The bank then works with the client organisation to develop the priority projects and these are incorporated into the loan application. This process

Fig. 1: The EBRD process.
Source: EEFIG Underwriting Toolkit

ensures that all commercially and financially viable improvements are incorporated, improves the client's cash flow (which reduces the lending risk) and increases the capital deployed. The process is shown in Fig. 1.

Financing Energy Efficiency in Commercial Buildings

During the due diligence process for acquisition or refinancing of a building, an investor or lender will typically review the building's financials, rent roll and history and require a Physical Needs Assessment (PNA) or comparable review. If significant deficiencies exist, the lender may even require that certain capital replacements be made as a condition of refinancing. It can be a relatively simple matter to make energy-efficiency assessments and ratings, such as Energy Performance Certificates part of that PNA and even to make performance standards part of a lender's requirements. Some banks, including ING and ABN Amro, have implemented such programmes and going further by providing tools to assist owners to identify energy-efficiency measures.

ING Real Estate Finance (ING REF) set an ambition of reducing CO_2 emissions from its Dutch portfolio by 15–20 per cent with a target of energy cost savings of EUR 50 million per year. This entailed targeting 3,000 Dutch clients with 28,000 buildings. ING paid for the development of an app which was offered to all clients—the app provides an analysis of the clients' energy use across their portfolio and identifies potential energy savings. If the potential energy savings exceed EUR 15,000, the client is offered a free site energy survey.

ING REF also provides advice to clients on what subsides are available (through a specialist third party) and ING REF offers 100 per cent finance for energy-efficiency improvements from ING Groenbank with a 0.5 per cent discount on normal interest rates.

Within the first two years, the app has been used to scan 18,000 buildings with a total floor area of 10 million m^2 (65 per cent of ING REF's portfolio). ING aims to empower 5,000 Dutch clients and roll out the app to other European countries.

ING REF has also instituted a new policy—if more than 50 per cent of a portfolio has an energy label of C or above, then the acceptable LTV is 5 per cent higher than otherwise. Furthermore, in December 2016, ING announced that they will offer only new financing for office buildings in the Netherlands that achieve an Energy Performance Certificate of C or above. This is in line with Dutch regulations that say from 2023, buildings must have a C rating or above in order to be rented as office space.

Specialised Energy Efficiency Funds

Multi-lateral banks, with their long interest in energy efficiency, have established specialised energy-efficiency funds in their areas of operations over many years; examples include the World Bank's Renewable Resources and Energy Efficiency (R2E2) Fund in the Western Balkans or the Romania Energy Efficiency Fund (FREE) funded by the World Bank and the Global Environment Facility (GEF). Over the last five to 10 years, a number of specialised energy-efficiency funds have been established using either public or private sector funding or a combination of both.

These funds offer a range of equity and debt-financing products to energy-efficiency projects, often projects implemented using Energy Performance Contracts. Examples include the European Energy Efficiency Fund, the London Energy Efficiency Fund (LEEF) and the SUSI Energy Efficiency Fund.

The European Energy Efficiency Fund (EEEF) is a public-private partnership focused on financing energy efficiency, small-scale renewable energy and clean urban transport projects at market rates. It is aimed at municipal, local and regional authorities and public and private entities aimed at serving those authorities. It was capitalised in 2011 with EUR 265 m with investments from the EC, the EIB, Deutsche Bank (DB) and Cassa Depositi e Prestiti SpA (CDP). EEEF invests in the range of EUR 5 m to EUR 25 m through a range of instruments including equity, senior debt, mezzanine debt, leasing and forfeiting loans. The fund is managed by DB, which provides Technical Assistance (TA) to assist potential investees to develop projects through a dedicated TA facility.

Property Funds Specifically for Energy Efficient Buildings

Property funds based on purchasing properties and making them more energy efficient have been established in a number of countries. The advent of Minimum Energy Performance Standards (MEPS), and their potential effects on property values have led to increased interest in this model of financing energy efficiency. Examples include the Credit Suisse European Climate Value Property Fund and the Low Carbon Workplace Fund.

The Credit Suisse European Climate Value Property Fund acquires existing commercial properties that have leased well in promising European markets and implements a system for controlling, measuring and monitoring energy consumption in cooperation with the Siemens technology group.

All properties in the portfolio are continually upgraded in terms of their energy efficiency on the basis of measurement data in order to systematically reduce overall energy consumption as well as CO_2 emissions. This ensures that alongside the sustainability of investment, the earning potential for the fund's investors is also strengthened. The remaining portfolio share for which the energy consumption cannot be reduced in a cost-effective manner is made 'carbon-neutral' once a year through the purchase of CO_2 certificates.

The Low Carbon Workplace Fund is a £208 million, unleveraged property fund which invests in commercial office space and invests to improve its energy performance. It is advised by Threadneedle Asset Management Limited, the Carbon Trust and Stanhope plc. It has achieved the following energy efficiency results across the eight buildings in the portfolio:

- Average EPC improvement from E to B
- BREEAM Excellent status awarded to all buildings
- 60 per cent more energy efficient than CIBSE's ECON19 office benchmark
- 35 per cent more energy efficient than Better Building Partnership's Environmental Benchmark

Secondary Financing

In order to grow the energy-efficiency financing market, it will ultimately be essential to have an active market in secondary financing in order to recycle capital. The secondary market is only now starting to emerge due to the relatively small scale of energy-efficiency finance market and lack of standardisation and aggregation of projects. Various secondary financing methods, forfaiting funds, securitisation and bonds are discussed here.

Forfaiting Funds

Energy service contracts, such as Energy Performance Contracts, produce long-term stable cash flows which can be an attractive asset for long-term investors. Forfaiting funds can re-finance EPC contracts, thus allowing the primary investors and banks to recycle their capital into new projects.

A pioneering energy efficiency forfaiting fund in Europe is LABEEF, the Latvian Building Energy Efficiency Fund. LABEEF has been established to purchase the cash flows from Energy Performance Contracts established to finance the upgrade of Soviet era housing blocks. The process is as follows:

- An ESCO signs a 20-year contract with the Home Owner Association
- The ESCO takes a loan from a financial institution
- The ESCO renovates the building, typically achieving energy savings of 45–65 per cent, while sub-contracting to construction companies and equipment providers
- The House Maintenance Company (which maintains the housing block) bills the same amount as before the renovation works and pays the ESCO a percentage of those bills, based on the realised savings
- The House Maintenance Company pays the reduced energy bill to the heat providers
- Once the project is implemented and savings are proved, an assignment agreement is signed between the ESCO and LABEEF. The ESCO receives discounted cash flow for the future receivables, minus an amount for operations and maintenance and a performance guarantee
- The cash flows from the homeowners, via the House Maintenance Company, to LABEEF which keeps paying the ESCO for operations & maintenance

While delivering greater levels of energy efficiency and comfort, this model is also addressing the physical deterioration of Soviet era housing, a problem which is extensive throughout Central and Eastern Europe.

The LABEEF is designed to be a EUR 30 million fund and in February 2017, it signed a EUR 4-million funding agreement with EBRD.

Securitisation

In 2014, Deutsche Bank closed the first ever securitisation of loans for residential energy efficiency with a USD 104 million bond in California. The 11-year, double-AA rated bond was priced at a fixed coupon of 4.75 per cent and was supported by Property Assessed Clean Energy (PACE) loans to householders. Since then, there have been follow-on deals with Renovate America alone, making seven bond issues with a total value of USD 1.35 billion.

Bonds

Bonds, particularly green bonds, have a large potential role in financing energy efficiency because energy-efficiency projects have a clear environmental benefit. Most specific energy-efficiency projects are too small for the issuance of a bond on a single-project or single-owner basis; a stand-alone energy-efficiency project of EUR 10 million is unusual and still too small for a debt capital market bond. Even if several such projects were identified, the development and execution of these projects and the uncertainty associated with the pace of draws on capital over time would make the use of bonds unwieldy.

Green bonds have, however, been used successfully to finance energy-efficient buildings, a notable example being Berlin Hyp which has a core focus on commercial real-estate finance in metropolitan areas in Germany. Its total real-estate finance portfolio is EUR 18.1 billion. Berlin Hyp finances energy-efficient buildings, which means buildings with an energy demand below the levels required by the German energy savings regulations and/or a good sustainability certification. As of February 2017, the green finance portfolio comprised 42 loans with an aggregate amount of EUR 2.02 bn. The portfolio has been refinanced with issuance of green bonds.

Bonds are likely to play an important role even in retrofit projects once a sufficient volume of projects can be aggregated. A set of standardised projects, originated and financed by utilising other forms of capital, such as equipment leases or loans, can be aggregated and refinanced through a bond issuance. As a hopeful sign of a market maturing, pooled retrofits have been refinanced by bonds in some instances in the United States.

Important questions regarding bonds for energy efficiency remain, including what characteristics make a bond for energy-efficiency projects distinct from other bonds, how to define and measure energy efficiency of the underlying projects and how to ensure the underlying projects are performing as planned? For new build projects, bond financing could only really be considered energy efficiency if the buildings or industrial facilities financed have an energy performance better than regulations, i.e., better than business-as-usual.

Financing of Specialised Energy Service Contracts

The growth of energy services contracting is an important aspect of energy efficiency. Different types of energy service contract exist but the best known is the Energy Performance Contract (EPC). An Energy Performance Contract (EPC) is a contractual arrangement between the beneficiary and the provider of an energy-efficiency improvement measure in which the provider, an Energy Service Company (ESCO), provides a guarantee of performance for the installed measures. The ESCO does not generally provide the required capital but usually works with established lenders to facilitate provision of finance, although the customer can also decide to directly finance the project with own equity. The ESCO's guarantee is meant to ensure that the savings are sufficient to pay debt service. If there is a shortfall, the host, but not the lender, has recourse to the ESCO.

In the USA and Europe, the majority of EPC contracts are with the public sector. The complexity of EPCs has led to the emergence of EPC facilitators in some market, as well as procurement frameworks to assist public sector agencies to develop and implement contracts and link projects to financing. An example is the UK's Carbon and Energy Fund (CEF) which focusses on projects in the National Health Service.

The Carbon and Energy Fund (CEF) was established in 2011, specifically to facilitate, develop and fund infrastructure upgrades within the National Health Service using Energy Performance Contracts. Since then, CEF has implemented more than 40 projects with a capital expenditure of more than GBP 150 million and annual cost savings of more than GBP 21 million. CEF has been expanded into Scotland and more recently, into Ireland. An example of a CEF project involves a consortium of three NHS Trusts in Liverpool. The combined capital cost was GBP 13 million with guaranteed energy savings of GBP 1.8 million with a 15-year EPC. The project was developed and delivered by Engie and financed by Macquarie. The CEF provides an important model as, though it is not a source of finance in itself, it generates a flow of bankable projects through working with public sector clients, building capacity and standardising project development.

Innovation in Energy Services Contracts

Although Energy Performance Contracts are the best known energy services contracts, other types of energy services contracts exist and there has been some innovation in contract types in the last few years.

Energy Supply Contracting (Chauffage)

In Europe, Energy Supply Contracts (chauffage) are traditionally more common than the EPC described above. Under these contracts, the contractor takes over the provision of an agreed set of energy services, most often heat (hence 'chauffage') but also potentially light, compressed air, etc. The host pays to the contractor some historical average of its energy cost. The contractor then takes responsibility for all elements of energy services, including purchasing fuel for the building and upgrading systems. The developer may choose to discount the historical bill charged to the building owner to ensure savings and incentivise the signing of the contract. The building owner has other motivations, however, typically receiving new equipment and a set of energy services that it might otherwise have to purchase. Chauffage contracts are typically long, 15 to 30 years or more, and are best for buildings where an owner is comfortable outsourcing all elements of the energy infrastructure, energy purchasing and operations & maintenance.

Efficiency Services Agreement

In an Efficiency Services Agreement (ESA), a developer retrofits the host property and the host property pays the developer the savings, typically with a negotiated discount to the facility's historical costs. Savings are measured against historical energy usage and operating expense, allowing for adjustment based upon current energy prices, weather and other factors. Where calibrated models and precise measurement are not possible, the savings may be stipulated. In contrast to a Managed Energy Services Agreement (MESA), the ESA provider does not take responsibility for utility payments, which remain in the hands of the host property.

The ESA developer may act as designer and installer of the project, engaging contractors directly, or outsource the function to an ESCO.

Managed Energy Services Agreement

In a Managed Energy Services Agreement (MESA), the developer assumes responsibility for payment of utility bills on behalf of the host asset. Rather than a bill based on savings, the host asset pays the developer an amount equal to the historical energy usage adjusted for current energy rates, weather and occupancy of the building. This approach typically requires a fully calibrated model reflecting 365 days of energy usage and capable of replicating historical usage with a high degree of accuracy. The formulae for calculating MESA bills based upon future rates, weather and occupancy are provided in the MESA contract.

The MESA developer does not typically assume responsibility for procuring energy, which otherwise could represent a conflict of interest; since the asset pays the developer based on historical usage multiplied by current rates, the developer would have a natural disincentive to source lower-cost energy. Typically the MESA makes payment of the energy bill a contractual obligation and an administrative function of the MESA developer, but it does not generally require that energy bills appear in the name of the developer. These bills typically remain in the name of the host asset.

Metered Energy-Efficiency Transaction Structure

The fundamental shift in the Measured Energy Efficiency Transaction Structure (MEETS) is that energy efficiency is metered. Metering is achieved by combining smart meter consumption data and building modelling to produce a dynamic baseline, against which savings are measured. Units of energy saved are then paid for on a per unit basis. The model has only recently emerged in the United States in a pilot transaction which funded additional energy-efficiency measures in a new build net zero building, the Bullitt Center in Seattle. The utility can fill the role of the developer, or the equity provider, or this can be undertaken by an experienced project developer working in partnership with capital providers.

A number of advantages are claimed for the MEETS structure, including:

- The deal structure resembles a Power Purchase Agreement, a well-understood instrument that can be financed
- It provides an incentive for the utility to sell efficiency
- The energy tenant agreement looks like standard real estate leases and therefore is easy to understand for real estate professionals
- Energy efficiency could become a tradable resource

Despite these apparent advantages, the MEETS structure has not yet been replicated although there is growing interest in the concept in the US and Europe.

Lighting as a Service (LaaS)

With the introduction of LED and internet-enabled lighting rapid paybacks can be achieved with lighting conversions and Lighting as a Service (LaaS) models are growing. In LaaS, the provider instals lighting upgrades at no cost to the client and finances the project and takes on maintenance of the system and lamp replacements. The client pays a fixed fee over the life of the contract. Taken to its logical extreme, the customer pays for a set level of lighting—'pay per lux' and has no interest in how that lighting level is produced. The falling cost of LED lighting will continue to improve payback periods for LED conversions howsoever they are financed and presumably help drive LaaS models. Navigant Research estimate that the global LaaS market will grow from USD 35.2 m in 2016 to USD 1.6bn in 2025.

Innovations in Market Infrastructure

Besides the product and contract innovations described above, there has been much needed innovation in what can be termed 'market infrastructure', systems and methodologies that enable a more active efficiency financing market.

The Investor Confidence Project

One of the major barriers to scaling up the flow of finance into energy efficiency is the lack of standardisation, particularly in the way that projects are developed and documented. This has been identified as a problem by the IEA, the Energy Efficiency Financial Institutions Group (EEFIG) and Michael Eckhart of Citi, who said; *"Energy-Efficiency projects do not meet the requirements of the capital markets. No two projects or contracts are alike."* The consequences of this lack of standardisation are:

- Greater performance risk
- Uncertainty over outcomes that limits demand
- Higher transaction costs
- Difficulties in building human capacity
- Difficulties in aggregating projects

The Investor Confidence Project (ICP)[7] is an international framework for reducing owner and investor risk, lowering due diligence costs, increasing certainty of savings achievement and enabling aggregation. It ensures transparency, consistency and trust-worthiness by utilising best practice and independent verification.

The ICP offers a project certification scheme for energy-efficiency projects in buildings, industry, street lighting and district energy called Investor Ready Energy Efficiency™ or IREE. IREE is equivalent to building performance standard, such as LEED and BREEAM, but for energy-efficiency projects. It is owned by GBCI who operate LEED, GRESB and other international sustainability indicators. Started in the US, by the Environmental Defense Fund, it was brought to Europe where it has been supported by European Commission Horizon 2020 funding, which has enabled the development and early adoption of the IREE system for buildings in all EU countries.

Under the IREE, projects are developed by credentialled Project Developers, firms that have undertaken training in the ICP methodology and whose engineers involved in the project development have demonstrated qualifications and experience. Then the project is certified by an ICP credentialed Quality Assurance Professional who is also trained in ICP and has relevant experience. The certification of the project feeds into the decision making or underwriting process of the project owner or provider of capital (which can be debt or equity or both). IREE projects must include an Operations and Monitoring Plan and a Measurement and Verification Plan to help ensure optimal performance as well as on-going performance measurement.

IREE brings benefits to all parties involved in developing, financing and implementing energy-efficiency projects. For building owners, IREE's independent review and certification of projects:

- Gives greater confidence in project development and achievement of planned savings
- Enables the comparison of projects
- Enables access to more project finance
- Can function as a 'tender in a box' and ready made underwriting criteria

For providers of investment capital (either third party or internal), IREE:

- Reduces due diligence costs
- Speeds up underwriting
- Opens access to quality projects through the Project Developer network
- Increases confidence in project fundamentals and engineering
- Provides standard document packs which enable the aggregation of projects

For project developers, IREE:

- Offers a repeatable process which aids quality assurance
- Enables more project approvals due to the independent third party review
- Offers a differentiation in the market
- Increases ability to connect with finance and insurance without additional transaction costs

For government programmes, IREE:

- Is ready to deploy
- Is based on internationally and nationally recognised and off-the-shelf technical standards
- Provides a readymade provider credentialling and training programme
- Allows the cost of quality assurance to be distributed across the market

Globally the ICP is supported by more than 400 allies including some of the largest project developers, utilities and investors. The network of

Project Developers and Quality Assurance Providers is growing, as are the number of IREE certified projects and programmes utilising IREE.

EEFIG–DEEP and the Underwriting Toolkit

The Energy Efficiency Financial Institutions Group (EEFIG)[8] was established in 2013 by the European Commission Directorate-General for Energy (DG Energy) and United Nations Environment Program Finance Initiative (UNEP FI). It created an open dialogue and work platform for public and private financial institutions, industry representatives and sector experts to identify the barriers to long-term financing for energy efficiency and propose policy and market solutions to them. EEFIG has engaged 120 active participants from 100 organisations to deliver clear and unambiguous messages.

In February 2015, EEFIG presented its landmark report, *Energy Efficiency—The First Fuel for the EU Economy: How to Drive New Finance for Energy Efficiency Investments*, which provided a significant advance in the understanding and knowledge about the issues of energy-efficiency financing. The findings of the *EEFIG Report* have contributed to actions such as G20 commitments and the European Commission has taken the *EEFIG Report* into full consideration in the development of energy-efficiency-related policies.

In continuation of the EEFIG 2015 findings, the De-risking Energy Efficiency Project Consortium, consisting of COWI, BPIE, EnergyPro, NTUA, Fraunhofer ISI and Climate Strategy & Partners, was formed to support EEFIG during 2016–2017 in its work addressing the fundamentals of energy-efficiency investments in the buildings and corporate sectors through two main work streams—the creation of an open source database for energy efficiency investments providing performance monitoring and benchmarking, and the development of common, accepted and standardised underwriting and investment framework for energy-efficiency investing.

In November 2016, the EEFIG's De-risking Energy Efficiency Platform (DEEP)[9] was launched with over 7,800 projects in an open-source, pan-EU database to improve the sharing and transparent analysis of existing energy-efficiency projects in buildings and industry. The DEEP now holds data on more than 10,000 projects.

In June 2017, the EEFIG Underwriting Toolkit[10] was launched. The Toolkit was produced with the following objectives:

- To help originators, analysts and risk departments within financial institutions better understand the nature of energy efficiency investments and therefore better evaluate both their value and the risks

- To provide a common framework for evaluating energy efficiency investments and analysing the risks that will allow training and capacity building around standardised processes and understanding
- To help developers and owners seeking to attract external capital to energy efficiency projects to develop projects in a way that better addresses the needs of financial institutions
- To foster a common language between project developers, project owners and financial institutions

The Toolkit covers the reasons why financial institutions should be interested in energy efficiency, ways of financing efficiency, the project life cycle and assessing value and risks of energy-efficiency projects. It includes an on-line resources section which provides background information on energy-efficiency technologies, contracts, organisations as well as additional case studies.

The EEFIG DEEP database helps to derisk energy efficiency projects and the Underwriting Toolkit is a capacity-building tool for financial institutions looking to expand deployment of capital into energy efficiency.

Innovation in Energy Markets

Energy efficiency has long been considered as something that has to be supported and encouraged by public funds or programmes. The design of energy markets often includes obligations on energy suppliers to invest in energy efficiency and these obligations are overseen by regulators supported by a programme evaluation industry. In a very real sense, there is no market for energy efficiency as a consumer cannot directly choose between buying units of energy and units of energy efficiency. There are only markets for the various types of products and services that produce efficiency, such as LED lighting, more efficient boilers or insulation. This is a barrier to achieving the full potential of energy efficiency and one that is being addressed by recent US innovations in several states which have introduced Pay for Performance (P4P) models. P4P requires the ability to meter efficiency either at a single building level or across a portfolio of projects. The MEETS contract referred to above is based on metered efficiency in a single building and offers the prospect of a real market for efficiency in which utilities, and others, can purchase long-term reliable supplies of efficiency in the same way that they procure energy supply. In another approach which seems to be gaining traction, the delivery of energy efficiency from portfolios of houses is being metered by the OpenEEMeter which collects smart meter data and produces normalised savings. OpenEEMeter[11] allows comparison of portfolios of different technologies as well as comparison of the performance of different contractors. These data-driven P4P models will build confidence in energy efficiency as a Distributed Energy Resource that can be contracted for and relied upon by utilities.

Conclusions

Accelerating the rate of improving energy efficiency is an essential part of our efforts to combat climate change. This will require a significant increase in the flow of investment into efficiency, probably by a factor of five, and this investment must predominantly come from the private sector as the public budgets are insufficient for the task ahead. Growing the level of investment represents a major opportunity for financial institutions but will require innovation in four areas—in energy-efficiency financing products, in energy service contracts, in market infrastructure and in energy market design. We are currently seeing innovation in all four, which offer great promise but we are only at the beginning of this transition and there is still much scope for further innovation and for scaling-up of existing innovations.

Steven Fawkes
30 July 2016

Note: This text has drawn heavily on the EEFIG Underwriting Toolkit for which Steven Fawkes was the principal author.

References

1   The numbers used here are illustrative only and not intended to represent actual situations, the cost-effective potential or a specific target.
2   https://deep.eefig.eu.
3   Amory B. Lovins. (1977). Soft Energy Paths: Toward a Durable Peace, Penguin Books.
4   Gerald Leach et al. (1979). A Low Energy Strategy for the UK, IIED.
5   Preliminary numbers show this increased to USD 231 billion in 2016; USD 133 billion in buildings.
6   CO_2 Estates (2016) MEES: The implications for rent reviews, lease renewals and valuation. http://www.CO$_2$estates.com/mees-the-implications-for-rent-reviews-lease-renewals-and-valuation/.
7   http://www.eeperformance.org.
8   http://eefig.eu.
9   https://deep.eefig.eu.
10 https://valueandrisk.eefig.eu.
11 See: openee.io.

Other Readings

EEFIG Energy Efficiency Financial Institutions Group Underwriting Guide. (2016). Available at http://bpie.eu/publication/eefig-underwriting-guide-value-and-risk-appraisal-for-energy-efficiency-financing/.

Electricity and Fuel. (2012). How Energy-Efficient Light Bulbs Compare with Traditional Incandescents. accessed Nov. 17, 2017 https://energy.gov/energysaver/how-energy-efficient-light-bulbs-compare-traditional-incandescents.

EU Commission. (2016). Boosting finance in energy efficiency investments in buildings, industry and SMEs.available at https://ec.europa.eu/energy/en/news/new-report-boosting-finance-energy-efficiency-investments-buildings-industry-and-smes.

DEEP Derisking Energy Efficiency Platform available at https://deep.eefig.eu.

Leach, G. (1979). A low energy strategy for the UK. IIED.

Lovins, A.B. (1977). Soft Energy Paths: Toward a Durable Peace, Penguin Books, 1977.

OpenEEMeter available at https://www.openee.io.

Stern, D.I. (2012). A multivariate cointegration analysis of the role of energy in the U.S. macroeconomy. Energy Econ. 22: 267–283.

Stern, D.I. (2003). Energy and economic growth, available at https://www.researchgate.net/profile/David_Stern/publication/228721215_Energy_and_economic_growth/links/02bfe50dacb1fe39e0000000.pdf.

4

Green Bonds: For You to Advertise only?

A Compact Guide Through the Current State of the Green Bond Market and the Conditions for its Further Development[#]

Stefan Klotz[1,3,*] and *Sabine Pex*[1,2]

Introduction

In recent years, green bonds have become the rising stars of the global bond markets not only for those who are interested in sustainable finance. Despite the fact that the market share of green bonds is still well below one per cent, the public showed strong interest in this kind of financial instrument which is supposed to be the answer of the financial industry to the global ecological challenges, especially to climate change. The kind of innovation linked to green bonds is remarkable: On the one hand, they are formally straightforward bonds which investors buy without taking notice of the fact. On the other hand, green bonds make use of innovative

[1] Asset Impact GmbH, Munich, Germany.
[2] Forum Nachhaltige Geldanlage (FNG), Berlin, Germany; pex@assetimpact.de., consulting@sabine-pex.de.
[3] VIF-Klotz Consulting, Munich, Germany.
[*] Corresponding author: s.klotz@vif-klotz.de
[#] In accordance with Taylor & Francis policy and our ethical obligations as researchers, we are reporting that we both are partners of Asset Impact GmbH. This company acts as initiator of the CROWD—Green Bond Impact Fund, a UCITS fund investing into green bonds. This company may indirectly be affected by the research reported in the enclosed paper; hence we do not expect any potential conflicts arising from that involvement.

concepts, such as transparency requirements or the decoupling of recourse scope and the proceeds which are earmarked for green projects. What is more, only a fuzzy definition exists as to which bond may be labelled as 'green'. Obviously, we currently witness green bonds finding themselves in some kind of adolescent phase and nobody should take it for granted that green bonds will end up as an established part of the financial world.

The paper is organised as follows. We start by describing the central features of green bonds as well as how their market developed during its short history of less than ten years. We continue this study by discussing whether and to what extent green bonds really help to make the world more sustainable and 'greener'. Then, we look at both the benefits and the costs linked with engaging in the green bond field, from the issuer's point of view as well as from the investor's. Come that far, we integrate those aspects by making a case for what will be necessary in order to see the green bond market develop further. We complete the paper by highlighting our conclusions, referring to open questions and suggesting ideas for empirical research topics.

Features of Green Bonds

The idea of issuing bonds dedicated to fund projects with positive environmental impact is about a decade old. The first green bond was issued by the European Investment Bank in 2007 (European Investment Bank 2007), with the World Bank following suit (World Bank Treasury 2008). Until 2012, the green bond market was worth a few billions of dollars niche filled by multilateral development banks. Then, different kinds of issuers started to pick up the idea, resulting in green bonds issued also by municipals, merchant banks and corporates, and such ones constructed as ABS as well. The emerging market obviously lacked clarity on the definitions and processes associated with green bonds. This was why a group of banks initiated the development of the Green Bond Principles (GBP) which were first released January 2014. At the same time, the green bond market powerfully accelerated with a total issuance of about 35 billion USD in 2014 (Climate Bonds Initiative 2016a,b). Currently, the total issuance of labelled green bonds sums up to about 150 billion USD (Environmental Finance 2016; Climate Bonds Initiative 2016b).

Measuring the issuance of green bonds leads to ambiguous results. This is because no mechanism exists which would distinguish whether a bond is a green one. The Green Bond Principles, being the most important reference for green bonds, label itself as 'voluntary process guidelines' (Green Bond Principles 2016b). They not only lack the power to impede misuse but also fall short from defining a minimum standard. While the 'use of proceeds' rather clearly demands that the utilisation of the proceeds should provide clear environmental benefits, the three other principles remain vague. Concerning the Process for Project Evaluation and Selection and the Management of Proceeds, the GBP 'encourage a high level of transparency'; for the reporting, a framework is provided (GBP 2016b). The recommendation of an external review, known as SPO (Second Party Opinion), is not one of the four principles. While confining itself to a recommendation framework is normal for a voluntary agreement, market participants are confronted with limited transparency. Accordingly, any issuing institution cannot be prevented from labelling its bond as a green bond even if an analysis would find a negative net sustainability impact of the bond.

Given that, the volume of green bonds with positive sustainability impact may significantly be less than the quoted 150 billion USD. Then again, the Climate Bonds Initiative claims that the multiple, a whopping 700 billion USD of climate-aligned bonds have already been issued, detecting a 'universe of bonds financing climate-aligned assets that do not carry a green label' (Climate Bonds Initiative 2016a,b). According to their analysis, bonds financing low-carbon transport represent about two-thirds of the unlabelled climate-aligned bonds (Climate Bonds Initiative 2016a,b).

Turning back to the labelled green bond market let us summarise some of its properties. Most issuers are banks, being public or private. Energy and utility companies are the only relevant group, besides the banking sector. That contrasts with the situation in the unlabelled climate-aligned bond market which is much more diverse in this respect. The labelled market is a high grade one with almost three-fifths being rated 'AAA' or 'AA' which is mostly due to the high importance development banks give to this market. Looking at currencies, USD and EUR dominate the field with more than 80 per cent of the total issuance (cf. Climate Bonds Initiative 2016a,b).

In their appendix, the GBP provide a very useful distinction between four types of green bonds (GBP 2016b). First, a 'Green Use of Proceeds Revenue Bond' is a non-recourse-to-the-issuer debt obligation mostly issued by government agencies. Instead, they are secured by the revenue from specific green projects. A 'Green Use of Proceeds Project Bond' is comparable in terms of direct exposure to the green project and without potential recourse to the issuer. Still, the project does not promise a constant stream of revenues. A 'Green Use of Proceeds Securitised Bond' basically adds an additional recourse access as familiar from covered bonds, ABS structures and the like. However, most green bonds can be assigned to the fourth type, the 'Green Use of Proceeds Bonds'. Those are standard recourse-to-the-issuer debt obligations for which the proceeds should be separated and used for eligible green projects.

The latter type is not only the prevailing type of green bond but most market participants think only of this type when mentioning green bonds. However, the combination of recourse to the issuer and separation of the proceeds implies that these bonds are 'standard bonds with green as a bonus feature', as the Climate Bonds Initiative puts it (Climate Bonds Initiative 2016c). Economists usually expect that there is no free lunch, therefore, such a bonus should come along with a price tag. The composition of this price tag will be illustrated below. However, for the future of the green bond market, it will be crucial that the green bonus will be appreciated sufficiently in order to cover those expenses.

Relevance of Green Bonds for ESG Investment and Sustainability Goals

Buying bonds is, of course, all but new for sustainable investors. For about a quarter of a century, they are used to judge the ESG performance of a bond's issuer. The new aspect of green bonds is their earmarking which shifts the attention from the issuer to the properties of the project(s) financed by the green bond. In fact, one of the open questions around green bonds is how relevant the ESG performance of the issuer should be for evaluation of the bond's sustainability impact. However, it is beyond controversy that green bonds offer the chance to assess their impact rather directly.

During the COP21 Conference in Paris, in December 2015 the 'Green Infrastructure Investment Coalition' (GIIC) was launched. Its aim is to support the financing of a rapid transition to a low-carbon and climate resilient economy. Green bonds are in the centre of the strategy to redirect huge financial resources into climate projects which will be crucial in order to reach the two degree target agreed upon in Paris. GIIC expects green bonds to be the key in tapping the capital at low costs (GIIC 2015).

From this perspective, the additivity of green bonds is the main criterion of success. Do green bonds significantly increase the amount available for climate-friendly projects? To put ourselves into the position to dare an answer we will analyse demand as well as supply in the current green bond market.

Green Bond Economics: The Investor's View

Let's examine the green bonus that investors can possibly find in the labelled green bond market. The analysis reveals that the bonus consists of at least five main aspects.

As a first advantage of the green bond label, those investors who seek environment-friendly assets can easily identify green bonds. There are several information systems providing lists of green bonds, e.g., Bloomberg or the website of the Climate Bonds Initiative.

Beyond this rather rough information that a bond is labelled to be green, the information about the projects which are financed by the bond's proceeds is of high interest to investors who are convinced of sustainable investment, being used to apply ESG criteria, and very selective when deciding about the impact on their investments.

There is a group of investors with the obligation to transparently report about their portfolio holdings. Such investors typically are concerned about their reputation, and therefore, try to avoid investments in assets with the potential for negative headlines. They do not only apply classical exclusion criteria (e.g., weapon producers) but try to turn from a defensive attitude to a more offensive approach driven by sustainability impacts. The echo the decarbonisation campaign earned showed how useful such an approach can be for developing a positive reputation. From the outside, this position of an issuer cannot be distinguished from an intrinsic attitude towards impact investing. However, important investors like Swiss Re or Deutsche Bank have announced to build up green bond portfolios for at least one billion USD. For such investors the green bond labelling is important because it allows them to prove the fulfilment of their announcement.

From a slightly different point of view, rational investors can be expected to optimise the risk-return-properties of the portfolios they manage. As several studies show, bonds associated with the above average ESG scores tend to exhibit less risk for a given return expectation, everything else being equal. This is even true after controlling for the financial rating (For a comprehensive presentation of corresponding papers, see Friede et al. 2015; oekom research and Klotz 2014). While there is no empirical evidence yet that green bonds reveal a similar risk advantage, obviously, it is straightforward to expect that.

But also such investors, who are not familiar with sustainable investing, are about to find themselves in the need to collect information about the ESG aspects of their portfolios. At least, this seems to be the road on which the international regulation is moving on. In 2015, the 'law on energy transition for green growth' was passed in France (LOI n° 2015-992 du 17 *août* 2015 *relative à la transition énergétique pour la croissance verte*). Its article 173 carries mandatory ESG and climate policy reporting to all asset owners on a 'comply or explain' basis, starting as early as 2016 and unfolding completely two years later. This regulation will exert influence throughout Europe as asset managers from country will have to support their French asset owners in this respect. Holding green bonds will significantly reduce the hassle this new regulation implies. France's initiative joins considerations within the European Union. Lately, in a green paper 'Building a Capital Market Union' ESG investments were mentioned as an investment category with high potential. In this context, the meaning of increased transparency on ESG issues was highlighted (European Commission 2015).

This chapter showed that almost any investor stands to benefit with the green bonus. The bonus consists primarily in the reduction of information costs in several respects. Furthermore, the green label can be used as a signal (as outlined by Spence 1973) supposed to establish a good reputation of the investor. Last but not least, regulation issues might cause a direct urge to invest in green bonds.

As green bonds currently are priced as their standard counterparts, i.e., *ceteris paribus* providing the same yield, the green label can, for most investors, be associated with a positive value spread. Consequently, one would expect, first, investors to concentrate their demand on green bonds, and second, to accept a lower yield (higher price) in exchange to the green label.

Green Bond Economics: The Issuers' View

An issuer is evidently confronted with the pros and cons when considering whether a new bond to be issued should be armed with a green label.

The most obvious possible advantage is an easier access to investors. Given the advantages, a green labelled bond offers to investors, issuing a green bond instead of a standard one should either attract more investors, or allow lowering of the issue's yield, or reducing the marketing costs for the new bond—or a combination of the three possibilities.

Second, being an institution issuing a green bond is a marketing measure by itself. As almost everybody consents to undertakings with positive ecological impact, it is worthwhile to stage own activities in this respect. While no rigorous empirical evidence exists on this aspect, one can point to the fact that a number of big banks issued, in a one-off style, one green bond with a negligible volume relative to the respective bank's total assets. At the same time, they tend to advertise their green activities. Obviously, there's a clear rationale for signalling not only for investors, but for issuers, too.

It should be mentioned that a signal cannot be sent only externally, but internally as well. For a management aimed at putting more emphasis on ESG topics, issuing a green bond may be a suitable project in order to influence one's own organisation. Besides that, political authorities may decide in favour of a labelled green bond in order to encourage corporates to decide in the same manner.

Of course, one must not forget that there are issuers whose corporate philosophy backs on the importance of sustainability. Such institutions have an intrinsic interest in issuing green bonds, more or less regardless of the costs the labelling evokes.

Those costs are of significant size, which arise from the obligations linked to a green bond label. First, the issuer has to lay the foundations for a separate accounting of the bond's proceeds. Second, the guidelines for evaluating the projects to be financed by the bond have to be determined, and the projects have to be assessed. Third, additional difficulties may arise, e.g., in the case of a green bond issued by a bank, ultimate borrowers may not agree to the transparency of their credit project. Fourth, an issuer will typically mandate a third party to write the recommended external review, causing direct costs as well as own effort to provide the information needed for it. Fifth, in order to be registered by the Climate Bond Initiative, a fee must be paid. After successfully issuing the labelled green bond, the issuer is required to regularly publish updates on the bond's projects. Beside the cost pool of the green labelling, fulfilling all these requirements normally retards the issue of the bond.

While we do not know exactly the size of this cost pool, we can assume that it drives the whole development of the green bond market.

Conditions for Becoming a Significant Market Segment

Having discussed the advantages and costs of labelling a green bond, let's briefly analyse the stability of the current market situation. As mentioned above, we can take it as a stylised fact that the green label spread is constantly zero, that is, a green bond yields identical to its standard counterpart. One possible explanation for this could be that issuers find enough investors much more easily if their bond is labelled as green. While this explanation cannot be rejected given the current state of empirical research, it is rather unlikely. For several years, the primary bond market easily absorbs new issues, being labelled as green or not. At least in these times of the ultra-easy monetary police regime, companies do not face considerable problems when endeavouring to raise debt capital. Accordingly, at least until now, they do not need a green label in order to satisfy their capital needs.

Then, a second possible explanation was that many issuers of labelled green bonds are intrinsically motivated. Unfortunately, this is even more unlikely. If so, we should be able to witness the transformation processes in the concerned companies. Obviously, this has not been the case until now.

Consequently, we must assume that it's marketing aspects which are the main cause for the acceleration in labelled green bond issuance. This assumption is backed by the evidence of the market. Just remember the guess published by the Climate Bonds Initiative that some 700 billion USD of climate-aligned bonds have been issued. To turn it the other way round, less than a quarter of climate-aligned bonds have been labelled as green bond. Let's not forget as well that we cannot observe a tendency to routinely issue green bonds in a row.

This finding is very bad news for future prospects of the green bond market. The key consideration says: If a market's base is marketing expenses, its scope is naturally limited. The improvement in an issuer's reputation is relatively high for the first green bond but the marginal utility of an additional green bond constantly decreases towards zero.

Should the current scenario remain basically unchanged, the share of labelled green bonds will not rise significantly nor reach a magnitude which could be associated with mainstream investing. Staying a niche phenomenon would then be the best perspective for green bonds; rather, one must expect that a faltering market, disappointing the hopes it had raised, will be shortlived.

For a decisively better fate, the market of labelled green bonds must reach a different equilibrium. The central characterisation to postulate for such an equilibrium would be that the additional costs an issuer faces for the green labelling must be covered for most individual bonds, at least in *a priori* expectations. This translates into a negative spread associated with green labelling, for reasons specified above, investors must be ready to accept lower yields. This was the condition for a self-supported growth of the labelled green bond market which could develop into a pronounced market segment.

Conclusion and Open Questions

This paper has sketched the development of the green bond market. Despite impressive growth rate, it is still a niche market. We have pointed out that the costs of green labelling form a serious obstacle to the market's growth. There is evidence that even if a green bond labelling takes place, the decision has quite often been driven by marketing considerations.

From these findings, our educated guess about the hitherto realised additivity of green bonds cannot turn out to be too optimistic. While there were certainly some issues that have felt tailwind from the green bond market development, it seems that a bulk of financed projects has simply been repacked into green bonds. While this was helpful in the beginning to kick-start the green bond market, now the market must prove that it's able to unlock new investment sources for ecological projects. However, objective empirical evidence is still lacking whether green bonds can increase the amount which is invested with ecological impact, or already did.

This empirical question is not the only one related to green bonds that is waiting to be answered. We also miss empirical analysis of the related aspect whether green bonds are easier sold than their standard counterparts. We also do not know enough about how an issuer decides about green bond labelling. This would be very important to design the framework of the green bond market. An additional idea for future empirical research is the risk profile of green bonds—can they state the finding that ceteris paribus an above average ESG performance of a company reduces the risk associated with its bonds?

These positive aspects of sustainable and impact investing constitute a stable tailwind for green bonds. However, from today's point of view, the only possible game changer is regulation. Without rules that internalise the external costs of pollution and CO_2 emissions, the green bond market will not be able to jump into a new equilibrium which can be associated with a much larger and established market position. This new equilibrium will be characterised by a negative yield spread compared to standard bonds. It should be mentioned that green bond investors would benefit from the emergence of such a spread by price advances of their existing green bond positions.

A further development of the green bond market will be of relevance for sustainability and impact investing as a whole. Green bonds have not only been the most relevant contribution to the plurality of this investment style, they have also inspired related new ideas: as recently as in summer of 2016, ICMA released the first guidelines for social bonds (ICMA 2016b). Beyond that, as Schneeweiss points out (2016), green bonds confront capital markets with an advanced level of transparency, enabling them to become more sustainable. It might turn out, according to Schneeweiss, that this advance in transparency will be green bonds' most relevant heritage. However, we tried to show how the green bond market could even be more beneficial.

References

Climate Bonds Initiative. (2016a). Bonds and Climate Change—the State of the Market in 2016.

Climate Bonds Initiative. (2016b). Blog on www.climatebonds.net. http://www.climatebonds.net/2016/08/market-blog-breaking-green-abs-goldwind-greenko-8x-oversubscribed-nafin-announces-cecep, accessed August 26th, 2016.

Climate Bonds Initiative. (2016c). Explaining green bonds. https://www.climatebonds.net/market/explaining-green-bonds, accessed August 26th, 2016.

Environmental Finance. (2016). Green bond market breaks through $150bn barrier. https://www.environmental-finance.com/content/news/green-bond-market-breaks-through-150bn-barrier.html, accessed August 26th, 2016.

European Commission. (2015). Commission Staff Working Document, Economic Analysis, accompanying the document: Communication from the Commission to the European Parliament, the Council, the European Economic and Social Committee and the Committee of the Regions. Action Plan on Building a Capital Markets Union. http://ec.europa.eu/finance/capital-markets-union/docs/building-cmueconomic-analysis_en.pdf.

European Investment Bank. (2007). EPOS II-The Climate Awareness Bond, EIB Promotes Climate Protection via Pan-EU Public Offering, Press release, May 1, 2007.

Friede, Gunnar, Timo Busch and Alexander Bassen. (2015). ESG and financial performance: aggregated evidence from more than 2000 empirical studies. Journal of Sustainable Finance & Investment 5(4): 210–233. doi: 10.1080/20430795.2015.1118917.

Green Infrastructure Investment Coalition. (2015). Green Infrastructure Investment Coalition Fact Sheet, dated 09.12.2015, accessed August 27th, 2016.

ICMA (International Capital Market Association). (2016a). Green Bond Principles, 2016. June 16, 2016.

ICMA (International Capital Market Association). (2016b). Social Bonds—Guidance for Issuers. June 16, 2016. http://www.icmagroup.org/Regulatory-Policy-and-Market-Practice/green-bonds/guidance-for-issuers-of-social-bonds/.

Légifrance. (2015). LOI n° 2015-992 du 17 août 2015 relative à la transition énergétique pour la croissance verte.

oekom research, A.G. and Stefan Klotz. (2014). The Importance of Sustainability Criteria in Assessing the Opportunities and Risks of Investing in Corporate Bonds. Available at http://www.oekom-research.com/index_en.php?content=studien.

Schneeweiss, Antje. (2016). Green Bonds—Black Box mit grünem Etikett? Suedwind Institut.

Spence, Michael. (1973). Job Market Signalling. Quarterly Journal of Economics 87(3): 355–374. doi:10.2307/1882010.

World Bank Treasury. (2008). World Bank and SEB Partner with Scandinavian Institutional Investors to Finance 'Green' Projects, Press release.

5

Pensions in a Time of Climate Change
The Inconvenient Truth about Fiduciary Duty

Bethan Livesey

In the 2006 film documentary, 'An Inconvenient Truth', Al Gore sets out in stark terms the global crisis presented by climate change. Climate change is going to change the world as we know it, Gore explains, unless we take action soon. Since 2006, thinking about climate change has accelerated to an even greater level of sophistication. It is now recognised as an issue with far-reaching consequences for all aspects of human life—from the physical changes to our planet to the social changes threatened by climate-related migration and the impact on our economies. However, in at least one area of finance, action has been taken only by a small cohort of leaders. The pension sector's response to climate change is disappointingly slow and inconsistent, especially in light of the long-term horizons of this industry. One frequently given reason for this is the alleged barrier posed by fiduciary duty. This article explains why this excuse has been exposed as invalid and considers what the real barriers to action may be.

This article is written from the UK perspective, but it is acknowledged that parallel arguments can be made in other jurisdictions. The UK pension system is complex, with both trust-based and contract-based elements. It is the author's view that the discussion applies across these two elements, although the term 'fiduciary duty' technically covers the former.

Pension fund administration and investment have become increasingly complex, in line with the increasingly fast-paced and intermediated nature

Head of Policy & Research ShareAction (Fairshare Educational Foundation) 16 Crucifix Lane, London UK, SE1 3JW; shareaction.org, bethan.livesey@shareaction.org.

of financial investment in the 21st century. However, in many respects, the laws governing the duties and powers of pension fund trustees in the common law system of England and Wales have remained rooted firmly in the past. This system is still underpinned by paternalistic concepts of trust law developed from private and family trust laws, where trust beneficiaries are kept at arms' length as grateful recipients of a trustee's superior knowledge and benevolence. Whilst this conception of the trustee-beneficiary relationship maps reasonably well on to a pension system in which an employer company provides a 'defined benefit' (final salary) pension backed by a covenant, it remains to be seen how well it can cope with the pensions of the future. These pensions will be 'defined contribution', meaning that the size of a pension saver's retirement pot is dependent on the size of contributions she (and her employer) make, the costs charged by those administering the scheme and the success of the investment strategy.

'There is good evidence that taking into account environmental, social and governance (ESG) factors in investment strategy can have a positive impact on investment returns. This evidence has increased as responsible investment has become more of a mainstream consideration. One of the most comprehensive meta-studies in this area found that the evidence points to a strong correlation between sustainable/ESG business practices and economic performance (Clark et al. 2015). For example, 88 per cent of the reviewed studies found that solid ESG practices result in better operational performance of firms.[1] Furthermore, sustainable firms (as measured by an aggregate sustainability score) tended to outperform less sustainable firms. Eighty per cent of studies showed a correlation between good sustainability business practices and superior financial market performance.[2] Recent data from MSCI shows a strong correlation between corporate performance and strong ESG related risk management—the MSCI EM ESG Leaders Index, which consists of 417 companies scoring highly on ESG factors, has consistently outstripped the MSCI EM benchmark since 2008 (Kynge 2017). It is not the case that every possible ESG factor will be relevant for every investment nor that a factor which is relevant at one point in time will remain relevant. What is important, however, is the recognition that ESG factors may present risks to investors and should therefore be considered alongside other risks.

To a significant proportion of the investment sector this will not be news. Asset managers in particular have adopted the mantle of promoting responsible investment. However, despite the substantial market buy-in to the need to take account of ESG factors from a financial risk standpoint,

---

[1]   Forty-five out of 51 studies on this topic.
[2]   Thirty-three out of 41 studies reviewed.

actual practice within the European asset management sector varies widely. A 2017 survey of the largest European asset managers' responsible investment practices shows a wide gulf between the top and the bottom ranking firms (for example, out of a possible 90, the top score awarded was 82, but the thirtieth ranked manager scored 29) (de Haas and Kieve 2017).

The rhetoric, at least, around ESG factors has spread within the asset management industry. However, uptake amongst pension funds has been slower. Within trust-based pension funds, one major factor in this has been the perceived role of fiduciary duty. Fiduciary duty is in some ways a very simple concept: in case law a fiduciary is described as 'someone who has undertaken to act for and on behalf of another in a particular matter in circumstances which give rise to a relationship of trust and confidence' (*Bristol & West Building Society v Mothew*). The most common formulation of a trustee's fiduciary duty is to act in the 'best interests' of its principal. Fiduciary behaviour, therefore, has a certain flavour, characterised by the imbalance in power and the dependency of one party on another. However, unpicking the exact constituent powers and behaviours that constitute fiduciary duty is not straightforward. It is not the purpose of this article to attempt to examine the nature of fiduciary duty, not least because this has been ably undertaken by the UK Law Commission. Its report, *Fiduciary Duties of Investment Intermediaries*, discusses at length the nature of fiduciary duty under the common law system of England and Wales (Law Commission 2014). It characterises the distinguishing duty of a fiduciary as one of loyalty, which may be broken down into a duty to avoid conflicts of interest and a duty to not make an unauthorised profit by reason of the fiduciary office.

Although the term 'fiduciary duty' is used within the European Union, this is a common law term not found within the majority of members states' legal systems. However, similar duties can be found in the widespread civil law application of parallel duties (PRI et al. 2015). In its report for the European Commission DG Environment, EY explains that these include duties to act in the best interests of beneficiaries, to act prudently and duties of loyalty, which often encompass duties to avoid conflicts of interest and to act impartially. It has been stated within the EU context that these duties do not exclude the consideration of ESG factors (EY 2015).

Parallels can be drawn with other jurisdictions which impose similar legal duties for those managing other people's assets. The important report into fiduciary duty and ESG undertaken by the Asset Management Working Group of the UNEP Finance Initiative explains that the US position is based on the application of the modern prudent investor rule

(UNEP Finance Initiative 2005). Like fiduciary duty, this incorporates a duty of care and a duty of loyalty.

It has been well-documented that some trustees and their advisers have characterised fiduciary duty as a barrier to consideration of factors beyond maximizing financial return (Berry 2011). This view has persisted despite over a decade having passed since it was clarified that fiduciaries investing in the context of pensions in the modern world should take ESG factors into account (UNEP 2005). Too often, the duty to act in beneficiaries' best interests has been reduced to a maxim to maximise profits, usually over the short-term. This characterisation overlooks two important features of pension investment—first, trustees have a duty of impartiality amongst beneficiaries, which is potentially breached by investment practices that overlook longer term risks to younger savers' investments; secondly, that the purpose of a pension fund is to provide beneficiaries with a retirement income capable of underpinning a decent standard of living, which is not necessarily in direct correlation to maximising the sum in their pension pot at the expense of all other impacts of investments.

Most importantly, however, the Law Commission (2014) found that the law does not require pension trustees to maximize returns over the short term. Instead, it found that the primary purpose of the investment power given to pension trustees is to secure the best realistic return over the long-term, given the need to control for risks (p. 95). The Law Commission concluded that these risks will include those presented by ESG factors. Trustees, it advised, should take into account such ESG factors where they are financially material. Furthermore, subject to a two-part test, trustees may take account of wider potentially non-financial or ethical factors. Parallel conclusions have been reached in the context of the European Union (EY 2015).

One of the most significant and most urgent environmental issues facing the modern world is climate change. Historically, climate change was seen as a niche ethical issue associated with environmental activism. Today it is regarded as a major factor relevant to the underlying stability of not only our planet, but also of the global economy. In 2015, the Governor of the Bank of England warned about the risks of potentially huge losses to investors if climate change is not taken seriously as an issue relevant to the financial markets (Carney 2015). The signing of the 2015 Paris Agreement signalled international recognition of the widespread risks posed by climate change. The Agreement aims to keep global temperature rises well below 2 degrees Celcius above pre-industrial levels. It will be necessary, in doing so, to significantly curb the current trajectory of warming, but the risks posed by not doing so are great. The Economist Intelligence Unit (2015) has estimated a total cost to the global economy of US$13.8 trillion in an environment of six degrees Celsius warming, which is equivalent to 10 per cent of the world's stock of manageable assets.

Climate change has serious financial implications for pension funds (and other asset owners). There are physical risks to assets from extreme weather events, as well as risks associated with the transition to a low carbon economy. Growing regulation could cause high carbon companies to lose value given the financial implications for business models built on risky or non-exploitable resources (Economist Intelligence Unit 2015). The global asset management firm, Schroders, has issued warnings about climate change risks, particularly in relation to policy and regulatory changes and the risks posed by the physical effects of climate change. It estimates that, on average, fifteen to twenty per cent of company cash flows are at risk (Mooney 2017).

However, the move to a low carbon economy also presents opportunities for pension funds. For example, the implementation of the Paris Agreement creates opportunities for asset owners to participate in the transition and to hedge against climate risks. Opportunities will arise from the need for investment in low carbon energy generation, infrastructure, agriculture and water and waste management.

Climate change has therefore moved from being a niche topic to being a topic for serious consideration in economic debate and policy. In light of this, it is surprising that pension funds have not widely taken steps to protect their assets under management against the risks posed by climate change nor sought to take advantage of the opportunities. Most concerning is the finding that only 5 per cent of 1,241 institutional investors across 13 European countries have even considered the investment risk posed by climate change (Mercer 2017), which is the very first building block to addressing the risk itself.

The Law Commission found that, far from being a barrier, trustees' fiduciary duties require them to take account of financially material factors or risks. The evidence is clear that climate change poses financially material risks to investments. It is therefore clear that trustees should be taking account of climate change as a risk to their portfolios. This is supported by a recent legal opinion in England (Bryant and Rickards 2016). The fact that the majority of funds are not taking climate change into account is extremely worrying. This is especially true given the fact that savers in defined contribution schemes will bear the investment risk of this investment decision. It is therefore important to investigate why pension funds are not taking climate change risk into account. Possible reasons worth exploring are: (1) trustees lack the understanding to do so; (2) trustees lack the capacity to do so; and (3) trustees lack the incentive to do so.

Lack of Understanding

Trust-based pension funds are constituted and administered in different ways. Some trusts are large with in-house capacity for asset management, others are small and outsource all significant functions to external advisers and managers. The newer form of master trusts introduced larger, multi-employer schemes into the sector.

Amongst these funds, there is a wide divergence in activity related to climate change risk. Whilst some pension funds are not even taking the first steps to understand climate risk, some pension funds are taking climate change risk seriously. For example, the UK's Environment Agency Pension Fund[3] has integrated responsible investment into its investment and decision making processes. The EAPF announced in July 2017 that it is in surplus (being 103 per cent funded). It recorded investment gains of 19.6 per cent in the year to March 2017, with five-year investment returns of 11.6 per cent. In the corporate sector, the HSBC pension fund has worked with Legal & General Investment Management to develop a default investment option designed with significant climate risk protection. Parallels can be drawn from the work of pension funds in other jurisdictions, particularly in Sweden and Denmark. For example, the fourth largest Danish pension fund, PKA, has demanded that companies take steps to protect their business models from climate change and has itself divested from some carbon-intensive companies.

The question is, therefore, what message the activities of these leader funds sends to the rest of the sector. The more the market moves towards the consideration of climate change risk, the greater the pressure will be on other funds to adopt such policies and practices. Until this pressure reaches a tipping point, it is reasonable to assume that the laggard funds are either considering climate risk but deciding not to act on it (for at least the present) or are not considering climate change risk at all.

These examples are important for two reasons—first, they demonstrate that both the law and the evidence can be interpreted (and, it is argued, should be interpreted) to allow an investment strategy that accounts for climate change risk; secondly, they show that addressing climate change risk is something which funds are being public about: it is difficult to imagine that trustees remain ignorant of the suggestion that climate change presents some kind of risk. Furthermore, pension regulators are signalling that pension fund trustees should take long-term risks such as climate change into account. Guidance from the UK's Pensions Regulator for trustees of DC schemes sets out the requirement to take account of

---

[3] This is not technically a trust, but the powers and duties of its governing board are the same as trustee boards in this area of law.

financially material ESG factors and specifically highlights the potential risk posed by 'climate change, unsustainable business practices, unsound corporate governance, etc.' (The Pensions Regulator 2016a). Fiduciary duty is most commonly regarded as a process test, in which trustees retain their discretion over the best course of action to take and exercise their duty by following due process and considering risks (PRI et al. 2015). To refuse to undertake consideration of climate change risk seems to be a decidedly risky strategy, given that their actions will presumably be judged against those of comparable funds in the market when assessed for reasonableness by a court of law.

Lack of Capacity to Act

If pension funds understand that there is an issue to be addressed when considering climate change, inactivity may be a result of a lack of capacity to act. There is evidence that many pension trustee boards lack the skills and capacity to navigate the complexities of investment. In its recent review of trusteeship, The Pensions Regulator flagged concerns about trustee competence and board governance in some schemes, particularly those which are smaller (The Pensions Regulator 2016b). It is interesting that the revolution in thought about the best way to run corporate boards has yet to permeate into the pensions sector. There is, instead, a risk of 'group think' amongst pension fund trustees. Interestingly, the role of member-nominated trustees is potentially powerful here. Although they may be lay-trustees, their presence goes some way to adding some diversity to the board. Research suggests that member-nominated or lay trustees perform an important oversight role within the trustee board (de Ste Croix 2015).

If a trustee board is under resourced, it is possible that it will place greater reliance on its advisers. Trustees are legally required to take proper advice, and in the UK, this role has fallen to investment advisers or consultants. However, recent studies have identified problems with the nature of this relationship. The UK's Financial Conduct Authority found that some pension funds, particularly smaller ones, struggle to monitor and/or challenge their advisers. Thirty-three per cent of respondents to the regulator's 2016 survey said that they 'only rarely' challenged their advisers (Financial Conduct Authority 2016). The same report flagged research by The Pensions Regulator which found that 24 per cent of trustees would never disagree with an investment adviser. There is a problem with the competitiveness of the market, with low levels of switching between advisers and poor oversight and understanding by trustees. This suggests that a key factor in raising the profile and understanding of climate change as a risk for pension trusts lies with the role of investment advisers.

One possible solution to the challenges posed by a lack of capacity and capability is a move towards larger funds. The Financial Conduct Authority identified 35,000 trust-based DC schemes in 2016, of which 33,000 had fewer than 11 members (Financial Conduct Authority 2016). The Pensions Regulator suggests that 1,000 members and above is the size at which pension funds demonstrate the quality of governance and other features which contribute to good member outcomes (The Pensions Regulator 2013). Larger funds, with higher value assets under management, have the advantage of being able to better resource their trustees. There is also the possibility of moving asset management in-house, which may be advantageous. Larger funds are able to also, potentially, invest in a wider range of assets, including illiquid assets such as infrastructure. A study of jurisdictions in which scale in pension funds has been encouraged shows that these funds may have better outcomes for members (de Ste Croix 2015). It seems possible that larger funds would be better equipped to address climate risk.

Lack of Incentive

Financial regulators, such as The Pensions Regulator and the Bank of England, have issued guidance and warnings about the risks posed by climate change. However, regulatory guidance does not have the full force of law and we have seen that the laggards in the sector have not been spurred to action. A move towards mandatory positive regulation has happened already in France, where Article 173 is now in force. The IORPs II Directive in the European Union is significant because it contains explicit references to ESG factors and mandates that EU member states allow occupational pension providers to consider ESG factors. The transposition of this directive into the laws of relevant EU member states will be important for moving the acceptance of ESG risks into the mainstream. However, the effectiveness of the resulting laws will have to go beyond mere advisory guidance, which is not widely catalysing action.

Perhaps the most potent incentive for pension trustees will come in two forms—the first will be when investment returns start to be affected by unmitigated climate risks; the second will be when beneficiaries, particularly in DC schemes, take legal action against trustees for breach of their fiduciary duties. The tragedy of these scenarios is that there will be no real winners in a world in which climate change has advanced.

The above factors point to the need for regulatory changes. The market can only do so much to encourage best practice across the pensions sector: the evidence strongly suggests that the laggards in the sector will not be moved on by market pressures. When considering what regulatory change is needed, it is necessary to remember that fiduciary duty is not a real barrier to the integration of financially material risks into investment strategies by pension funds. What is needed is clarity, not law change. Policymakers (government and regulators) should ensure that the law is as clear as possible in setting out what is expected of trustees in respect of ESG (and wider) risks. This would mean that the excuse of fiduciary duty is removed and the wider issues can be addressed, if necessary, through further regulatory change. For example, there should be regulatory consequences for laggard funds ignoring the evidence that climate change is a risk. If pension funds recognise the risk, but do not feel able to act because of capacity constraints, such as size or training, these constraints should be removed. If regulatory levers are needed to do this, that would provide the necessary incentive for action. Overall, the message needs to be that those who regulate are ready to protect the best interests of ordinary savers, where pension funds fail to do so.

Reference

Berry, C. (2011). Protecting our best interests. FairPensions.

Bristol & West Building Society v Mothew [1998] Ch 1 at 18 per Lord Millett.

Bryant, K. and Rickards, J. (2016). The legal duties of pension fund trustees—Abridged Opinion. Available at: https://www.documents.clientearth.org/library/download-info/qc-opinion-the-legal-duties-of-pension-fund-trustees-in-relation-to-climate-change/[Accessed 29 July 2017].

Carney, M. (2015). Breaking the tragedy of the horizon. [Speech] Lloyds of London, 29 September. Available at: http://www.bankofengland.co.uk/publications/Pages/speeches/2015/844.aspx [Accessed 26 July 2017].

Clark, G. and Monk, A. (2012). Principles and Policies for In-House Asset Management. Available at: SSRN: https://ssrn.com/abstract=2189650 or http://dx.doi.org/10.2139/ssrn.2189650.

Clark, G., Feiner, A. and Viehs, M. (2015). From the stockholder to the stakeholder: how sustainability can drive financial outperformance. University of Oxford and Arabesque Partners.

De Haas, N. and Kieve, T. (2017). Lifting the Lid: Responsible Investment Performance of European Asset Managers. ShareAction.

de Ste Croix, C. (2015). Realigning Interests, Reducing Regulation. ShareAction.

Economist Intelligent Unit. (2015). The Cost of Inaction: Recognising the Value at Risk from Climate Change.

Environment Agency Pension Fund. (n.d.). Tackling climate risk. Available at: https://www.eapf.org.uk/investments/climate-risk/climate-risk-strategy [Accessed 29 July 2017].

EY. (2015). Resource Efficiency and Fiduciary Duty of Investors. European Commission DG Environment.

Financial Conduct Authority. (2016). Asset Management Market Study Interim Report.

Kynge, J. (20 July 2017). Investors in companies that do good do better. London, Financial Times.

Law Commission. (2014). Fiduciary Duties of Investment Intermediaries.

Mercer. (2017). 2017 European Asset Allocation Report.

Mooney, A. (16 July 2017). Schroders issues climate change warning. London, Financial Times.

Nusseibeh, S. (2017). The Why Question. Available at: https://www.the300club.org/wp-content/uploads/2017/03/300-Club-COMMENTARY-0217-The-why-question-Saker-Nusseibeh-FINAL-060317.pdf [Accessed 25 July 2017].

PRI, UNEP FI, UNEP Inquiry & UN Global Compact. (2015). Fiduciary Duty in the 21st Century.

The Pensions Regulator. (2013). Trust-based Pension Schemes Features Research.

The Pensions Regulator. (2016a). Managing DC Benefits—Investment Governance Guidance. Available at: http://www.thepensionsregulator.gov.uk/trustees/investment-management-in-your-dc-scheme.aspx#s22313 [Accessed 29 July 2017].

The Pensions Regulator. (2016b). 21st Century Trusteeship and Governance—Discussion Paper Response.

UNEP Finance Initiative. (2005). A Legal Framework for the integration of environmental, social and governance issues into institutional investment.

6

Innovative 21st Century Water Utilities

Robert C. Brears

Introduction

As the century progresses, water utilities managing public water systems are facing increasing pressure from a wide range of social, technological, economic, environmental and political trends that challenge their ability to provide a sustainable, reliable and affordable water service that meets customers' expectations in the future (UKWIR 2011). Response to these stresses will require water utilities to undertake substantial technological and management innovations. However, water utilities have typically been slow to evolve and incorporate new innovative solutions into existing systems due to a number of barriers, including technologies lacking economies of scale for widespread implementation, lack of political will or coordination in implementing innovative initiatives as well as regulations that essentially favour status quo technologies over new, more efficient technologies (Kiparsky et al. 2013; Copeland and Carter 2017; Brears 2016). Nonetheless, failure to implement technological and management innovations will expose water utilities to a variety of risks including environmental degradation, public health risks from poor quality water and reductions in the level of service customers have come to expect (Speight 2015). This chapter will first outline the multiple challenges that water utilities are facing in this century before introducing the definition of innovation and various types of innovations available as water utilities. Finally, the chapter will discuss a variety of technological and management innovations that water utilities have implemented around

Founder of Mitidaption and Urban Water Security Center; rcb.chc@gmail.com the world to enhance the environment, provide new services, replace aging infrastructure and lower operational costs and carbon emissions.

Multiple Challenges to Water Utilities

Water utilities are faced with multiple challenges in ensuring a sustainable, reliable, and affordable water service that meets customers' expectations in the future including climate change, rapid economic and population growth as well as urbanisation impacting the availability of water supply in addition to rising commercial, technological and public pressures to protect the environment, provide new services, replace aging infrastructure and lower operational costs and carbon emissions.

Climate Change

Climate change will lead to fluctuations in precipitation, ground and surface water levels as well as water quality, for example, the Food and Agricultural Organization (FAO) predicts that for each 1°C of global warming 7 per cent of the world's population will see a decrease of 20 per cent or more in renewable water resources (FAO 2016). At the same time, climate change will lead to water quality deterioration due to increased temperature, increased sediment, nutrient and pollution loadings from heavy rainfall, increased concentration of pollutants during droughts and disruptions of treatment facilities during floods (Brears 2016). The providing of water- and wastewater-related services contributes to greenhouse gas (GHG) emissions as they require significant energy inputs. In China, average GHG emissions from urban water utility operations accounted for 41 MT CO_2-equivalent, with 58 per cent coming from energy use, 40 per cent from treatment processes and 2 per cent from chemical usage (Zhang et al. 2017). Meanwhile, it was estimated that if the Los Angeles Department of Power and Water (LADWP) reduced its use of coal and increased its use of natural gas and renewable energy when providing of local water services, the utility could experience a reduction in carbon intensity by 54 per cent (Fang et al. 2015).

Economic Growth

By 2050, the world's economy will grow to four times its current size. While this growth will result in a less than proportional increase in water demand, the global economy will still require 55 per cent more water. For instance, global water demand for the manufacturing sector will increase by 400 per cent from 2000 to 2050, while industrial demand for water will increase, with the sector's water demand proportional to the country's income level; ranging from 5 per cent of water withdrawals in low-income countries to more than 40 per cent in high-income countries (UN-Water 2014; OECD 2012b; UNESCO 2012).

Population Growth

The world's population of 7.6 billion in 2017 is expected to reach 8.6 billion in 2030, 9.8 billion in 2050 and 11.2 billion in 2100. Between 2017 and 2050, half of the world's population growth will occur in just nine countries: India, Nigeria, the Democratic Republic of the Congo, Pakistan, Ethiopia, the United Republic of Tanzania, the United States of America, Uganda and Indonesia (United Nations 2017). Population growth nonetheless is a contributor to water scarcity as an increasing population means greater demand for water for domestic, industrial and municipal uses. In fact, the OECD projects that by 2050 domestic water demand will increase by 130 per cent (OECD 2012a). In Texas, the population is expected to increase by more than 70 per cent between 2020 and 2070, from 29.5 million to 51 million. This will result in water demand increasing by 17 percent, from 18.4 million acre-feet per year in 2020 to 21.6 million acre-feet per year in 2070 (Texas Water Development Board 2017).

Rapid Urbanisation

Global demand for water is projected to exceed supply by 40 per cent in 2030 and 55 per cent in 2050 due to a variety of trends including rapid urbanisation (OECD 2012c; UNEP 2016). For instance, by 2030, 5 billion people will be living in urban areas with hundreds of millions living in one of the world's 41 mega-cities, up from 28 today (United Nations Population Fund 2016; United Nations 2014). Already, one in four cities are water stressed due to geographical and financial constraints of importing water from distant sources (McDonald et al. 2014). For example, the Middle East and North Africa (MENA) region is one of the most rapidly urbanising regions in the world with the urban population growing at 2.4 per cent per annum (World Bank 2014), yet the MENA region is one of the most water-scarce in the world: in 1950, the per capita renewable water resources were 4,000 cubic metres per year and this has dropped to 1,100 metres in 2007 and is likely to drop further to 550 by 2050 (World Bank 2007).

Rising Energy Costs

Energy is a significant cost factor in the provision of water and wastewater treatment services, for instance, in the UK, the water industry's electricity costs make for 13 per cent of total costs (Rothausen and Conway 2011).

Over the next 25 years, water utility electricity costs will more than double, mostly due to desalination projects, large-scale water transfer projects as well as increasing demand for wastewater treatment (and higher levels of treatment) (IEA 2016). In Australia, the cost of electricity and increasing energy intensity of water supply is likely to result in a five-fold increase in annual electricity costs for water utilities by 2030 (Cook et al. 2012). As such, energy conservation and efficiency will become issues of increasing importance for many water utilities (Copeland and Carter 2017).

Aging Infrastructure

In many cities around the world, a large portion of the water infrastructure is approaching, or has already reached, the end of its useful life, with aging infrastructure often resulting in high water loss from physical leakage (Lam et al. 2017). In an earlier World Bank study, it was estimated that around 32 billion cubic metres of treated water physically leaks from urban water supply systems around the world each year (World Bank 2006). In addition, sewage as well as groundwater surrounding pipes, which often contain contaminants, can enter leaking pipes and travel throughout the water distribution network causing public health concerns, for example, outbreaks of gastrointestinal illness (Fox et al. 2016; Säve-Söderbergh et al. 2017). The required investment to rebuild these networks has to come on top of other water investment needs including investments needed to comply with standards for drinking water quality (AWWA 2012). Faced with increasing capital needs and potential funding shortfalls, many water utilities are increasing their rates they charge for water services in the immediate future (AWWA 2017). However, there is evidence that customers' willingness to pay for any infrastructure upgrade is negatively affected by the cost of the proposed improvement (Tanellari et al. 2015).

High Customer Expectations

Water utilities are under increasing pressure to show customers the value for the rates paid and to enhance customer engagement and participation in various programmes (NACWA 2017). This has resulted in end users of water services transitioning from being captive consumers of a uniform product delivered under fixed circumstances to end users that demand they be able to choose different products and services, for example, purchasing rain-water harvesting systems. This effectively turns the consumer into a co-constructor of new water infrastructure, helping to support water innovations while at the same time demanding these systems to be delivered and subsidised by the water utility or municipal agencies (Hegger et al. 2011). Furthermore, water users are demanding that global water-using practices become more sustainable, which in turn provides support to water conservation initiatives developed by their local providers (Hegger et al. 2011).

Innovation

In the context of water utilities, innovation can be defined as *"the creation, development and implementation of a new product, technology, service, tariff design or process of production with the aim of improving efficiency, effectiveness or competitive advantage. It includes new ways of acquiring or deploying inputs, such as financial resources. The change may be incremental or fundamental"* (Speight 2015). It should be noted that the definition includes the following:

- It deals with both products and processes
- It refers to the creation, development, implementation of a new product/process developed either in-house or by other companies and sectors
- All products and processes to be new or novel
- The aim is to improve efficiency, effectiveness or increase competitive advantage

The characteristics of innovation in the water industry are summarised in Table 1.

Table 1. Characteristics of innovation in the water industry.

Definition	Characteristic
Products and processes	Refer to both goods and/or services where goods are an actual end product sold to the customer and services are how the product is sold and supplied to the customer. Processes include technological processes in the production sector
Development and existing innovations	Innovations can be new and developed in-house or make use of existing innovations. In-house innovations include research and development (R&D) and other activities, including applied research to gain new knowledge and development of new products or processes. Already-existing innovations adopted by other firms or organisations are mainly non-R&D activities, including identifying new innovative solutions (process, products), buying technical information, know-how or skills, developing human skills, investing in equipment, software, reorganising management systems and business activities, developing new methods of marketing and selling its goods and services

(Speight 2015)

Innovation and Novelty

A key aspect of the definition of innovation is that it must contain a degree of novelty, specifically:

- *New to the firm*: The innovation must be new to the firm. A product, process, marketing method or organisational method may already have been implemented by other firms, but if it is new to the firm (or in the context of products and processes it is significantly improved), then it is an innovation for that firm
- *New to the market*: Innovations are new to the market when the firm is the first to introduce the innovation to the market, where a market is defined as the firm and its competitors and it can include a geographic region or product line
- *New to the country*: An innovation is new to the country when the firm is the first to introduce the innovation for all domestic markets and industries
- *New to the world*: An innovation is new to the world when the firm is the first to introduce the innovation for all markets and industries internationally

Innovative Inputs and Outputs

There are two types of innovation: inputs and outputs. Innovation inputs consist of all the resources dedicated to promoting innovation and includes new strategies, knowledge, capital and human resources and even environmental public policy components, such as water and wastewater fees and charges, new technologies, for example, energy recovery from wastewater, as well as innovative infrastructure, for instance, providing alternative water supplies. Innovative outputs include customer value and efficiency measures, better customer service as well as information, images and ideas that increase the efficiency of the existing water supply system (London Economics 2009).

Innovative Inputs

Water utilities have implemented a variety of innovative inputs including water and wastewater tariffs, as well as new infrastructure to ensure a sustainable, reliable and affordable water service that meets customers' expectations in the future.

Water Pricing

Economic theory suggests that demand for water should behave like any other goods—as price increases, water use decreases. Water utilities use a variety of different price structures, all of which send different conservation signals to individuals and communities. Pricing structures include a flat rate for water usage regardless of volume used, a volumetric rate that is based on the volume of water used at a constant rate, an increasing block rate that contains different prices for two or more pre-specified quantities (blocks) of water, and a two-part rate involving a fixed and variable component with the fixed part covering infrastructure costs and the variable amount based on the volume of water consumed (Sibly 2006; Policy Research Initiative 2005; Brears 2016).

Singapore's Water Price Revision

Singapore's Public Utilities Board (PUB) is revising its water prices in two steps, on 1 July 2017 and on 1 July 2018 as a result of increased investments in water infrastructure, coupled with rising operational costs (Table 2). PUB is upgrading its water system to make it more resilient, especially in light of challenges posed by climate change. The revised water price will enable the utility to cater to future demand, enhance water security and continue to deliver a high-quality and reliable supply of water to customers. Over the next two years, the key revisions in the water price are:

- A 30 per cent increase in water price, phased over two years, starting from 1 July 2017
- Restructuring of the Sanitary Appliance Fee and the Waterborne Fee into a single, volume-based fee

Table 2. Singapore's water price revision.

		Current		From 1 July 2017		From 1 July 2018	
		Water price ($/m³)		Water price ($/m³)		Water price ($/m³)	
		0–40 m³	> 40 m³	0–40 m³	> 40 m³	0–40 m³	> 40 m³
	Tariff	$1.17	$1.40	$1.19	$1.46	$1.21	$1.52
Potable water	Water Conservation Tax (% of water tariff)	$0.35 (30% of $1.17)	$0.63 (45% of $1.40)	$0.42 (35% of $1.19)	$0.73 (50% of $1.46)	$0.61 (50% of $1.21)	$0.99 (65% of $1.52)
Used water	Waterborne Fee	$0.28	$0.28	$0.78	$1.02	$0.92	$1.18
	Sanitary Appliance Fee	$2.80 per fitting		Combined into Waterborne fee		Combined into Waterborne Fee	
Total price		$2.10	$2.61	$2.39	$3.21	$2.74	$3.69

(PUB 2017)

Cape Town's Water Scarcity-based Tariffs

Because Cape Town is situated in a water-scarce region, the city imposes water restrictions on a permanent basis, with the level of water restrictions dependent on dam storage levels. Cape Town has three levels of water restrictions:

- Level 1 (10 per cent water savings): Normally in place
- Level 2 (20 per cent water savings): Applicable when dam levels are lower than the norm
- Level 3 (30 per cent water savings): Applicable when dam levels are critically low

Since 1 November 2016, Cape Town has been under Level 3 (30 per cent water savings) which restricts water usage activities including the prohibition of residents using sprinkler systems, watering their gardens, and washing their cars with hosepipes with municipality-supplied drinking water. To reduce water consumption, Cape Town, from 1 December 2016 until further notice, charges all residential, commercial and industrial water uses Level 3 (30 per cent savings) tariffs. For domestic water users, the first 6,000 litres remains free, but the next block rates increase significantly (Table 3). Meanwhile, commercial and industrial users, who normally are charged R18.77, including VAT per thousand litres (under Level 1 water savings), are charged the level 3 charge of R25.35 per thousand litres (Table 4) (City of Cape Town 2016a; City of Cape Town 2016b).

Table 3. Cape Town's residential water tariffs.

Water 2016/17 (domestic full) Steps	Unit*	Level 1 (10% reduction) Normal tariffs Rand (incl. VAT)	Level 2 (20% reduction) During level 2 restrictions Rand (incl. VAT)	Level 3 (30% reduction) During level 3 restrictions Rand (incl. VAT)
Step 1 (> 0 ≤ 6 kl)	/kl	R 0.00	R 0.00	R 0.00
Step 2 (> 6 ≤ 10.5 kl)	/kl	R 14.89	R 15.68	R 16.54
Step 3 (> 10.5 ≤ 20 kl)	/kl	R 17.41	R 20.02	R 23.54
Step 4 (> 20 ≤ 35 kl)	/kl	R 25.80	R 32.65	R 40.96
Step 5 (> 35 ≤ 50 kl)	/kl	R 31.86	R 48.93	R 66.41
Step 6 (> 50 kl)	/kl	R 42.03	R 93.39	R 200.16

*1 kl is a thousand litres

Table 4. Cape Town's commercial and industrial water tariffs.

Commercial & Industrial water use (Standard)	Unit	Level 1 (10% reduction) Rand (incl. VAT)	Level 2 (20% reduction) Rand (incl. VAT)	Level 3 (30% reduction) Rand (incl. VAT)
Water	Per kl	R18.77	R21.82	R25.35

Waste Reduction and Resource Recovery

Water utilities can implement circular economy innovations that aim to design out waste throughout the value chain, rather than relying on solutions at the end of a product's life. This can be achieved through activities that include reduction in the quantity of materials required to deliver water- and wastewater-related services; reduction in the use of energy in providing water- and wastewater-related services; reduction in the use of materials that are hazardous or difficult to recycle and creation of a market for secondary raw materials (Brears 2015).

Scottish Water's Waste-to-Energy Project

As part of Scottish Water's contribution towards developing the Scottish circular economy and lower operational costs in its water distribution system, the utility is partnering with Sainsbury's to provide recycling facilities for waste cooking fat and oil, which is a major cause of sewer blockages and flooding: fat, oil, and grease (FOG) cause 20 per cent of the nearly 37,000 sewer blockages reported per year. Sainsbury's is trialling dedicated FOG collection points at seven store car parks located in Edinburgh, West Lothian and Fife, where customers can drop off containers of waste oil in an easy and clean way. So far almost 5,000 litres of waste oil has been collected and recycled. Olleco—a resource recovery company—transports the waste oil to one of its processing centres where FOG is removed from its containers, heated, cleaned and filtered before it is converted into biodiesel for use in road vehicles (Scottish Water 2017).

Anglian Water's Waste Reduction and Resource Recovery Efforts

Anglian Water has implemented a waste reduction programme across its whole business. Since 2007, the utility has operated a 'business swap shop' on its intranet where different parts of the company advertise spare equipment to release storage space and avoid costs of purchasing new equipment unnecessarily. Meanwhile, sludge from the water utility's Wing Water Treatment Works in Rutland is now diverted away from a landfill and used as biofuel at the nearby Castle Cement plant at Ketton while methane created during the water recycling treatment process is used as fuel in combined heat and power units. Finally, 90 per cent of biosolids—by-product of the water recycling treatment process—is recycled for agricultural use (Anglian Water 2017).

Developing Alternative Water Supplies

Due to the financial costs of maintaining and replacing aging infrastructure, some cities are examining alternative ways of providing water, including developing rain-water harvesting (capturing and storing of rain-water for beneficial use), grey water (untreated used water that has not come into contact with toilet waste, such as water from showers and laundry machines) and recycled water systems (reusing treated wastewater for beneficial purposes). The additional benefit of developing alternative water supplies is that it enables water utilities to reduce the costs of treating potable water (chemical, energy, etc.) for non-potable uses (Brears 2016; ASCE 2017).

Pure Water San Diego Program

To lower operational costs and become more resilient to climate change, the City of San Diego is embarking on its phased, multi-year Pure Water San Diego Program that will see recycled water provide one-third of the city's water supply locally by 2035 and reduce the city's ocean wastewater discharges by more than 50 per cent. Instead of wastewater being treated at Point Loma and discharged into the ocean, the Pure Water Program will direct wastewater flows away from Point Loma and use proven water purification technology to produce safe, high-quality purified drinking water. Specifically: (1) wastewater is treated to recycle water standards at an existing water reclamation plant; (2) recycled water is treated at a pure water facility, resulting in purified water; (3) purified water is sent to an existing reservoir and blended with imported and local water supplies; (4) water is treated further at an existing drinking water treatment plant; and (5) potable water is distributed to customers via the city's existing water supply system (City of San Diego 2017).

Recycled Water for New Housing Estates

In Melbourne, City West Water's West Wyndham Recycled Water Project aims to deliver high quality, Class A recycled water to housing estates in the Wyndham area, as well as a number of open spaces managed by the Wyndham City Council. Currently, recycled water—a mix of drinking water and recycled water—is supplied to around 3,570 homes in the area. The aim of the West Wyndham Recycled Water Project is to create a supply of 100 per cent recycled water in 2017. The recycled water will come from Melbourne Water's Western Treatment Plant, where it will be further processed and sent to homes and open spaces in the Wyndham West area through a dedicated 'purple pipe' recycled water system. Class A recycled water can be used for toilet flushing, car washing on grassed areas, garden watering, filling water features, providing drinking water for pets and washing machines. It should not be used for drinking, cooking or food preparation, bathing or showering and swimming (City West Water 2017).

Innovative outputs

Water utilities have implemented a variety of innovative outputs including retrofit programmes, subsidies and rebates to encourage the uptake of water-efficient technologies, public education and customer-centric system initiatives to ensure a sustainable, reliable and affordable water service that meets customers' expectations into the future.

Retrofit Programmes

Retrofit programmes involve the distribution and installation of replacement devices to physically reduce water use in homes and offices. The most common retrofits are toilet retrofits, involving customers replacing their older toilets with newer low-/dual-flush toilets, and the distribution of showerheads and faucet aerators (devices, when inserted into taps, reduce the flow of water) to households and offices (Georgia Environmental Protection Division Watershed Protection Branch 2007; Michelsen et al. 1999; Pennsylvania State University 2010). Water-saving devices can be distributed by water utilities in numerous ways, including door-to-door delivery of water-saving kits to households or direct installation by trained technicians or plumbers (Pennsylvania State University 2010).

South West Water's Free Water-Fixtures

To reduce stress on limited supplies from climate change, South West Water has begun offering its customers free water-saving kits to enable households to take control of their water usage. With a belief that small changes can cumulatively lead to a big difference, the water utility is giving away kits that contain a variety of water-fixtures and information as summarised in Table 5 (SaveWaterSaveMoney: South West Water 2017).

Table 5. South West Water's free water-fixtures.

Water-saving Fixture	Description
Hippo 9	Every time a toilet is flushed, the Hippo will save 2–3 litres of water. This is for toilets installed before 1991
Hippo 7	The smaller version is for cisterns installed between 1991 and 20001 and save around 1 litre per flush
ShowerSave	Sets a constant flow rate of 7.5 litres per minute and saves energy too
Shower timer	The 4-minute sand timer is a simple tool to help shorten shower times and save water and energy costs
Spraymagic tap insert	Saves on average 36 liters per day. Fits on most hand basin taps with circular outlets
Neoperl tap inserts	Saves on average 36 litres. Fits on most hand basin taps with screw-fit nozzle outlet
Top tips leaflet	Includes more water-saving tips for a water-wise home

New York City's Water Conservation Kits

New York City's Department of Environmental Protection (DEP) is making available free water-saving kits to private homeowners and individual apartment tenants who live in New York City. The kit contains retrofit fittings including low-flow showerheads, faucet aerators and different gravity tank toilet saving-devices that, if installed to replace higher consumption fittings, can reduce water consumption and associated energy costs. The kit also includes dye tablets used for detecting gravity toilet tank leaks as well as a brochure on how to perform a home water survey (NYC DEP 2017).

Subsidies and Rebates

Subsidies and rebates (incentives) are used to modify customers' behaviour in a predictable, cost-effective way, i.e., reducing wastage and lowering water consumption by providing, for example, subsidies for newer, more water-efficient devices. In particular, incentives are commonly used to encourage the uptake of water-efficient appliances, as positive incentives are found to reduce the gap between the time the incentive is presented and behavioural change as compared to disincentives (Brears 2016).

LA's Water Technical Assistance Program

LADWP has developed the Water Technical Assistance Program that offers commercial, industrial, institutional and multi-family customers a customised approach to reducing their water and energy bills. Through the program, LADWP works one-on-one with customers to modernise their facility with the latest water-efficient equipment. The program offers up to $250,000 in financial incentives for pre-approved equipment and products that demonstrate water savings. The actual incentive amount is based on the water savings accomplished by the project, with the incentive calculated at $1.75 per 1,000 gallons of water saved over a number of years—not to exceed the installed cost of the project—with customers receiving a rebate following verification of installation and operation of pre-approved projects (LADWP 2017).

Denver Water's Commercial Rebate for Cooling Towers

Denver Water's Cooling Tower Performance Rebate Program helps businesses upgrade their cooling tower controls and optimise their efficiency. Denver Water will reward the customer 50 per cent of project cost, of $18.50 per 1,000 gallons saved below a determined previous three-year consumption average. Savings are calculated from meter readings provided by the customer during the performance year. The maximum pay-out is $40,000. Overall, if an 800-tonne cooling tower increases its cycles of concentration from five to eight, the building could save an estimated 194,000 gallons of water a year and be eligible for a $3,589 incentive payment or 50 per cent of project costs. Additional savings come from decreased utility costs, which amount to $1,500 in water and sewer and more than $1,000 in chemical savings (Denver Water 2017).

Public Education

Water utilities can use public education to persuade individuals and communities to conserve water resources. In particular, water utilities can influence an individual's attitude and behaviour towards water resources by increasing their knowledge and awareness of environmental problems associated with water scarcity (Steg and Vlek 2009; Najjar and Collier 2011; Policy Research Initiative 2005). Meanwhile, water utilities can promote water conservation in schools to increase young people's knowledge of the water cycle and encourage a sustainable use of scarce resources (Brears 2016).

San Francisco's Racy Water Conservation Messages

Over the past few summers, the San Francisco Public Utilities Commission (SFPUC) has implemented a head-turning water conservation strategy that involves using bold, risqué, multilingual water conservation advertisements to change the behaviour of water-users in the city. The SFPUC's racy public awareness advertisements, featured in or on newspapers, bus shelters, buses and billboards, were designed to get the heart racing with creatively crafted messages that blare out for customers to 'Jiggle it' when looking for leaks, 'Make it a quickie' when having a shower, and 'Doing it' by replacing old toilets and getting paid for it (San Francisco Public Utilities Commission 2017).

United Utilities' School Education Programme

United Utilities in the United Kingdom runs a varied educational programme aimed at primary and secondary school children. The focus of the programme is to deliver fun, interactive lessons that tie into the national curriculum and leave a lasting memory for students and teachers. Through an educational provider, the utility delivers interactive water-efficiency workshops in primary schools across the region, providing students with an introduction to the water table and the importance of saving water, not flushing the wrong things down the toilet as well as practical water conservation tips for the home and garden. In addition, the utility has created an interactive online 'All about water' game which enables students to learn about the water cycle including where it comes from; how it is caught; how drinking water is prepared; how water is distributed into homes; where it is used; how dirty water is cleaned and how cleaned water is returned back to nature (United Utilities 2017a; United Utilities 2017b).

Customer-centric Systems

To ensure water is managed in a more sustainable and efficient manner, water utilities are implementing customer-centric systems including smart sensors, smart meters and online monitoring applications that enable customers to understand where, when and why they use water.

Dubai Electricity and Water Authority's Smart Meters

Dubai Electricity and Water Authority (DEWA) is installing 1.2 million smart meters across the Emirate, enabling customers to receive real-time information on water as well as energy consumption. This will enable customers to monitor actual consumption to better understand and manage bills. In addition to providing current consumption data, DEWA's smart meters will provide customers with historical consumption data as well as a breakdown of consumption processes that use water and energy (DEWA 2017a; DEWA 2017c). This will enable customers to identify water and energy efficiencies in their homes. The smart meter data is delivered to customers' smartphones or tablets via DEWA's Smart App, allowing them to view billing information, graphs to check and compare consumption as well as set caps for both water and electricity consumption (DEWA 2017b; TechTrade Asia 2016).

MyWaterToronto

Toronto Water has developed the MyWaterToronto water meter programme in which customers can view their water use information anytime, anywhere, from a computer or mobile device. Customers can log on to their MyWaterToronto to view their total and average water use by day, month or year in an easy-to-read graph or chart format. Boxes can also be checked to add extra details including temperature and precipitation, so that water users can better understand why they have used more or less water during a particular time period (Toronto Water 2017).

Conclusions

Water utilities are faced with multiple challenges including climate change, rapid economic and population growth as well as urbanisation which impact the availability of water supply in addition to raising commercial, technological and public pressure to protect the environment, provide new services, replace aging infrastructure and lower operational costs and carbon emissions. In response, water utilities have implemented a variety of innovative inputs to ensure the delivery of a sustainable, reliable and affordable water service that meets customers' expectations in the future, including water and wastewater tariffs to cover rising investment costs and conserve water, and new infrastructure to enhance resilience to climate change, reduce waste, and recover resources as well as deliver alternative water supplies. Examples of this include Singapore's PUB revising its water price upwards as a result of increased investments in future-proofing its water infrastructure in addition to meeting rising operational costs; Cape Town increasing its water tariffs in line with water conservation restrictions; Scottish Water partnering with the private sector to recycle waste into biodiesel; Anglian Water implementing a waste reduction programme throughout its whole operations, in addition to turning sludge into biofuel for a nearby industrial plant, recovering methane for energy production and recovering biosolids for agricultural fertiliser; San Diego developing water recycling facilities to provide one-third of the city's water supply and City West Water in Melbourne developing a recycled water system for non-potable water uses on a housing estate. Meanwhile, water utilities have implemented a variety of innovative outputs to ensure the delivery of a sustainable, reliable and affordable water service that meets customers' expectations in the future, including retrofit programmes to facilitate water and energy savings, subsidies and rebates to encourage the uptake of water-efficient technologies, public education to raise awareness on the water cycle and customer-centric system initiatives to enable customers to view water-consumption data and make conservation decisions; examples include South West Water providing free water-saving fixtures and conservation tips to customers; Los Angeles providing one-on-one assistance to commercial customers to install water-efficient technologies; Denver offering commercial rebates for installing water-efficient cooling towers; New York City's DEP making available free water-saving kits for homeowners and apartment tenants to save water and energy; San Francisco creating racy advertisements to gain attention on conserving water; United Utilities' development of fun, interactive lessons for students that involve water-efficiency workshops and an interactive online water game; DEWA's new smart meters providing customers, via their smartphones and tablets, with real-time information on their water and energy consumption; and Toronto Water's online programme that allows customers to view their water consumption trends and understand their consumption trends.

References

Anglian Water. (2017). Reducing waste [Online]. Available: http://www.anglianwater.co.uk/environment/our-commitment/performance/reducing-waste.aspx.

ASCE. (2017). Aging U.S. water infrastructure presents engineering, financial challenges [Online]. Available: http://www.asce.org/magazine/20160809-aging-u-s--water-infrastructure-presents-engineering,-financial-challenges/.

AWWA. (2012). Buried no longer: Confronting America's water infrastructure challenge. Available: http://www.awwa.org/Portals/0/files/legreg/documents/BuriedNoLonger.pdf.

AWWA. (2017). 2017 State of the Water Industry Report. Available: https://www.awwa.org/portals/0/files/resources/water%20utility%20management/sotwi/awwa2017sotwi.pdf.

Brears, R. (2015). The circular economy and the water-energy-food nexus. NFG policy paper series [Online]. Available: http://www.asianperceptions.fu-berlin.de/system/files/private/pp715-water-energy-food-nexus.pdf.

Brears, R.C. (2016). Urban Water Security, Chichester, UK; Hoboken, NJ, John Wiley & Sons.

City of Cape Town. (2016a). Commercial water restrictions explained [Online]. Available: http://www.capetown.gov.za/Work%20and%20business/Commercial-utility-services/Commercial-water-and-sanitation-services/2016-commercial-water-restrictions-explained.

City of Cape Town. (2016b). Residential water restrictions explained [Online]. Available: http://www.capetown.gov.za/Family%20and%20home/residential-utility-services/residential-water-and-sanitation-services/2016-residential-water-restrictions-explained.

City of San Diego . (2017). Pure Water San Diego [Online]. Available: https://www.sandiego.gov/water/purewater/purewatersd.

City West Water. (2017). West Wyndham recycled water project [Online]. Available: https://www.citywestwater.com.au/about_us/major_projects/west_wyndham_recycled_water_project.aspx.

Cook, S., Hall, M. and Gregory, A. (2012). Energy use in the provision and consumption of urban water in Australia: an update. Available: https://publications-csiro-au.ezproxy.otago.ac.nz/rpr/download?pid=csiro:EP122271&dsid=DS4.

Copeland, C. and Carter, N. (2017). Energy-water nexus: the water sector's energy use. Congressional Research Service [Online]. Available: http://www.ourenergypolicy.org/wp-content/uploads/2017/02/R43200.pdf.

Denver Water. (2017). Cooling Tower Performance Rebate Program [Online]. Available: https://www.denverwater.org/business/rebate/cooling-tower-performance-rebate-program.

DEWA. (2017a). Be water smart [Online]. Available: https://www.dewa.gov.ae/en/customer/sustainability/spread-the-message/be-water-smart.

DEWA. (2017b). A Smart App. For a smarter tomorrow [Online]. Available: https://www.dewa.gov.ae/en/customer/innovation/smart-initiatives/app-download-page.

DEWA. (2017c). Smart Applications via Smart Grid and Meters [Online]. Available: https://www.dewa.gov.ae/en/customer/innovation/smart-initiatives/smart-applications-via-smart-meters-and-grids.

Fang, A.J., Joshua, P.N. and Joshua, J.C. (2015). The energy and emissions footprint of water supply for Southern California. Environmental Research Letters 10: 114002.

FAO. (2016). Coping with water scarcity in agriculture: A global framework for action in a changing climate. Available: http://www.fao.org/3/a-i5604e.pdf.

Fox, S., Shepherd, W., Collins, R. and Boxall, J. 2016. Experimental Quantification of Contaminant Ingress into a Buried Leaking Pipe during Transient Events. Journal of Hydraulic Engineering 142: 04015036.

Georgia Environmental Protection Division Watershed Protection Branch. (2007). Water conservation education programs. Available: http://www1.gadnr.org/cws/Documents/Conservation_Education.pdf.

Hegger, D.L.T., Spaargaren, G., Van Vliet, B.J.M. and Frijns, J. (2011). Consumer-inclusive innovation strategies for the Dutch water supply sector: Opportunities for more sustainable products and services. NJAS—Wageningen Journal of Life Sciences 58: 49–56.

IEA. (2016). A delicate balance between water demand and the low-carbon energy transition [Online]. Available: http://www.iea.org/newsroom/news/2016/november/a-delicate-balance-between-water-demand-and-the-low-carbon-energy-transition.html.

Kiparsky, M., Sedlak, D.L., Thompson, B.H. and Truffer, B. (2013). The innovation deficit in urban water: The need for an integrated perspective on institutions, organizations, and technology. Environmental Engineering Science 30: 395–408.

LADWP. (2017). Custom water conservation projects (TAP) [Online]. Available: https://www.ladwp.com/ladwp/faces/wcnav_externalId/a-w-cstm-wtr-prjct-tap?_adf.ctrl-state=kg8odqt9w_30&_afrLoop=526711373240641.

Lam, K.L., Kenway, S.J. and Lant, P.A. (2017). Energy use for water provision in cities. Journal of Cleaner Production 143: 699–709.

London Economics. (2009). Innovation in the Water Industry in England and Wales: Final Report : Cave Review of Competition and Innovation in Water Markets. Available: https://londoneconomics.co.uk/wp-content/uploads/2011/09/40-Innovation-in-the-Water-Industry-in-England-and-Wales.pdf.

McDonald, R.I., Weber, K., Padowski, J., FlÖrke, M., Schneider, C., Green, P.A., Gleeson, T., Eckman, S., Lehner, B., Balk, D., Boucher, T., Grill, G. and Montgomery, M. (2014). Water on an urban planet: Urbanization and the reach of urban water infrastructure. Global Environmental Change 27: 96–105.

Michelsen, A.M., Mcguckin, J.T. and Stumpf, D. (1999). Nonprice water conservation programs as a demand management tool. JAWRA Journal of the American Water Resources Association 35: 593–602.

NACWA. (2017). Envisioning the digital utility of the future. Available: http://www.nacwa.org/docs/default-source/conferences-events/2017-summer/17ulc-digital-utility-r6.pdf?sfvrsn=2.

Najjar, K. and Collier, C.R. (2011). Integrated water resources management: Bringing it all together. Water Resources Impact 13: 3–8.

NYC DEP. (2017). Free home water conservation kits. Available: http://www.nyc.gov/html/dep/pdf/bcs/home-water-conservation-kit-app.pdf.

OECD. (2012a). Environmental outlook to 2050: The consequences of inaction. Key findings of water. Available: https://www.oecd.org/env/indicators-modelling-outlooks/49844953.pdf.

OECD. (2012b). OECD Environmental outlook to 2050: the consequences of inaction. Available: http://www.oecd.org/env/indicators-modelling-outlooks/oecd-environmental-outlook-1999155x.htm.

OECD. (2012c). OECD Environmental outlook to 2050: The consequences of inaction highlights. Available: https://www.oecd.org/env/indicators-modelling-outlooks/49846090.pdf.

Pennsylvania State University. (2010). Water conservation for communities. Available: http://extension.psu.edu/natural-resources/water/conservation/water-conservation-home-study/why-conserve-water/communitywaterconservation.pdf.

Policy Research Initiative. (2005). Economic instruments for water demand management in an integrated water resources management framework. Ottawa, ON [Online]. Available: http://publications.gc.ca/collections/Collection/PH4-18-2005E.pdf.

PUB. (2017). Water price [Online]. Available: https://www.pub.gov.sg/watersupply/waterprice.

Rothausen, S.G.S.A. and Conway, D. (2011). Greenhouse-gas emissions from energy use in the water sector. Nature Climate Change 1: 210–219.

San Francisco Public Utilities Commission. (2017). Conservation [Online]. Available: https://sfwater.org/index.aspx?page=136.

Säve-Söderbergh, M., Bylund, J., Malm, A., Simonsson, M. and Toljander, J. (2017). Gastrointestinal illness linked to incidents in drinking water distribution networks in Sweden. Water Research 122: 503–511.

SaveWaterSaveMoney: SOUTH WEST WATER. (2017). Free water savings products [Online]. Available: https://www.savewatersavemoney.co.uk/southwest/free-water-saving-products.

Scottish Water. (2017). Sustainability report 2016. Available: http://www.scottishwater.co.uk/-/media/about-us/images/corporate-responsibility/a63157swsustainabilityreporthr.pdf?la=en.

Sibly, H. (2006). Efficient urban water pricing. Australian Economic Review 39: 227–237.

Speight, V.L. (2015). Innovation in the water industry: barriers and opportunities for US and UK utilities. Wiley Interdisciplinary Reviews: Water 2: 301–313.

Steg, L. and Vlek, C. (2009). Encouraging pro-environmental behaviour: An integrative review and research agenda. Journal of Environmental Psychology 29: 309–317.

Tanellari, E., Bosch, D., Boyle, K. and Mykerezi, E. (2015). On consumers' attitudes and willingness to pay for improved drinking water quality and infrastructure. Water Resources Research 51: 47–57.

TechTrade Asia. (2016). Dubai Electricity and Water Authority reports more using self-service capabilities [Online]. Available: http://www.techtradeasia.info/2016/09/dubai-electricity-and-water-authority.html.

Texas Water Development Board. (2017). 2017 state water plan. Available: http://www.twdb.texas.gov/waterplanning/swp/2017/.

Toronto Water. (2017). MyWaterToronto [Online]. Available: https://www1.toronto.ca/wps/portal/contentonly?vgnextoid=ae3d143ac42c2510VgnVCM10000071d60f89RCRD.

UKWIR. (2011). Research and innovation mapping study for the UK water research and innovation framework. Available: https://www.theukwaterpartnership.org/research-and-innovation-mapping-study-for-the-uk-water-research-and-innovation-framework/.

UNEP. (2016). Half the world to face severe water stress by 2030 unless water use is "decoupled" from economic growth, says International Resource Panel [Online].

Available: http://www.unep.org/NewsCentre/default.aspx?DocumentID=27068&ArticleID=36102.

UNESCO. (2012). Managing water under uncertainty and risk. Available: http://www.unesco.org/fileadmin/MULTIMEDIA/HQ/SC/pdf/WWDR4%20Volume%20 1-Managing%20Water%20under%20Uncertainty%20and%20Risk.pdf.

United Nations. (2014). World's population increasingly urban with more than half living in urban areas [Online]. Available: http://www.un.org/en/development/desa/news/population/world-urbanization-prospects-2014.html.

United Nations, D.E.S.A., Population Division. (2017). World Population Prospects: The 2017 Revision, Key Findings and Advance Tables. Available: https://esa.un.org/unpd/wpp/Publications/Files/WPP2017_KeyFindings.pdf.

United Nations Population Fund. (2016). Urbanization [Online]. Available: http://www.unfpa.org/urbanization.

United Utilities. (2017a). All about water [Online]. Available: http://www.unitedutilities.com/corporate/responsibility/communities/education/all-about-water/.

United Utilities. (2017b). Education [Online]. Available: http://www.unitedutilities.com/corporate/responsibility/communities/education/.

UN-Water. (2014). Partnerships for improving water and energy access, efficiency and sustainability. Available: http://www.un.org/waterforlifedecade/water_and_energy_2014/pdf/water_and_energy_2014_final_report.pdf.

World Bank. (2006). The challenge of reducing Non-Revenue Water (NRW) in Developing Countries: How the private sector can help: A Look at performance-based service contracting. Available: https://siteresources.worldbank.org/INTWSS/Resources/WSS8fin4.pdf.

World Bank. (2007). Making the most of scarcity: Accountability for better water management results in the Middle East and North Africa. Available: http://siteresources.worldbank.org/INTMNAREGTOPWATRES/Resources/Making_the_Most_of_Scarcity.pdf.

World Bank. (2014). Africa's urban population growth: trends and projections. Available: http://blogs.worldbank.org/opendata/africa-s-urban-population-growth-trends-and-projections.

Zhang, Q., Nakatani, J., Wang, T., Chai, C. and Moriguchi, Y. (2017). Hidden greenhouse gas emissions for water utilities in China's cities. Journal of Cleaner Production 162: 665–677.

Part 2
Social Impact Finance

7

Social Impact Incentives (SIINC)

Enabling High-Impact Social Enterprises to Improve Profitability and Reach Scale

Bjoern Struewer, Rory Tews and *Christina Moehrle**

- -

Summary

Premium payments for real impact can systematically close the gap between financing demand and supply. Social Impact Incentives (SIINC) empower social enterprises to raise large amounts of investment and to grow sustainably while creating positive social impact at scale.

Roots of Impact and the Swiss Agency for Development and Cooperation co-developed Social Impact Incentives (SIINC)—an innovative, blended finance model enabling high-impact social enterprises to improve profitability and reach scale. With SIINC, social enterprises are rewarded for real impact achieved. They earn additional revenues by monetising positive externalities. As a consequence, social enterprises receive a boost in their profitability once the impact performance is achieved. This profitability boost, in turn, attracts investors to provide the necessary capital for scaling.

Roots of Impact http://roots-of-impact.org.
Emails: bstruewer@roots-of-impact.org; rtews@roots-of-impact.org
* Corresponding author: cmoehrle@roots-of-impact.org.

SIINC is A Simple, Flexible and Entrepreneurial Solution

SIINC builds strongly on the entrepreneurial drive that social enterprises display when addressing the world's most pressing social and environmental challenges. The basic mechanism of SIINC is very straightforward—an outcome payer—usually a public funder or philanthropic organisation, agrees to act as a key customer to the enterprise, paying premiums for its social contribution. These premiums are then disbursed to the social enterprise in addition to its regular revenues. Thus, impact is incentivised very directly: it becomes linked to the social enterprise's levels of profitability and raises its attractiveness for investors.

These temporary SIINC payments have a catalytic effect on all parties involved: they accelerate the social enterprise's process of achieving long-term financial viability while offering the outcome funder and the impact investor strong, ongoing social returns on the resources they invest.

Another important feature is that there is no need to set up a special purpose vehicle or any other kind of dedicated structure. SIINC simply requires a contractual agreement between two parties to be tailored around their specific needs. For long-term impact, the key to success is developing the business while ensuring that the organisation is optimised for social performance. With SIINC, the final goal is to get both bottom lines fully 'synched'. This basic effect is illustrated below:

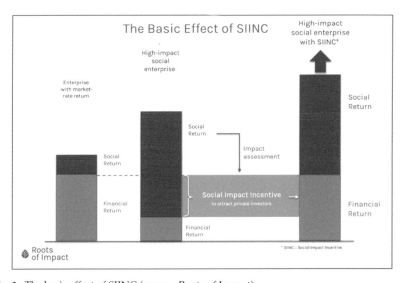

Fig. 1. The basic effect of SIINC (source: Roots of Impact).

Pilot Project in Latin America

After careful preparation, SIINC went live in December 2015 with a pilot project in Latin America and the Caribbean. The project is led by Roots of Impact and implemented in partnership with the Swiss Agency for Development & Cooperation (SDC), the Inter-American Development Bank (and its OMIN facility), as well as New Ventures and support from Ashoka. The first two candidates, Clinicas del Azúcar and Village Infrastructure Angels closed SIINC contracts in April/May 2017, with Clinicas del Azúcar showing first results substantially above outcome targets in early 2018.

PART 1: SHIFTING THE FOCUS FROM DEMAND TO SUPPLY

PART 1: SHIFTING THE FOCUS FROM DEMAND TO SUPPLY

SIINC Creates Leverage by Modifying and Integrating Three Proven Concepts: Venture Capital, Social Impact Bonds and Results-Based Financing

SIINC emerged from a modification of three well-known concepts: Venture Capital, Social Impact Bonds (SIBs) and other Results-Based Financing models. The real innovation of SIBs (sometimes known as 'Pay-for-Success') was combining the pay-for-results logic with pre-financed activities. This created an unseen investability of impact interventions, mostly in the field of preventive measures. Roots of Impact and the SDC took this idea one step further by melding it with the attitude of a venture capitalist, i.e., a market-based mechanism. The revenue streams of a social business, social enterprise or impact-oriented business, no matter how the target is labeled, are generated in conjunction with impact. This important switch recognises the fact that business is not only a significant driver of economic development, but also an efficient channel for entrepreneurial creativity and innovative impact solutions. Thus, SIINC becomes an entrepreneurial model: once a social enterprise grows, it will enjoy economies of scale. This, in turn, will reduce the overall cost for the desired impact.

SIBs and most results-based financing models are basically driven by demand. The outcome payer makes the promise to render a project financially worthwhile by rewarding effective solutions to a given problem. One important consequence is that a market for a pre-defined set of results comes into existence. This approach fits particularly well with enterprises which don't have much potential for business activity and where cost-savings can be tracked through strong evidence base-lines of costs versus results. In the classic SIB model, for example, the outcome payer only has to pay when results are achieved in full. More recently, SIBs have also evolved and are becoming more flexible. Partial payments[1] for partial impact delivery as well as other more flexible elements are now part of the solution.

What is really new in the SIINC mindset is that the focus switches from demand to supply. Highly effective social enterprises are selected to have their impact incentivised. With stronger financial projections, they immediately become more 'investable' and able to attract the necessary capital for scaling. Thus, the outcome payer does not agree to pay for a given set of outcomes; instead, he or she agrees to directly support an increase in the impact supplied by the social enterprise. Also, there is no pre-defined investor in the model any more: the enterprise is able to freely engage with financiers that are best suited to meet its needs. This marks the essential switch from demand to supply. Impact will be generated long after the original outcome funder has ceased to provide payments. The social entrepreneur enjoys more freedom and society benefits from ongoing positive impact.

In essence, SIINC transforms the role of the outcome payer to that of an 'impact venture capitalist'. Similar to the traditional finance world, the VC supports the investee in improving performance and maximising scale, which leads to greater business efficiency. With SIINC, this effect is simply transferred to another dimension, i.e., to social impact.

PART 2: HOW TO CREATE A SIINC INTERVENTION

SIINC offers the potential to align the interests of investors, investees and outcome payers and to catalyse more capital into solutions that work effectively.

There are three distinct actor groups involved in a typical SIINC transaction:

- Social enterprises seek investments in order to scale operations and generate more positive social impact

---

[1] http://govlab.hks.harvard.edu/files/siblab/files/social-impact-bonds-a-guide-for-state-and-local-governments.pdf?m=1419347623.

- Public and philanthropic funders are driven by the motivation to maximize the positive impact generated by their funds
- Impact investors target reasonable social and financial returns on their investments

SIINC has the capacity to align the interests of each of these three groups. The outcome funder agrees to pay premiums not to the investor, but directly to the social enterprise based on its social performance. This, in turn, makes the enterprise attractive enough to catalyse investment from impact investors. Such an arrangement is at the core of entrepreneurial thinking: what kind of investment will be taken from whom is open. The following graph outlines the basic SIINC model and the roles of each of the three groups involved:

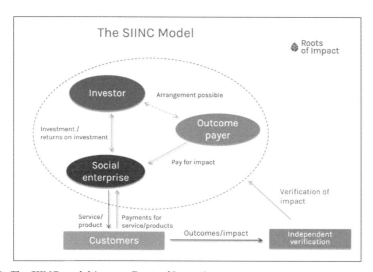

Fig. 2. The SIINC model (source: Roots of Impact).

In general, SIINC is structured as straightforward as possible. A Special Purpose Vehicle or other kinds of overlay structures are not required. In the basic model, there is a payment agreement between the outcome payer and the social enterprise alongwith pre-defined social performance indicators. The investment contract between the social enterprise and the investor is structured individually to meet the specific needs of both. There can be additional arrangements between the investors and the impact payers, but this is not a must. In the second step, an impact base-line is established, with payments triggered by organisational metrics directly related to the impact performance. Finally, the ongoing payments are structured and linked to impact, while an independent verification of the impact assessment system ensures that the results are as reliable as possible.

How to Address Long-term Sustainability

A natural question is what the end game of a SIINC intervention may look like—how about the 'exit'? Basically, when a SIINC intervention comes to an end (this may be after two to five years), the social enterprise should have reached financial sustainability through market activity and/or public contracts. Either scale plus paying end-users have made it economically viable or public bodies have been convinced of the solution's effectiveness and will pay for the service, or for the results.

PART 3: SELECTING THE RIGHT TARGETS

The SIINC mechanism aligns both bottom lines of an enterprise—income and impact—while scaling. High-impact social enterprises often struggle to secure growth capital for one reason or another. Frequently, they operate in difficult, unproven markets. On top of that, they are often serving customers with minimal and inconsistent livelihoods. The SIINC scheme successfully boosts the viability of such growth-stage enterprises. Once an enterprise attracts capital, it is able to build capacity, increase revenues and achieve lower per-unit costs. This effect is irrespective of whether the unit in question is a product or a unit of a service provided. In an ideal-case scenario, impact investors see an increase in marginal impact in relation to the increase in net income per unit. This 'ideal double bottom-line business' can be visualised as follows:

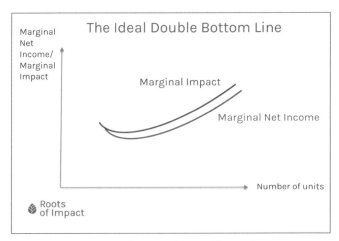

Fig. 3. The ideal double bottom line (source: Roots of Impact).

Scenario One

The original idea for SIINC was to deal with cases where the marginal net income did not increase at the same rate as the marginal impact. This happens, for instance, when high initial costs are associated with expansion and margins are simply too low to pay the cost of scaling. In other words, the enterprise remains a high-impact operation but its investability is limited. SIINC helps to bridge this very gap.

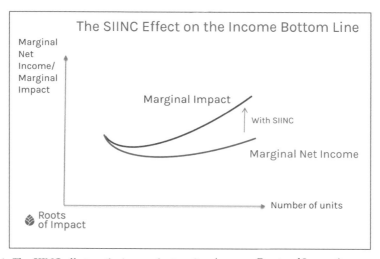

Fig. 4. The SIINC effect on the income bottom line (source: Roots of Impact).

We refer to this as scenario one. Here, a SIINC deal is designed to increase the marginal net income to levels that are attractive to investors and therefore, catalyses a round of investment. In practice, there was no shortage of scenario one applicants during the SIINC pilot programme, on the contrary, the idea of rewarding a social enterprise for its impact was apparently very compelling, but also attracted other types of candidates for a second scenario.

Scenario two

There is one characteristic that raised the second wave of interest during the pilot project—SIINC is not a traditional grant or subsidy, nor is it milestone-based; instead, it is a bilateral deal that rewards impact performance. The social enterprise must agree upon a set of enterprise-internal metrics which will be used to trigger payments. These metrics are designed to capture aspects of its impact. At the same time, they should be useful for the business operations as well. So when the metrics get rewarded, the incentive is to focus on improving them.

Right from the beginning, the idea was born that SIINC could be adapted to large corporates. It could be a tool to leverage their platform for social impact at a massive scale. But there are further interesting applications for SIINC between the two extremes of the spectrum—between the relatively small but highly effective social enterprises and the large corporates. What if impact-conscious organisations would use the SIINC model as a means of ensuring that their impact increases disproportionate to their income while scaling significantly? This would mean that their operation's marginal impact increases at least in parallel with their marginal net income per unit—an effective method of preventing mission drift or even of generating a further deepening of impact.

Such a scenario is particularly valid when a model has achieved (or has the potential for) strong financial performance. These enterprises often receive much interest from investors, but they can come under strong pressure to focus on more lucrative markets or segments. The result would be an erosion of the marginal impact as the operation scales, a threat that SIINC is able to address. Of course, one could be cynical and say that social enterprises are just looking for more funds. But the consequence of a SIINC deal on the social enterprise's strategy shouldn't be overlooked. The enterprise has to (re-)focus its business model on maintaining and deepening its levels of impact. The following graph illustrates this scenario two:

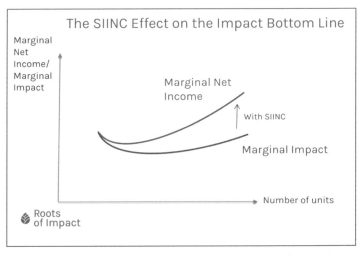

Fig. 5. The SIINC effect on the impact bottom line (source: Roots of Impact).

In reality, the two scenarios are not far removed from each other. It is simply a question of perspective and the related development stage. SIINC supports either highly mission-driven entrepreneurs who are struggling with their commercial business model, or it addresses commercially viable businesses with impact-conscious leaders who are looking for ways to deepen their social contribution.

PART 4: DESIGNING THE IMPACT ROADMAP

SIINC is based on an individual impact roadmap with tailored, enterprise-specific metrics. When designing productive outcome metrics, flexibility is the key. As the SIINC intervention is based on a specific deal negotiated and agreed upon by the involved parties, measuring and tracking the impact follows no fixed pattern. Deciding unilaterally on a set of metrics would risk to create friction between the parties involved. Instead, the SIINC solution builds on an individually developed impact roadmap: it lays out a detailed plan for the evolution of impact metrics to be tracked. These metrics are then used as payment triggers over the course of the SIINC deal. The premise underpinning the roadmap is that there must be a commitment from the enterprise to an increasing level of sophistication in the metrics and processes over the course of the entire intervention.

Strategies for Impact Roadmaps

The process begins with an evaluation of the metrics—which metrics are currently tracked by the enterprise and what are the processes behind? If they are sufficient to act as a strong proxy for the impact which the outcome payer wishes to promote, then they are selected for the opening-phase payment triggers. A base-line is used to assess performance up to now and the agreed-upon base-line payment amount is linked to them. If the enterprise ends up underperforming, then the payments will be below the base-line payment. If the enterprise outperforms, then they can get premium beyond the base-line, up to a capped amount.

The direction that the impact roadmap takes is dependent to a large extent on the strategy that the enterprise envisages regarding scaling and financing: what are its medium-term plans for servicing the most impactful segments of the market at scale? To date, we have identified two broad strategy types: market-based strategies and public-body strategies.

- In the case of a market-based strategy, the impact plan centres on combining business with impact metrics; in other words: the focus is placed on developing business-based impact metrics. Ensuring that the enterprise can continue to service this market segment depends on how much they know about their customers and how best to serve them from a business perspective. In this way, the business opportunity represented by this segment becomes more appealing and the probability that investors will buy into the strategy is maximised.

- With a public-body strategy, the target market segment usually cannot afford whatever good or service the social enterprise is offering. But it may well require it. The idea is to use the SIINC intervention as a basis for generating a strong enough argument that a public body (e.g., regional government or social insurance agency) will agree to contract the social enterprise to facilitate a continued provision to that market segment moving forward.

As mentioned above, both the strategies require a commitment on the part of the enterprise; it has to improve the sophistication of the metrics and processes involved. The roadmap should lead, for example, from a focus on output metrics to including outcome metrics. Nevertheless, the impact measurement doesn't have to be very complex or expensive. This mindset has much in common with Acumen's 'Lean Data'[2] as it seeks to hit the sweet spot at the intersection of useful business and impact metrics. Of course, such a transition does not happen overnight. Much consideration must be given to which metrics to track and how, as resources are going to be very stretched at that stage of organisational development.

In general, the entire process of implementing SIINC can be sliced down to three major phases: (1) identification, assessment and preparation, (2) investment readiness and transaction management, and (3) impact measurement and monitoring. The following graph details the individual tasks that typically need to be performed in each phase of the SIINC process:

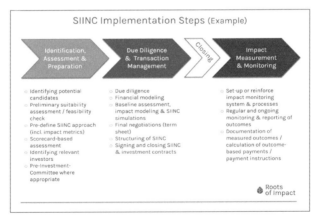

Fig. 6. SIINC implementation steps (example) (source: Roots of Impact).

---

[2] http://ssir.org/articles/entry/the_power_of_lean_data.

PART 5: SIINC IN PRACTICE—VILLAGE INFRASTRUCTURE ANGELS

Village Infrastructure Angels (VIA)[3] is a social enterprise with the vision to give poor communities across the globe access to safe, affordable and renewable energy. Yet it is confronted with the typical fate of pioneers: a highly innovative and scalable business model meets an investor market that is too shy to enter uncharted territory and take a high level of perceived risk—an ideal case for SIINC.

Access to Energy for All

Access to energy for all is a pressing issue and ranks very high on the United Nation's 2030 Sustainable Development Goals agenda. Around one billion people around the globe lack access to electricity, burning one US$ per week per household with kerosene lamps. This translates into more than US$ 10 billion spent per year. The side effects can be devastating: burning kerosene is the number one attributor to fire-related, often fatal injuries. It is also suspected to have serious health effects due to indoor smoke, predominantly on children. Yet well-planned and -managed solar power solutions, like VIAs, allow communities to run mills, pump water, equip schools and electrify clinics—a scope of impact that reaches well beyond the simple task of lighting.

To date, the staff of VIA was able to provide more than 2 million people with clean, affordable and safe solar energy. By adding agro-processing mills and solutions for other day-time appliances, the social enterprise has the goal to specifically empower women by saving hours of manual labour for the benefit of more productive work and time to support children's education.

VIA's Honduras Pilot

VIA's pilot project started in September 2014 with 150 households and focussed on isolated areas of the least-served department of Gracias a Dios. There, many donor-funded projects involving rural electrification have failed to reach due to a combination of low prioritisation from the government and a lack of funds to reach all households. Another factor is the government's motivation to bring access to areas of highest population density first. Also, designing cost-effective village power systems that do not depend on subsidies is a major, widely unresolved challenge. Studies,

---

[3]   www.villageinfrastructure.org.

such as the Climate Investment Funds Investment Plan, therefore, estimate that 10 per cent of Honduran villages will not be connected to the national grid in the foreseeable future. The necessity of isolated power systems [mini-grids or solar home systems (SHS)] will affect 80,000 households (400,000 people), out of which only 14,000 have access to such solutions today.

VIA's pilot project has demonstrated that there is a strong demand for leasing SHS in the Gracias a Dios region. One precondition, however, is that the technology is working correctly; another that people have jobs and other income sources to meet the repayments. The social enterprise integrated these important insights into its model: Beneficiaries are allowed to pay with their products and goods when using agro-processing community mills on top of pay-as-you-go lighting and phone-charging solutions.

All in all, VIA's business model includes selecting, purchasing, installing and ensuring correct operation and maintenance of mini-grids, light agro-processing solutions and solar home systems (SHS). It also features important innovations, such as 'pay-as-you-go technology' (PAYG): The households leasing the SHS purchase a unique code similar to phone credit top-ups that, once entered into the SHS via a keypad, will allow the system to work for a 30-day period. This technology is being adapted by VIA to also work in the higher power solar mills.

VIA's main Challenge and the SIINC Solution

VIA's main challenge is not the scalability of the model—it is to crowd-in the necessary investment to roll-out its solution across Honduras and beyond. This is where SIINC came into play: By providing payments for verified performance based on carefully-designed impact metrics, VIA has the potential to enhance its revenues and de-risk its financial bottom line. This is a major argument for impact investors who so far were hesitant to support the highly promising yet risky pioneer business model.

The SIINC rationale was clear from the beginning: to specifically support the wider roll-out of the solar-powered community mills, a true innovation in VIA's business model. Agro-milling is a very male-centric business in developing countries today. Enabling women to use cleaner, simpler, safer and quieter solar-powered micro-milling technology, therefore, offers great room for female empowerment. In addition, it saves women substantial time that they previously spent on manual labour.

Designing VIA'S Impact Metrics

The set of impact metrics for SIINC was defined accordingly. It focuses on three impact key performance indicators (Impact KPIs) that include female empowerment in their design:

(1) First, lease contracts signed with female agents (micro entrepreneurs) at the village level serve as one of the triggers for SIINC payments. Within this Impact KPI, new contracts signed with female agents for both lighting and milling will be favoured. Contracts for milling are remunerated higher than those covering lighting facilities only. Both, SHS and solar-powered milling are affordable to low-income household due to the pay-as-you-go technology. This KPI recognizes that VIA is making microfinance loans in deep rural areas where no microfinance has previously reached, which increases financial inclusion.

(2) The second Impact KPI is the number of hours of manual labour saved by women in local communities. Currently, staple crops are processed by hand in a time-consuming process. The SIINC mechanism rewards VIA for the time saved by women on these activities. The Impact KPI is derived from the effective operation of the mills and strongly reflects the benefits for the female population. Ongoing payments will be made in proportion to the number of hours saved, with a minimum as well as a maximum payment defined in the SIINC mechanism.

(3) The third Impact KPI is the amount of additional economic value created for the communities. This is measured through the goods provided in lieu of payment—an offer VIA has come up with to allow households to pay for the milling service with hand-made goods. This approach enables women to convert some of the time saved through the mills, providing an impulse to produce more locally-crafted goods. SIINC payments will be relative to the increase in economic output and are again provided with a cap.

The following graph summarises the essence of these three Impact KPIs:

Fig. 7. SIINC impact metrics for VIA (source: Roots of Impact).

Through the SIINC transaction, VIA will now be able to prove its model in tough business conditions and position itself for a broader roll-out across Honduras and the Latin American region. The SIINC payments are limited to a maximum period of four years. After that time, VIA's operations in Honduras are expected to be financially self-sustainable. By including an innovative barter-style model, even the poorest members of the local communities will gain access to milling services. All in all, the SIINC mechanism ensures that under-served communities will enjoy products and services that they would otherwise never be able to access.

Outlook: Harnessing the SIINC Potential

Increasing the effectiveness of impact investing is key to unlocking the full potential of market-based solutions. SIINC is an innovative Blended Finance solution that pursues this important goal. In the current market environment, there is a significant mismatch between investors' expectations and the actual needs of social entrepreneurs. Consequently, the current practice of impact investing and social entrepreneurship is not fulfilling its potential. Blended Finance is one solution to this dilemma and an approach that the Swiss Agency for Development and Cooperation and Roots of Impact are committed to pursue. There is a growing desire in development finance to use public, development and philanthropic funds in ways which are able to 'crowd in' private investment. The key in making blended finance successful is to develop mechanisms that combine different sources of capital in a mission-aligned manner. Yet the characteristics and effectiveness of incentive mechanisms are different. The Centre for Global Development, for example, concludes, "Pay-for-Success instruments are less distortionary and produce better results for a lower expected cost than other incentive programmes."[4]

According to the Global Impact Investing Network (GIIN),[5] over 80 per cent of impact investors aim for market- or near-market returns. At the

Comparison of Blended Finance Instruments

	Guarantees	Subsidies	Pay for success
Avoid moral hazard in project selection	✗	✓	✓
Better performance management	✗	✓	✓
Improve targeting	✗	✗	✓
Promote contestability	✗	✗	✓
Avoid the costs of optimism bias	✗	✗	✓
Build public support	✗	✗	✓
Reduce monitoring and evaluation costs	✗	✗	✓

Source: Center for Global Development working paper 402, May 2015

Fig. 8. Comparison of blended finance instruments (source: Center for Global Development).

---

[4]   Centre for Global Development. (2015). Working Paper 402. Guarantees, Subsidies, or Paying for Success? Choosing the Right Instrument to Catalyze Private Investment in Developing Countries.

[5]   https://thegiin.org/research/publication/annualsurvey2017.

same time, there are constant complaints about a lack of suitable investees. Of course, there are sectors, business models and activities where social impact readily joins profitability. But many highly effective and efficient solutions to social and environmental challenges evolve at points along the risk/return spectrum which are not (yet) in line with the mainstream capital market. This is where the spotlight should go if large-scale social issues are to be effectively solved.

Another stumbling block is the lack of commitment to a rigorous measurement and monitoring of impact. The majority of investors today allocate little effort or resources to track, manage, report or optimise the impact generated through their activities; only a tiny number of funds have some form of impact-related incentives.

Shaping finance for positive impact

'Roots of Impact is an impact finance advisory firm working with public funders, philanthropists and impact investors globally to finance private sector innovations and enterprises with strong potential for positive impact. We are dedicated to designing and implementing effective solutions and programs for financing social impact at scale and are driven by the desire to maximize the impact on every dollar granted or invested. For more information: www.roots-of-impact.org

---

The advantage of the SIINC model is that it does not need a paradigm shift to work. It acknowledges the realities of the market while offering a means to spur an evolution: managing, deepening and reporting real impact, and, of course, consistently channelling capital towards solutions with proven social contribution. Producing impact roadmaps in collaboration with impact investors and philanthropic funders allows them to engage with investees to devise impact-evolving strategies. Developing outcome metrics prepares the basis for funds to begin drawing up their own impact reporting processes.

Hopefully, the SIINC interventions themselves will show that strategies for deepening impact can lead to an opening up of further markets. The vision is clear—stronger long-term commercial performance, fully in-line with impact.

Key Terms

Blended Finance:
Blended Finance is the strategic use of development finance and philanthropic funds to mobilize private capital flows to emerging and frontier markets".

World Economic Forum

Pay-for-Success (PFS):
"PFS is an innovative contracting and financing model that leverages philanthropic and private dollars to fund (social) services upfront, with the government, or other entity, paying after they generate results."
Corporation for National and Community Service

"What makes recent PFS initiatives distinctive is that they are focused not simply on creating additional financial incentives for contractors to produce better outcomes, but more broadly on overcoming the wide set of barriers that are hindering the pace of social innovation."
H. Azemati, M. Belinsky, R. Gillette, J. Liebman, A. Sellman, A. Wyse/John F. Kennedy School of Government, Harvard University

Suggested Readings

Acumen. (2015). The Lean Data Field Guide. http://acumen.org/wp-content/uploads/2015/11/Lean-Data-Field-Guide.pdf.

Centre for Global Development. (2015). Working Paper 402. Guarantees, Subsidies, or Paying for Success? Choosing the Right Instrument to Catalyse Private Investment in Developing Countries. http://www.cgdev.org/publication/guarantees-subsidies-or-paying-success-choosing-right-instrument-catalyze-private.

ClearlySo. (May 12th 2016). A German Innovation I Hope We Don't Overlook, by Rodney Schwartz. https://www.clearlyso.com/category/blog/ (originally published on Third Sector).

Global Impact Investing Network, JP Morgan Chase & Co. (2015). Eyes on the Horizon. https://thegiin.org/knowledge/publication/eyes-on-the-horizon.

Global Impact Investing Network (2018). Annual Impact Investor Survey, https://thegiin.org/research/publication/annualsurvey2017.

Harvard Kennedy School Social Impact Bond Technical Assistance Lab. (2013). Social Impact Bonds—A Guide for State and Local Governments. http://govlab.hks.harvard.edu/files/siblab/files/social-impact-bonds-a-guide-for-state-and-local-governments.pdf?m=1419347623.

ImpactAlpha. (2016). Social Impact Incentives Aim to Tilt Businesses Toward the Needs of the Poor, by Dennis Price. http://impactalpha.com/social-impact-incentives-aim-to-tilt-businesses-toward-the-needs-of-the-poor/.

Stanford Social Innovation Review. (2013). Up for Debate: When Can Impact Investing Create Real Impact by Paul Brest and Kelly Born (William and Flora Hewlett Foundation). http://ssir.org/up_for_debate/article/impact_investing.

Stanford Social Innovation Review. (2016). The Power of Lean Data by Sasha Dichter and Tom Adams (Acumen) and Alnoor Ebrahim (Harvard Business School). http://ssir.org/articles/entry/the_power_of_lean_data.

UNCTAD. (2014). World Investment Report 2014. Investing in the SDGs: An Action Plan. http://unctad.org/en/pages/PublicationWebflyer.aspx?publicationid=937.

WEF, OECD. (2015). Blended Finance Vol. 1—A Primer for Development Finance and Philanthropic Funders. http://www3.weforum.org/docs/WEF_Blended_Finance_A_Primer_Development_Finance_Philanthropic_Funders_report_2015.pdf.

8

Social Impact Bond

Beyond Financial Innovation

Rosella Carè

- -

Introduction

Defined as financial assets whose objective is to attract investors to fund social programs by providing them an incentive if the project meets its predefined targets, Social Impact Bonds (SIBs) have rapidly become the most discussed instruments in the social finance landscape (Nicholls and Tomkinson 2015; Rizzello and Carè 2016; Schinckus 2017).

SIBs are not traditional bonds but can be considered contracts in which finance, service delivery and, supposedly, risks are devolved from the public to the private sector (Disley et al. 2011; Costa et al. 2014; Godeke and Resner 2012; Fraser et al. 2016).

In particular, the bonds are based on the idea that private investors can inject their capital into traditionally public activities or initiatives by producing more cost-effective practices in both sectors. The best candidates for private funding are programs with large upfront costs, those that serve large numbers of people, and those with a strong evidence base.

Considered the next step in the marketization of public sector delivery (Joy and Shields 2013; Dowling and Harvie 2014; Cooper et al. 2016), this particular financial innovation monetizes the benefits of social interventions and can be used to enhance the transparency and evaluation of the expenditures made by government (Schinkus 2015).

This chapter provides an overview of the most prominent characteristics of SIBs by focusing, in particular, on the implication that

Department of Legal, Historical, Economic and Social Science, University Magna Graecia of Catanzaro (Italy) - 88100 Catanzaro (Italy); care@unicz.it the development of the market may have for both the public and private sectors. At the same time, it describes the role of financial institutions and the importance of the development of impact metrics and standards of evaluations.

Impact Investing and Social Impact Bonds

Impact investing is defined by the Canadian Task Force on Social Finance (2010, p. 5) as:

> *'the active investment of capital in businesses and funds that generate positive social and/or environmental impacts, as well as financial returns (from principal to above market rate) to the investor'.*

This definition emphasizes two main aspects:

(i) the simultaneous presence of two different kinds of returns, of which the first is related to a social or environmental dimension and the second refers to a financial dimension; and

(ii) the intention to actively place capital in business activities by expecting something that extends beyond a merely financial return.

Impact investing is based on the concepts of blended return and shared value and, thus, on the idea that social returns and financial returns may be maximized at the same time (Weber 2016; Weber and Felmate 2016) (Fig. 1).

Impact investors extend beyond the traditional socially responsible approach because their ambitions are to actively place capital in businesses or projects, with the aim of promoting environmental or social objectives (Nicholls 2010; Hummels 2016).

At the same time, Impact investing differs from Socially Responsible Investing (SRI) because this latter screens the investment moving from environmental, social, and government factors (the most well-known ESG factors), whereas impact investors seek to make positive and measurable impacts in addition to the traditional financial returns (Geobey and Weber 2013; Weber 2016).

The academic literature shows significant variations in the conceptualization of Impact investing, and many authors highlight that impact investing has many names (Hebb 2013; Hochstadter and Scheck 2015; Trotta et al. 2015; Rizzello and Carè 2016), including double and triple bottom line, mission-related investing, program-related investment, blended-value, and economically targeted investing. However, it is reasonable to believe that the overlap between concepts and terms could be due to the emerging nature of the phenomena.

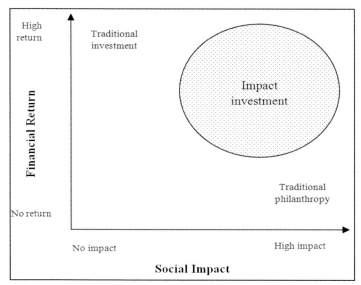

Fig. 1. Traditional investment, traditional philanthropy and impact investment.
Source: our elaboration

Table 1. Main definitions of impact investing.

Bugg Levine and Emerson (2011, p. 10)	"The idea behind impact investing is that investors can pursue financial returns while also intentionally addressing social and environmental challenges".
Jackson (2013, p. 609)	"Impact investing involves the placement of capital in enterprises or projects intended to produce social or environmental as well as financial returns".
Wood et al. (2013, p. 75)	"Impact investment is investment with the intent to create measurable social or environmental benefits in addition to financial return".
Monitor Institute (2009, p. 3)	"Investments that generate social and environmental value as well as financial return".
Global Impact Investing Network (2017)	"Impact investments are investments made into companies, organizations, and funds with the intention to generate social and environmental impact alongside a financial return".

Table 1, which is not intended to be exhaustive, provides an overview of some of the definitions of impact investing provided by academics, practitioners, and international organizations.

It is interesting to note that in the definition provided by the Global Impact Investing Network (GIIN), impact investing has four main characteristics:

1) the intention to have a positive social or environmental impact;
2) the expectation of a financial return;

3) a wide range of asset classes, ranging from below-market instruments to market-rate investments (cash equivalents, fixed income, venture capital, and private equity); and

4) the measurement of social and environmental performance.

Further specifications regarding what impact investing entails are provided by the World Economic Forum (2013, p. 6), which defines impact investing 'as an investment approach that intentionally seeks to create both financial return and positive social or environmental impact that is actively measured'. This definition emphasizes the following (World Economic Forum 2013; Brandstatter and Lehner 2015):

a) impact investing is an investment approach and not a stand-alone asset class. In the wide range of impact investing opportunities, the financial instruments span from equity to bonds; and

b) outcomes must be measured for the investment to be considered an impact investment.

Nicholls (2010, p. 81) includes impact investments in the realm of social investments and explains how these reflect systemic investor rationality, which typically strives to balance means-ends and value-driven rationalities by seeking returns that benefit both the investor and the investee/beneficiary.

Many authors have attempted to clarify the boundaries of this emerging investing approach (Hochstadter and Scheck 2015; Rizzello et al. 2016).

With regard to the asset classes and financial instruments that are available for impact investing, Hochstadter and Scheck (2015) clarify that a number of practitioner reports explicitly state that impact investing can occur across asset classes. At the same time, examples of asset classes and financial instruments include debt, equity, guarantees, and deposits (e.g., O'Donohoe et al. 2010) or more innovative structures, such as Social Impact Bonds (SIBs) (O'Donohoe et al. 2010; Addis et al. 2013).

Rizzello et al. (2016) offer an extensive bibliometric analysis on the academic literature of impact investing by providing an interesting map of its landscape. In particular, the authors note three main "domains" of research in this field: sustainable finance, impact entrepreneurship and public policy in the social sector (Rizzello et al. 2016). SIB(s) are included in this last domain, which also includes important terms such as Social Policy, Politics of Austerity, Social Outcome, New Public Management, Payment by Results, and Pay for Success; nonetheless, SIBs have a key role in connecting all three domains (Trotta et al. 2015).

The SIB model represents a new PPP model for the nonprofit sector (Joy and Shields 2013, p. 45) and is characterized by the following: (i) the participation of private and public actors in Public Private Partnership(s); (ii) an initial monetary investment; and (iii) an action program (Trotta et al. 2015).

Moreover, the SIB model is based on the relationship between the involved parties in the commissioning and the provisioning of social services (Nicholls and Tomkinson 2013; Palandijan and Hughes 2014; Arena et al. 2016) and on common interests between a wide range of stakeholders such as governments, private organizations, investors, and financial intermediaries (Kim and Kang 2012; Nicholls and Tomkinson 2013; Arena et al. 2016).

Despite several 'definitions' that can be retrieved in both the academic and practitioner literature, they all agree on the basic idea that SIBs can address social issues (Wieland 2015) (Table 2).

In fact, although the core model is fairly standardized, many terms are used around the world. In particular, SIBs are called pay-for-success bonds in the US and social benefit bonds in Australia (Brandstatter and Lehner 2016).

Initially developed in 2010 with the launch of the Peterborough program (Box 1), SIBs have quickly spread internationally and across different sectors (Clifford and Jung 2016).

Currently, according with the Social Finance's database, 74 SIBs have been launched, and more than 70 are in a development phase with total raised capital of $ 278 million. SIBs are actually available in the following countries: Australia (3), Austria (1), Belgium (1), Canada (3), Germany (1), Finland (1), France (2), India (1), Israel (2), Netherland (7), New Zealand (1), Peru (1), Portugal (1), South Korea (1), Sweden (1), Switzerland (1), the UK (32) and the US (14) (Fig. 2).

Table 2. Main definitions of Social Impact Bond.

Joy and Shields (2013, p. 40)	"SIBs are a financial product used to encourage private, philanthropic and/or public investors to provide upfront capital to support project-oriented service delivery by public, private, or non profit actors, or a combination of these actors".
Schinckus (2017, p. 729)	"Social impact bonds are new financial assets whose objective is to invite investors to fund social programs by providing them an incentive if the project meets its predefined targets".
Social Finance (2016, p. 12)	"Social Impact Bonds are public-private partnerships that drive resources toward effective social programs that measurably improve lives".

Box 1. The HMP Peterborough SIB.

In September 2010, the UK promoted the first world's SIB by raising, through the non-profit intermediary 'Social Finance', 5 million pounds from private capital markets to reduce the rate of reoffending among 1000 prisoners at Peterborough prison (Disley et al. 2011; Fox and Albertson 2011; Fox and Albertson 2012; Jackson 2013; Disley and Rubin 2014; Nicholls and Tomkinson 2015; Trotta et al. 2015; Clifford and Jung 2016). The program was aimed at reducing the re-offending rates among short-sentenced prisoners leaving Peterborough Prison. The prevention of each individual prisoner returning to the prison system was estimated to save the state $50,000, with a total government savings of $5 million for 100 prisoners being prevented from returning to prison (Godeke and Resner 2012; Jackson 2013). The Ministry of Justice and the Big Lottery Fund have had the role of outcome payers, and One Service, the organization created by Social Finance UK specifically for the SIB, was the entity that negotiated with social enterprise partners (such as St. Giles Trust, Ormiston, SOVA, YMCA, and Mind) for providing services (Disley et al. 2011; Disley and Rubin 2014; Trotta et al. 2015). The target population was divided into three cohorts, each composed of approximately 1,000 men who had been discharged from short prison sentences at HMP Peterborough (Nicholls and Tomkinson 2013; Trotta et al. 2015). The re-offending measure used was the frequency of re-conviction events (Social Finance 2016).

In the HMP Peterborough Social Impact Bond, the outcome-based payments were scheduled at the end of each of the three cohorts if the reduction in re-offending was 10% or, if not, at the end of the program. In the latter case, the threshold of the reduction rate in reoffending considered for payments was 7.5% across all cohorts. Payments were capped at £8 million. This sum of the maximum payment was equivalent to a maximum annual implied IRR of approximately 13% (Disley et al. 2011; Disley and Rubin 2014; Disley et al. 2015; Jolliffe and Hedderman 2014; Ministry of Justice 2014; Trotta et al. 2015).

After two years of operation, in 2013, the project released interim results showing that the rate of reoffending had declined in Peterborough, whereas the national rate had risen. However, as emphasized by Jackson (2013, p. 612), *"the interim study could not pinpoint which elements of the Peterborough delivery agent's services contributed to this trend, nor whether or how this trend might be sustained over a longer timeframe"*. The results for cohort 1, published in 2014, highlighted an 8.4% reduction in the frequency of reconviction events (Jolliffe and Hedderman 2014; Ministry of Justice 2014; Disley et al. 2015). This result was below the 10% target required to trigger an early outcome payment for the first cohort. The HMP Peterborough closed at the end of June 2015 after two cohorts, and investors are on track for payment in 2016 if a 7.5% reduction is achieved across the project (Social Finance 2016). The policy reform called "Transforming Rehabilitation" (Ministry of Justice 2013a; Ministry of Justice 2013b; Ministry of Justice 2013c) caused the cancellation of the third cohort of the SIB (Trotta et al. 2015). Under this reform, supervision is mandatory for those released from prison sentences of less than 12 months and, consequently, for the target group of the Peterborough pilot.

SIBs target social issues such as criminal justice (7), homelessness (13), child and family welfare (9), early childhood education (8), workforce development (28), health (7), environment and sustainability (1), and adults with complex needs (1) (Social Finance 2017).

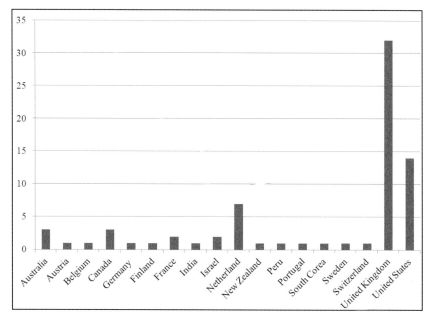

Fig. 2. SIBs launched per Country (as of June 2017).

Contractual Arrangements in Social Impact Bonds

Currently, there are no SIBs that are replicable to scale and in holistic or integrated combinations (OECD 2016); however, by analyzing the existing schemes, two main models, depending on how the payments relate to outcomes, can be identified (Gustaffson-Wright et al. 2015). The first model refers to a single SIB. In the second model, governments establish social impact bond funds to finance several SIBs. An example is provided by the "Fair Chance Fund" launched in UK in 2014 to address youth homelessness. The Fund, which consists of £10 m from the Department for Communities and Local Government (DCLG) and £5 m from the Cabinet Office, has been distributed in the form of seven Social Impact Bonds (SIBs) with the same duration (36 months) and outcome funder (U.K. Department for Communities and Local Government and the Cabinet Office) (Table 3).

From Table 3, two major aspects emerge:

1) the public sector commissioner establishes a rate card for payment per outcome that is identified through research that examines the cost

savings or the reduced remedial assistance that each outcome can yield; and

2) investors can provide debt or equity investments.

SIBs involve a set of contracts (Nicholls and Tomkinson 2015; Arena et al. 2016) between a set of actors (Fig. 3).

As noted by Godeke and Resner (2012, p. 5),

"A SIB is not a bond and does not have a set repayment schedule or interest rate. A SIB is a multi-stakeholder partnership based on contracts that define the targeted outcomes, risk sharing and payment mechanisms among the partners. The government's obligation to pay SIB investors is a contractual obligation; it is distinct from a general obligation, moral obligation or revenue bond".

Table 3. SIBs launched through the "Fair Chance Fund".

SIB Name	Total investment raised (£)	Maximum return
Local Solutions	0.55 million	Each type of outcome can only be claimed once. The total value of outcome payments claimable for support provided to an individual participant is limited to £17,000. There is also a cap on total outcome payments from the Department for Communities and Local Government for each project.
Your Chance	0.62 million	
Home Group	0.498 million	
Fusion Housing	0.940 million	
Rewriting Futures	1.03 million	
Ambition East Midlands	0.480 million provided by two Senior Investors (including retail investors that benefited from Social Investment Tax Relief)[1] and 0.12 million provided by Subordinate investors	Each type of outcome can only be claimed once. The total value of outcome payments claimable for support provided to an individual participant is limited to £17,000. There is also a cap on total outcome payments from the Department for Communities and Local Government for each project.
Aspire Gloucestershire	0.484 million, of which 0.390 million was provided by Senior Investors (including retail investors that benefited from Social Investment Tax Relief) and 0.060 million provided by Subordinated Investors	The investment from the senior investors is a debt investment with a set interest rate (not publicly available). The SITR investors are not eligible for this payment. Subordinate Investors made an equity investment and will be paid what is in the SPV after the senior investors have been repaid. In this case, returns could vary widely.

---

[1] Social Investment Tax Relief was created by the UK Treasury in 2014 and provides a 30% income tax break to individual investors investing in eligible social organizations.

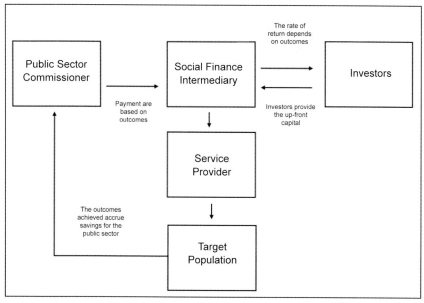

Fig. 3. The SIB model.

A SIB involves a contractual agreement for the provision of public services by a private sector consortium, an 'optimal' risk-sharing between the public sector and the private sector, and an innovative design and delivery of public services by the private sector. The implementation of a SIB contract begins when the Commissioner identifies a target population and a desired outcome and enters into a contract with a Social Finance Intermediary. Subsequently, the Social Finance Intermediary agrees to provide the up-front capital to finance the program (Arena et al. 2016; Child et al. 2016) by representing the central node of the SIB network (Child et al. 2016) and involving private investors that provide the financial support for the service delivery. If the scheduled outcomes are achieved, the Commissioner provides the resource to the Social Finance Intermediary to reimburse the investors at a fixed rate of interest. Conversely, if the outcomes are not achieved, the Commissioner does not provide the resource, and the investors receive no forms of reimbursement. The key elements of SIB are as follows:

1) Selecting a service to be addressed;
2) One or more commissioners;
3) Identifying a target group of the population;
4) Evidence-based outcomes;
5) A series of contracts between the involved parties;

6) Private Investors;
7) One intermediary or special purpose company;
8) One or more service providers;
9) One or more independent evaluators;
10) Repayment by a public body; and
11) Potential public expenditure savings.

SIBs are not suitable for all services. However, SIBs are likely to be appropriate when the desired outcome is clear and measurable (e.g., reducing recidivism), the government is seeking to transfer financial risk, there is a desire to catalyze the market for innovative financing and savings are cashable.

The combination of partners is part of the innovation (OECD 2016). In particular, this funding mechanism enables:

(i)   the public sector to commission innovative services that require new delivery approaches and to share the risk of exploring these new approaches;

(ii) one or more service providers to benefit from increased flexibility in delivering the agreed outcomes; and

(iii) investors to finance activity designed to achieve significant social outcomes by providing working capital.

Though this kind of contract, stakeholders could potentially have different benefits (Table 4).

By linking the various stakeholders, outcome metrics are the foundation of the SIB contract (Cooper et al. 2016). Outcome metrics are used to judge whether the interventions funded are having their intended

Table 4. Potential benefits per stakeholders.

Public Sector Commissioner	Investors	Philanthropists and charitable foundations
To achieve better value for money in service delivery	To align their investments with their desire for social impact	To extend the value of their contribution by investing and reinvesting their capital instead of always providing irrevocable donations or grants
To share financial and performance risks with investors		
To improve the quality and quantity of delivered services		
To increase transparency, accountability and performance	Investment diversification	

impact and, thus, to produce a means of measuring impact in a way that is rigorous and robust (Social Finance 2015).

The definition of the outcome metrics is typically done through the following process:

- Identification of the outcomes that represent the creation of social value, specific to the social issue being addressed;
- Identification of a baseline or a counterfactual;
- Valuation of the outcomes, in accordance with the objectives of the commissioner;
- Creation of a means of measuring and attributing the impact of the intervention on the outcomes that is both objectively accepted by all parties involved and perceived as being acceptable by all parties including the wider community; and
- Evaluation of the impact (Social Finance, 2015, p. 10).

To determine the effectiveness of the model, a reputable third-party evaluator must track and measure the success of the interventions (Bafford 2014).

OPEN QUESTIONS IN THE SIB MODEL

The Concept of Risk in a SIB Contract

SIBs represent a new asset class that allows investors to diversify portfolios with investments that should have minimal correlation with equity and bond markets (European Commission 2014).

Investors interested in social impact bonds represent a wide array of institutions, foundations, and individuals seeking new ways to solve social problems have a high tolerance for risk, including principal loss and lack of liquidity, and can wait out the long-term pay-out time frames of three to five years or longer (Costa et al. 2012). From the investor perspective, risk is a central aspect because it determines the rate of return required. In a SIB contract, the principal risk relates to the possibility that the project fails to meets its outcomes (e.g., the Rikers Island SIB case described in Box 2) or the government reneges on its commitment to pay (e.g., the Peterborough SIB case described in Box 1) (Tekolste et al. 2016). However, much of the risk in a SIB project originates from the complexity of the arrangement.

Risks can be classified, according to their nature, into three main levels:

(i) The macro level, which consists of external risks. This kind of risk is often associated with political and legal conditions, economic and

Box 2. The Rikers Island SIB.

Following the UK's first experience, the Rikers Island SIB was launched in the United States in August 2012, when Goldman Sachs Bank's Urban Investment Group (UIG) announced a $9.6 million loan to support the delivery of therapeutic services to 16- to 18-year-olds incarcerated in the New York City jail (Olson and Phillips 2013). The initial target population was young men ages 16-18 entering the jail with a length of stay of more than 7 days who were at risk of reoffending. Toward the end of the program, the target population was expanded to include 19- to 21-year-olds.

The program was named the "Adolescent Behaviourial Learning Experience program" (ABLE) and focused on improving social skills, personal responsibility, and decision making through cognitive behavioral therapy delivered to adolescents before their release from Rikers Island. The intervention was led by the Osborne Academy and the Friends of Island Academy (subcontractor). The Rikers Island experience was the first public-private partnership following a Social Impact Bond model to involve a large financial institution (Rudd et al. 2013). The public private partnership involved the City of New York, Manpower Demonstration Research Corporation (MDRC), the Osborne Association, Bloomberg Philanthropies, and Goldman Sachs with the main aim of leveraging high-quality nonprofit capacity, private-sector capital, and philanthropic support to address a pressing community challenge. To reduce the investor risk, Bloomberg Philanthropies guaranteed $7.2 M of this investment (Rudd et al. 2013; Olson and Phillips 2013). The Vera Institute of Justice was commissioned to conduct an independent quasi-experimental evaluation of the project. MDRC tested the program from February to June 2012. In January 2013, after a pilot period, the program expanded to serve all young people in the target population. The program ran for three years, from September 2012 to August 2015 (Olson and Phillips 2013; Rudd et al. 2013; Berlin 2016).

Thereafter, Rikers Island SIB's initiative was discontinued as of August 31, 2015, and no payments were made to investors (Goldman Sachs), thus triggering Bloomberg Philanthropies' $6 m guarantee (Social Finance 2016). The evaluator (Vera Institute) determined that the program did not lead to reductions in recidivism for the participants (Vera Institute 2015). The Vera Institute's final report highlight that: "the change in recidivism for the eligible 16- to 18-year-olds, adjusted for external factors, was not statistically significant when compared to the matched historical comparison group. Furthermore, the 19-year-olds *and the study group (16- to 18-year-olds) displayed similar trends in rates of recidivism over time, indicating that any shifts were the result of factors other than the ABLE program. The program did not reduce recidivism and therefore did not meet the pre-defined threshold of success of a 10 percent reduction in recidivism bed days"*. The Rikers Island SIB was based on the general goal of permanently reducing the number of jail beds operated and, thus, saving money per bed. By considering the fixed costs, the savings were calculated for the reductions of beds with a minimal basis of 100 jail beds. Thus, the total amount was approximately $4,600 per jail bed for reductions of fewer than 100 beds but approximately $28,000 per jail bed for reductions of 100 beds or more (Rudd et al. 2013). These parameters make it very difficult to achieve substantial financial savings in the first three years of program operation due to the need to serve a sufficient number of people to produce a sufficiently broad effect (Rudd et al. 2013).

social conditions and arises from risk events occurring beyond the boundaries of the SIBs programs;

(ii) The meso level, which includes risks occurring within the boundaries of the project; and

(iii) The micro level, which represents the risks arising from the relationship between the private and public sectors.

Table 5. Risks in SIB contracts.

Macro level	Meso level	Micro level
Regulatory Risks	Programmatic Risks	Partnership Risks
Policy Risks	Operational Risks	
	Evaluation Risks	

Table 5 provides an overview of the main risks that may occur in a SIB contract.

Regulatory or policy risks may occur when new policies and new legislation come into force by changing the operating setting of the SIB. The typical example is represented by the Peterborough SIB case (see Box 1) where the policy reform called "Transforming Rehabilitation" caused the cancellation of the third cohort of the SIB because under this reform, supervision for people released from prison sentences of less than 12 months is mandatory and, consequently, applicable for the target group of the Peterborough pilot.

Programmatic risks may occur when the program does not work. In this case, the best example is represented by the Rikers Island SIB (see Box 2), where the established parameters made it very difficult to achieve substantial financial savings in the first three years of program operation due to the need to serve a sufficient number of people to produce the desired effect. Operational risks may occur when the program is not executed as scheduled in the design phase, and evaluation risks may arise when errors occur in measuring results. Finally, partnership risks refer to the possibility that partners do not fulfill their obligations (Tekolste et al. 2016).

The presence of philanthropies can potentially reduce the risk of losses for investors and intermediaries. A classic example is related to the Rikers Island SIB where Bloomberg Philanthropies provided a guarantee of $7.2 million, thus securing the investment of Goldman Sachs. The example of Rikers Island suggests that private investors are likely more risk-averse than some SIB proponents have claimed and require government or philanthropic funds to guarantee or underwrite their investment to reduce their risk exposure if they choose to invest in a SIB (Fraser et al. 2016).

The analysis of the existing literature reveals a research gap regarding measuring and quantifying risks in the SIBs practices.

Assessing the Value for Money of SIBs in the Public Perspective

A key challenge for governments is to find a rigorous and feasible method of evaluating whether SIBs can provide a superior approach in delivering welfare services compared with traditional methods. From the public perspective, SIBs allow a government or agency to privatize the up-front costs of social innovations and the associated risks, reduce taxpayer expenditure in the short-term and eliminate the risk of government money being spent on interventions that do not deliver the desired outcomes (Fox and Albertson 2012, p. 356).

In this view, a SIB project needs to be linked to cashable savings by the public sector commissioner; therefore, the value for money calculation is used. Value for money (VFM) is usually explained in terms of economy, efficiency and effectiveness (Glynn 1985; Glynn and Murphy 1996). The assessment of VFM requires estimating the future financial and non-financial benefits of the projects (Glynn and Murphy 1996; Hyndman and Anderson 1995). The VFM approach was developed as a benchmark to assess the comparative merits of using a mixed private—public approach to deliver a project relative to other procurement options (Siemiatycki and Farooqi 2012). The most formalized approach to measure VFM was initially developed in the United Kingdom and has since been adopted in various forms as part of the public-private partnerships (PPPs) procurement in many countries such as Australia, Canada, and other emerging PPP markets (Siemiatycki and Farooqi 2012). In the public sector, the VFM is generally estimated by comparison against a Public Sector Comparator (PSC).

The PSC is a theoretical calculation of the total costs for the public sector of developing and operating an infrastructure and/or service. The PSC is basically the sum of cash-flows for a pre-determined duration, incorporating the efficiency gains arising from the manager learning curve and the retained risk and assuming a public management model (Cruz and Marques 2013, p. 27). However, calculating the PSC is complicated by the need to calculate and discount all relevant cash flows in addition to estimating the cost of risks transferred to the private sector (Grimsey and Lewis 2005). Arguably, it may not be possible to 'objectively' assess the claimed benefits of SIB contracts in terms of VFM. The final costs of SIB contracts may not be fully identified and measured *a priori*. The purpose of valuing benefits is to consider whether a SIB's benefits are worth its costs (UK Cabinet Office). The benefits can be classified as follows: (i) cashable savings to the commissioner; (ii) non-cashable benefits to the commissioner; (iii) cashable savings to other public sector bodies; (iv) non-cashable benefits to other public sector bodies; and (v) social benefits.

At the same time, cost-benefit analysis seeks to assess the net value of a policy or project to society as a whole, and the evaluation of non-market impacts is an essential element of this. In a public project, there are costs and benefits at different points in time, and a discounting procedure is required to express all of this in the project's present value. Consequently, discounting is a critical step in determining whether a public project is socially desirable and makes the costs and benefits with different time paths comparable (Zhuang et al. 2007). A social discount rate reflects the society's relative valuation of today's well-being versus the future well-being (Zhuang et al. 2007) as well as the opportunity cost of public sector investment in terms of the rate of return to the marginal private sector investment displaced (Pearce and Ulph 1995).

Cost-benefit analysis is being increasingly applied to the study of social programs and for predicting and valuing the effects of a variety of welfare services that generate benefits not only for the program participants but also for the rest of society (Temple and Reynolds 2015). As remarked by Temple and Reynolds (2015, p. 13), the method of cost benefit analysis *"underlies the great current interest in social impact borrowing among private investors, policymakers, and service providers. Analysts' ability to separate out government cost savings from the rest of the benefits accruing to program participants and the public provides valuable information to all of the involved parties regarding the feasibility of this funding mechanism"*.

However, despite the diffusion of practices such as cost-benefit analysis and value for money calculation, much remains to be done to quantify the effective positive impact of SIBs in terms of public savings and value created.

Evaluating Social Returns

The theme of measurement is embedded in impact investing (Reeder et al. 2015), and the state of measurement of non-financial performance is weak (Saltuk et al. 2013; Reeder et al. 2015; Bengo et al. 2016). As stated by Schinckus (2015), the literature addressing the financial valuation of SIBs focuses mainly on the posterior estimation of social impact and on a mere contextual cost-benefit analysis; however, a prior financial formulation of these assets would be useful to attract potential investors. The limited number of actual SIB arrangements makes it difficult to analyze the characteristics that will define SIBs and, more specifically, to analyze the existing evaluation metrics.

In recent years, many instruments, such as the Impact Reporting and Investment Standards (IRIS) and the Global Impact Investing Rating System (GIIRS), have been developed by academics and practitioners to measure and compare social value creations (Kroeger and Weber 2016).

IRIS is a catalogue of publicly available standardized performance metrics (more than 550) that cover the social, environmental, and financial performance of companies, organizations, or funds, and GIIRS is a rating methodology that grants a maximum of five social impact stars to rated companies and funds (Kroeger and Weber 2016).

Based on the consideration that exclusively using financial parameters cannot measure the full impact of activities, SROI is a methodological framework for measuring and explaining changes via a much broader concept of value (Brandstatter and Lehner 2016).

SROI is a methodological framework for estimating the value created by a specific intervention across three main dimensions: social, economic and environmental (Fischer and Richter 2017). According to this model, the preliminary steps are to (i) identify the key stakeholders; (ii) define the key social objectives; and (iii) draw an "impact map". In particular, the impact map is drawn by moving from the following logic thread: input (total costs in the projects)—output (quantitative effects)—outcome (direct and indirect changes in communities and stakeholders)—impact (outcomes discounted by what would have occurred without the intervention) (Amati et al. 2017). The SROI model monetizes the various impact components and sets the financial value of such monetization in comparison to the financial investment made (Grabenwarter 2016, p. 83).

The SROI is basically a cost-benefit analysis (Jackson 2013) based on proxies and assumptions that are then monetized (Nicholls 2009). The monetized social value (that may be created or reduced) is then compared to the resources invested into the program (Kroeger and Weber 2016). Technically, the SROI is calculated by dividing the net present value of benefit projections by the net present value of investment for a specific period (Kroeger and Weber 2016).

The use of SROI can take two particular forms:

- evaluative: in which the analysis is retrospective and based on observed outcomes; or
- forecast: in which the model is used to estimate the social value that may be created under varying circumstances (Gustafsson-Wright et al. 2015; Nicholls et al. 2015; Fisher et al. 2017).

However, SROI presents one main limitation, which is the difficulty of attributing a financial dimension to soft, qualitative and subjective outcomes (Amati et al. 2017).

The issue of measuring social impact represents one of the central points of interest for the development of the SIB market.

The Potential Role of Banks

Banks can play an essential role both in the financial structuring of a SIB and in providing this instrument to investors. In recent years, many financial intermediaries have shown interests in SIBs. Banks such as ABN AMRO, Goldman Sachs (GS), Santander Bank, and UBS have invested their capital in SIB projects. By providing risk capital, grants or other program-related investments, banks are the best candidates to finance SIBs. Thus, since 2001, Goldman Sachs has developed a Social Impact Fund. The GS

Social Impact Fund is an impact investing vehicle that has invested over $5.0 billion of GS capital in impact investing opportunities to date. The Fund's objective is to provide clients with access to "double bottom line" investments that can offer both a financial return and a measurable social impact.

After the experience with the Rikers Island SIB (described in Box 2), GS invested in three other SIBs through its Fund. Table 6 provides an overview of SIB projects funded by Goldman Sachs.

Table 6 highlights that GS acted as senior lenders in all their funded SIBs. Banks can provide financial resources for consultancies and SIBs simultaneously, giving them an opportunity to exercise the banks' corporate social responsibility.

The role of banks in the development of the SIBs market could be potentially analyzed under two lenses. First, banks can potentially push the diffusion of SIBs within their customer's portfolios and thus improve the number of potential investors in outcomes-based programs. Second, banks could potentially act as financial advisors in the arrangement of a SIB program by using their skills in financial modelization to provide investors with an estimation of risks and returns. However, considering this aspect, we cannot forget that SIBs are not bonds but contractual arrangements between a series of public/private actors.

Table 6. SIBs funded by Goldman Sachs (as of June 2017).

SIB Name	Senior Lenders	Subordinate Lenders	Other Funders
Chicago, IL	Goldman Sachs Social Impact Fund and Northern Trust Company	J.B. and M.K. Pritzker Family Foundation	/
Massachusetts Juvenile Justice	Goldman Sachs	Living Cities and the Kresge Foundation	Laura and John Arnold Foundation, New Profit, The Boston Foundation
Salt Lake County, UT	Goldman Sachs	J.B. and M.K. Pritzker Family Foundation	/
Rikers Island*	Goldman Sachs	/	/

*To reduce investors' risks, Bloomberg Philanthropies guaranteed $7.2 M of this investment.

LOOKING FORWARD: BUILDING A SOCIAL IMPACT BOND MARKET

Therefore, the SIB market is in a marketplace-building phase. There is no doubt that the social impact bond market has experienced significant growth since the launch of the first SIB in Peterborough; however, many questions remain to be addressed. In particular, the main challenges can be classified into four main categories: measurement, accountability, sustainability, and financialization (Fig. 4).

The theme of accountability can be explored by following a double perspective. The first is related to the critical importance of strengthening accountability and transparency in the public sector, and the second is related to the role that the improved accountability may have in attracting investors and donors to fund prevention programs. The topic of efficiency and efficacy in the public sector has, over the last several years, has been placed at the center of political and doctrinal debate. All sectors of public intervention have shown growing interest in monitoring performances, with the intent to obtain better margins of functionality. The implementation of New Public Management (NPM) has had a significant impact on the public sector. As suggested by Hood (1995), this development can be claimed to be part of a broader shift in the received doctrines of public accountability and public administration (PA). The existence of inefficiency may suggest that public service resources could be better used elsewhere in the economy or that more outputs could be generated within the public services without additional resources (Smith

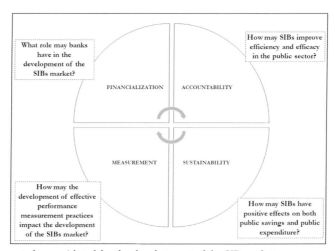

Fig. 4. Issues to be considered for the development of the SIB market.
Source: our elaboration

et al. 2005). Through SIBs, governments are more likely to be willing to spend money on programs that can improve people's lives by sharing the related risks with the private sector. In particular, recent budget constraints have made it difficult for governments to promote innovative preventive services, and SIBs help address that problem by promoting increased accountability (Rudd et al. 2013).

However, by exploring the field of SIB, it is clear that content of the account is reduced to specific organizational performance measurements (Cooper et al. 2013). In particular, Cooper et al. (2013, p. 6) highlight that *"what is unusual about SIBs is that certain aspects of financial risk are separated out of the equation, are borne by the party providing the financing, and are made contingent on the performance of a third party, the service provider. The practice of providing the account is thus reduced to a calculation directed towards a diverse set of stakeholders, each of whom has different interests".*

Thus, the theme of accountability is related to the themes of sustainability and measurement. In particular, the theme of sustainability can be explored by posing a simple question: 'what is the relationship between SIBs and public expenditures/public savings?' In addition, the theme of measurement can be explored with the question 'how we can measure the performance of a SIB?'. These two questions are strictly related. The role of impact measurement is central for the market development of SIBs. In fact, performance measurement practices that focus only on specific aspects or on the interest of specific stakeholders and not overall metrics are available. The result matches those given by Cooper et al. (2013), who perform separate calculations for a diverse set of stakeholders, each of whom has different interests. Moreover, the development of overall performance metrics could potentially attract the interests of private investors.

Banks could potentially have a central role in developing performance measurement practices that can capture the attention of small and private investors and thus help the development of the market.

Concluding Remarks

This chapter describes the major characteristics of SIBs and the main challenges that should be addressed for specific market development. The growth of this market reveals promising opportunities not only for the public sectors but also for impact investors and banks. Furthermore, the chapter noted that the SIB research field needs further development and proposes a research agenda consisting of four main themes that need to be addressed in the future.

Future research in this area needs to be interdisciplinary and to borrow from the domains of public policy, accountability, and finance.

References

Addis, R., McLeod, J. and Raine, A. (2013). Impact—Australia: Investment for social and economic benefit. Canberra: Department of Education, Employment and Workplace Relations.

Amati, T., Arena, M., Bengo, I. and Caloni, D. (2017). Social impact measurement and management: Between theory and practice. pp. 371–388. *In*: Lou West, L. and Worthington, A. (eds.). Handbook of Research on Emerging Business Models and Managerial Strategies in the Nonprofit Sector, IGI Global.

Arena, M., Bengo, I., Calderini, M. and Chiodo, V. (2016). Social impact bonds: Blockbuster or flash in a pan? International Journal of Public Administration 39(12): 927–939.

Bafford, B. (2014). The feasibility and future of social impact bonds in the United States. Sanford Journal of Public Policy, 3.

Bengo, I., Arena, M., Azzone, G. and Calderini, M. (2016). Indicators and metrics for social business: a review of current approaches. Journal of Social Entrepreneurship 7(1): 1–24.

Berlin, G.L. (2016). Learning from Experience: A Guide to Social Impact Bond Investing. MDRC.

Brandstetter, L. and Lehner, O.M. (2015). Opening the market for impact investments: The need for adapted portfolio tools. Entrepreneurship Research Journal 5(2): 87–107.

Bugg-Levine, A. and Emerson, J. (2011). Impact investing: Transforming how we make money while making a difference. Innovations 6(3): 9–18.

Canadian Task Force on Social Finance. (2010). Mobilizing private capital for public good. Retrieved from: https://www.marsdd.com/wp-content/uploads/2011/02/MaRSReport-socialfinance-taskforce.pdf.

Child, C., Gibbs, B.G. and Rowley, K.J. (2016). Paying for success: An appraisal of social impact bonds. Global Economics and Management Review 21(1): 36–45.

Clifford, J. and Jung, T. (2016). Social Impact Bonds: Exploring and Understanding an Emerging Funding Approach. The Routledge Handbook of Social and Sustainable Finance, Routledge: London.

Cooper, C., Graham, C. and O'Dwyer, B. (2013). Social impact bonds: can private finance rescue public programs? In Accounting, Organizations and Society Conference on Performing Business and Social Innovation through Accounting Inscriptions.

Cooper, C., Graham, C. and Himick, D. (2016). Social impact bonds: The securitization of the homeless. Accounting, Organizations and Society 55: 63–82.

Costa, A., Leoci, P. and Tafuro, A. (2014). Social Impact Bonds: implications for government and non-profit organizations. Review of Business and Economics Studies (2): 58–65.

Costa, K., Shah, S., Ungar, S. and The Social Impact Bonds Working Group. (2012). Frequently Asked Questions: Social Impact Bonds, Washington: Centre for American Progress.

Cruz, C.O. and Marques, R.C. (2013). Infrastructure public-private partnerships: decision, management and development. Springer Science & Business Media.

Disley, E. and Rubin, J. (2014). Phase 2 report from the payment by results Social Impact Bond pilot at HMP Peterborough. London: Ministry of Justice.

Disley, E., Rubin, J., Scraggs, E., Burrowes, N. and Culley, D. (2011). Lessons learned from the planning and early implementation of the Social Impact Bond at HMP Peterborough. London: Ministry of Justice. Retrieved from https://www.gov.uk/government/uploads/system/uploads/attachment_data/file/217375/social-impact-bond-hmp-peterborough.pdf.

Dowling, E. and Harvie, D. (2014). Harnessing the social: State, crisis and (big) society. Sociology 48(5): 869–886.

European Commission. (2014). Social impact bonds private finance that generates social returns. Retrieved from http://www.europarl.europa.eu/EPRS/538223-Social-impact-bonds-FINAL.pdf.

Fischer, R.L. and Richter, F.G.C. (2016). SROI in the pay for success context: Are they at odds? Evaluation and Program Planning 64: 105–109.

Fox, C. and Albertson, K. (2011). Payment by results and social impact bonds in the criminal justice sector: New challenges for the concept of evidence-based policy? Criminology & Criminal Justice 11(5): 395–413.

Fox, C. and Albertson, K. (2012). Is payment by results the most efficient way to address the challenges faced by the criminal justice sector? Probation Journal 59(4): 355–373.

Fraser, A., Tan, S., Lagarde, M. and Mays, N. (2016). Narratives of promise, narratives of caution: A review of the literature on Social Impact Bonds. Social policy & administration.

Global Impact Investing Network. (2017). About impact investing. Retrieved June 5, 2017, from http://www.thegiin.org/cgi-bin/iowa/resources/about/index.html.

Glynn, J.J. (1985). Value for money auditing. An international review and comparison. Financial Accountability & Management 1(2): 113–128.

Glynn, J.J. and Murphy, M.P. (1996). Public management: Failing accountabilities and failing performance review. International Journal of Public Sector Management 9(5/6): 125–137.

Godeke, S. and Resner L. (2012). Building a Healthy & Sustainable Social Impact Bond Market: The Investor Landscape. Available at: https://www.missioninvestors.org/system/files/tools/social-impact-bond-investor-landscape-godeke-consulting-dec-2012.pdf.

Godeke, S. and Resner, L. (2012). Building a Healthy & Sustainable Social Impact Bond Market: The Investor Landscape. New York: Godeke Consulting.

Grabennwarter, U. (2016). Measuring impact. A debate about the concept of profit and value. *In*: Vecchi, V., Balbo, L., Brusoli, M. and Caselli, S. (eds). Impact Investments. Principles and Practice of Impact Investing: A Catalytic Revolution. Greenleaf publishing.

Grimsey, D. and Lewis, M.K. (2005, December). Are public private partnerships value for money? Evaluating alternative approaches and comparing academic and practitioner views. In Accounting forum. Elsevier 29(4): 345–378.

Gustafsson-Wright, E. and Gardiner, S. (2015). Policy recommendations for the applications of impact bonds. Retrieved from: https://www.brookings.edu/wp-content/uploads/2016/07/SIB20Policy20Brief201web-1.pdf.

Gustafsson-Wright, E., Gardiner, S. and Putcha, V. (2015). The potential and limitations of impact bonds: Lessons from the first five years of experience worldwide. Global Economy and Development at Brookings.

Hebb, T. (2013). Impact investing and responsible investing: what does it mean?. Journal of Sustainable Finance & Investment 3(2): 71–74.

Höchstädter, A.K. and Scheck, B. (2015). What's in a name: An analysis of impact investing understandings by academics and practitioners. Journal of Business Ethics 132(2): 449–475.

Hummels, H. (2016). The emergence of a new beacon in investing? *In*: Vecchi, V., Balbo, L., Brusoli, M. and Caselli, S. (eds). Impact Investments. Principles and Practice of Impact Investing: A Catalytic Revolution. Greenleaf publishing.

Hyndman, N.S. and Anderson, R. (1995). The use of performance information in external reporting: an empirical study of UK executive agencies. Financial Accountability & Management 11(1): 1–17.

Jackson, E.T. (2013). Evaluating social impact bonds: questions, challenges, innovations, and possibilities in measuring outcomes in impact investing. Community Development 44(5): 608–616.

Jolliffe, D. and Hedderman, C. (2014). Peterborough Social Impact Bond: Final Report on Cohort 1 Analysis. Retrieved from https://www.gov.uk/government/uploads/system/uploads/attachment_data/file/341684/peterborough-social-impact-bond-report.pdf.

Joy, M. and Shields, J. (2013). Social impact bonds: the next phase of third sector marketization? Canadian Journal of Nonprofit and Social Economy Research 4(2): 39.

Kim, J. and Kang, S. (2012). CSO-State Partnerships and Social Finance: Smart Social Capital and Shared Incentives towards public-private partnership efficiency using social impact bonds. International Studies Review, (4).

Kroeger, A. and Weber, C. (2016). Advantages and disadvantages of a new comparability method, IRIS, GIIRS, and SROI. Routledge Handbook of Social and Sustainable Finance.

Ministry of Justice. (2013a). Transforming Rehabilitation: A revolution in the way we manage offenders. London: Ministry of Justice. Retrieved from https://consult.justice.gov.uk/digital-communications/transforming-rehabilitation.

Ministry of Justice. (2013b). Transforming Rehabilitation: A strategy for reform. Retrieved from https://consult.justice.gov.uk/digital-communications/transforming-rehabilitation/results/transforming-rehabilitation-response.pdf.

Ministry of Justice. (2013c). Transforming Rehabilitation: a summary of evidence on reducing reoffending. London: Ministry of Justice. Retrieved from https://www.gov.uk/government/uploads/system/uploads/attachment_data/file/243718/evidence-reduce-reoffending.pdf.

Ministry of Justice. (2014a). Peterborough Social Impact Bond HMP Doncaster Payment by Results pilots Final re-conviction results for cohorts 1. London: Ministry of Justice. Retrieved from https://www.gov.uk/government/uploads/system/uploads/attachment_data/file/341682/pbr-pilots-cohort-1-results.pdf.

Monitor Institute. (2009). Investing for social and environmental impact. Available at: http://monitorinstitute.com/downloads/what-we-think/impact-investing/Impact_Investing.pdf.

Nicholls, A. (2010). The institutionalization of social investment: The interplay of investment logics and investor rationalities. Journal of Social Entrepreneurship 1(1): 70–100.

Nicholls, A. and Tomkinson, E. (2015a). Risk and return in social finance: "I am the market" *In*: Nicholls, A., Paton, R. and Emerson, J. (eds.). Social Finance, Oxford University Press.

Nicholls, A. and Tomkinson, E. (2015b). The Peterborough Pilot Social Impact Bond in (edited by) Nicholls A., Paton, R., e Emerson, J. Social Finance, Oxford University Press, 2015.

O'Donohoe, N., Leijonhufvud, C., Saltuk, Y., Bugg-Levine, A. and Brandenburg, M. (2010). Impact investments: An emerging asset class. New York, NY: J.P. Morgan.

OECD. (2016). Social Impact Bonds: state of play & lessons learnt. Retrieved from: https://www.oecd.org/cfe/leed/SIBs-State-Play-Lessons-Final.pdf.

Olson, J. and Phillips, A. (2013). Rikers Island: the first social impact bond in the United States. Community Development Investment Review (01): 097–101.

Palandijan, T. and Hughes, J. (2014). A strong field framework for SIBs. Stanford Social Innovation Review.

Pearce, D.W. and Ulph, D. (1995). A social discount rate for the United Kingdom. Norwich: CSERGE.

Reeder, N., Colantonio, A., Loder, J. and Rocyn Jones, G. (2015). Measuring impact in impact investing: an analysis of the predominant strength that is also its greatest weakness. Journal of Sustainable Finance & Investment 5(3): 136–154.

Rizzello, A., Caré, R., Migliazza, M.C. and Trotta, A. (2016). Social impact investing: A model and research agenda. *In*: Lehner, O. (ed.). Routledge Handbook of Social and Sustainable Finance, Routledge.

Rizzello, A. and Carè, R. (2016). Insight into the social impact bond market: An analysis of investors. ACRN Oxford Journal of Finance and Risk Perspectives 5.3 (2016), 145–171.

Rudd, T., Nicoletti, E., Misner, K. and Bonsu, J. (2013). Financing Promising Evidence-Based Programs: Early Lessons from the New York City Social Impact Bond. MDRC.

Saltuk, Y., Bouri, A., Mudaliar, A. and Pease, M. (2013). Perspectives on Progress: The Impact Investor Survey. Global Social Finance, JP Morgan and the Global Impact Investing Network, London, January, 7.

Schinckus, C. (2015). The valuation of social impact bonds: An introductory perspective with the Peterborough SIB. Research in International Business and Finance 35: 104–110.

Schinckus, C. (2017). An essay on financial information in the era of computerization. Journal of Information Technology 1–10.

Siemiatycki, M. and Farooqi, N. (2012) Value for money and risk in public–private partnerships. Journal of the American Planning Association 78(3): 286–299.

Social Finance. (2015). DESIGNING EFFECTIVE OUTCOME METRICS AND MEASUREMENT SYSTEMS. Retrieved from http://www.socialfinance.org.uk/wp-content/uploads/2015/02/Tech_Guide_2_Designing_Effective.pdf.

Social finance. (2016). Social Impact Bonds—the early years. Retrieved from http://www.socialfinance.org.uk/wp-content/uploads/2016/07/SIBs-Early-Years_Social-Finance_2016_Final-003.pdf.

Social Finance UK. (2014a). Peterborough social impact bond reduces reoffending by 8,4%; investors on course for payment in 2016. Retrieved from: http://www.socialfinance.org.uk/wpcontent/uploads/2014/08/Peterborough-First-Cohort-Results.pdf.

Social Finance UK. (2017). Impact Bond global database. Retrieved from: http://www.socialfinance.org.uk/database/.

TeKolste, R., Eldridge, M. and Hawkins, R. (2016). Managing Investors' Risk in Pay for Success Projects. Washington, DC: Urban Institute.

Trotta, A., Caré, R., Severino, R., Migliazza, M. C. and Rizzello, A. (2015). Mobilizing private finance for public good: challenges and opportunities of Social impact bonds. European Scientific Journal, ESJ 11(10).

Weber, O. (2016). Impact investing. *In*: Lehner, O.M. (ed.). Routledge Handbook of Social and Sustainable Finance. Routledge.

Weber, O. and Feltmate, B. (2016). Sustainable Banking: Managing the Social and Environmental Impact of Financial Institutions. University of Toronto Press.

Whitfield, D. (2015). Alternative to Private Finance of the Welfare State: A global analysis of Social Impact Bond, Pay-for-Success & Development Impact Bond Projects. Adelaide: Australian Workplace Innovation and Social Research Centre and European Services Strategy Unit.

Wieland, O.L. (2015). Modern financial markets and the complexity of financial innovation. Universal Journal of Accounting and Finance 3(3): 117–125.

Wood, D., Thornley, B. and Grace, K. (2013). Institutional impact investing: practice and policy. Journal of Sustainable Finance & Investment 3(2): 75–94.

World Economic Forum. (2013). From Ideas to Practice, Pilots to Strategy—Practical Solutions and Actionable Insights on How to Do Impact Investing. Retrieved from: http://www3.weforum.org/docs/WEF_II_SolutionsInsights_ImpactInvesting_Report_2013.pdf.

Zhuang, J., Liang, Z., Lin, T. and De Guzman, F. (2007). Theory and Practice in the Choice of Social Discount Rate for Cost-benefit Analysis: A Survey. Retrieved from http://hdl.handle.net/11540/1853.

9

Swiss Investments for Development

Characteristics of a Market with Strong Growth Dynamics

Julia Meyer[1,*] and *Kelly Hess*[2]

Introduction

Historically, Switzerland has a strong track-record in fostering development in less privileged countries, be it through public-sector activities, NGO work or—more recently—through financial service providers channelling private funds into developing countries. Switzerland has become an important hub of specialised investment teams, where extensive know-how has been built up on investing in less developed markets of this world to service basic needs (i.e., access to financial services, energy infrastructure or education), while at the same time seeking market returns.

Especially in the light of the milestones reached in 2015 during four important international conferences defining new frameworks to address some of the world's current pressing issues and emphasising the role of private companies—namely, at the conference in Sendai (March 2015) the first framework for disaster-risk reduction was adopted; in Addis Ababa (July 2015) the international community finalised a framework on 'Financing for Development'; New York saw the adoption of the ambitious Sustainable Development Goals and the Agenda 2030

---

[1] Center for Sustainable Finance and Private Wealth, Department of Banking and Finance, University of Zurich.
[2] Swiss Sustainable Finance, Zurich Switzerland; Kelly.Hess@sustainablefinance.ch.
[*] Corresponding author: julia.meyer@bf.uzh.ch

(September 2015); and lastly, in Paris the decision to limit climate change to 1.5–2 degrees was finally agreed upon by all nations (December 2015)—it is imperative to analyse what investment approaches can be best used to foster an inclusive economy and protect natural resources. With its strong background in supporting development, we cite Switzerland as an example to better understand the mechanisms currently used in this field of the private sector.

Given the growing need for investments to finance development, the role of the financial sector has gained public attention, both at the international and national levels. Projects, such as the UNEP Inquiry, looking into how the financial system can contribute to a green and sustainable economy, have led to intense discussions on the role of financial players in contributing to sustainable development. At the same time, financial service providers increasingly recognise the opportunities resulting from such investments.

The financial sector, therefore, has the fundamental role to develop tools and instruments that build a bridge between the real economy looking for affordable and stable funding and investors seeking long-term investments and attractive returns. As many of the required investments, e.g., in infrastructure or education, are at the intersection of public service and private business, the public sector also plays a crucial role in making such endeavours attractive for private investors on a risk/return level. While in the long term it is prices—and with that public policy—that are key, there are already mechanisms in the form of technical assistance, de-risking or co-investing at hand for the public sector to create a fertile ground for private investments and contribute to an efficient cycle for more sustainable development.

The contribution of this paper is twofold—first, it provides an overview of the Swiss market in investments for development. Through a survey, unique data was collected on the size, dynamics and characteristics of sustainable investments managed by specialised asset managers, banks or institutional investors with the focus on building up sustainable economies in low- and middle-income countries. Second, the paper points out the importance of this investment segment in general and identifies key characteristics and possible success factors as well as obstacles that affect the growth and acceptance of the industry.

The structure of the paper is as follows. The next section introduces the definitions used and the methodology applied. The subsequent section presents the results of a market survey conducted among Swiss institutions in 2015, both at the level of the institution as well as at the product level. The last section concludes the paper and provides some input for future analyses.

Data and Methodology

Definitions

The idea behind the analysis of this specific market segment was developed within a workgroup established by Swiss Sustainable Finance (SSF)[1] in 2015. The workgroup facilitated the exchange and collaboration between experts from different types of investment vehicles, academia, the public sector and SSF. Aiming to gain a better overview of this fast-growing segment and the different tools and instruments available, the definition developed and used in this paper for 'investments' highlights three necessary elements: intention, target region and return.

- Investments for development must demonstrate a clear intention to improve the social, environmental and/or economic situation within the investment region
- Investments for development target countries in developing or so-called low- and middle-income frontier countries[2]
- Last but not least, investments for development target a performance in line with market returns

This definition is more focused than the frequently used concept of impact investing (e.g., Hebb 2013), adopted by institutions such as the Global Impact Investing Network (GIIN) or Eurosif. Figure 1 illustrates the definition of investments for development in comparison with other forms of impact investments.

Fig. 1. Investments for development as a sub-category of impact investing—investments with a clear intention to improve social/environmental/economic situation.

---

[1] Swiss Sustainable Finance (SSF) is an association founded in 2014 with the aim to strengthen the position of Switzerland in the global marketplace for sustainable finance by informing, educating and catalysing growth. SSF has representation in Zurich, Geneva and Lugano, and unites over 90 members and network partners from financial service providers, investors, universities and business schools, public sector entities and other interested organisations. More information can be found at www.sustainablefinance.ch.

[2] The classification published on the website of the World Bank as of 10.1.2016 is used to distinguish low-oncome (lower and upper), middle-income and high-income countries.

Whilst no specific market return is defined, this choice excludes venture philanthropy and similar investments that focus on impact and sacrifice returns. Similarly, all investments targeting developed countries are not considered in this new investment category.

The investors involved in this segment include most investor groups, such as institutional asset owners, retail investors, public entities, family offices and high net worth individuals (HNWI). Investments are made directly in institutions in the respective industries, or indirectly through financial intermediaries using standard instruments, such as funds or mandates. They may come purely from the private sector, from public entities only, or can involve public-private partnerships and are typically based on asset classes such as private debt, private equity and/or real assets.

The value proposition of such investments clearly resides in the fact that there is a dual outcome. Firstly, a market financial return is paid back to the investors, whilst secondly, the investments offer a benefit in the form of a tangible contribution to development, often measured by specific key performance indicators. The investment cycle which creates a return and repays capital at the end of the investment period allows continuance of subsequent investments and therewith continuous impact.

Sample of the Market Survey

The first survey on Swiss investments for development was sent out to a broad sample of institutions, including asset managers, foundations, banks, pension funds, family offices and others in November 2015. The majority of respondents to the survey consisted of asset managers (60 per cent), but also included two foundations, two banks, one pension fund and one other type of institution (Fig. 2). Not every question was answered by all the 15 respondents; we therefore indicate the sample size (n) for each sub-section and figure. Survey guidelines and invitations to participate were sent out by SSF. The invitations were distributed to a total of 57 institutions, of which 15 participated in the survey, six institutions replied that they had no activities in this field and were, therefore, considered ineligible for the analysis; 10 declined to participate and 26 institutions did not respond. This represents a participation rate of 30 per cent of the 51 eligible companies, which largely meets the expectations. Companies that refused to participate mentioned high sensitivity of data and limited resources as reasons for non-participation.

This report collects investment data from different types of institutions involved in the field of investments for development, an industry where intermediary financial institutions are common. It thus needs to address the issue of potential double-counting of assets. For example, if a pension fund invests through an investment vehicle managed by a specialised

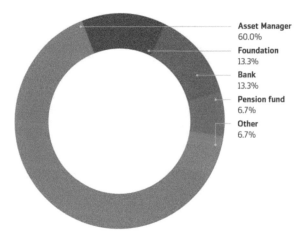

Asset Manager
60.0%

Foundation
13.3%

Bank
13.3%

Pension fund
6.7%

Other
6.7%

Fig. 2. Investments for development survey respondents by type of organisation (n = 15).

asset manager, and they both reply to the survey, those respective assets would be integrated twice in the results. In order to avoid such double-counting, the survey used the following categories to clearly differentiate the assets being managed directly and indirectly:

Total direct investments for development (assets managed internally)

- managed funds
- managed mandates and accounts
- assets invested directly (i.e., project, institution, etc.)

Total indirect investments for development (assets managed by third party)

- externally managed funds
- externally managed mandates and accounts

The report looks at different types of sectors and industries and applies a slightly modified industry classification than the one developed for J.P. Morgan's (2015) impact investor survey. Investments for development are thus differentiated into 15 categories.[3]

Regarding the investment for development products, the definition does not consider public equities and debt from emerging and frontier markets

---

[3]   Agriculture and food, education, energy, environment, financial services, microfinance, financial services, microinsurance, health, housing/community development, infrastructure, conservation, information and communication technology, manufacturing, water and others.

as part of investments for development. This is because these types of investments are typically in companies with a global reach where there is a smaller direct effect on the economy of the target markets. These investments are normally subsumed under broader classifications of ESG or sustainable investment categories (for instance, under ESG integration or Best-in-Class).

The survey results primarily give an overview of the current Swiss market for investments for development, but also include some projections for the market based on respondents' market views. The study explicitly only considers assets being managed in Switzerland; however, those investments can originate from Swiss or international sources.

Results of Market Survey

Swiss Market Size

The survey respondents (n = 14) report a total of USD 9.85 billion assets under management for investments for development as of September 2015,[4] with the size of the investments differing largely, ranging from USD 6.5 million to USD 3.1 billion (Table 1).[5] USD 8.68 billion assets under management were reported at the end of December 2014. This

Table 1. Total assets under management by survey respondents (n = 14, as of December 2014).

Category	Volume (Billion USD)	Share of Investments for Development
Assets managed directly by respondents		
Managed funds	4.00	46.1%
Managed mandates and accounts	1.14	13.1%
Assets invested directly	0.40	4.6%
Total direct investments	**5.54**	**63.8%**
Assets invested through intermediaries		
Externally managed funds	2.87	33.0%
Externally managed mandates and accounts	0	0%
Total indirect investments	**2.87**	**33.0%**
Unspecified	**0.27**	**3.2%**
TOTAL investments for development	**8.68**	**100%**
Additional assets under advice	**2.33**	**n/a**

---

[4]   Figures are collected for December 2014, except for the total assets under management, where respondents also indicate the level for September 2015.

[5]   All currencies are converted to USD using the exchange rate for December 2014 and September 2015 respectively; source: www.oanda.com.

indicates a considerable growth rate of 13.5 per cent over the first nine months of 2015, which would imply a compound annual growth rate of 18.4 per cent for 2015. The total reported assets at the end of 2014 were USD 8.68 billion, of which USD 5.54 billion in assets were invested directly by the respondents into products, USD 2.87 billion indirectly through intermediaries and USD 0.27 billion was not specified. Additionally, the respective institutions advise[6] on USD 2.33 billion assets (Table 1). Some of the indirectly invested assets are potentially double-counted. However, due to the structure of the respondents, with less than a quarter being asset owners, it is unlikely that a large share of third-party managed assets are also represented within the direct investments of the banks and asset managers. Furthermore, in case indirectly managed assets flow through non-Swiss intermediaries, double-counting is not an issue. It is, therefore, fair to assume that double-counting is negligible and total investments for development in 2014 amounted to USD 8.68 billion in Switzerland. Among the 13 respondents, the majority (nine respondents) indicate between 90 per cent and 100 per cent of total firm-wide assets as devoted to investments for development. Three investors have below 20 per cent of their total assets in investments for development and one between 20 per cent and 40 per cent.[7] This data shows the important presence of firms specialising in investments for development in Switzerland and its potential competitive advantage in the global market.

On a global level, J.P. Morgan (2015) reports USD 60 billion assets under management, including all types of impact investments as well as investments by development-finance institutions. When narrowing down the analysis to investments for development, a total of USD 30 billion is currently expected to flow into the sector on a global level.[8] This indicates that with USD 8.68 billion, almost one-third of the global market for investments for development is managed through institutions in Switzerland. The 2015 FNG market study reports USD 8.82 billion assets under management in impact investments for the Swiss market by the end of 2014. Bearing in mind that investments for development are defined more narrowly for this study than impact investments, the estimated Swiss market size (USD 8.68 billion) compared to the FNG results, indicates that this survey manages to cover a very large part of the Swiss investments for development market.

---

6   Assets under advice are not included under total assets under management for this study.
7   Two respondents did not provide this information.
8   This number is based on estimations by responsAbility Investments and GIIN Impact Base.

Asset Allocation

Sector and Industry

The majority of assets under management of the respondents (80 per cent) flow into the financial services sector, with a focus on microfinance (Fig. 3).[9] 10 of the 15 respondents report activities in microfinance, of which five are currently specialised in the field, having over 97 per cent of their investments in microfinance. The following industry sectors are also important in Switzerland: energy (6.1 per cent) with seven respondents, agriculture and food (4.5 per cent) with six respondents and manufacturing (3.2 per cent) with three respondents being invested. Six respondents are engaged in investments in education, but with rather small exposures leading to a share of only 1.6 per cent of all investments for development.

In comparison, the study by Eurosif (2014) finds that 55 per cent of impact investments in Europe are made in microfinance. The global J.P. Morgan (2015) report finds housing to be the largest sector with 27 per cent, followed by microfinance with 16 per cent of all global impact investments reported. One reason for the lower prevalence of microfinance in the global studies compared with the current Swiss study is that the global studies also include investments in the developed/industrialised countries where the need for microfinance is lower. Similarly, housing investments likely represent a higher percentage of total investments in the global studies, as low-income housing projects are common forms of impact investments in developed/industrialised countries.

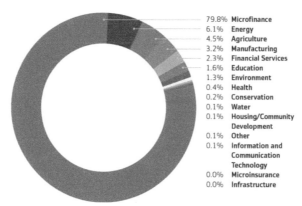

79.8%	Microfinance
6.1%	Energy
4.5%	Agriculture
3.2%	Manufacturing
2.3%	Financial Services
1.6%	Education
1.3%	Environment
0.4%	Health
0.2%	Conservation
0.1%	Water
0.1%	Housing/Community Development
0.1%	Other
0.1%	Information and Communication Technology
0.0%	Microinsurance
0.0%	Infrastructure

Fig. 3. Sector and industry exposures (% of assets under management) of survey respondents (n = 14).

---

[9] Microfinance was not defined in detail for the purpose of the survey. The distinction between financial services to micro-customers as opposed to SMEs (small and medium enterprises) lacks clarity and probably both types of services are captured in this category.

The results confirm that microfinance is an important theme for Swiss institutions focussing on investments for development. This is consistent with the latest *Swiss Microfinance Investments Report*, describing investments solely through Swiss microfinance investment vehicles (MIVs) and finding that Switzerland manages 38 per cent of global microfinance investments (Symbiotics/CMF 2016). Unlike the *Swiss Microfinance Investments Report*, survey respondents of the current analysis also included institutions not specialised in microfinance (i.e., institutional investors, general asset managers). Nevertheless, the strong representation of Swiss MIVs in this survey may result in an overestimation of the microfinance share among all investments for development.

Structure of Portfolio

The majority of assets are invested through direct investments in private debt (Fig. 4), followed by indirect investments in private debt (together totalling 77.8 per cent of all assets under management). Comparing the findings of this survey with the global impact investing market, according to the J.P. Morgan survey (2015), two aspects can be highlighted: firstly, the share of private debt of 40 per cent found for the global impact investment market is significantly lower than the above-mentioned 77.8 per cent for the Swiss market; secondly, the global impact investing market has a stronger focus on private equity, with a share of 33 per cent of all assets under management. By contrast, the Swiss market is characterised by a much smaller fraction of private equity investments (7.9 per cent direct and 3.0 per cent indirect).

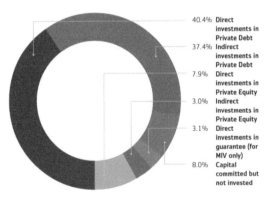

Fig. 4. Structure of the managed portfolio of survey respondents: share of aggregated assets under management (n = 10).

Characteristics of the Investments

The majority of the invested volumes originate from institutional investors (39.8 per cent) followed by public investors (29.5 per cent) (Fig. 5). Retail investors also represent a considerable average share across the respondents, with 20.4 per cent. This result is noteworthy, as retail investors typically invest smaller amounts than institutional or public investors. Consequently, the number of retail investors involved must be large. This is explained by the inclusion of two asset manager respondents in the survey, which have issued products particularly attractive for retail investors (i.e., easy to invest, liquid, etc.). Retail investors are not targeted by all the institutions participating—three survey respondents largely focus on public investors, two target solely high net worth individuals (HNWIs) and one only concentrates on private institutional investors. Generally speaking, all survey respondents, except three, have a narrow focus, managing assets from one or two types of investors.

The results demonstrating the importance of institutional and public investors in this market, with a combined share of approximately 70 per cent, are comparable to the findings of the study on overall Swiss sustainable investments (63 per cent) (FNG 2015). The global study on impact investments finds private investors (HNWIs, family offices, retail investors) to have a smaller stake in the market, with 21 per cent (J.P. Morgan 2015). These findings could indicate that Swiss private investors are more interested in the sector of investments for development, or that the market is easier to access for them than in other regions.

On average, 29 per cent of the investments by survey respondents are provided in local currency (i.e., in the currency of the respective developing/frontier country) (n = 11). Among those investing in local currency, on average a share of 12.2 per cent is not hedged against currency fluctuations, albeit hedging varies largely between respondents, ranging between 0 per cent and 100 per cent; especially for developing countries,

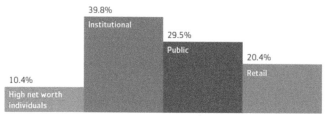

Fig. 5. Distribution of investor types among survey respondents according to the value of investments (n = 12).

currency hedging is not easily available and if so, mostly at a high cost. The investment opportunities differ with regard to currency exposure, hedging strategies and costs. These factors are important for potential investors who, on the one hand, want to understand the associated risk and, on the other, want the possibility of being exposed to exotic currencies, which might be part of the investment strategy for certain investors.

Questions regarding the portfolio quality, in particular the level of provisioning and write-offs,[10] were answered by eight of the 15 respondents. Those eight institutions have used provisioning in 2014 with an average of 3.82 per cent, with a minimum of 0 per cent and maximum levels over 25 per cent. With regards to write-offs during the period, the average was 1.9 per cent, again with large differences ranging between 0 per cent and over 15 per cent.

Regional Allocation

Among the 15 survey respondents, seven provide information on the regional allocation of their assets (USD 2.9 billion[11]) on a country level. In total, the reported investments for development are very well diversified regionally and flow into 96 different countries.

Nevertheless, the assets are largely concentrated in the top 10 countries (60 per cent of all assets) and respectively in the top 20 countries (80 per cent of all assets). Figure 6 shows the 30 largest country exposures by volume in USD million. Cambodia receives the largest share of assets invested by the seven institutions (USD 285 million) followed by India (USD 249 million) and Peru (USD 238 million). The large exposures in these three countries are driven by four survey respondents only. The large share of microfinance in the data used for this section probably explains the focus on these three countries as they all receive top scores with regards to the regulatory environment for financial inclusion (Economist Intelligence Unit 2015).

All 30 top countries targeted are categorised as low-income, lower middle-income or upper middle-income countries according to the classification listed on the website of the World Bank (as of 10.1.2016). Looking at the volume invested in those countries, the majority of the assets (51.2 per cent) flow into lower middle-income countries, 35.5 per cent

---

[10] Provisioning is the accounting process used when an expense is recognised to reflect critical investments that are expected to (partially) fail. As soon as the failure of an investment is certain, a write-off occurs, where an investment (earning asset) is removed from the books and its book value is written down to zero (Fitch 2000).

[11] Some of the seven respondents did not provide the regional allocation for their whole portfolio in investments for development.

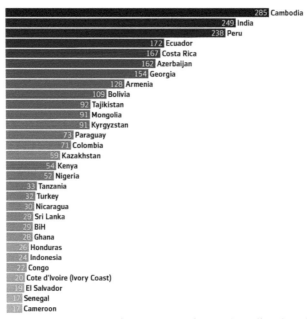

Fig. 6. Largest 30 country exposures of survey respondents, USD million (n = 7).

in upper middle-income countries and also a share of 13.2 per cent in low-income countries.

Regarding the regional distribution of assets under management (in terms of investment volumes), the majority flows into the regions Latin America and the Caribbean (32.4 per cent), Europe and Central Asia (27.9 per cent), followed by East Asia and the Pacific (15.1 per cent) (Fig. 7). According to the global study on impact investments, the majority of global assets flowing into developing countries target Sub-Saharan Africa, followed by Latin America and the Caribbean and Eastern Europe, Russia and Central Asia (J.P. Morgan 2015). 2.2 per cent of reported investments flow into high-income countries, which are not applicable in this report. Nevertheless, the volume flowing into high-income countries is small and only 14 such countries were targeted, with the largest exposure in Hong Kong, followed by Russia, Poland and Switzerland with an average exposure of USD 4.5 million. Furthermore, all the respondents active in high-income regions have very small exposures in these countries.[12]

---

[12] Examples of exposures in high-income countries would also include investments in larger institutions with activities in different countries being headquartered in a high-income country.

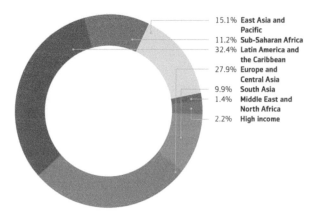

15.1% **East Asia and Pacific**
11.2% **Sub-Saharan Africa**
32.4% **Latin America and the Caribbean**
27.9% **Europe and Central Asia**
9.9% **South Asia**
1.4% **Middle East and North Africa**
2.2% **High income**

Fig. 7. Regional distribution of survey respondents' assets under management (%) (n = 7).

Social and Environmental Indicators

According to the definition coined in this report, investments for development should involve a clear intention to improve the social, environmental and/or economic situation within the investment region. Similar to other fields of socially responsible investments, it is very difficult to measure and capture this intention and even more so, the resulting impact. In fact, there are international organisations (i.e., Global Social Impact Investment Steering Group, OECD social impact investment project) currently dedicated to developing common definitions and standards and facilitating data collection.[13] In the microfinance sector, as one specific area of impact investment, approaches to evaluate social performance at the level of investment fund are undertaken (e.g., SPI 4 ALINUS[14]), but there is currently no widely-accepted consensus on a set of metrics or standards to be applied across different fields of impact investments. Therefore, the questions on non-financial performance in the survey were kept rather general, especially because they should be applicable to different types of institutions and investment sectors.

Results show that most respondents except for one (not stating an answer) have a tool or methodology in place to assess social and/or environmental performance. 71 per cent of these also have a specific team responsible for social performance measurement. The majority of those respondents measure social performance using proprietary metrics

---

[13] http://www.keepeek.com/Digital-Asset-Management/oecd/finance-and-investment/social-impact-investment_9789264233430-en#page14.

[14] http://www.cerise-spi4.org/alinus/.

(40 per cent). Others use metrics in line with IRIS[15] (20 per cent) or other methodologies (33 per cent). On a global level, IRIS indicators seem to have even more importance, with 60 per cent of respondents being involved in impact investments stating to have their metrics aligned with IRIS (J.P. Morgan 2015).

Similarly, environmental issues seem to be closely monitored by survey respondents, with 78.6 per cent of the respondents (n = 14), having defined an environmental exclusion list that they comply with, and almost all respondents (92.3 per cent or 12 of the 13 institutions replying to this question) stating that they review environmental issues of investee companies. The majority of respondents (69.2 per cent) also actively inform their investors about ESG issues (n = 9).

Product-specific Information

Return, Risk and Liquidity

Financial performance data was collected at the product level in order to ensure comparison of data. Ten of the participating institutions provided information at the product level and six on more than one product. In total, information on 33 products was supplied; among them, 29 funds, three direct investments and one managed account. As previously discussed, most products use private debt or private equity instruments for investment (Table 2). The managed account and the three direct investments are invested through private debt instruments. Among the funds, the majority placed their assets in private debt (51.7 per cent), followed by private equity (24.1 per cent), and direct investments (20.7 per cent).

Total expense ratios range between 1.4 per cent and 3.5 per cent – averaging 2.4 per cent.[16] These observations do not include private equity vehicles, which do not provide this information. Target returns differ largely across the 22 different products providing information on this question, ranging between 3 per cent and 7 per cent, with an average of 4.5 per cent per annum and one private equity product targeting a return of 20 per cent. Product performance is valued on a monthly, quarterly or annual basis, except for one direct investment that is valued daily. 32.1 per cent of the products (nine of the 28 products for which this information is provided) come with the offer of technical assistance for the investees.[17]

---

[15] IRIS metrics are managed by the Global Impact Investing Network (GIIN) with the intent to measure social, environmental and financial performance (https://iris.thegiin.org/metrics).

[16] The average TER is calculated based on the number of products and not weighted by volume.

[17] All products providing target return information are organised either as direct investments or funds. One PE fund providing information was excluded (20 per cent target return).

Table 2. Fund characteristics reported by survey respondents (n = 29).

		Number of Funds	Per cent of Funds
Investment instrument (29 PRODUCTS)	Private debt:	15	51.7%
	Private equity:	7	24.1%
	Direct investments:	6	20.7%
	Unspecified	1	3.5%
Total expense ratio (10 PRODUCTS)	Average:		2.4%
	MIN:		1.4%
	MAX:		3.5%
Target return[17] (22 PRODUCTS)	Direct investment/private debt (21 Products):		
	Average:		4.5%
	MIN:		3.0%
	MAX:		7.0%
	Private equity (1 Product):		20%
Liquidity (23/24 PRODUCTS)	Subscription		
	Monthly:	14	58.3%
	Biannual:	1	4.3%
	Closed-end:	9	37.5%
	Redemption		
	Daily:	3	13.0%
	Monthly:	8	34.8%
	Quarterly:	4	17.4%
	Biannual:	1	4.3%
	Closed-end:	7	30.4%

With regards to liquidity, the majority of investment products offer monthly subscription (58.3 per cent) and redemption (34.8 per cent) possibilities. Nevertheless, a large share of products are organised as closed-end products (37.5 per cent) for which the investment period is fixed. Three products offer a daily redemption possibility.

The assets invested directly (three products) are either fully unhedged or partially hedged against currency risk, whereas the managed account is fully hedged. Half of the funds are fully hedged against currency risks, 23.3 per cent partially and 26.3 per cent are fully unhedged. This result could indicate that some of the products are not using local currency and therefore, hedging is not required.[18]

---

[18] The share of local currency was not recorded at the product level through the survey.

The three direct investments are offered only to high net worth individuals and the managed account is targeting private-sector institutional investors only. Among the funds, the majority also target private-sector institutional investors (63.0 per cent) and HNWIs (18.5 per cent), 11.1 per cent focus on public investors and 7.4 per cent, namely two products, are open to retail investors.

Social Performance Measurement

The survey captures the types of social performance indicators that are measured at the product level for 15 products. Typically, respondents analyse two to three indicators to assess the social impact of their products. Most frequently, the indicators used focus either on the share of female clients or employees, or the number of beneficiaries served, by counting either end-clients (borrowers, jobs, beneficiaries) or institutions (facilities) served.

The results also include the absolute value of these indicators, but this information is not examined in detail here due to lack of comparison or aggregation across different products. It is very difficult to compare social performance measurement across investment vehicles in one sector (Krauss/Meyer 2015) and so it is even more challenging and would require a large data base to compare social performance across different sectors and investment product types. Nevertheless, it is remarkable that for almost half of the products reported (45.5 per cent), specific social performance metrics are measured at the product level. Three of the metrics mentioned are clearly specified for the microfinance sector only, one for education, one for health and the remaining six indicators would be applicable for different sectors (Table 3).

Table 3. Social indicators for different sectors.

Sector	Indicators
Microfinance	Female active borrowers as percentage of total active borrowers Number of active borrowers financed Median loan size of end-borrower
Education	Educational facilities served
Health	Healthcare facilities served
Different sectors	Total number of female employees Total number of employees Private capital mobilised Number of end-beneficiaries pro rata Jobs supported Taxes paid

Projections

The survey respondents involved in investments for development are optimistic overall about the future growth of this market segment. Out of 13 responses received, a majority of 53.8 per cent expect that the performance of this market will slightly or clearly improve above the current level, while 38.5 per cent expect a stable development over the next three years. Furthermore, all expect their own assets under management to grow considerably over the next three years. Total assets are expected to grow to USD 14.1 billion in three years, equivalent to a compound annual growth rate of 15.9 per cent over the next three years. This seems to be a conservative estimate, as the growth rate measured last year was higher (18.4 per cent).

Conclusions and Outlook

This first analysis of the Swiss investments for development market gives a general overview of a diverse and growing market, focussing specifically on asset allocation, investment characteristics and performance of certain investments.

Overall, the Swiss market for investments for development is worth around USD 10 billion, with investments ranging between USD 6.5 million and 3.1 billion and a compound annual growth rate of 18.4 per cent for 2015. This indicates firstly, the considerable growth which has perpetuated since a few years and secondly, the important market position of Switzerland, holding about 30 per cent of the global market of investments for development.

A very large portion of this (approx. 80 per cent) currently flows into microfinance, as this sector is one of the most established sources for investments for development, and Swiss institutions have been pioneers in this field. With Switzerland managing about one-third of all global microfinance assets (Symbiotics 2015), it is well positioned to build on this experience and expand even further into investments for development. Compared with the global investments for development market, the Swiss market is less diversified regarding sector and asset class exposure, with high exposures to microfinance and private debt. There would be room for innovative Swiss players to re-orient towards other sectors and/or other asset classes, which again, could provide significant growth potential. An example of this growth potential is the increasing importance of syndicated loans, seen, for instance, in the recent landmark USD 250 syndication loan to Lanka Orix Leasing group of Sri Lanka, where three Swiss institutions played an important role.[19]

---

[19] LOLC plc. 2016 (http://www.lolc.com/news.php?id=225).

The regional spread of investments over 96 different countries is a positive sign that such investments can be widely applied. There is a large concentration within countries with sound regulatory environments conducive to foreign investments. Thus, supportive local regulatory frameworks and stable economic and political environments are important factors for investors to channel their funds towards these countries. Based on this, it will be interesting to see the regional distribution of Swiss investments for development as foreign markets evolve over time.

Swiss investment products in this segment manage to attract a fair share of retail investors (more so than in other countries). Yet, against the backdrop of tightening financial regulations, it has generally become more difficult to establish products that are authorised for public distribution. In order to further meet the apparent demand from retail investors for such investments, it is crucial not to build up more regulatory hurdles for public distribution, but instead, eliminate some of the existing ones.

The average reported target return of 4.5 per cent per annum illustrates that investments for development can be an interesting add-on to an investment portfolio. In the current low-interest environment, investors are looking for new opportunities. An increasing appetite for investments for development is, therefore, a logical consequence, which is reflected in the above-average growth rates.

Lastly, information on the product level, especially the non-financial information, was difficult to access. There is a lack of consensus regarding the environmental and social performance of products and adequate indicators. It will be imperative for products in this area to be transparent and have clear reporting to investors in order to track and communicate measurable outcomes. Success will strongly depend on the ability of the industry to provide evidence that its efforts lead to concrete benefits to local economies, contributing to sustainable development while providing returns to investors.

This current report covers 15 different Swiss actors, the majority being specialised asset managers in this area. In time, more players will enter the market and there will be further growth within larger financial organisations. A future study will, therefore, most likely cover more actors, both because of a growth in the number of players and due to an even higher response rate.

There is a wide gap between the variety of investments undertaken by practitioners and the research and knowledge being gathered on a national and global level. This study contributes to further insights into this interesting emerging investment segment, aiming to raise awareness about the importance of this sector for the current Swiss financial market, as well as the notable growth potential and chances to innovate and create further investment opportunities.

Acknowledgements

We thank the Swiss Sustainable Finance workgroup 'Investments for Development' and mainly Frédéric Berney and Sabine Döbeli for their valuable support and meaningful inputs. We also thank Annette Krauss for important comments on the first draft of the study.

References

Demirgüç-Kunt, Asli, Leora Klapper, Dorothe Singer and Peter van Oudheusden. (2015). The Global Findex Database 2014, Measuring Financial Inclusion around the World. Policy Research Working Paper, World Bank Group, Development Research Group.

Draxler, Alexandra. (2014). International Investment in Education for Development: Public Good or Economic Tool? International Development Policy | Revue internationale de politique de développement 5.1.2014.

Economist Intelligence Unit. (2015). Global Microscope 2015: The Enabling Environment for Financial Inclusion. An index and study by the Economist Intelligence Unit.

Eurosif. (2014). European SRI Study 2014. Paris. Online at: http://www.eurosif.org/wp-content/uploads/2014/09/Eurosif-SRI-Study-20142.pdf.

Fitch, Thomas. (2000). Dictionary of Banking Terms. Barron's Business Guides, Fourth Edition, USA.

Forum nachhaltige Geldanlagen (FNG). (2015). Marktbericht nachhaltige Geldanlagen 2015, Deutschland, Österreich und die Schweiz. Berlin Mai.

Hebb, Teresa. (2013). Impact investing and responsible investing: What does it mean? The Journal of Sustainable Finance and Investment 3(2): 71–74. doi: 10.1080/20430795.2013.776255.

J.P. Morgan (2015). Eyes on the Horizon, the Impact Investor Survey, Global Impact Investing Network (GIIN)/Global Social Finance, 4 May 2015.

Krauss, Annette and Julia Meyer. (2015). Measuring and Aggregating Social Performance of Microfinance Investment Vehicles. CMF Working Paper, Series, No. 03-2015.

Symbiotics/Center for Microfinance. (2015). Swiss Microfinance Investments Report. Online at http://www.cmf.uzh.ch/publications.html.

Symbiotics. (2015). Symbiotics 2015 MIV Report. Online at http://www.syminvest.com / papers.

Part 3
Social Entrepreneurship and Technology

10

Sitting at the Edge Looking for a Way to Create Scaled and Meaningful Impact

Tanya Woods*

Introduction

Good entrepreneurs always have a pitch ready to invite investors and clients to support their ideas and projects. With that in mind, here is one for you:

"We have some big problems and they have been around for a long time. Hunger, poverty, unequal access to education and health care, pollution and climate change, conflict and human rights violations persist globally. These challenges are increasingly complex, and the status quo approach is too slow. We can and must do better. With your support, our team will apply some the most intelligent technology solutions available today—big data, artificial intelligence, and blockchain—in a globally accessible and gamified online product offering that not only gets to the root of these issues but also enables you to be a better person, neighbour and citizen in the process. Our team will exponentially increase the value of every dollar you invest in our project as we aim to reach billions of people, enhancing their well-being

* Tanya is the Chief Impact Officer and CEO at KindVillage.com, an award winning social impact technology company using technology and community partnerships to address some of the humanity's biggest challenges to enhance the well-being of all global citizens. Tanya has co-founded 3 non-profits, has sat on numerous charitable and community boards, and is currently the Social Entrepreneur in Residence at Algonquin College in Ottawa, Canada. She is an experienced international lawyer, policy strategist and has assisted international companies, governments and groups to enhance their economic and social ecosystems using technology and applied innovation. Say hello to her at: tanya@kindvillage.com.

too. Invest in us, because we will achieve our mission to create sustainable positive changes everyone can benefit from."

So, would you invest? Lots of big technology buzz words, many of which you may not have ever heard of or really understand. For some folks, this is a pretty big and bold pitch. It is intriguing because it shows vision and it fulfills many, if not all, of the opportunity boxes investors want to see (or at least what entrepreneurs think investors want to see)—bold vision, actionable plan, exponential return on investment wrapped in a 1-minute elevator pitch. It sounds intriguing, but is it too good to be true?

Five years ago, I would have been skeptical and wondered how many episodes of Silicon Valley this dreamer has watched in the last week on Netflix. Today, I would be more likely to invest not just money, but my time, knowledge, goods and abundant enthusiasm to keep this person going, and to help them focus on creating an excellent solution. I also know that if this entrepreneur's pitch is properly executed, what she is proposing is possible in the next 3–5 years. She is ambitiously taking on altruistic and humanitarian goals that we (and she) can only learn from if she fails. In the case that she succeeds, we will all reap the benefits (social and economic) and the ripples from her success will hopefully add speed to the rising tide of social impact innovations globally. In both cases, the outcomes are better than the status quo and worth the money, time and support to help her succeed.[1]

Still not sure how you might react to this social entrepreneur pitching to you? Well, I challenge you to consider for a moment the possibility that we have everything on the planet that we need to overcome all of humanity's biggest challenges today. All of the resources, knowledge, and tools are here and ready to be applied to create global social impact and improve humanity's well-being. The only missing piece is *you*, who we need to help us catalyse the process to solve these complex challenges.

This chapter is a pitch for your support, and to some extent is presented as such. The chapter highlights big challenges facing social impact entrepreneurs and the social impact innovation ecosystem. It also offers a snapshot view of the social and market potential that exists today in the social impact ecosystem. Finally, it addresses some of the obstacles that must be overcome to further develop and scale impactful solutions that will future-proof your well-being and that of humanity.

---

[1] Failing forward is important. This means that each time we experiment or test new approaches or innovations we are treating them like experiments—considering the context or environment you are working in, the methodology applied, and feedback provided by the process to ensure we are left with learning to build upon going forward. As we begin to apply technologies to address big challenges there will be many failures. The important lesson from failure is not to see it as a negative, but rather pull out the positive learning opportunities from it to move forward.

THE PITCH

Big Issues and Biggest Challenge

When it comes to the biggest issues (or problems) affecting humanity on the grand scale, individuals often think of hunger, poverty, and lack of health care or education.[2] Globally, people also tend to look to large international or domestic organizations and government for insight, leadership and support.[3] In part, this response has been conditioned because the big issues are overwhelming in scale. For individuals generally, and social impact entrepreneurs specifically, it can be very hard to see how individuals can make a meaningful difference on issues of such magnitude. Similarly, with so many different facets to these issues, it can be difficult to know enough to feel empowered to take a view on how to begin to address them. Today we are increasingly accustomed to googling the answers we need and downloading an app to make tough tasks easier; but, there is no app to fix hunger, poverty, human injustice, climate change, healthcare, education, and inequality—yet.

After more than 7 decades since the establishment of the United Nations, one of the oldest and most representative international organizations in the global social impact ecosystem, it is time to reflect and consider these big issues, what progress has been made, and what we need to be doing now to create significant and scaled improvements.

The Big Issues

As a starting point for anyone interested in creating or supporting social impact efforts, it is helpful to consider the views of two of the largest, and most vocal, international organizations define our biggest issues— The United Nations ("UN") and The World Economic Forum ("WEF").[4] As a forum for dialogue, the promotion of peace and an organization empowered to act on the issues confronting humanity in the 21st century, we tend to trust that UN is well placed to articulate thoughtful and expert perspectives on the issues we face and how we may address them. The UN and its 193 member states and stakeholders have identified 17 Sustainable Development Goals (SDGs) that require priority level attention from all country leaders, businesses and citizens. The 17 SDGs provide implicit

---

[2] The "big issues" or "problems" as referred to in this chapter include the issues impeding the attainment of the SDGs globally, but also, the goal of well-being as articulated by the WEF. Of note: "issues", "problems" are used shorthand throughout and refer to this.

[3] Support could be financial, strategic planning, or any other resources needed to address the issue or challenge.

[4] For historical and mandate information see: http://www.un.org/en/about-un/; https://www.weforum.org/; http://www.oecd.org/about/.

insight into what the issues are and what the end goals should be when taking action to address them.

The SDGs have been stated as follows:

1. End poverty in all its forms everywhere;
2. End hunger, achieve food security and improved nutrition and promote sustainable agriculture;
3. Ensure healthy lives and promote well-being for all at all ages;
4. Ensure inclusive and equitable quality education and promote lifelong learning opportunities for all;
5. Achieve gender equality and empower all women and girls;
6. Ensure availability and sustainable management of water and sanitation for all;
7. Ensure access to affordable, reliable, sustainable and modern energy for all;
8. Promote sustained, inclusive and sustainable economic growth, full and productive employment and decent work for all;
9. Build resilient infrastructure, promote inclusive and sustainable industrialization and foster innovation;
10. Reduce inequality within and among countries;
11. Make cities and human settlements inclusive, safe, resilient and sustainable;
12. Ensure sustainable consumption and production patterns;
13. Take urgent action to combat climate change and its impacts;
14. Conserve and sustainably use the oceans, seas and marine resources for sustainable development;
15. Protect, restore and promote sustainable use of terrestrial ecosystems, sustainably manage forests, combat desertification, and halt and reverse land degradation and halt biodiversity loss;
16. Promote peaceful and inclusive societies for sustainable development, provide access to justice for all and build effective, accountable and inclusive institutions at all levels; and,
17. Strengthen the means of implementation and revitalize the global partnership for sustainable development.

The SDGs list is long, ambitious, and clearly takes stock of a number of global issues and objectives that we (as humanity) should be supportive of. The SDGs are also reflective of participating government perspectives and discussions that aim to set guideposts for domestic priorities and international efforts.

The work of the World Economic Forum (WEF) also provides valuable insight for anyone trying to gain perspective on the big issues. The WEF engages a variety of stakeholders and has committed to improving the state of the world. As a self-described independent and impartial organization, the Forum strives in all its efforts to demonstrate entrepreneurship in the global public interest while upholding the highest standards of governance. Regarding the big issues, the WEF's stated objective is "reducing inequality and accelerating real, meaningful and widespread inclusive [economic] growth […] the most urgent challenges of our age."[5]

While aligned, both leading global organizations take high-level perspectives that do not immediately offer a clear indication as to the root causes of the issues or the solutions and innovation required to overcome them and achieve the desired goals. The large issue statements also do not explicitly reflect or provide localized nuances that are critical for nations to resolve their own challenges and most effectively assist in aiding in international efforts. While a macro view is helpful to gather context, it hasn't proven to create large-scale social impact in a timely manner, perhaps due to the obscurity that attaches. The macro view speaks to government and it puts the issues on a pedestal of sorts. However, broad and non-instructive language doesn't engage individuals or speak to social impact entrepreneurs who want to use their time and talents in an intentional manner to create the measured social and economic outcomes that we claim to desire to see. Some have also critiqued that the over-emphasis on government and large global organizations to solve humanities big issues has created a "lack of capacity and social permission to conduct public experiments [which] has led society down a path where the most vulnerable cannot access the best possible services and solutions." (Rajasekaran at 12)

Social impact entrepreneurs are committed to addressing big issues and solving big problems. The clearer the root causes of these problems are, the higher the odds are that they will get addressed or, at the very least, that progress will be made through experimentation and entrepreneurial efforts. In consideration of the big issues discussed in this chapter, and taking the most micro perspective as an individual, one wonders what the UN and WEF would articulate as the set of problems and root causes impeding our global ability to achieve the stated goals today. Further begging the questions of whether these organizations are even equipped to offer these insights and provide guidance to individuals should they ask for it?

---

[5]   World Economic Forum, "Social Innovation: A Guide to Achieving Corporate and Societal Value" (25 February 2016) at 1. To be transparent, as a social impact entrepreneur and global citizen, I agree whole-heartedly with this statement.

Individuals living in their local communities have different perspectives and often a clearer understanding regarding the root causes of the problems that impact their local communities. By approaching our biggest issues at this micro level, new and clearer opportunities to create social impact to resolve or improve the big issues and root causes will expectedly emerge and ultimately enable greater systemic change at a more rapid pace. Put plainly, a micro-level approach that focuses on individuals is more likely to succeed in creating large systemic social impact by enabling and empowering individuals in villages, communities, and countries to achieve a state of socio-economic well-being by *their* definition.

To succeed, such a micro-level approach must engage individuals by gathering their views and empowering them to address the root causes of the big issues they face locally (wherever they live) while concurrently measuring the changes and impact they create for their communities. For the last 5 years, the team of technologists at my organization, The Kind Village, have been working to find ways to empower individuals to create localized impact on their big issues. With an ambitious goal of being able to empower 7.5 Billion people in a meaningful, inclusive way by 2030, our team experiments with technology as an outreach tool to engage individuals and enable them to achieve impact and improve community well-being. Our theory of change is simple: empower individuals in local communities by giving them access to technology, information and tools that enable them to improve their own communities; and, community by community measure and share community achievements to achieve overall global improvements on the big issues. To date, we see promise in our theory of change, but the constant and most important factor to ensure success is the participation of individuals.

The Biggest Challenge: Harnessing the Power of Individuals to Create Positive Global Impact

We live in an imperfect and diverse world that can be slow to change. Depending on where one is positioned (e.g., locally and socio-economically) their individual and community perspective on the "big issues" will likely be very different than those of different backgrounds; however, all views are needed. To create scaled progress on the issues globally, it is imperative that we are inclusive of the varying individual perspectives and enable individuals to engage with the issues.

In recent documentary, Poverty Inc. (2014), a variety of aid efforts around the world were examined and, in certain cases, there was more harm done to local economies and livelihoods than the good that NGOs, governments and charities were providing. Resident entrepreneur,

Herman Chinery-Hesse, shared a perspective that is both insightful and important to consider:

"I see multiple colonial governors [of the international development establishment]. We are held captive by the donor community. The West has made itself the protagonist of development, giving rise to a multi-billion dollar poverty industry. From TOMs Shoes to international adoptions, from solar panels to U.S. food aid [these groups must] ask the tough question: Could I be part of the problem?"

Considering whether a solution, regardless from whom it is offered, is perpetuating or creating a problem is a difficult reflective exercise for anyone because the outcomes may not be as initially hoped or planned for. Ultimate honesty with oneself is required to move forward toward ultimate success in all cases where positive social impact is the goal. Such a critical exercise is, as the film highlights, applicable to the global and local social impact ecosystem—whether NGO or government employees, politicians, charity workers, entrepreneurs or neighbours—and is encouraged, as a regular course of action before, during and after efforts are made if we are to truly consider and measure the ultimate impact outcomes we seek.

Such reflection is critical to success and progress when one considers strategy, next steps and future efforts. Put another way, failing to ask these questions often, increases the likelihood that resources may not be appropriately allocated and solutions may not be best designed to achieve the maximum impact on the issues at hand. Taking this a step further, failure to document this review exercise and failing to share the results of the assessment with local community stakeholders, further shuts out the potential to harness the collective power of those individuals being "aided", who could be working to collaboratively re-think and re-iterate better solutions based on localized knowledge and existing community resources.[6]

To best understand how reflective assessment may look in practice, one may consider how the Kind Village team develops its social impact technology solutions. First, the team aims to take a holistic view of the big issues. Rather than assume we understand them, the team focuses on creating sets of tough questions seeking individual and community feedback. Some of the critical questions we frequently ask include:

---

[6] A recent study undertaken by Germany and India, identified that a lack of comprehensive information for all organizations active in the local ecosystems has created a need for greater transparency and information sharing between all stakeholders. The study also provides a number of recommendations regarding of the potential role of the social enterprise ecosystem in India to contribute to the country's inclusive growth agenda. See: GIZ, "Enablers For Change—A Market Landscape of the Indian Social Enterprise Ecosystem" (Government of India and Government of Germany Co-Publication), September, 2012 at: www.giz.de/en/downloads/giz2012-enablers-for-change-india-en.pdf.

- Do I really understand the full context and environment within which my "help" or support will be given and how it will be received or perceived? If not, what more do I need to know to fill in the gaps?
- How well do I understand the root problem I am working on? And, how will I track the measured outcomes—good and bad?
- How is my effort part of the solution? What is the need on a micro and macro scale? How is the need addressed today and why? How might I be contributing to other unintended problems (e.g., flattening a local (emerging) market or merchant)?
- How can I use my effort to empower individuals and communities locally to develop their own solutions to achieve their defined state of well-being? What have they said that they need?
- Is the support that I can provide what is needed and being asked for by the communities being support?
- How can I enhance support efforts to make them more impactful on the big issues and more beneficial to the communities I am trying to support?

While some of these questions are difficult to answer, as a technology company and as social impact entrepreneurs, we must be constantly adaptive and humble in our thinking and iterative in our approach to big issues. In fact, the process of constant self-evaluation is native to technology companies and entrepreneurs that succeed. Which is why asking the hard questions and being open to all of the feedback—good, bad, or otherwise—is the secret to developing a great solution that people will like, trust and adopt. Effectively, community feedback is gold—but you need to be encouraging it, listening for it and learning from it.

In the case of facilitating systemic change and scaled social impact, one must ensure that a healthy feedback loop is in place to inform and guide a successful social impact and innovation strategy. The feedback collected will also help prioritize and ensure resources can be allocated where they will have the most benefit and will help with identifying the types of social innovation needed to achieve shared impact goals. Not only does a feedback loop enable iterative development, but it also empowers individuals to speak up and participate in the process—whether receiving or giving support or simply observing an issue at a distance.

Today, there is no primary or established feedback loop in the global social impact ecosystem that draws insights, intelligence or feedback from local communities. We are still seeing a very "colonial" or hierarchical structured system—with power and decision-making about our big issues being largely led by governments and NGOs. In addition, as is often the critique of large organizations, there is a real and perceived lack of transparency regarding discussions and practices applied to address the big issues. There are a number of reasons transparency is lacking, but it is certain that, the complex and siloed organizational infrastructure (no one group has the full answer or story); obscure and challenging communication norms (an average person will never jump up to read a 120 page report with jargon-filled language); and, resistance to publicly share vulnerability (not being open with the public that there is no known solution for an issue or that the status quo approach is no longer sustainable), are core to creating and perpetuating this critique.

As a result, individual citizens are awake to the fact that there are big issues. They also tend to want to help, but they are not clear on how they can help and whether, or how, their efforts made a difference or impact. In addition, for those individuals living in time-starved societies with competing pressures demanding their attention, these people also don't have a lot of time to figure out what they should be doing to make a difference on the issues. They lack information and frameworks to guide, manage and measure their efforts. They are not fully empowered or fully engaged and as a result, collectively we are not fully benefitting from their potential value. Combined, these facts set out a significant problem that needs attention if we hope to achieve the SDGs or any issue obscuring the path toward individual well-being.

To encourage global social impact and progressive social innovation, the biggest and smallest players alike must overcome challenges created by, outdated perspectives, organizational models and the persistent failure to share feedback in an open, measured and iterative social impact framework. If successful at open collaboration, we expect that individual and ecosystem engagement will improve and participation in both the feedback loop and socially innovative solutions will be enhanced in local communities. Indeed, active, regular engagement is the key to our shared success on the big issues. The more people who are on the same page with clarity of purpose and actions required, the better the outcomes and the faster the speed at which we get remarkably further on the big issues and reach our shared sustainable future of well-being.

As stated by the UN and the WEF, the goals and challenges each organization articulates can be seen as an invitation for deeper exploration. However, as explained above, it is important to realize that these big issues are just the starting point. The primary and most pressing challenge to overcome is engaging individuals globally and inspiring them to deepen their knowledge on community issues in a manner that incents them to work together to create scaled and successful social impact and social innovation. Catalysing this process requires a plan that will enable and empower individuals anywhere to play a role in addressing their big issues locally while working to ultimately achieve a state a well-being for all.

The Monumental Opportunity—Why Now?

We are witnessing a unique moment in time when key decisions makers—consumers, business leaders, government and financial investors—are conscious of what global economic collapse looks like and the devastating longer term economic and social "ripples" that follow.

Coincidentally, we are also witnessing the power of enabling technologies to scale and facilitate meaningful change, including social impact and noteworthy economic shifts.[7] By all accounts, evidence is showing that the context behind this intense global climate is a perfect catalyst for utter chaos or positive systemic change and improvement, if we capitalize on the opportunities in front of us.

Economic, Social and Political Climates are Ripe for Systemic Change

We are wedged between two critical sets of events that, when considered together, create an unparalleled contextual backdrop for social innovators to thrive, social innovation to flourish and individuals to truly be empowered to create solutions for challenges that have plagued humanity globally and solutions that will future-proof our own human sustainability.

The first event is the Financial Crisis which began in 2008 and the second "event" is now, at the dawn of the Fourth Industrial Revolution. As a result of both, we are witnessing growing geo-political divides; looming risk of economic downturn due to globalized, cost effective enabling technological solutions; citizen unrest that is resulting in personal and collective inflection points and lifestyle pivots (Moreno 2017; Pankaj 2016); and a rise in empathy, conscious decision making and a strong desire for more connected and collaborative civic engagement.[8]

---

[7] Consider decentralization through blockchain, extreme intelligence capabilities though data analytics and artificial intelligence, and experiential learning and production through virtual reality, augmented reality and mixed reality technologies. Such enabling technologies create opportunity and also shift power and control to groups or individuals able to engage. The ability to innovate is happening at a pace and moment in time where exponential benefits to humanity are possible, as are abuses and misguided applications. Cautious consideration by all stakeholders is imperative and should be ongoing throughout our advancement into the Fourth Industrial Revolution. For those unfamiliar with the concept, Wikipedia is a great place to being your research.

[8] This is well documented by journalists around the world. The challenges are unique with their own contextual settings, the level of citizen unrest, whether BREXIT, Trump or otherwise related, is palpable and loud enough to be heard several times round the world. People are mad, activated and vocal and they want to enhance their engagement with their governments. Engagement is often attributed as a quality of millennials, but it is multi-generational. See Cone Communications 2017.

The Financial Crisis Set the Tone

The Financial Crisis is largely known to be the most significant economic collapse since the Great Depression; many lives globally were impacted by financial ruin, jobs lost, and economies flattened. The Crisis is significant in this context because the ultimate result, beyond a massive economic tsunami, was the utter obliteration of citizen trust (Swagel 2013). Citizens around the world became disenfranchised and troubled that business, and specifically the for-profit financial services sector and its shareholders, managers, and regulators, had disrupted their well-being and sense of security while they were left powerless.

Today, despite the fact that we live in a vast, homogeneous global market, which is more literate, interconnected and prosperous than at any other time in history—we still find ourselves being cast as living in an age of anger, mistrust and cynicism as "authoritarian leaders manipulate the cynicism and discontent of furious majorities" (Mishra 2016). Not surprisingly, recent political results in the US, EU and UK provide further evidence of this sentiment or, at the very least, add fuel to the pre-existing fire.[9]

The opportunity and great potential for social innovation lies amidst the discontent—people want change, they want something new, they want better relationships with decision makers and community leaders. Which is, in part, evidenced by the large social movements catalyzed by the Crisis demanding better from business and governments.[10] Individuals are also increasingly making values-based decisions.[11] Whether relating to employment or more commonly purchasing decisions where they have the power to demand and support large-scale social and economic improvements led or empowered by businesses that align with their values and priorities.[12]

---

[9] "Brexit", "Frexit", the Scottish referendum to leave the UK, the Catalonian vote to leave Spain, and the ongoing unrest following Donald Trump's election in the United States.

[10] For example, Occupy Wall Street. The rise of blockchain technology and crypto-currency are also attributed as a citizen movement in response to the Financial crisis.

[11] The focus on values-based decisions is not a passing trend. In fact, it is see as an indicator of an emerging Trillion dollar social impact economy that is as important to consumers as it is to the investment community. On January 18, 2018, Larry Fink, the CEO of Blackrock, published a letter to the CEOs and board members of publicly traded companies urging them to consider their impact and practices: https://www.blackrock.com/corporate/investor-relations/larry-fink-ceo-letter.

[12] Today one may consider Benefit Corporations (B Corps) as an example of values focused businesses. Efforts like B Corps, designed to reshape corporate structures to focus on profit and social purpose (versus just profit), provide a legal framework that shareholders and consumers can count on to hold companies accountable for their actions and give social impact investors' confidence that more than profit is being considered. There are over 2000 B Corps, including those in countries where the legal structure of Benefit Corporations isn't even recognized.

Citizen-driven social innovation and social entrepreneurship is also proliferating to address frustrations and failures across sectors. While social entrepreneurship is a less known subset of entrepreneurship—often because the role of entrepreneur was strictly business and profits focused versus socially supportive or purpose driven—global policy makers seem generally open to supporting the values, opportunities, and economic promise entrepreneurs bring to a shifting socio-economic landscape (Fallows 2016).

Whether driven by fear, sustainability, curiosity, survival, or an opportunity to do something that was only once a dream, social entrepreneurs around the world are re-imagining the tools we use daily, and solving persistent issues that challenge millions and billions of people locally and globally.[13] Challenges to the status quo, show no signs of stopping, creating a global socio-political-economic climate ready for positive change and ripe for an increase in social innovation.

The Fourth Industrial Revolution Sets the Pace

The Fourth Industrial Revolution ("4IR") is upon us. It is not a science fiction movie or myth, rather the 4IR is the next wave of industrialization characterized by technology fusing the physical, digital and biological worlds, while impacting all disciplines, economies and industries and embedding itself deeper into our economies, communities and daily lives (Schwab 2016).

Products and projects like the ubiquitous mobile supercomputer, intelligent robots, self-driving cars, neuro-technological brain enhancements, genetic editing, blockchain apps and digital crypto-currencies are the early advancements of the 4IR. The evidence of dramatic innovation and change is all around us and it's happening at exponential speed.

The opportunity is upon us now to design our future with social impact products and social impact outcomes in mind. But where do we begin? Who do we need to collaborate with? Who partakes in the research and design of effective, more efficient technology driven solutions? Who will design the process to help engage groups to collaborate, and how will they know they have succeeded? All of these questions need immediate consideration to set the stage going forward. And certainly "a combination

---

[13] Daniel Pink (Pink 2009) offers great perspective on what drives human behaviour and motivates action. At p. 21, Pink reflects on the open source movement, where people have taken vows of poverty to participate in projects that "burnish their reputations and sharpen their skills", while enhancing their earning power because of their intrinsic motivation. In fact, Pink finds that "enjoyment-based intrinsic motivation, namely how creative a person feels when working on the project, is the strongest and most persuasive driver" and being in this state of optimal challenge is called "flow"—a place where social entrepreneurs thrive.

of competency, culture and craft intentionally applied to continuously learn, evaluate, refine and conduct practical experiments in order to enhance social wellbeing" is necessary, as is a strong feedback loop and impact measurement framework (Rajasekaran 2016 at p. 8). But the devil is in the details. We should expect to encounter tougher questions, making it all the more important to be reflective, consider our values and ask the difficult questions about our futures and actions today—often.

Klaus Schwab is the founder and executive chairman of the World Economic Forum. Schwab observes that other industrial revolutions liberated humankind from animal power, made mass production possible and brought digital capabilities to billions of people. As the 4IR rolls out, Schwab cautions that the pace and scope of the resulting shifts and disruptions mean that we live in a time of great promise and great peril. We can connect billions more people to digital networks, dramatically improve the efficiency of organizations and even manage assets in ways that can help regenerate the natural environment, potentially undoing the damage of previous industrial revolutions. But, we need to be mindful that organizations may be unable to adapt; governments could fail to employ and regulate new technologies to capture their benefits; and shifting power will create important new security concerns; inequality may grow; and societies fragment (Schwab 2016).

These cautions are important to keep in mind and provide all the more reason to ensure that all groups are collaborating openly, sharing insights and referring to iterative frameworks feedback loops as we approach rapid technological evolution. For social impact entrepreneurs, innovators and investors, the principle of "do no harm" applies across the board and critical questions must be asked to ensure that as a community we approach innovation in a responsible way.

This is not the time for ego or power struggles if we hope to have a bright future.

It is truly time to evaluate the status quo and where we have failed domestically and internationally, as government and NGOs, and as individuals and global citizens. This is an age for innovation and it comes at a time when the need is great, and likely increasing as our global population grows from 7.5 billion toward 11 billion.

The leaders of the future are likely unknown despite current rankings. Innovation does not happen overnight and no one group has a full picture view of what is being developed today or to come years from now.

Consider for a moment that a developed country like Canada faces increasingly complex social, ecological and economic challenges and currently spends 7% of its GDP, or roughly $300 billion, on social outcomes and programs that are not producing "better, more lasting impact" (Rajasekaran 2016 at p. 8). Like many other countries, Canada has a robust government infrastructure, a large number of charities and non-profits supporting communities and individuals, and a population of individuals known to value kindness, community and peace. But, they are not working together in a fully collaborative, transparent or supportive way—old silos, program structures, service offerings, and attitudes persist making the promise of a social impact revolution all the more important and necessary to future-proof the stability of the country. In truth, at any given moment, there is little to no understanding of the domestic status quo on the panoply of social and economic issues impeding the wellbeing of citizens and there is no measurement framework to measure or guide progress or collaborative efforts. The lack of impact measurement framework is a global challenge all countries face at the moment, and that a number of groups and governments are working to address—including my team at Kind Village.[14]

Social Enterprises are in Demand, Creating Social Impact and Generating Profit

Global business leaders are undertaking social impact commitments, going beyond CSR and marketing efforts, to show added value to their customers and shareholders.

While the reasons may vary, the impacts are notable. However, growth has not come as quickly as one might expect. Harvard economists Michael Porter and Michael Kramer note that,

> "A big part of the problem lies with companies themselves, which remain trapped in an outdated, narrow approach to value creation. Focused on optimizing short-term financial performance, they overlook the greatest unmet needs in the market as well as broader influences on their long-term success. Why else would companies ignore the well-being of their customers, the depletion of natural resources vital to their businesses, the viability of suppliers, and the economic distress of the communities in which they produce and sell?" (Kramer and Porter 2016).

---

[14] The importance of a social impact measurement framework that every once can understand and apply to daily decision-making cannot be underscored enough. This is not only going to be helpful to impact investors but will also inform policy-making, social programming and investment strategies once developed. Governments, academics, economists, sector groups and even social entrepreneurs (including Kind Village) are working on developing metrics to help groups set goals and targets around social impact. It is one thing to demand a progress report for big goals, but it is another to provide that report in a way that is meaningful, transparent, and indicative of true progress beyond GDP. Projects like the Social Progress Index are insightful, as is the Gross National Happiness framework when trying to quantify "wellbeing" in economic and social terms. Both frameworks, go beyond reducing outcomes to fiscal calculations which do not reflect the greater social emphasis in a concept like "well-being". See: https://www.socialprogressindex.com/ and http://www.grossnationalhappiness.com/.

In Canada, MaRS Catalyst Fund Investment Director, Kathryn Worstman, emphasizes the urgency for a shift in business leadership, noting that, "We are working on scarce resources, health inefficiencies and high unemployment. We need all efforts, as governments alone can't solve our social and climate problems, we need for-profit businesses to solve these problems" (Worstman 2016).

"Conscious consumerism" is also on the rise globally and the number of social impact businesses is increasing in an effort to attract the support of this growing base of consumers using their purchasing power to reward good business actors locally and globally. In 2012, $2.1 Trillion in global revenue was attributed to social enterprises (Eggers and Macmillan 2013 at p. 37), and in 2017, Facebook announced that 100 million people on Facebook are part of "very meaningful" groups addressing social impact issues globally and in their communities (Zuckerberg 2017).

The interest and support by consumers and individuals is noteworthy and indicates that now is the time to get involved, if you aren't. In fact, a recent study indicated that **91%** of global consumers expected companies to do more than make a profit, but also operate responsibly to address social and environmental issues; **84%** of consumers said they sought out responsible products whenever possible; and **90%** would boycott a company if they learned of irresponsible or deceptive business practices (Cone 2015).

The result to date is clear and businesses of all sizes are starting to listen and respond to consumer demands and values. In its most recent 2017 Global CSR Study, Cone Communications acknowledges 2017 as:

> "the year that corporate social responsibility (CSR) was redefined. Although CSR will always be grounded in business operations— from water conservation to supply chain transparency—recently, the stakes have gotten a lot higher. … In order to lead as a responsible company, it's simply not enough to [impactfully and sustainably] address internal operational challenges—business must take the lead to push progress on issues that go straight to the hearts and minds of [citizens] and communicate company values in a way that's relevant and authentic. Now is the time not only to stand for, but stand up for something that matters."

Rick Ridgeway, a Vice-President at the apparel company Patagonia, articulates the viewpoint of social impact company well:

> "Businesses and business leaders have a responsibility to be activists…now more than ever. It's incumbent upon all businesses to rise to the occasion, and it's in their self-interest…to understand the most fundamental of connections: that without a healthy planet supporting healthy societies, none of them are going to have healthy

markets. If none of them can see long term, they don't really deserve to be in their positions of leadership" (Ridgeway 2017).

Ridgeway is also articulating some core concepts of "shared value" management, most commonly attributed to Harvard economists, Michael Porter and Mark Kramer. By Porter's definition, "shared value" is a management strategy in which companies find business opportunities in social problems. With philanthropy and CSR, efforts focus on "giving back" or minimizing the harm business has on society; in the case of shared value company leaders focus on maximizing the competitive value of solving social problems in new customers and markets, cost savings, talent retention, and more (Porter and Kramer 2011). There is long-term benefit to businesses that incorporate social impact or shared value frameworks into their operations. Studies have shown that companies more committed to social performance ultimately outperform counterparts on return on assets and return on equity (Kanter and Eccles 2011; Eccles et al. 2011; Mennel 2013).

In 2013, the OECD reported that "overall, social enterprises appear to be more active in comparison to commercial enterprises in launching new services or products, albeit with innovation taking place mainly in the services sector and that three-quarters of the social enterprises operates in areas relevant to the EU 2020 growth strategy" (OECD 2013 at p. 8).

Eggers and Macmillan of Deloitte reported that in 2012, $2.1 Trillion in global revenue was made by social enterprises and they predicted a constant increase by 15% year over year (Egger and Macmillan 2013 at p. 37). That same year, the UK reported an £18.5 billion contribution (roughly $37 billion USD) from social enterprises.

The EU and UK are not the only growth markets—growth is being seen and predicted around the world—Australia reported 20,000 social enterprises, generating 2–3% of GDP and employing 200,000 people with a predicted sector growth rate of 4% of GDP and employment of 500,000 Australians within the next decade (Smith 2017).[15]

That said, the United Kingdom is a global leader harnessing and catalyzing success from social entrepreneurship, social enterprise and social innovation and as such worthy of closer consideration.

Technology is Mature Enough Today to "Help"

Today, in 2017, with some distance from those dark days of the Crisis, we can look back at what was and now see some renewed energy in global

---

[15] In this case "social enterprise" is defined as driven by a public or community cause (be it social, environmental, cultural or economic), derives most of its income from trade (not donations or grants), and uses the majority (at least 50%) of profits to work towards its social mission.

economies as they recover. However, we are not out of the woods just yet. This is not to say that there will be another crisis quite like the one in 2008, but we are now sitting in front of the Fourth Industrial Revolution. As discussed above, the 4IR is identified in part by the proliferation of new and advanced enabling technologies that impact all disciplines, economies and industries, and have the power to systemically and fundamentally

---

**The Market Opportunity for Social Enterprise
Case Study: United Kingdom[16]**

In 2015, the Social Enterprise UK reported the following statistics on its very young (less than 5 years old) social enterprise ecosystem.

- 49% of all social enterprises are five years old or less. 35% are three years old or less–more than three times the proportion of SME start-ups. In terms of new business formation in the UK, social enterprise is where the action is.

- The proportion of social enterprises that grew their turnover over the past 12 months is 52%. A greater proportion of social enterprises are growing than mainstream SMEs (40%).

- 50% of social enterprises reported a profit, with 26% breaking even. Almost all use the majority of those profits to further their social or environmental goals.

- 31% of social enterprises are working in the top 20% most deprived communities in the UK, applying focus where it is needed.

- The proportion of social enterprises that export or licence their IP has grown to 14%. For over 1⁄3 of these, international trade accounts for between 11% and 50% of income.

- 73% of social enterprises earn more than 75% of their income from trade; for-profit business is the majority of social enterprises.

- 27% of social enterprises have the public sector as their main client and source of income, an increase on 2013 and 2011. 59% of social enterprises do some business with the public sector.

- The number of social enterprises introducing a new product or service in the last 12 months has increased to 59%. Among SMEs it has fallen to 38%.

- 40% of social enterprises are led by women; 31% have Black Asian Minority Ethnic directors; 40% have a director with a disability; creating strong leadership in diversity and inclusivity.

- 41% of social enterprises created jobs in the past 12 months compared to 22% of SMEs. 59% of social enterprises employ at least one person who is disadvantaged in the labour market. For 16% of social enterprises, this group forms at least half of all employees. These are important jobs.

- The average pay ratio between social enterprise CEO pay and the lowest paid is just 3.6:1 for FTSE 100 CEOs, this ratio stands at 150:1; social enterprises are paying fairly.

---

[16] This study is the most comprehensive research undertaken into the state of the sector to date. The report shows that social enterprises in the UK are thriving, outperforming their mainstream SME counterparts in nearly every area of business: turnover growth, workforce growth, job creation, innovation, business optimism, and start-up rates. The findings show that in a time of public sector austerity and globally networked markets, social enterprises are providing real answers to the significant social and environmental problems we face.

alter the ways that we, as humans, interact with our environment and the things and people around us today.

Thanks to enabling technologies, an unprecedented number of individuals can also now be empowered to advance their own well-being and the well-being of those around them. Smart technologies, peer-to-peer technologies and the sharing economy have provided evidence of global potential. We can borrow cars, share houses, give away things we don't need and exchange our own digital currencies to get what we need and want. By sharing, we need to own less, can create efficiencies, and reduce tendencies of over-consumption and waste. Better still, is the recent emergence of the "caring" or "social impact" economy that is showing strong signs of growth and potential as noted above. In the last decade, different social and technological innovations have contributed substantially to the improvement of living standards and enhanced the diversity, quality and safety of products in the market (Schacht 2008 at pp. 1–2; Cooter et al. 2011; EC 2011 at p. 30).

While globalization and digitization have taught us lessons, both economic and social, on what is possible, the truth is that we have no idea of the full potential for change that awaits us. While we appreciate connectivity, access to global information and the power of networks, perhaps, the most important lesson to learn from our experience to date is that in a global and digitized world, the most powerful group of influencers are individuals—which is why we must engage them and capture their attention to create scalable social impact. If not today, certain going forward, individuals will yield all of the power—not government, not industry, but individuals. And the biggest challenge for government and business will be to harness that power and persuading individuals to support global objectives like tackling our big issues set out above.

But if the people are not happy, do not trust in the objectives or the people leading the organizations and projects, winning over individual support may be impossible. Indeed, we are living in a climate where transparency is in demand, trust is scarce, and everyone can become a leader of the next biggest thing they can imagine. But successful innovators, including social innovators, must work hard to convince consumers, users, governments and regulators that such innovation is worthy of adoption.

Today, enabling technologies are rolling out faster than we can learn them, and it is these technologies that actually make much of the scaled social impact solutions, and almost anything, possible. Today, a watch, like the Apple watch, can serve as one's phone, calendar, entertainment device, personal assistant, calculator, security system and health monitor; this was not the possible 10 years ago. Soon enough your glasses will do all of this and allow you to feel like you are standing beside someone on the other side of the planet, as Microsoft's Hololens promises. Not far off, there will be no cords or screens, and you will be able to fly your own personal aircraft to work or have a driverless car shuttle you around a country faster than an airplane could fly you to your destination—as Hyperloop promises. Surely, if we can create all of this, we should be able to get food to the billions in need.

While these solutions are approaching market readiness, they haven't yet scaled and there are a number of reasons why scaling may take some time before they considered market ready. High production cost for mass-market distribution, concerns from regulators about how to safely introduce these new innovations into the marketplace, and, the under-estimated concern of governments and incumbent players about the possible impacts all of this could have on … the economy, their bottom lines, and their positions of power with status quo. The challenges facing social innovation are similar. But, the disruptive force of social impact innovation is immense and truly life changing at full scale, possibly exceeding other forms of innovation. In fact, fully scaled, wide-spread social innovation ecosystems are likely to decentralize and disrupt long established norms, power and governance hierarchies, on the path to empowering individuals. Such a degree of disruption, is welcomed by some and highly threatening to others—but that doesn't mean social innovation is bad or wrong or should be stifled it just means it is "disruptive"; which is key to creating systemic change and what we need most if we are to achieve the SDGs or any other social impact goals. Today, technologies are in place and mature enough to assist with scaled social innovation—we just need to create the space and environments that will allow the social innovators to get to work.

The Plan and Your Involvement

There are a growing number of mainstream publications, movements, institutions and organizations raising awareness for the exponential potential and value of social innovation to solve humanity's biggest challenges, like those embodied in the SDGs. Yet, despite the increase in global thought leadership, most practicing social entrepreneurs continue to be challenged to justify their value and efforts to investors, governments, and industry partners; all the while receiving little support, particularly in places that are risk adverse or entrenched in traditional social support hierarchies.[17]

---

[17] Common "traditional social support hierarchies" would include societies that look only to government to offer social support to citizens directly and indirectly through charities. Progressive social support hierarchies can be characterized by having a variety of actors offering assistance, e.g., community members know that can get food from traditional places like food kitchens, food banks but also from restaurants and neighbors and other local community venues—responsibility for local hunger is widely shared and not the role of a few types of groups or organizations. Such a model would hold in all other "big issue" cases.

Break Down Silos and Champion Inclusivity

My plea to you, the reader, is to help me and my fellow social entrepreneurs breakdown silos and champion inclusivity every chance you get. Globally, social impact entrepreneurs and innovators are facing systemic perception and relational biases. Decades of experience in western or developed countries show that most citizens expect government, NGOs, charities and non-profits, and religious organizations to address humanity's big challenges, whether local or global. Hunger, poverty, unemployment, health care access, education are not generally the responsibility of businesses and certainly not that for your "average" entrepreneur or citizen.[18] As such, definitions and norms are being haphazardly applied to social entrepreneurship in a way that promotes continued exclusion rather than inclusion of everyone interested helping to address the big issues.

In part, exclusion may be occurring because the value proposition for social innovation is hard to capture. Consider that, social innovation is generally not tangible, return on investment is not immediately obvious or quick, and seeing value in future efforts requires a long view and further enlightenment or awareness of the issues and potential scope for broad impact. Investing in these ventures is not typically comfortable for the risk adverse or those seeking measured returns on their investment. While not a recent phenomenon (hospices, mutual aid associations and benefit societies can be traced back to centuries ago), social innovation is still a seemingly foreign concept when detached from religious institutions and treated as a new field or sector—making it undeniably a recent construct (Ranchordás 2015 at pp. 16–17).

In some cases, countries are working to build supportive government and business ecosystems for social impact innovation, but progress has generally been slow and lacks boldness or vision. Successful approaches must be inclusive and feature new and progressive policies, programs and funding programs for all applicants; and the UK and EU governments are leading efforts in creating models that support social impact ecosystems.

The EU has a stated definition for "social innovation" and describes it broadly as "the design and implementation of creative ways of meeting social needs" (Ranchordás 2015 at pp. 16–17). This definition stands in line with the general acknowledgement that a true social innovation is generated when the benefits to society of a product or process have

---

[18] Most entrepreneurs fail, and the incredible successes of a few, like Richard Branson, Mark Zuckerberg, and other well-known tech success stories, continues to be the special exception, not the norm. This is important to appreciate when considering how many entrepreneurs are recognized and operating globally—while difficult to calculate, the Global Entrepreneurship Network indicates in its 2017 Impact Report it included roughly 9 million entrepreneurs globally.

substantially more social than private value. "The distinctive character of social innovation lies on the inventor's main intrinsic motivation: social change. The social value generated by social innovative programs or policies is not a mere by-product but rather its primordial goal" (Ranchordás 2015 at pp. 16–17). Globally, there is less contention around the term "social innovation", although in many cases national governments have yet to adopt a firm perspective or establish supportive programming that aligns with the overall goal to build social value by easing current points of tension in existing social systems.

However, slightly more contentious is the precise terminology and definitions used when referring to "social impact entrepreneurs" and "social enterprise". It should come as no surprise that there is sector disagreement going on regarding what these terms actually mean and who qualifies to be included in them; put another way, who is in the club and who is not. This is important to recognize when supporting or building a successful social impact ecosystem, in that all aspects of the design must consider the broader goals, which must include principles like absolute inclusivity to succeed at scale.

In some cases, social entrepreneurs (and entrepreneurs generally) have been sidelined is through age-restrictive policies and programs. For example, a recent article from the UN New Center acknowledged the importance of communicating the SDGs and highlighted the need to localize communications and empower local groups to take on the goals. While the article was clear, it also provides a good example of a typical communication misstep regarding social innovation—alienating allies. The article propagated the view that youth are the "best allies" in SDG achievement. In an interview, Cristina Gallach, the UN Under-Secretary-General for Communications and Public Information, explained that youth "are aware the planet is not going well and they might inherit something really bad so they want to be part of the transformation: They know the goals will be achieved when they are adults, when they will be at the peak of their lives" (Gallach 2017). Whether the ageist undertones are intentional or not, youth are often cited by cause groups and governments as the answer to our biggest challenges and offered countless programs opportunities to activate youth to get involved with causes. While youth engagement is great, the stark contrast of similar offerings and support for anyone over 28 feeds into an indirect message that the "rest of us" shouldn't bother or don't matter.[19]

---

[19] The average age of the world's population is rapidly approaching 30 and is expected to reach 37 by 2050. In the developed world, this average is much higher. Skewing programs to youth under 30 fails to harness the knowledge and experience of multi-generational societies, and misses a key opportunity to facilitate collaborative and empathy driven solutions. Only by working in diverse teams will we truly be able to create the most useful and beneficial solutions to our shared challenges.

Over-emphasis on any demographic comes at a cost—it alienates everyone beyond it and fails to catalyze our immense human capital existing in the rest of the population who could be mobilizing, applying their skills and know-how, and taking up leadership roles on the issues today. Putting aside individuals with experience, failures, knowledge, judgment, and skill, not encouraging multi-generational, diverse, multi-experiential collaborations is a misstep for social innovation practice and policy; not least because it artificially narrows the potential reach and applicability of social innovation at scale. A solution created by one group for one group, is only really serving one group—what good is that for everyone else? As such it must be discouraged in messaging surrounding programming, support and calls to action—particularly those made by the organizations standing behind a goal of equality and inclusivity like the UN and many national governments.

In fact, social innovation can come from anywhere, because it is often based on lived experiences and deeper personal values. In social entrepreneurship, the truth is that everyone has a role to play and has something important to contribute. It is also the case that to create optimal social entrepreneurial ecosystems, we need to champion absolute inclusivity and we must treat inclusivity as a practice to be applied in everything we do, including how we communicate publically, how we shape policies and programs, and who we invite to the table to collaborate. And yes, inclusivity means everyone.

The term "social enterprise" is also plagued with dispute. Some reserved it strictly for use by non-profits and charities, while others use it only for for-profit social impact businesses, and further, others define it as any entity working to achieve social objectives—whether for profit or not.[20] The point is that there is no consensus. The lack of consensus creates a barrier to engagement for anyone who may want to explore and innovate in this space. Definitional challenges may occur because of a limited availability to financial programs and benefits for "social enterprise" or the perception of scarcity or dilution of available funding.

---

[20] Defining "social enterprise" is an ongoing challenge that hopefully will correct itself in short order. A greater consideration is by limiting what is a social enterprise, for example, that is must be charity or non-profit, inadvertently this will also limit the potential outputs as it fails to create incentive for business—which is results and profit driven—to partake. Those using narrow definitions, or none at all are encouraged to think big and create a wide open space to capitalize on the full potential of the emerging sector.
See variety of definitions of social enterprise here: http://www.centreforsocialenterprise.com/what-is-social-enterprise/; http://www.businessdictionary.com/definition/social-enterprise.html;http://www.thegoodtrade.com/features/what-is-a-social-enterprise;YunusCentreat: http://www.muhammadyunus.org/index.php/social-business/social-business; Innoweave and the J.W. McConnell Family Foundation at: http://www. innoweave.ca/en/modules/social-enterprise.

They may also occur as one group attempts to exert or preserve control by excluding the other. Whatever the reason, exclusivity has no place in the mission to create global social impact.

The discord amongst key stakeholders, invites governments globally to consider their socio-economic goals and agree to a broad and inclusive terminology to ensure maximum growth and benefit is realized from this emerging sector. Organizations like the OECD, WEF and UN remain suitable venues for countries to share best practices, sector knowledge and social impact results.

Another way to enhance inclusivity is through funding programs and opportunities. Globally, investors, foundations and governments who fund social enterprises are invited and encouraged to consider how they can diversify their funding programs to support all types of social enterprise—non-profit, for-profit and other hybrid structures of organizations. While legal structures are helpful in establishing organizational frameworks and accountability. However, exclusion from funding opportunities because of legal structure (i.e., for profit or non-profit) remains a challenge and stifles the scope and speed of possible social innovation and social improvements. Funders are encouraged to place emphasis on the problem being solved, the approach being taken, and the broad impact potential of the project—regardless of corporate structure.

With the varied scope of definitions carving out boundaries and barriers for what counts and who can help, you, as the reader, are encouraged to champion inclusivity and the position that broad and flexible definitions enabling all entities to come to the table and share their efforts, in support of the global wellbeing of others, is the best approach.[21]

Anticipate Patient Growth and Expect Unknown Social and Economic Returns

Barriers to advancing social innovation do not solely rest on the shoulders of traditional decision-makers. Technology innovators are equally challenged when building social innovation solutions; and particularly when trying to reflect community values and localized objectives.

Executing a social impact vision requires patience and perseverance, empathy, and a strong grasp on community values. In the case of Kind Village, patience and perseverance have allowed our team to stay the course as we aim to effect global systemic change. Empathy is what we rely on to understand how to approach tough issues in a respectful

---

[21] Stanford Center for Social Innovation offers a good starting point, broad enough that everyone can feel included, but focussed enough to keep everyone on task toward a great social mission: https://www.gsb.stanford.edu/faculty-research/centers-initiatives/csi/defining-social-innovation.

and inclusive way. We also set egos aside to ensure we are aligned with community values as we consider how we will disrupt the status quo to introduce new (technology) solutions to reduce some of the biggest challenges facing humanity today. There is no room for fear (or ego) in this process, and anyone who is truly keen on creating systemic change must be ready for what they will learn, encounter and have to overcome to make such a scaled impact—especially in the case of social impact technology.

As Professor Suchit Ahuja explains:

"We see many technology entrepreneurs and innovators approach their solutions with ambitious, sexy, very advanced technology designs. But they sometimes forget to ask the important questions: Will the people I am trying to help be able to use this and will they feel comfortable using this? These are questions you can only answer if you appreciate the stakeholder groups and the environmental constraints they [the stakeholders] have to face. Mimicking the best and sexiest ("top down" or unilaterally designed) technology solutions—like Airbnb—and expecting them to just be adopted and solve everything simply won't work" (Ahuja 2017).

The challenge of designing innovation that is loved and adopted is one shared by many technology entrepreneurs and professionals alike. The additional considerations required to ensure that not only adoption, but also social impact, is achieved are significantly more difficult and tend to take longer to incubate and scale. These constraints can be technological or related to connectivity, cost, and perception barriers. Bigger fundamental questions must be considered like: Do users trust the technology? Does it matter who delivers the solution to users? And, at what point is the solution market ready and financially self-sustaining?

Professor Ahuja adds that,

"A lot of ground work generally needs to be done to effect change using technology. The right way, the most likely to succeed at being impactful and beneficial to the most people, requires patience, perseverance and stakeholder input and support. It is slow, long and challenging, but the results are significantly more impactful on the challenges they are addressing. This is the right way and my research and case studies show this" (Ahuja 2017).

To succeed, social impact technology innovators must be open to learning, failure and acceptance of what is known and obvious, and what is less known and less obvious, to achieve a strong design framework and desired outcomes—which can take time. Similarly, investors and supporters of social impact entrepreneurs must also appreciate these challenges to better anticipate milestone projections and understand the potential for iteration and prospective returns on their investments.

Many investors we have met are unfamiliar with the social impact ecosystem and apply standard technology investment approaches to social impact technologies. While this is helpful in so far as it provides a framework to assess an investment relationship, it is less helpful when it does not bring in all of the contextual nuances unique to social impact innovation.

For example, consider the internet for the value it offers to reduce costs to users for any given product or service. That value of scaled distribution of consumer goods and services online is expected, and well understood. Social impact entrepreneurs appreciate that value, but also may view the value of the internet lying in its capacity to make something (knowledge, service, goods) that is needed accessible to individuals that have limited or no access (Belk 2014). As a communication platform, the internet is also immensely powerful in creating opportunities to learn more about many more communities, without the need to be physically present to gain beneficial insight. In the sharing economy, the internet has also enabled greater access to a shared pool of resources and has decreased the need for private ownership or capital investment in certain "shareable" goods— which levels the playing field for many economically; and these creates economic, social and environmental benefits.

The European Commission has recognized this economic shift as the "collaborative economy" marked by "a deep socio-economic trend that is fundamentally changing the way we live our lives. From freelancing platforms changing the way we work to food-sharing platforms changing the way we share and connect in local communities, collaborative businesses are leading the way to new economic and social interactions within member states and across Europe" (Vaughn and Davario 2016).

The "collaborative" economy (or sharing-caring economy, or social impact economy, howsoever named depending on where you are) is estimated to have contributed 4 billion euros and facilitated transactions worth 28 billion in Europe in 2015, which is expected to increase, making this a highly interesting space to work in, and invest in (Vaughn and Davario 2016).

Ultimately with patient innovators and investors, using feedback and an inclusive approach, it is expected that the "collaborative" or "social impact" economy will see remarkable momentum in the next decade— impacting the economy globally, be it via the labor market (job creation), goods and services markets (better products, less waste), or improved resource allocation and efficiencies overall (DeGroen and Maelli 2016). This is value that is difficult to measure, but very important to consider when investing and supporting social impact entrepreneurs and social innovation.[22]

Invest

It is time to move social impact innovation and its entrepreneurs from the edge into the mainstream, and much work has yet to be done. For example, even with the progressive approach taken in the UK, 49% of social enterprises operating in public sector markets say they're yet to see their work arrive in tender documents—placing them at a disadvantage; and, 44% don't feel financially supported as strongly as small business— highlighting the need to ensure that appropriate funding is available and given a high degree of attention so social impact ecosystems can grow and thrive.[23]

In the case of governments, it is a leadership position to state that a government will champion and fund social innovation, given few have to date. However, the announcement of support itself is not as important as the strategic manner in which government undertakes the exercise of championing the support efforts, funding and incenting investment capital to the efforts, and executing strategic programs and policies to support a healthy social impact ecosystem. As technology entrepreneurs know, the idea might get you started, but it is the execution of the idea that actually matters—inadequate resources, poor execution and poor product will result in ultimate failure. Failure and risk of failure are not typically a reputational objectives of government, and so what governments really need are intrapreneurs and entrepreneurs to work with them, to understand the challenges and then innovate solutions together. Doing this requires open access to all knowledge, resources and data, and a willingness to fail forward fast.[24]

Social entrepreneurs often empathize with one another about having to spend a significant amount of their time searching for support (financial

---

[22] There are guides available that provide helpful impact investing frameworks to being exploring how to assess value and approach. Once such guide is: P. Plastik et al., "Investing Strategically in Social-Impact Networks: A Guidebook for Foundations" (2015, Innovation Network for Communities (INC) and Island Press) at: https://www.cgbd.org/investing-strategically-in-social-impact-networks-a-guidebook-for-foundations/Another excellent resource for information is 3ci, a Canadian organization working to inspire more impact investing and tools and resources to facilitate these: https://carleton.ca/3ci/projects-and-initiatives/impact-investingsocial-finance/ (last viewed July 1).

[23] 44% of social enterprises sought funding or finance in the last 12 months and 39% believe its lack of availability is a barrier to their sustainability. Just 5% of SMEs think access to finance is a barrier, see: Social Enterprise UK, "The State of Social Enterprise Report 2015".

[24] The Government of Canada has begun to implement innovation labs inside Departments to build collaboration and innovation between intrapreneurs and entrepreneurs. The model is in its infancy, however, anecdotally, it is showing signs of great potential.

or otherwise), explaining the unique value proposition they bring to humanity and their partners, and seeking validation for the meaningful and important work they are choosing to undertake, for the betterment of their communities, countries, and the world. As a social entrepreneur, who empathizes with my peers, these regular challenges seem curious and out of step with what should be received with encouragement, excitement, and support—not least because if executed well, a socially impactful business or innovation will lift some of the fiscal and programming burdens off of government, which ideally brings benefit to all tax payers and citizens.[25] As such, it is key that governments put in place measures that provide an enabling ecosystem for social enterprises, not only at start-up stage but also beyond, to get the capital and investment they need to realize the larger gains they hope to achieve. Such measures may include policies promoting social entrepreneurship, building enabling legal, regulatory and fiscal frameworks, providing sustainable finance, offering business development services and support structures, supporting access to markets and supporting further research into the sector (OECD 2013).

In the case of investment and access to capital, as has already been stated, social entrepreneurs are stultified by traditional forms of financing. Donations and grants are not widely available or large enough to permit significant growth. Virtually no access exists to capital markets, creating little flexibility to experiment at various stages of growth. Making the single biggest obstacle to scale social impact solutions that address our big issues, a lack of effective funding models and agreed upon metrics to measure success (Cohen and Sahlma 2013). As Harvard Business School's Robert Kaplan and Allen Grossman have stated, investments in social causes will remain chronically inefficient unless the social sector comes up with transparent ways to measure, report, and monitor social outcomes (Kaplan and Grossman 2010).[26]

With this in mind, here is the call to action to all investors—which includes YOU. Investment at all levels, in a variety of forms, is needed now if we hope to capitalize on the opportunity in front of us to innovate and reduce, if not overcome, some of humanities biggest issues plaguing

---

[25] Working with social enterprises and promoting their development can result in short and long-term gains for public budgets through reduced public expenditures and increased tax revenues compared with other methods of addressing social needs. Social enterprises can also often be more effective in meeting public goals than either purely private or purely public sector actors because of their local roots and knowledge and their explicit social missions.

[26] Kaplan and Grossman also note that in recognizing the need for such transparency, the Rockefeller Foundation joined with many of the most important social venture investors in launching a major effort to finance the development of institutional machinery and infrastructure for social enterprise capital markets. Of note, while there is activity being done to create measurement frameworks, there is no agreed upon standard—which perpetuates the challenge.

local communities around the world. Investment of time, skills, funds, knowledge and insights to help propel social impact innovation forward— wherever you are, whoever you are—is valuable and in demand. As financial investors, be open to all projects that cross your path, as they present opportunities to learn more about the issues and possible ways to create real and sustainable impact for many people. Consider setting aside, if only for a moment, the crass and regimented assessment normally applied to business investments and be open to considering value creation more broadly. An investment of money in the social impact space may or may not return more money to an investor, which is true of almost any financial investment, but that is not to say that it won't have an impact along the way and create value. The shared learning, engagement with community, incremental achievements of the social entrepreneurs you invest all matter and are valuable. This value is not just realized between investor and social entrepreneur, but it is also realized by everyone participating in the social impact ecosystem because it is a show of support and encouragement that paves the way forward toward a better life for all. An investment in social impact is an investment in the foundation necessary to build stronger and more sustainable communities.

Finally, regardless of whether you have capital to invest, every individual in all of their capacities has a role to play if they invest in social impact objectives, social enterprises, and social entrepreneurs. If you are a consumer, demand better products and services and support those businesses that are responding to social impact priorities. If you work in Government, ask more questions and assess if your programs really demonstrate an all-in commitment to scaled and inclusive social impact growth—if not, change them. If you work for or run a charity, consider what you need to make your programs more efficient and effective and ask yourself, what information do you know that you could share to better inform the community of the needs that exist. If you are an investor, champion social impact investments and educate your investor community on the potential and value that exists in this space. If you are anyone that wants to see our social impact ecosystems evolve, please engage in discussion with your community and its leaders to see how you could create a supportive and robust social impact ecosystem that drives economic and social benefits to all.

At a moment in time where history cannot chart our path forward, why shouldn't we take risks to ambitiously design the future we want for ourselves, our families and our neighbours? Why not try being bold and ambitious by sharing our ideas and building supportive social impact communities? Humans have the capacity for great empathy, for great innovation and for great progress.

Collectively we can create new trends, global mindset shifts, and impact. We must take a moment and be less ego-driven, the era of "me first" is over and the sharing-caring economy is in full swing. Now is the time to invest.

Conclusion

In Sum

Humanity continues to face big issues that challenge the ability for individuals to achieve a state of wellbeing. The complexity and nuances in each community about these issues are understood in some ways and still require deeper exploration in others. People, including social entrepreneurs, are increasingly more interested in learning and addressing these challenges, but the status quo social impact ecosystem is still very much a hierarchical model lacking extreme innovation and transparency.

At this juncture in time, devastating economic loss is globally known and recent in many minds, following the financial collapse. Similarly, the rapid scale of digital and enabling technologies is also known and presents opportunities to use technologies to scale socially impactful solutions to those who need them most. Government, NGOs, charities and non-profits in the social impact ecosystem are turning their attention to business and individuals to help innovate, deliver and address our big issues, but they are doing this with little support, financial or otherwise, to offer—which will not yield proportionate results to meet demand and need.

We have hit a tipping point and the status quo and weak supports must shift. Businesses, social entrepreneurs and individuals are ready to assist where they can, but they need broad, committed support from the larger ecosystem of players who typically run and fund the social assistance, charity and economic ecosystems. The time for these groups to pivot and support social entrepreneurs is now.

My Closing Ask

Entrepreneurs are often told that investors don't typically invest in the idea, but rather in the person. I, the social entrepreneur, am asking you to invest in me because I need your help.

For a moment, let us agree that a monetary return on your investment should be viewed as an added incentive for both you, the investor, and I, the social entrepreneur. Let us also acknowledge that a high tolerance for risk is needed to support social entrepreneurs like me, and social innovation, like the work done by my company, Kind Village. Let us also agree that this is a long game, and whether we fail forward or outright succeed with our solution, the ultimate outcome will be progressive and get us closer to a better future. There are no widgets for sale in this plan, only a strategic solution to better the future and act on our commitment to driving change to improve the wellbeing of others.

And so, here is the closing ask (an important part of any pitch) on behalf of social entrepreneurs, just like me:

> "We share this planet. Technologies like the Internet have made us more connected than ever, and have allowed us to better understand some of the experiences lived by our global neighbours. The big issues challenging humanity are known and an army of social entrepreneurs and citizens are ready to help.
>
> We are tired living on the edge looking in at the status quo waiting for permission to do big things that will matter and improve the well-being of our neighbours. While we may not be household names with millions of followers, we have incredible and diverse teams and communities activated in the social impact ecosystem with full force around the world.
>
> Our socially impactful solutions offer unique value propositions to benefit charities, non-profits, governments, consumers and citizens. We love feedback loops because we are fearless innovators and comfortable being vulnerable and failing forward as we work, with your support, to help create a sustainable global impact on humanity's biggest issues.
>
> We need your knowledge, networks and capital but we can't guarantee you 10x financial payout on your investment, and very few could. However, we can promise you that we will harness every opportunity to create exponential growth while working 125% to bring a game changing social innovation to market and help future-proof your well-being and that of others. We also promise that if we fail completely, we will share what we learned with the community; and, when we succeed we will share the success so many people benefit, including you.
>
> We hope that you will generously support our relentless work to build a better world that enables, empowers and realizes global social impact at scale.
>
> We are ready to catalyze big change, and we need you and your investment of time, skill, knowledge and capital to help us succeed. Will you change the world with us?"

So are you in? If you are brave enough, please send me a note.

References

Adam Levene. (2016). Beyond Disruption: The Age of the Impact Entrepreneur, in Wired Magazine https://www.wired.com/insights/2014/10/the-age-of-the-impact-entrepreneur accessed December 3, 2017.

Belk, R. (2014). You are what you can access: Sharing and collaborative consumption online. Journal of Business Research 67(8): 1595.

Cone. (2015). Cone Communications/Ebiquity Global CSR Study at: http://www.conecomm.com/research-blog/2015-cone-communications-ebiquity-global-csr-study, accessed June 10, 2017.

Cone. 2017. Cone Communications CSR Study (May 17, 2017) at: http://www.conecomm.com/2017-cone-communications-csr-study-pdf.

Daniel, H. Pink. (2009). Drive (penguin, 2009).

De Groen, W. and Maelli, I. The Impact of the Collaborative Economy on the Labour Market (June 3, 2016) Centre for European Policy Studies at: https://www.ceps.eu/publications/impact-collaborative-economy-labour-market.

EC. (2011). European Commission, European 2020: A European strategy for smart, sustainable and inclusive growth, COM (2010) 2020; OECD, 'Regions and Innovation Policy' (OECD 2011) 30.

Fion Smith. Profits with Purpose: Can Social Enterprises Live Up to Their Promise? (15 June 2017) at: https://www.theguardian.com/sustainable-business/2017/jun/15/profits-with-purpose-can-social-enterprises-live-up-to-their-promise.

Gallach. (2017). UN New Release. Communicating SDGs' key to achieving global development targets—senior UN official (2 March 2017) citing Cristina Gallach, the UN Under-Secretary-General for Communications and Public Information. March 2017.

Global Entrepreneurship Network. (2017). Impact Report: http://genglobal.org/content/about-gen.

Government of India. (2016). For Change—A Market Landscape of the Indian Social Enterprise Ecosystem (Government of India and Government of Germany Co-Publication), September, 2012 at: www.giz.de/en/downloads/giz2012-enablers-for-change-india-en.pdf, accessed December 3, 2017.

Gross National Happiness Framework. (2016). https://www.socialprogressindex.com/ and http://www.grossnationalhappiness.com/ and http://www.sciencedirect.com/science/article/pii/S0195925510000648, accessed December 3, 2017.

Innovation in the Sharing Economy. Minnesota Journal of Law, Science & Technology (Winter 2015) at pp. 16–17. Suchit Ahuja, Adjunct Professor, Management Information Systems, Smith School of Business, Queens University (interviewed 2017 June 30).

James Fallows. The Looming Entrepreneurial Boom: Kauffman Weighs In, February 22, 2016, The Atlantic at: https://www.theatlantic.com/national/archive/2016/02/entrepreneurship-and-making-across-the-country/470385/.

Jeff Bussgan. (2016). Impact Entrepreneurship, available at https://www.huffingtonpost.com/jeff-bussgang/impact-entrepreneurship_b_8930582.html, accessed December 3, 2017.

John Mennel et al. (2013). The roadmap toward effective strategic social partnerships, Deloitte, October 16, 2013. https://dupress.deloitte.com/dup-us-en/topics/social-impact/the-roadmap-toward-effective-strategic-social-partnerships.html, accessed December 3, 2017.

Kasia Moreno. Top Thought Leadership Trends In 2017 And Beyond, in Forbes (Mar 23, 2017) at: https://www.forbes.com/sites/forbesinsights/2017/03/23/top-thought-leadership-trends-in-2017-and-beyond/#3e0add133595.

Kathryn Worstman. (2016). In MaRS Catalyst Fund focuses on the 'double bottom line'—social impact and returns, March 16, 2016. Financial Post: http://business.financialpost.com/investing/investing-pro/mars-catalyst-fund-focuses-on-the-double-bottom-line-social-impact-and-returns/wcm/17c706eb-3897-42d7-8463-f5d4734b1c1d, accessed December 3, 2017.

Klaus Schwab. (2016). Fourth Industrial Revolution (Crown 2016).

Litan, E. and George, L. Priest. (2011). The importance of law in promoting innovation and growth, in The Kauffman Task Force on Law Innovation and Growth. Kauffman Kansas City, available at www.kauffman.org/-/media/kauffman_org/research… and…/2011/…/rulesforgrowth.pdf, accessed December 3, 2017.

Moss Kanter and Robert Eccles. (2011). How Great Companies Think Differently. Harvard Business Review, November 2011.

OECD. (2011). Regions and Innovation Policy, p. 30.

OECD. (2013). Policy Brief on Social Entrepreneurship Entrepreneurial Activities in Europe (2013) at: http://www.oecd-ilibrary.org/employment/entrepreneurial-activities-in-europe-social-entrepreneurship_5jxrcml2kdtd-en.

Pankaj Mishra. (2016). Welcome to the Age of Anger (2016 December 8) at: https://www.theguardian.com/politics/2016/dec/08/welcome-age-anger-brexit-trump.

Phillip Swagel, Financial Crisis Reading List, New York Times, July 15, 2013: https:// economix.blogs.nytimes.com/2013/07/15/financial-crisis-reading-list-2/?mcubz=0 and Bookscrolling.com's list at: http://www.bookscrolling.com/best-books-learn-financial-crisis/accessed 2017 June 11.

Porter, M.E. and Kramer, M.R. (2011). Creating Shared Value. Harvard Business Review (Jan–Feb 2011).

Rick Ridgeway, Vice-President, Patagonia quoted in Conscious Company, May–June, 2017 at 21.

Robert Cooter et al. (2011). The importance of law in promoting innovation and growth. *In*: The Kauffman Task Force on Law Innovation and Growth (Kauffman Kansas City 2011) available at www.kauffman.org/-/media/kauffman_org/research… and…/2011/…/ rulesforgrowth.pdf, accessed December 3, 2017.

Robert Eccles et al. (2011). The impact of a corporate culture of sustainability on corporate behaviour and performance, available at http://trippel.sdg.no/wp-content/uploads/2014/09/Eccles-HBR_The-Impact-of-a-Corporate-Culture-of-Sustainability1.pdf, accessed December 3, 2017.

Robert Kaplan and Allen Grossman. The Emerging Capital Market for Nonprofits (HBR, October 2010) at: https://hbr.org/2010/10/the-emerging-capital-market-for-nonprofits.

Sir Ronald Cohen and William, A. Sahlman, Social Impact Investing Will Be the New Venture Capital, Harvard Business Review Online, January 17, 2013 at: https://hbr.org/2013/01/social-impact-investing-will-b.

Social Enterprise UK. (2015). The State of Social Enterprise Report 2015, https://www.socialenterprise.org.uk/state-of-social-enterprise-report-2015, accessed 15 June 2017.

Sofia Ranchordáa. (2015). Does Sharing Mean Caring? Regulating.

United Nations, Sustainable Development Goals available at: https://sustainabledevelopment.un.org/?menu=1300 (last visited June 4, 2017), accessed December 3, 2017.

Vaughan, R. and Daverio, R. Assessing the size and presence of the collaborative economy in Europe (2016, PWC) at: http://ec.europa.eu/DocsRoom/documents/16952/attachments/1/translations.

Vinod Rajasekaran. (2016). Getting to Moonshot: Inspiring R&D practices in Canada's social impact sector (Social Innovation Generation, November 1, 2016) p. 12 at: www.sigeneration.ca/moonshot, accessed December 3, 2017.

WEF—World Economic Forum. (2016). The big Issues, available at: https://www.weforum.org, https://www.weforum.org/agenda/2016/01/what-are-the-10-biggest-global-challenges/.

Wendy, H. Schacht, Cooperative R&D: Federal Efforts to Promote Industrial Competitiveness (Report for Congress, RL33526, Congressional Research Service 2008), pp. 1–2.

Wikipedia, https://en.wikipedia.org/wiki/Fourth_Industrial_Revolution, accessed 2017 June 24.

William, D. Eggers and Paul, Macmillan. (2013). The Solution Revolution: How Business, Government, and Social Enterprises are Teaming Up to Solve Society's Toughest Problems (2013, Harvard University Press).

World Economic Forum. (2016). Schwab Foundation for Social Entrepreneurs: Social Innovation: A Guide to Achieving Corporate and Societal Value (25 February 2016) http://www3.weforum.org/docs/WEF_Social_Innovation_Guide.pdf.

Zuckerberg, M. (2015). Letter to shareholders—Cone Communications/Ebiquity Global CSR Study at: http://www.conecomm.com/research-blog/2015-cone-communications-ebiquity-global-csr-study.

11

Preliminaries for Ecosystems: From Doing Well to Doing Good

Pathways of Personal Transformation and Entrepreneurial Action

*Anaïs Sägesser**

- -

From Doing Well to Doing Good

We can be very successful within our economic systems *'doing well'* without working for the well-being of humanity and the planet *'doing good'*. There is a gap between doing well and doing good and this gap can be large. This relates to the fact that our economic systems take money as the metrics of everything which is seen in GDP, growth (and not development) units used to govern ourselves and the difficulty to integrate the 'good' in these systems: the good remains an externality, i.e., it is not captured by our usual metrics and hence is not used to drive what we do.

Observations in regard to this have not changed in spite of the introduction of alternatives indicators like Human Development Index (HDI, introduced in 1990 and reworked in 2010) or Gross National Happiness. As most exchanges are being handled via monetary flows, measurement of success and 'doing well' continues to being measured so.

Working on building sustainable financial innovation it is necessary to ensure that these innovations truly contribute to the flourishing of mankind on this planet and thus arise from the motivation to do good.

STRIDE - unSchool for Entrepreneurial Leadership; anais.saegesser@stride-learning.ch

As sustainability has been used in an economic context to allow for long-term continuous growth, it is in this context that it is not automatically associated with doing good.

From Innovation to Scaling

The term 'innovation' has been over-used and hailed as holy grail to solve almost all of our societal problems. The impact perspective has in this context often been lost, especially when looking at what kind of ideas to support financially. Innovation is not an end in itself but only one of many available means. What is more important is to analyse carefully which interventions, new or old, are working to establish a culture of learning and from that, bring impact to scale. Innovation should not be pursued without having scaling in mind.

To scale something is typically a trade-off between speed and level of control. Thus the willingness to potentially let go (also some potentially larger financial returns) to allow something to scale much faster is worth taking into account. There has been a strong discourse on scaling in management literature, where it is strongly related to growth of a company or more recently, with internet-based companies to exponential growth. At the same time, there is a running discourse in the social sector about replicability of projects and how to sustainably build impact by creating new ecosystems or public-private partnerships. Seelos/Mair (2017) reveal in their analysis of organisations the much overlooked nexus between investments that might not pan out (innovation) and expansion based on existing strengths (scaling). The real bottleneck though is scaling, and not innovation. Managing this tension between innovation and scaling is a difficult balancing act that fundamentally defines an organisation and its impact. In their framework, they link the problem of space (what knowledge) to the identity space (why knowledge) and solution space (how knowledge). The identity space is where the reason 'why' sits, the mission statement and values of an organisation.

The Call for New Values

Values translated into action lie at the core of what we are looking to address. Keeping our planet and societies in a safe operating space requires speeding up transitions in several domains—economic, social, environmental, personal and spiritual, which, in turn, require changes in individual behaviours and lifestyles, in policies and social equity; indeed in our social practices.

"I used to think the top environmental problems were biodiversity loss, ecosystem collapse and climate change. I thought that with 30 years of good science we could address those problems. But I was wrong. The top environmental problems are selfishness, greed and apathy... ... and to deal with these, we need a spiritual and cultural transformation—and we scientists don't know how to do that."

Gus Speth

What we need to do is work towards a cultural and spiritual transformation tackling the issues of selfishness, greed and apathy. The greatest threat to human well-being is the attitude that someone else will take care of it.

As stated in the World Business Council for Sustainable Development WBCSD Vision 2050 and more recently in the FOEN paper, Go for Impact, issued by the Federal Office for the Environment Switzerland (FOEN), there is a need for new values. WBCSD Vision 2010 said: "Strategic planning towards sustainability requires engaging people in profound change. An inner shift in people's values, aspirations and behaviours guided by their mental models, leads to an outer shift in processes, strategies and practices."

The Pathway of Personal Transformation

Prof. Tanja Singer (in collaboration with Mind & Life Institute), leading the social neurosciences department at the Max Planck Institute of Human Cognitive and Brain Sciences, found that through a continuous practice of certain types of meditation (especially the compassionate aspect) our neuronal structures can be altered. This alteration can be seen in MRIs (Magnetic Resonance Imagining, a standard technique in modern medicine) and can take place even in adulthood. Their research showed that the observed impact of meditation does not only alter the neuronal structure, but leads also to a shift in our predominant motivational system. Thus, instead of having consumption as the predominant motivational system which leads to a self-interest behaviour, if a meditation on compassion is pursued this will change to 'care', which consequently triggers a pro-social behaviour.

Meditation holds thus, according to Singer, the potential to change our 'stable preferences' (whether you are altruistic or egoistic in your predominant behaviour) as economists would call them. This leads necessarily to re-thinking of the neo-classic economic models based on a *homo economicus* and brings us to a caring economy—an economic system in which genuine caring for people and nature is the top priority.

This holds the potential of changing the system from its very core—the actors.

"You cannot solve problems with the same thinking used to create the problems."

Albert Einstein

One potential pathway of arriving at these 'new values' as asked for earlier is thus the pathway of meditation or personal transformation. Personal transformation is, however, a continuous process and a continuous effort. This, as well as then the 'new' values, are both supported and reinforced by societal practice. Humans as essentially social beings who need the reinforcement and support of community.

As values drive behaviour, though we all do not consistently live up to all of our values, change can be addressed from within rather than by trying to nudge it and succumb people to the same manipulation that got us into this situation that threatens the very existence of humanity.

Reconnecting

The process of meditation is also a process of reconnection. Reconnection being a central part of the theory of change in which the urge for taking action stems from the deep knowledge and living life through connection with all.

"The human being is a part of the whole called by us as universe, a part limited in time and space. He experiences himself, his thoughts and feelings as something separated from the rest, a kind of optical delusion of his consciousness. This delusion is a kind of prison for us, restricting us to our personal desires and to affection for a few persons nearest to us. Our task must be to free ourselves from this prison by widening our circle of compassion to embrace all living creatures and the whole of nature in its beauty."

Albert Einstein

In meditation, we start by connecting with oneself and can then continue to connect with others, nature and the universe.

The Quest for Meaning

The search for meaning—the 'why'—has become the quest of our time, though often the individual is wrongly placed in the centre of this quest rather than playing the role or contributing to the whole. The search for meaning and purpose will never be successful if it is only directed towards one's own short-term satisfaction, be it from material or spiritual 'consumption'. But we can find meaning by looking at the wider canvas of things and what each of us can contribute to entirety. If this becomes the focus or centre of our work and life (with work and life not being separated the two uniting into one purpose) and we perform each act not because anyone tells us to do so nor because we expect some kind of reward but rather because it is the right thing to do, then we will be able to joyfully and purposefully live our life.

This quest for meaning is also fuelled through sensing and/or acknowledging the fact that our economic system continues to destroy our basis of living. The aspiration to become rich and consume to support a hedonistic lifestyle is not what makes people happy, nor is the attainment sustainable for humanity.

Frequently people say that they wish to contribute to a better society but simply have no idea of their own to create their own position or own role in it. Social or impact-driven entrepreneurship is part of the solution but from the view of support organisations, what is being asked of these new entrepreneurs is to work within the boundaries and limited mindset of the old system addressing problems with the same means that caused the problem in the first place, that is, looking for growth and maximisation of profit. Critical reflection in terms of incentives set in venture support systems is required along with careful project support selection. The challenge is to create a new system with a wider mind-set while still working on the old one. This, however, should not provide any reason not to engage in action and continue working towards a world that works for all.

To bring 'doing good' to scale, we need to induce a transformation in both ourselves (reconnection) and the systems in which we live.

For a person to build trust in the pathway and purpose chosen, he or she must first try to reconnect with her/himself. The connection means, first and foremost, being present (see also Scharmer) in the moment and fully accepting where one currently stands (does not imply losing the ambition to go beyond) and embracing the resources, including one's own body. Strength cannot be borne by rejecting one's body, thoughts or emotions. This may sound simple but those people who have distanced themselves from the social media, virtual or gaming realities, advertisements, stories or tales of perceived expectations and are happy, are those who are rare to find. This happiness with the present becomes powerful if it leads to a connection with others, nature and the universe. In other words, being happy with oneself through a hedonistic selfish approach to life of 'doing well' but not considering truly about 'doing good' and contributing to the whole, knowing about one's place in the world and realising being a part of the world is not what quest means. The quest is what provides both grounding as well as the urge to contribute to a greater good and move beyond the target of individual well-being.

From Personal Transformation to Societal Action

The inner journey towards oneself can be referred to as 'Personal Transformation' (see also Ricard 2015). Personal transformation stands for the process of reconnecting to oneself and developing consciousness of one's own values and belief systems. It further encompasses setting this on an ethical foundation through a practice of compassion, which allows reconnection with others, nature and beyond.

The theory of change behind personal transformation means community building and civil action, which can also mean entrepreneurial action. Individual and collective action are closely interlinked and often interdependent. Thus the preliminary settings that allow a personal transformation can be very much influenced by the setting and framing of the surroundings and as vice versa. There is an urgent call to taken responsibility, foster entrepreneurial action and among other things, find new ways of doing business.

As the support system for venture support continues to grow, we observe that few people engage in new ideas and take risks that would truly contribute to well-being of humanity. Thus the venture support organisations are increasingly struggling to find a sufficient number of great teams and ideas to incubate or accelerate. This is partly due to the focus on doing well; on the notion that every action needs to give monetary value and the narrow view emerging from the predominant customer-centric approach (e.g., lean, design thinking) in the start-up world. In a purely customer-centric approach, where there has to be an individual customer need (or in the technical term a 'pain reliever' or 'gain creator') for everything, we neglect what is good for all of us despite having no immediate *individual* value. The conflict between individual and collective benefits and utility, that is, between individual value maximisation and collective value maximisation, is described by the rationality trap. There is often an implicit assumption that public good can result from a combination of private interests where climate change is often not the issue.

Rationality trap describes the clash between what is rational (individual rationality) for the individual and what is rational for all individuals (collective rationality). It describes situations where aggregation of rational individual behaviour does not lead to collective optimum. One simple example is fire in a cinema hall. While it is rational for each individual to run to the exit as quickly as possible, but this individual behaviour creates clogging of the exits. Climate change is another example of this gap and of course, also an example of the free-rider problem which occurs when a party receives the benefits of a public good without contributing to its cost for example, addressing climate change creates collective value while a single person may not attribute direct individual added value to it. Asking potential change agents to address grand societal problems purely by taking a customer-centric view and scaling through the currently predominant system of market economy may not account for interaction of several participants in dynamic systems and therefore, neglect the rationality trap. The rationality trap as a reason for market failure is often described by economists as a failure to internalise price externalities for public goods. The rationality trap and the consequential lack of internalisation of external costs has led to systemic problems, such as climate change.

Need for Collaboration

Although the pathway of personal transformation is propagated in this chapter, its aim is to go beyond the individualistic perspective. There have been too many accounts of 'heropreneurs' (see Papi-Thornton 2016) aiming to save the world on their own, without either understanding the underlying challenge or the existing solutions but driven by a hero's quest for glory. What we need is more collaboration and stepping back from glorification of individual achievements. Once I manage to connect to myself, 'I', I then need to connect to the other 'you'. Only from this dyad 'I' and 'you' can we then move on to the collective 'we'.

> *"Never doubt that a small group of thoughtful, committed citizens can change the world; indeed, it's the only thing that ever has."*
>
> Margaret Mead

Change can start from small but it must go beyond promoting the agenda, image or power of an individual. What was stated above about a caring economy moves exactly beyond the homo economicus with an anticipated behaviour of maximisation of individual benefit, to a behaviour that is beneficial for all. For this it is also helpful to transcend the arrogance of assuming to know everything alone. Acting in communities of collaboration, we need to go one step further—by beginning from what works for an individual, a team, a group to a network, a movement and eventually to all beings.

Pathways to Change

Assuming that all people essentially have a thirst for fulfilment, happiness and avoidance of suffering, this then creates the basis for applying this concept as an approach which leads to an improvement in society.

Between taking an approach where humans are fully self-determined and determined by the system stands the approach of addressing change through societal practices. Our societal practices, the way we are doing things, need to undergo scrutiny and potentially be altered. Starting with practices, both as systems and units of analysis, make change possible for individuals as both observers and practitioners.

Addressing the enormous societal and human-caused environmental challenges at hand which are threatening our existence on this planet requires a transformation. As we want to neither opt for a transformation by design nor leave it to disaster (see also Welzer) we must opt for a multitude of simultaneous approaches and thus allow also for diversity of pathways and methods. The two approaches being introduced here, which are closely interlinked, are personal transformation and entrepreneurial action.

The Need for Entrepreneurial Action

Entrepreneurial action, understood as taking responsibility for something and acting accordingly, can express itself through everyday action, intrapreneurship or building a start-up. If one were to merely look at the rising number of start-ups concentrated in so-called hotspots, one would assume that taking responsibility is on the rise. This is, however, only partly so as start-ups and their support organisations are increasingly demanding state support and safety nets for entrepreneurs whilst enjoying an increasing pot of funding available.

Entrepreneurial action is a pathway to contribute to world-making by changing society through change in practices and to 'make history'. Successful entrepreneurship is in this context understood as implementing societal change—that is, a change in practice—successfully (see Spinosa et al. 1997). Practice refers to the way things are done, like the practice of commuting or having breakfast. Successful entrepreneurship is thus about changing the way something is done in society, 'the way in which we understand and deal with ourselves and with things' (Spinosa), the way a practice is changed. Changing societal practices can be done for the benefit of all or just a particular business; an example is how Gilette changed the understanding of manhood. Shaving went from being a careful practice that required a sharp blade that was valued and cared for to being a convenience that could be taken care of with a throw-away blade. Men no longer, at least in this aspect of manhood, needed to care for things but could make a single use and then throw away objects at their will.

The concept of world-making through entrepreneurial practice is thus only helpful if it is for the 'good'. Thus again the underlying intention is the key. Only with the intention of doing good, with the fundaments of ethics, is entrepreneurial action a valid approach towards addressing some of the most urgent challenges of our time.

As systems and economies are transforming at a slow pace, there are a few traditional job openings for people wanting to contribute something positive to our society. This emphasises the need for people to take entrepreneurial action and embracing their responsibility.

Education as a Catalyser of Transformation

"Education is the most powerful weapon which you can use to change the world."

Nelson Mandela

As global challenges, like climate change, have a great urgency, it is not enough to look at education only of our children but we must include education of ourselves and those people in power in a position to actually take action. This encompasses building the financial ecosystems in order to address climate change. The current leaders are all professionals and one way to address them is through executive education or business schools.

Much has been written on the role of business schools in shaping our financial ecosystem, especially in the aftermath of the financial crisis. But with MBAs being no longer prized by the employers, their transition needs to continue. The fundamental change which needs to happen is that business school education is moved away from looking at 'what the economy needs' and 'how to do business successfully' to the question of 'how to successfully build or change social practices' by building executive education on the principles of 'what does the world need'. A range of alternative business schools has thus emerged (such as Kaospilots, Thnk, STRIDE-unSchool for Entrepreneurial Leadership or also Schumacher College, which has been around for 25 years) and many existing business school have started to significantly reshape their programmes (e.g., Business School Lausanne is now offering a Master in Sustainable Finance).

If we start with ourselves when rethinking leadership, by starting from 'self'-leadership, and acknowledge that each one of us is also a source of inspiration to others, we can truly embark on a pathway of change.

Back to Good

Doing good is also related to a constantly inquisitive mind and looking at the consequences of one's action. The intention of doing good must thus be deeply rooted and cannot stem from another superficial wish to please the ego and being able to say that one is doing good. This means that one's values need to be congruent to the values behind the action one engages in (including the values of, e.g., a particular enterprise). Thus 'good' from an innermost intention comes when we are no longer attached to the fruits of our own work. It is then unimportant whose contribution leads to how much change or good. Our actions become a selfless service to the greater good.

Suggested Readings

Billeter, Salomon. (2016). Claims Contagion—the 'Me Too' Effect in Liability. Blog Contribution.

Gismondi et al. (ed.). (2016). Scaling Up: The Convergence of Social Economy and Sustainability.

Hacker, Robert: Scaling Social Entrepreneurship: Lessons Learned from One Laptop per Child.

Harnish, Verne. (2014). Scaling Up: How a Few Companies Make It...and Why the Rest Don't (Rockefeller Habits 2.0).

Maurya, Ash. (2016). Scaling Lean: Mastering the Key Metrics for Startup Growth.

Ostrom, Elinor. (1990). Governing the Commons: The Evolution of Institutions for Collective Action.

Papi-Thornton. (2016). Tackling Heropreneurship.

Ricard, Mathieu. (2015). Altruism: The Power of Compassion to Change Yourself and the World.

Ries, Erich. (2011). The Lean Startup.

Sägesser, Anaïs. (2016). Personal Transformation: Progressing to the Internal. Blog contribution.

Scharmer, Otto. (2016). Leading from the Future as it Emerges, Second Edition.

Seelos, Christian and Mair, Johanna. (2017). Innovation and Scaling for Impact: How Effective Social Enterprises Do It. Christian Seelos & Johanna Mair

Singer, Tanja et al. (2015). Caring Economics.

Sommer, Bernd and Welzer, Harald. (2014). Transformations design.

Spinosa, Charles et al. (1997). Disclosing New Worlds: Entrepreneurship, Democratic Action, and the Cultivation of Solidarity.

Stern, Nicholas. (2006). What is the Economics of Climate Change in WORLD ECONOMICS, Vol. 7, No. 2, April–June 2006.

Vihalemm, T. and Keller, M. (2016). Social practices as sites of social change. *In*: From Intervention to Social Change: A Guide to Reshaping Everyday Practices.

Zimmer, Daniel. (2017). Scaling-up Scaling-out: Lessons from Exponential Organisations. Blog contribution.

Online Sources

http://www.economist.com/whichmba/nothing-special-mbas-are-no-longer-prized-employers [accessed Apr 11, 2017].

Part 4
Regional Focus ESG in China

12

Regulating CSR Disclosure
Quantity or Quality in Practice?

Shidi Dong,[1] *Lei Xu*[2,*] and *Ron McIver*[2]

Introduction

In this chapter, we examine the effectiveness of CSR regulation on the quantity and quality of disclosure of listed mining firms in a rapidly growing, developing economy, that is of China.

Globally the mining sector has become a focus of CSR debates due to its exploitation of non-renewable resources (Cowell et al. 1999; IIED 2002 and 2012). Not surprisingly, the mining sector, as well as its oil and gas counterparts, have significantly increased commitment to CSR disclosures since 1999. In developed countries, a growing awareness of CSR, which has guided middle-aged and middle-income professionals to make socially responsible investment decisions, has also raised expectations on disclosures (Perez-Gladish et al. 2013). A result of this attention in developed countries is that the mining sector has led other sectors in providing CSR disclosures. For example, Cowan et al. (2010) and Roca and Searcy (2012) find that US and Canadian mining firms take initiatives, such as integrating comprehensive indicators into CSR disclosures, and produce the best CSR reports.

---

[1] School of Management, Shenyang University of Technology, China.
[2] School of Commerce, University of South Australia, Adelaide, Australia.
* Corresponding author: lei.xu@unisa.edu.au

That CSR disclosure is relatively widespread is evidenced in the results of KPMG's triennial surveys between 1999 and 2011 (KPMG 2006 and 2011), which suggest that an average of 86 per cent of mining firms surveyed have disclosed CSR information over this period (Table 1). Also, the mining sector has achieved top scores for professional internal systems, external accountability and quality of communication.

While widespread, there is significant divergence in the level of CSR disclosures globally. This is despite such authorities as the United Nations Rio Conference on Sustainable Development (2012) advising the mining sector to continuously improve its accountability and transparency. Comparisons of the CSR disclosures by Fortune Global 500 and Fortune 500 Mining and Oil firms confirm noticeable differences across countries (Roberts Environment Centre 2010). In particular, mining firms in developing countries tend to disclose less information. Additionally, while the mining sector as a whole covers 31 per cent of global reporting initiatives (GRI) indicators in its environmental reports, more than half of mining firms only disclose one indicator, total water usage (Guenther et al. 2007). Thus, there has been noticeable quantity and quality variation in industry CSR disclosures.

China's developing economy's rapid growth has placed significant pressures on its natural resources, protection of the environment and on maintenance of social harmony. Public media has reported deteriorating environmental conditions, including the 'Top 10 Pollution Events by Listed Firms' (Xinhua News 2011). Environmental and social concerns have,

Table 1. CSR Disclosure Survey Results.

Year	1999	2002	2005	2006	2008	2011	Average
Number of countries	11	19	16	9	22	34	18.5
Firms from BRIC countries[a]	n/a	n/a	n/a	yes	yes	yes	n/a
G250 (Cross-sector)[b]	35%	45%	52%	n/a	79%	95%	61.2%
Mining (G250)[b]	100%	100%	n/a	59%	100%[d]	84%	85.8%
Oil and Gas (G250)[b]	63%	58%	80%	n/a	76%	69%	69.2%
N 100 (Cross-sector)[c]	24%	23%	33%	n/a	45%	64%	37.8%
Mining (N100)[c]	47%	33%	52%	n/a	43%[e]	n/a	44%
Oil and Gas (N100)[c]	53%	38%	52%	n/a	53%	n/a	49%

Source: KPMG (2006, 2011)
Note: a, Firms from Brazil, Russia, India and China are included
       b, Global top 250 firms is referred as G250
       c, National top 100 firms is referred as N100
       d, Global top 250 firms reporting business risks of climate change
       e, National top 100 firms reporting business risks of climate change

frequently, forced mining firms to stop production to attend to various stakeholder requests, in turn signalling pressure on world market prices.

To meet concerns over environmental and social issues associated with activities of mining and other firms, China introduced a range of explicit corporate social responsibility (CSR) regulations. These deal with sustainable exploitation of resources and define firms' social responsibilities. As part of its social harmony policy, China requires that its firms, particularly state-owned enterprises (SOEs), disclose CSR information. China's State Council has also introduced specific legislation to regulate corporate behaviour. Key CSR legislation includes 2008 *Guidelines to State-owned Enterprises on Fulfilling Corporate Social Responsibilities* and 2009 *Improve Social Responsibility Reporting System and Strengthen Information Disclosure and Responsibility Communication.* Other government agencies have developed rules on CSR disclosure as a component of new regulation. Both the Shanghai Stock Exchange (SHSE) and the Shenzhen Stock Exchange (SZSE) have imposed CSR regulations on listed firms: 2006 *Guidelines on Listed Firms' Social Responsibility*; 2008 *Guidelines on Environmental Information Disclosure*; and 2008 *Notice on Strengthening Social Responsibility of Listed Firms.* Additionally, both the SHSE and SZSE cover CSR disclosures in their Corporate Governance Index List (CG list). In the light of these regulatory changes, two key questions need to be addressed:

What impact have China's CSR regulations had on the level of CSR disclosure by firms in environmentally and socially sensitive industry sectors, such as mining?

Situ and Tilt (2012) argue that such regulatory pressure has been effective and contributed to a rapid increase in the number of CSR disclosures by Chinese listed firms. CSR disclosures increased from 32 in 2006 to 663 in 2010 (KPMG 2011), with China contributing 15 per cent of new CSR disclosures globally later in this period (China WTO Tribune 2011). However, the Chinese Academy of Social Science (CASS 2012) has questioned the quality of recent CSR disclosures. Furthermore, Gao (2009) has proposed that CSR disclosures in China be closely examined, given a possible weakening of the cultural impacts of Confucianism associated with internationalisation and globalisation of the economy. As a result, firms may pay less attention to social responsibilities in their pursuit of economic benefits. For example, in the absence of international scrutiny, China's coal mines have remained the most dangerous business entities in the world, continuing to deprive many employees of their lives (Li 2007).

While the debate over the efficacy of China's CSR disclosure requirements and its role as a major developing economy primarily motivate our study, we believe that several other considerations support additional analyses of China's case.

First, mining is recognised internationally as one of the most environmentally and socially sensitive sectors. Mining companies play an important role in providing raw materials and fuel for an economy's growth, as well as regional employment where resources are located. At the same time the sector's exploitation of non-renewable natural resources has resulted in increased requirements for CSR disclosures (Adams et al. 1998; Kolk et al. 2010). By examining these firms' CSR disclosures, we may measure the effectiveness of CSR regulation as well as identifying firms' priorities in achieving a balance between economic benefit and social responsibility.

Second, CSR initiatives developed by mining firms often contribute to the development and sustainability of a country (Mutti et al. 2012). The mining sector has been identified as a best-practice leader in adopting, streamlining and improving CSR disclosures to meet increased stakeholder demand for this information (Deloitte 2012). By examining CSR disclosures on this sector, we may gain a better understanding of the general status of CSR disclosures in a country. This is particularly important in the context of the further study of developing economies, for which there is less information on the impact of CSR disclosure requirements.

Third, despite the fact that China, the second largest economy in the world, has been active in the introduction of CSR regulation in recent years, there is lack of CSR literature about China and its mining firms. Additionally, despite the perception of Chinese firms' importance, few of the cited studies have significant coverage of Chinese companies. For example, the Roberts Environment Centre (2010) study largely focusses on developed countries, such as Australia and Switzerland, and includes only one Chinese firm. This is surprising in light of the fact that, with the mining sector being so closely tied to demanding environmental and social issues, China has had to regulate the sector in pursuit of sustainable growth (World Bank 2008). However, this may partly reflect that Chinese firms have only recently started to provide CSR disclosures, meaning a lack of information for statistical measurement has been a primary challenge for academic studies (Tu 2007; Wang and Qin 2010; Kolk et al. 2010).

Finally, China's mining firms are playing increasingly important roles in the world. They are highly active acquirers in resource-abundant regions, such as Australia, Canada and Africa. Thus, Chinese mining firms may bring their standards in corporate social behaviour to target countries through their global investments. However, given that the China Securities Regulatory Commission (CSRC) introduced the potential for foreign ownership into the stock market following China's entry into the World Trade Organisation (WTO), foreign investors may be influencing Chinese mining companies' commitment to CSR.

In addressing the above key questions, this chapter examines the CSR disclosures of listed mining firms in China. To do so, we utilise a manually collected dataset based on firms drawn from China's SHSE and SZSE, covering the 2007 to 2010 period. Our methodology involves identification of the information in corporate announcements on the level and content of firms' CSR commitments, and the application of content analysis to allow quantitative analysis of the characteristics of the information disclosed. We find that China's mining firms have significantly increased the level of CSR disclosures in response to the introduction of regulations governing CSR disclosure. However, the poor quality of CSR disclosures is shown to be a concern, suggesting that, in general, China's mining sector demonstrates a low level of real commitment to CSR. Therefore, strengthened CSR regulation appears to be needed to ensure that China's growth is sustainable in future.

The rest of the chapter is structured as follows: Section 2 provides a brief review of literature allowing development of our hypotheses; Section 3 presents the research sample and methodology; Section 4 discusses the results and Section 5 concludes the chapter.

Literature and Hypotheses

Modern legitimacy, institutional and stakeholder theories provide the bases for much of the discussion on CSR behaviour and disclosures. Legitimacy theory suggests a firm's activities will be conducted in order to achieve approval (legitimacy) from key groups within the society. Unequal power between these groups may, however, impose difficulties in defining the set of expectations with which to achieve or maintain legitimacy (Archel et al. 2009). Institutional theory reflects the ideas of legitimacy theory, proposing that a firm responds to institutional pressures so as to meet legitimacy requirements imposed by key groups in society. CSR disclosures, therefore, provide an opportunity to examine the firm's response to pressures in its institutional environment (Chen and Roberts 2010). Stakeholder theory explicitly defines the social groups that the firm must address, suggesting that it acts upon the expectations of its customers, suppliers, employees, financers, communities, the government, etc. (Gray et al. 1996).

Legitimacy, institutional and stakeholder theories share common ground, in that a firm has to adopt and maintain practices, such as CSR disclosure to conform to the requirements of powerful stakeholders (Mitchell et al. 2011). Through disclosures the firm interacts with other parties in a political, social and institutional context (Deegan 2006). Disclosures, therefore, reflect a firm's management of its relationships with powerful stakeholders and provide a way to achieve strategic targets

(Parmar et al. 2010). We, therefore, focus on the impact of meeting the requirements of select key stakeholders in our analysis.

As noted above, there has been some evidence of increasing CSR disclosures in China, reflecting a required response to directives and requirements imposed by the State Council. The China WTO Tribune (2011) survey finds that mining firms, representing 4.9 per cent of its sample, obtain the highest scores for disclosures based on indicators of product (49.3 per cent), environment (37.7 per cent), and supply chain (28.6 Per cent). Following KPMG (2011) and the China WTO Tribune (2011), An et al. (2011) find that the number of CSR disclosures has increased at an unprecedented speed and that the trend accelerated in 2009. In the light of these findings, we develop our first hypothesis.

H1: Regulatory change has been effective in increasing the quantity of Chinese mining firms' CSR disclosures

The quality of CSR disclosures is also a subject of concern in the existing literature. Liu and Anbumozhi (2009) argue that there is a positive relation between regulation and the quality of CSR disclosures. Both KPMG (2011) and Cheung et al. (2012) report that the largest Chinese firms have improved the quality of their CSR disclosures. However, Zeng et al. (2010) argue that Chinese manufacturing firms selectively disclose CSR information. CASS (2012) finds that 61.7 per cent of the Top 100 Chinese firms disclose the lowest level of, or no, CSR information, while Kuo et al. (2012) report that 41 per cent of Chinese firms fail to communicate any understandable information. Alon et al. (2010) compare CSR disclosures in Brazil, Russia, India and China and find that Chinese firms provide the least information. In the light of these studies, we develop our second hypothesis.

H2: Regulatory change has been less effective in increasing the quality of Chinese mining firms' CSR disclosures than the quantity of these disclosures

The industrial regulator, such as the stock exchange, is one of the most important stakeholder groups in supporting CSR disclosures in China. Therefore, Chinese firms are more likely to respond to their pressures than other stakeholders (Li et al. 2013; Cooke and He 2010). In the Chinese context, both the SHSE and SZSE have required listed companies to disclose CSR information if they are also to be included in the Corporate Governance Index (CG Index). As a result, the six listed mining firms covered by the CG Index listed will be under additional regulatory pressure from stock exchanges. Therefore, we believe that:

H3: China's listed mining firms, that are also in the CG Index, will provide both a greater quantity and better quality of CSR disclosures than other listed Chinese mining firms

Similarly, Chinese firms listed overseas may have better CSR disclosures as they are subject to 'external monitoring' by foreign regulators and investors (Cheung et al. 2012). In the light of the overseas context, we develop the fourth hypothesis.

H4: Cross-listed Chinese mining firms will provide both a greater quantity and better quality of CSR disclosures than mining firms only listed on the SHSE and SZSE

Research Sample and Methodology

Research Sample

To examine China's listed mining firms' CSR disclosures, we construct and utilise a proprietary dataset. Our sample covers all 47 of China's listed mining firms over 2007 to 2010. This includes 30 SHSE listed firms and 17 listed on the SZSE. Appendix A provides summary information on each of these firms, including names, stock IDs and stock exchange listing. All firms' announcements during 2007 to 2010 were manually collected, providing 220 CSR disclosures in total. Our sample period coincides with the post-introduction and evolution periods of CSR regulation in China.

We observe a rapid increase in the number of firms disclosing CSR information and in their total disclosures. Table 2 shows that 77 per cent of mining firms disclosed CSR information in 2007, through annual reports, with almost all firms providing CSR information through annual reports by 2010. However, mining firms have been less willing to provide separate CSR reports. At only 45 per cent, this suggests that China's mining sector firms are less likely than those in developed countries to provide separate CSR reports.

Methodology

We apply content analysis to the systematic examination of Chinese mining firms' CSR disclosures to allow quantitative analysis of the level and characteristics of the content of firms' CSR commitments. Content analysis allows patterns in firm-level information to be identified by coding qualitative and quantitative information into predefined categories (Guthrie et al. 2004).

Selection of the information unit for coding purposes is the key component in content analysis (Neuendorf 2002; Krippendorff 2004). Measurement based on the presence or absence of certain disclosure items helps to separate firms disclosing some (although possibly minimal) information from those disclosing no information (Cormier et al. 2005; Guenther et al. 2007). However, the measurement of the presence or

Table 2. The Number of Mining Firms Disclosing CSR 2007–2010.

		Disclosing through Annual Report				Disclosing through CSR Report				Through Annual Report + CSR Report			
		2007	2008	2009	2010	2007	2008	2009	2010	2007	2008	2009	2010
SHSE	No. of firms	26	26	26	27	4	13	13	13	4	13	13	13
	% of sample	86.67%	86.67%	86.67%	90.00%	13.33%	43.33%	43.33%	43.33%	13.33%	43.33%	43.33%	43.33%
SZSE	No. of firms	10	12	14	17	0	3	8	8	0	3	8	8
	% of sample	58.82%	70.59%	82.35%	100.00%	0.00%	17.65%	47.06%	47.06%	0.00%	17.65%	47.06%	47.06%
Total	No. of firms	36	38	40	44	4	16	21	21	4	16	21	21
	% of sample	76.60%	80.85%	85.11%	93.62%	8.51%	36.17%	44.68%	44.68%	8.51%	36.17%	44.68%	44.68%

Note: SHSE, the Shanghai Stock Exchange
SZSE, the Shenzhen Stock Exchange

absence, of a type of information does not distinguish between firms disclosing one sentence and those disclosing 50 (Hackston and Milne 1996; Bouten et al. 2011). Existing studies suggest that the sentence is the most reliable information unit for measurement and coding (Raar 2002; Bouten et al. 2011). The number of sentences in CSR disclosures can be quantified with less judgement and thus less error than other possible measurements, such as lines or proportions of a page (Unerman 2000; Hackston and Milne 1996). Thus it should be utilised as the unit of measurement for quantitative analysis (Unerman 2000). In addition, use of sentences as the measurement unit allows the analysis of specific issues from disclosures (Deegan et al. 2002).

Qualitative measurement is also an important component in content analysis. Reliance on the number of sentences may be misleading as it does not analyse the actual content. This requires that quantitative measurement be augmented by qualitative analysis (Guthrie et al. 2004). To this end, development of a CSR disclosure quality index, which refers monetary, non-monetary and narrative information is suggested (Raar 2002; Guthrie et al. 2008; Dong and Burritt 2010). However, a weakness is that the index developed may not capture the context in which the disclosure is made, or differentiate between the firm's elaboration on CSR targets and its achievements (Bouten et al. 2011). An objective index of the quality of CSR disclosure must acknowledge two types of disclosed information: general category and performance indicator. General disclosures convey monetary, non-monetary and narrative information, as well as descriptions of commitments, policies and achievements; performance indicators identify the level of achievement of firms' CSR targets (Clarkston et al. 2008).

In the light of the Chinese cultural and legislative contexts, the Chinese Academy of Social Science followed GRI standards and published the 2009 China CSR Report Preparation Guide (2009 CASS Guide). The Guide identifies the most comprehensive CSR indicators and resolves potential conflicts with international standards. Appendix B illustrates the classification scheme of this Guide. In addition, CASS suggests grouping Chinese firms into five categories: best-practitioner, leader, follower, starter and bystander. Table 3 lists the five categories and corresponding benchmarks. In this study, we adopt the 2009 CASS Guide as our basis for content analysis and allocate sample firms into the five categories.

With reference to China's corporate announcement framework, quantitative measurement of CSR disclosures is based on the number of sentences and qualitative measurement by estimating a scoring index (Skouloudis et al. 2012; Roca and Searcy 2012) as suggested above. The meaning and content of sentences is identified according to the 2009 CASS Guide, and the disclosed information coded for both quantitative and

Table 3. CASS Categories of CSR Disclosures.

Status	Characteristics
Best practitioner	Most socially responsible firms with comprehensive CSR management systems and the highest level of CSR information disclosure
Leader	Leading firms with continuously improved CSR management systems and comprehensive CSR information disclosure
Follower	Firms that began pursuing CSR practices and disclose substantial CSR information
Starter	Firms that have not established complete CSR management systems and only disclose certain CSR information, with a substantial gap relative to leaders and followers
Bystander	Firms with the lowest level of CSR information disclosure

qualitative measurements. The 2009 CASS Guide suggests that 14 items be covered by general categories and 61 items by performance indicators. The qualitative measurement of CSR disclosures covers 75 items in total. We allocate a score between zero and six to each of the 75 items to develop a disclosure quality index, which may have a maximum score of 450. Table 4 illustrates the scoring of items in development of the disclosure quality index.

Table 4. Development of the CSR Disclosure Quality Index.

Disclosures	Disclosure Status	Scores (0–6)
General Categories		
General information	Not disclosed	0
	Disclosed as narrative	1
	Disclosed as non-monetary	2
	Disclosed as monetary	3
Substance of information	Disclosed as value and commitment	1
	Disclosed as initiatives and policies	2
	Disclosed as performance and achievement	3
Performance indicators	Not disclosed	0
	Disclosed	1
	Disclosed relative to peers/rivals or sector	2
	Disclosed relative to previous period	3
	Disclosed in absolute and normalised form	4
	Disclosed relative to target	5
	Disclosed at disaggregated level (i.e., plant, business unit, geographic segment)	6

Results and Discussions

Quantitative Measurement

Table 5 presents the results of our quantitative measurement. The mining sector, as a whole, has increased the quantity of its CSR disclosures as expected in response to regulatory requirements. Average disclosures have increased for firms in both the SHSE and SZSE, with the increase for firms in the SHSE being more pronounced through annual or specific CSR reports. Table 5, therefore, provides support for our first hypothesis.

Across all sample firms the average annual report provides 16 sentences of CSR information, while the average CSR report has 95 sentences, with the average being 38 sentences related to CSR disclosures across both types of report. However, the extent of CSR disclosures by China's mining firms varies substantially, with most firms providing less than the average level of CSR disclosures as indicated by the medians (12.5, 55 and 18 sentences). Additionally, firms on the SHSE provide more CSR disclosures, with the average number of sentences per disclosure more than doubling (27 to 60) between 2007 and 2010. Firms on the SZSE behave differently to their SHSE counterparts, tending to disclose much

Table 5. Quantitative Measurement Results on CSR Disclosure.

		Annual Report	Annual Report Avg.	CSR Report	CSR Report Avg.	CSR Disclosures	Avg. Per Disclosure
	2007	476	18.31	344	86.00	820	27.33
	2008	509	19.58	1140	87.69	1649	42.28
SHSE	2009	547	21.04	1579	121.46	2126	54.51
	2010	569	21.07	1845	141.92	2414	60.35
	Sub-total	2101	20.01	4908	114.14	7009	47.36
	2007	98	9.80	0	0.00	98	9.80
	2008	106	8.83	167	55.67	273	18.20
SZSE	2009	91	6.50	389	48.63	480	21.82
	2010	136	8.00	403	50.38	539	21.56
	Sub-total	431	8.13	959	50.47	1390	19.31
	Sum	2532	16.03	5867	94.63	8399	38.18
All Firms	Min	0	/	12	/	0	/
	Median	12.5	/	55	/	18	/
	Max	47	/	352	/	352	/

less CSR information with average disclosure increasing from a low of 10 sentences in 2007 to 22 sentences in 2010, with average disclosures only being about one-third that of a SHSE listed firm.

Table 5 also highlights the difference in informativeness of CSR relative to annual reports.

For SHSE firms, the 46 CSR reports have 4,908 sentences in total, while the 105 annual reports have only 2,101 sentences. An average CSR report has 114 sentences, compared to an average annual report with 20 sentences. The average number of sentences in CSR reports increased from 86 to 142 sentences over 2007 to 2010. The average number of sentences in an annual report increased more slowly, from 18 to 21. Less than half of the mining firms on the SHSE that provided CSR reports disclosed more information than all the firms through annual reports.

The 17 firms on the SZSE disclosed a total of 431 sentences in annual reports and 959 sentences in CSR reports. In contrast to firms on the SHSE, between 2007 and 2010, firms on the SZSE reduced the number of CSR sentences in their annual reports from 10 to eight. Although CSR reports increased in number from zero to eight, CSR information also declined from an average of 56 sentences to 50. This suggests that mining firms on the SHSE lead in CSR disclosures.

Qualitative Measurement Result

Table 6 presents our qualitative measurement results. For firms on the SHSE, the average value of the CSR disclosure quality index increased from 31 to 59 between 2007 and 2010. The CSR quality index of an annual report increased from 24 to 29 over the sample period. The average quality index of a CSR report improved faster than that of the annual report, growing from 77 to 121. Similar to the quantitative measurement result, firms on the SHSE continuously improved the quality of their CSR disclosures over the sample period.

Measures for firms on the SZSE demonstrate differences in improvement. The annual report quality index grew from 174 to 211, while the CSR report index grew from zero to 607. However, the measure for average CSR disclosure quality shows little if any improvement. The average annual report quality index declined from 17 to 15, with a low of seven in 2009. The average CSR report quality index displays considerable volatility, rising from zero in 2007 to 91 in 2008, and then falls to around 75—a level it maintains. The average CSR disclosure quality index only increased from 17 to 22. This result suggests that mining firms on the SZSE have been reluctant to improve the quality of their CSR disclosures. Therefore, Table 6 does not support our second hypothesis and demonstrates the importance of the listing authority (SHSE or SZSE) in improving the quality of reporting.

Table 6. CSR Disclosure Qualitative Measurement Results.

		Annual Report	Annual Report Avg.	CSR Report	CSR Report Avg.	CSR Disclosures	Avg. Per Disclosure
SHSE	2007	630	24.23	309	77.25	939	31.3
	2008	720	27.69	1219	93.77	1939	49.72
	2009	714	27.46	1453	111.77	2167	55.56
	2010	774	28.67	1577	121.31	2351	58.78
	Sub-total	2838	27.03	4558	106	7396	49.97
SZSE	2007	174	17.4	0	0	174	17.4
	2008	167	13.92	273	91	440	18.2
	2009	187	6.5	597	74.63	784	21.82
	2010	211	15.07	607	75.88	818	21.56
	Sub-total	739	8.13	1477	77.74	2216	19.31
All Firms	Sum	3577	16.03	6035	94.63	9612	43.69
	Min	0	/	0	/	0	/
	Median	18	/	79	/	25.5	/
	Max	54	/	180	/	180	/

The disparity between quality indexes of firms on the SHSE and their SZSE counterparts is significant. The average quality index for an annual report on the SHSE is 27, more than three times that on the SZSE. The average CSR report has a quality index of 106 on the SHSE, still significantly higher than 78 on the SZSE. The average quality index comparison between the SHSE and SZSE is 50 versus 19. Similar to our quantitative measurement findings, mining firms on the SHSE have a higher quality of CSR disclosure.

Considering the information summarised in Tables 5 and 6, we find that China's mining sector has significantly increased CSR disclosures, with the average number of sentences more than doubling over the sample period. This reflects both the number of firms disclosing CSR information and the amount of information disclosed. However, our qualitative measurement suggests that although more mining firms are disclosing more CSR information though it is of poor quality. The maximum values for the quality indexes of the annual and CSR reports are 54 and 180, respectively, far below the maximum potential value of 450 for CSR disclosure. When assessed against the characteristics in Table 3, the mining sector falls in the starter category, suggesting that mining firms have started disclosing CSR information but have not yet established complete CSR management systems.

Extended Quantitative and Qualitative Measurement

We have identified the presence of significant disparities amongst sample firms despite evidence of the overall poor quality of disclosures. Of the 47 sample firms, three on the SZSE disclosed no information. In comparison, some firms perform much better. By grouping and comparing mining firms disclosing CSR information, we may explore a firm practice under different regulatory pressures.

We group the remaining 44 firms that revealed CSR information into four groups: those on the Corporate Governance Index List (CG list) announced by the SHSE and the SZSE, firms cross-listed overseas (CL), ordinary firms listed on the SHSE and ordinary firms listed on the SZSE. Both CG list and CL firms are under additional regulatory pressure to disclose CSR information. There are two firms on both the CG and CL lists, which are grouped under the CL grouping to avoid overlaps amongst the groups.

Table 7 presents results for each group of firms. As suggested in our analysis in Tables 5 and 6, the larger SHSE listed mining firms have out-performed those on the SZSE, having double the scores for quantity and quality of firms on the SZSE. This conforms to our findings in 4.1 and 4.2. However, mining firms on the CG list do not show a higher quantum or quality of CSR disclosures than ordinary SHSE listed firms. The average quantitative result of CG list firms is 20, lower than the 30 for those on the SHSE. The mean quality result of CG list firms is 30, also lower than the 39 of SHSE firms. Therefore, Table 7 does not support our third hypothesis. However, CG list firms disclosed CSR information throughout the entire sample period—a major difference from the other firms.

CL firms are the best performers in CSR disclosures, both in quantity and quality. The mean values of annual report, CSR report and all quantitatively measured disclosures of CL firms are more than double those of ordinary SHSE firms, being 25 versus 18, 135 versus 66, and 76 versus 30, respectively. Disclosures by CL firms are also of better quality than those ordinary SHSE firms. Mining firms listed overseas demonstrate the highest quantity and quality of CSR disclosures. Therefore, Table 7 supports our fourth hypothesis.

Firms on the CG list are only better than the ordinary firms on the SZSE. Foreign investors in the A-share market may have little impact on

Table 7. Extended CSR Measurement Results.

		Quantitative Result			Qualitative Result		
		Annual Report	CSR Report	All Disclosures	Annual Report	CSR Report	All Disclosures
SHSE	2007	283	121	404	379	84	463
excl. CG	2008	321	413	734	470	524	994
excl. CL	2009	334	498	832	479	616	1095
	2010	341	557	898	513	707	1220
	Sub-total	1279	1589	2868	1841	1931	3772
	Mean	17.76	66.21	29.88	25.57	80.46	39.29
	Min	0	23	0	0	46	0
	Median	16.5	40	21	25	73	31.5
	Max	43	221	221	52	148	148
SZSE	2007	80	0	80	138	0	138
excl. CG	2008	97	88	185	143	159	302
excl. CL	2009	78	323	401	151	473	624
	2010	124	348	472	185	498	683
	Sub-total	379	759	1138	617	1130	1747
	Mean	6.32	54.21	15.38	10.28	80.71	23.61
	Min	0	0	0	0	0	0
	Median	6	36	7.5	9	70	12
	Max	23	179	179	47	180	180
CG	2007	46	0	46	77	0	77
excl. CL	2008	23	79	102	57	114	171
	2009	62	138	200	69	184	253
	2010	43	55	98	58	109	167
	Sub-total	174	272	446	261	407	668
	Mean	10.88	38.86	20.27	16.31	67.83	30.36
	Min	3	18	3	5	37	5
	Median	8.5	37	9	16.5	66	18.5
	Max	27	79	79	26	114	114

Table 7 contd. ...

... Table 7 contd.

		Quantitative Result			Qualitative Result		
CL	2007	165	223	388	210	225	435
incl. CG	2008	174	727	901	217	695	912
	2009	164	1009	1173	202	777	979
	2010	197	1288	1485	229	870	1099
	Sub-total	700	3247	3947	858	2567	3425
	Mean	25	135.29	75.9	30.64	106.95	65.87
	Min	7	12	7	16	8	8
	Median	26.5	112	32.5	28.5	115.5	47.5
	Max	47	352	352	54	156	156

Note: SHSE, SZSE are the Shanghai and Shenzhen Stock Exchanges
 2007–2010 show the aggregate CSR disclosures by the subgroup firms
 CG, firms on the Corporate Governance Index List announced by the SHSE and the SZSE
 CL, firms listed both on the SHSE/SZSE and overseas

firms' CSR disclosures. This finding suggests that mining firms on the SHSE, which are of larger size, outperform firms on the SZSE. Corporate governance reform in China, which covers CSR in its surveillance, has had little impact over CSR disclosure quality but some impact over quantity. In addition to firm size, firms listed overseas are under strict regulations in developed countries.

Conclusion and Implications

This chapter has examined CSR disclosures by mining companies in a major developing economy, i.e., China. Our choice of the mining sector reflects that, globally, this industry is a focus of CSR debates (Cowell et al. 1999; IIED 2002, 2012), and also often a leader in developing CSR initiatives at the country level (Mutti et al. 2012). Our choice of China reflects a number of factors—lack of literature on its CSR disclosure; mining's importance to China's growing economy and its increasing global role in the industry. We find that explicit regulation has effectively contributed to the quantity of disclosures of China's listed mining firms over the 2007 to 2010 period, following the progressive introduction of regulatory requirements in this area in 2006. However, disclosure quality remains a source of concern. Most of China's listed mining firms disclose limited information and demonstrate a low level of CSR commitment.

Comparing mining firms under different regulatory pressures, we find that while higher standards of corporate governance, as required for inclusion in the SHSE and SZSE Corporate Governance Index List, has a positive impact on the quantity of disclosure in China but, it has not had a similar impact on the quality of CSR disclosures.

Firm size appears to be a significant factor in CSR disclosures in China, with firms listed on the SHSE producing a greater quantum of CSR disclosure than those on the SZSE. This may also reflect that large firms receive greater public scrutiny, or that larger firms are more likely to be able to engage in and report on multiple aspects of their CSR performance given their greater resource base.

We find that it is only where strict regulation is imposed on firms, as is the case for firms that are cross-listed, that both the quantity and quality of CSR disclosures improve jointly and significantly. For China, differences between cross-listed and locally listed firms may reflect an under-resourcing of regulatory departments, incomplete integration of regulations, or shifting policy agendas (Hilson and Haselip 2004). This would suggest that China needs to consider imposing compulsory elements in its CSR reporting and to provide resources to closely audit mining firms' CSR performance. Alternatively, if cross-listing's impact in improving CSR disclosure quality reflects specific demands from investors in higher income countries, over time China's mining companies may face similar pressures from local investors. With increasing incomes, citizens are more likely to be better informed, and both willing and able to impose demands on corporations for improved CSR reporting and performance (Gnyawali 1996). However, recent environmental disputes between cross-listed mining firms and residents outside China also suggest that China's mining sector may have a long way to go.

Finally, while our analysis has considered a range of factors—stock exchange, governance quality and cross-listing—our analysis has been limited by the small size of the sample. A larger sample of firms across a broad range of industries will allow future studies to provide statistical evidence of the impact of other important factors on CSR disclosure in the case of China. These include concentrated and state-ownership, foreign investment, industry and the cultural context on firm CSR disclosures. Both the SHSE and SZSE can provide unique samples for such studies.

Appendix A: List of Mining Firms as of the End of 2010.

Stock ID	Name of Firm	Stock Exchange
000053	SHENZHEN CHIWAN PETROLEUM SUPPLY BASE CO., LTD	Shenzhen
000552	GANSU JINGYUAN COAL INDUSTRY AND ELECTRICITY POWER CO., LTD	Shenzhen
000655	SHANDONG JINLING MINING CO., LTD	Shenzhen
000758	CHINA NONFERROUS METAL INDUSTRY CO., LTD	Shenzhen
000762	TIBET MINERAL DEVELOPMENT CO., LTD	Shenzhen
000780	INNER MONGOLIA PINGZHUANG ENERGY RESOURCES CO., LTD	Shenzhen
000933	HENAN SHEN HUO COAL INDUSTRY AND ELECTRICITY POWER CO., LTD	Shenzhen(CG)
000937	JIZHONG ENERGY RESOURCES CO., LTD	Shenzhen
000968	TAIYUAN COAL GASFICATION CO., LTD	Shenzhen
000983	SHANXI XISHAN COAL AND ELECTRICITY POWER CO., LTD	Shenzhen(CG)
002128	HUOLINHE OPENCUT COAL INDUSTRY CORPORATION LIMITED OF INNERMONGOLIA	Shenzhen
002155	CHENZHOU MINING GROUP CO., LTD	Shenzhen
002207	XINJIANG ZHUNDONG PETROLEUM TECHNOLOGY CO., LTD	Shenzhen
002340	SHENZHEN GREEN ECO-MANUFACTURE HI-TECH CO., LTD	Shenzhen
002353	YANTAI JEREH OILFIELD SERVICES GROUP CO., LTD	Shenzhen
002554	CHINA OIL HBP SCIENCE&TECHNOLOGY CO., LTD	Shenzhen
300084	LANZHOU HAIMO TECHNOLOGIES CO., LTD	Shenzhen
300157	LANDOCEAN ENERGY SERVICES CO., LTD	Shenzhen
300164	TONG OIL TOOLS CO., LTD	Shenzhen
300191	SINO GEOPHYSICAL CO., LTD	Shenzhen

600028	CHINA PETROLEUM & CHEMICAL CORPORATION	Shanghai
600123	SHANXI LANHUA SCI-TECH VENTURE CO., LTD	Shanghai
600139	SICHUAN WESTERN RESOURCES HOLDING CO., LTD	Shanghai
600188	YANZHOU COAL MINING COMPANY LIMITED	Shanghai(CG)/NY/HK/SG
600348	YANG QUAN COAL INDUSTRY (GROUP) CO., LTD	Shanghai
600395	GUIZHOU PANJIANG REFINED COAL CO., LTD	Shanghai
600397	ANYUAN COAL INDUSTRY GROUP CO., LTD	Shanghai
600489	ZHONGJIN GOLD CORPORATION, LIMITED	Shanghai
600497	YUNNAN CHIHONG ZINC & GERMANIUM CO., LTD	Shanghai
600508	SHANGHAI DATUN ENERGY RESOURSES CO., LTD	Shanghai
600546	SHANXI COAL INTERNATIONAL ENERGY GROUP CO., LTD	Shanghai(CG)
600547	SHANDONG GOLD MINING CO., LTD	Shanghai
600583	OFFSHORE OIL ENGEERING CO., LTD	Shanghai
600971	ANHUI HENGYUAN COAL INDUSTRY AND ELECTORICITY POWER CO., LTD	Shanghai
600997	KAILUAN ENERGY CHEMICAL CORPORATION LIMITED	Shanghai
601001	DATONG COAL INDUSTRY CO., LTD	Shanghai
601088	CHINA SHENHUA ENERGY CO., LTD	Shanghai(CG)/HK
601101	BEIJING HAOHUA NENRGY RESOURCE., LTD	Shanghai
601168	WESTERN MINING CO., LTD	Shanghai(CG)

Appendix A contd. ...

... Appendix A contd.

Stock ID	Name of Firm	Stock Exchange
601666	PINGDINGSHAN TIANAN COAL MINING CO., LTD	Shanghai
601699	SHANXI LU'AN ENVIRONMENTAL ENERGY DEVELOPMENT CO., LTD	Shanghai
601808	CHINA OILFIEDLD SERVICE LIMITED	Shanghai/HK
601857	PETROCHINA CO., LTD	Shanghai/HK/NY/UK
601898	CHINA COAL ENERGY COMPANY LIMITED	Shanghai/HK
601899	ZIJIN MINING GROUP CO., LTD	Shanghai/HK
601958	JINDUICHENG MOLYBDENUM CO., LTD	Shanghai
900948	INNER MONGOLIA YITAI COAL CO., LTD	Shanghai/HK

Note: CG, the listed firm is on the Corporate Governance Index List announced by the SHSE or the SZSE;
HK, the listed firm is also listed on the Hong Kong Stock Exchange;
NY, the listed firm is also listed on the New York Stock Exchange;
UK, the listed firm is also listed on the London Stock Exchange;
SG, the listed firm is also listed on the Singapore Stock Exchange.

Appendix B: The Classification Scheme Based on China's CSR Report Preparation Guide (2009 CASS-CSR Guide).

CASS-CSR Disclosure Category
GENERAL CATEGORIES STRATEGY AND ANALYSIS
Statement from the most senior decision maker of the organisation (e.g., CEO, chair, or equivalent senior position) about the relevance of sustainability to the organisation and its strategy
Value/Mission/Goal
Awards received in the reporting period
Summary of key performance
GOVERNANCE AND MANAGEMENT
CSR management procedures and progress of governance body for overseeing the organisation's identification and management of economic, environmental and social performance
CSR management system (e.g., CSR department, personnel, certification, implementation)
Subscription to international standards; initiatives
Membership in associations (e.g., industry association, national and international advocacy organisation)
CSR training and education (e.g., CSR seminars, conferences, courses, programmes, etc.)
Internal control and risk management system
Explanation of the precautionary approach
Non-compliance: Significant fines and non-monetary sanctions for non-compliance with laws and regulations
STAKEHOLDER ENGAGEMENT
Key topics and concerns that have been raised through stakeholder engagement, and how the organisation has responded to, including through its reporting approach to (internal and external) stakeholder engagement
Senior management participation

Appendix B contd.…

... Appendix B contd.

CASS-CSR Disclosure Category
PERFORMANCE INDICATORS MARKET PERFORMANCE (M)
M1 Investor
SOCIAL PERFORMANCE (S)
S1 Government
S1.1 Responding to governmental policies
S1.2 Payment to government (Tax contribution)
S1.3 Support employment
S2 Employee
S2.1 Compliance with employment contract
S2.2 Social pension provided
S2.3 Composition of governance bodies and breakdown of employees per category according to gender, age group, minority group membership, and other indicators of diversity
S2.4 Ratio of basic salary of men to women by employee category
S2.5 Employee turnover
S2.6 Employee training and education for career development
S2.7 Employee communication and feedback
S2.8 Employee satisfaction
S3 Production safety
S3.1 Education, training, counseling, prevention, and risk-control programs in place regarding occupational health and safety
S3.2 Rates of injury, occupational diseases, lost days, and absenteeism and number of work related fatalities by region
S3.3 Contractor safety

S4 Community
S4.1 Impact of nature, scope, and effectiveness of any programs on community
S4.2 Local hiring
S4.3 Local based supplier
S4.4 Charity and donation
ENVIRONMENTAL PERFORMANCE (E)
E1 Environmental management
E1.1 Environmental management system
E1.2 Training and awareness
E1.3 Environmental impact assessment
E1.4 Environmentally friendly production and product (e.g., R&D, equipment, technology)
E1.5 Total environmental protection expenditures and investment
E1.6 Biodiversity protection
E1.7 Land use
E1.8 Reclamation and Rehabilitation
E2 Energy saving
E2.1 Energy saving policies, initiatives and technologies
E2.2 Energy consumption/saving
E2.3 Water consumption/saving
E 2.4 Usage of renewable energy
E2.5 Circular economy policy
E2.6 Research on new energy and clean production

Appendix B contd. ...

... Appendix B contd.

CASS-CSR Disclosure Category
E3 Emission
E3.1 Policies, initiatives and technologies of reducing greenhouse gas emissions and reduction achieved
E3.2 Policies, initiatives and technologies of reducing other air emission waste
E3.3 Total weight of other air emission and reduction achieved
E3.4 Policies, initiatives and technologies of water discharge
E3.5 Total water discharge
E3.6 Policies, initiatives and technologies of waste disposal
E3.7 Total weight of waste (by type and disposal method)
E3.8 Waste recycled
E3.9 Noise

References

Adams, C., Hill, W. and Roberts, C. (1998). Corporate social reporting practices in Western Europe: Legitimating corporate behaviour? British Accounting Review 30(1): 1–21.

Alon, I., Lattemann, C., Fetscherin, M., Li, S. and Schneider, A. (2010). Usage of public corporate communications of social responsibility in Brazil, Russia, India and China BRIC. International Journal of Emerging Markets 5(1): 6–22.

An, J., Bai, J., Wan, W., Shen, X., Chen, Y. and Guo, P. (2011). A Journey to Discover Values: A Study of Sustainability Reporting in China. http://www.syntao.com. Accessed on 3/11/2012.

Archel, P., Husillos, J., Larrinaga, C. and Spence, C. (2009). Social disclosure, legitimacy theory and the role of the state. Accounting, Auditing & Accountability Journal 228: 1284–1307.

Bouten, L., Everaert, P., Liedekerke, L., Moor, L. and Christiaens, J. (2011). Corporate social responsibility reporting: A comprehensive picture? Accounting Forum 35: 187–204.

Chen, J. and Roberts, R. (2010). Toward a more coherent understanding of the organisation—Society relationship: A theoretical consideration for social and environmental accounting research. Journal of Business Ethics 97: 651–665.

Cheung, Y., Jiang, K. and Tan, W. (2012). 'Doing-good' and 'doing-well' in Chinese publicly listed firms. China Economic Review 23: 776–785.

China WTO Tribune. (2011). Golden Bee Research on Corporate Social Responsibility Reporting in China. International Research Center for Social Responsibility & Sustainable Development of Peking University, December 2, 2011.

Chinese Academy of Social Science. (2012). Research Report on Corporate Social Responsibility in China. Social Sciences Academic Press.

Clarkson, P., Li, Y., Richardson, G. and Vasvari, F. (2008). Revisiting the relation between environmental performance and environmental disclosure: An empirical analysis. Accounting, Organisations and Society 33: 303–327.

Cooke, F. and He, Q. (2010). Corporate social responsibility and HRM in China: A study of textile and apparel enterprises. Asia Pacific Business Review 16: 355–376.

Cormier, D., Magnan, M. and Velthoven, B. (2005). Environmental disclosure quality in large German companies: economic incentives, public pressures or institutional conditions? European Accounting Review 14(1): 3–39.

Cowan, D., Dopart, P., Ferracini, T., Sahmel, J., Merryman, K., Gaffney, S. and Paustenbach, D. (2010). A cross-sectional analysis of reported corporate environmental sustainability practices. Regulatory Toxicology and Pharmacology 58: 524–538.

Cowell, S., Wehrmeyer, W., Argust, P. and Robertson, J. (1999). Sustainability and the primary extraction industries: theories and practice. Resources Policy 25: 277–286.

Deegan, C. (2002). The legitimising effect of social and environmental disclosures—A theoretical foundation. Accounting, Auditing & Accountability Journal 15(3): 282–311.

Deegan, C. (2006). Financial Accounting Theory. Australia: Sydney: McGraw-Hill.

Deegan, C., Rankin, M. and Tobin, J. (2002). An examination of the corporate social and environmental disclosures of BHP from 1983–1997: A test of legitimacy theory. Accounting, Auditing and Accountability Journal 15(3): 312–343.

Deloitte Touche Tohmatsu. (2012). Tracking the Trends 2012: The Top 10 Trends Mining Companies may Face in the Coming Year. http://www.deloitte.com/assets/DcomGlobal/Local%20Assets/Documents/DTT_ERS_MMStudy_0405061).pdf accessed 25/11/2012).

Dong, S. and Burritt, R. (2010). Cross-sectional benchmarking of social and environmental reporting practice in the Australian oil and gas industry. Sustainable Development 18: 108–118.

Gao, Y. (2009). Corporate social performance in China: evidence from large companies. Journal of Business Ethics 89: 23–35.

Global Reporting Initiative. (2006). Sustainability reporting guidelines G3. http://www. globalreporting.org. (Accessed 10/9/2013).

Gnyawali, D.R. (1996). Corporate social performance: An international perspective. Advances in International Comparative Management 11: 251–273.

Gray, R., Owen, D. and Adams, C. (1996). Accounting and Accountability: Changes and Challenges in Corporate Social and Environmental Reporting. London: Prentice Hall.

Guenther, E., Hoppe, E. and Poser, C. (2007). Environmental corporate social responsibility of firms in the mining and oil and gas industries: current status quo of reporting following GRI guidelines. Greener Management International 53: 7–24.

Guthrie, J., Cuganesan, S. and Ward, L. (2008). Industry specific social and environmental reporting: the Australian food and beverage industry. Accounting Forum 32: 1–15.

Guthrie, R., Yongvanich, K. and Ricceri, F. (2004). Using content analysis as a research method to inquire into intellectual capital reporting. Journal of Intellectual Capital 5(2): 282–293.

Hackston, D. and Milne, M. (1996). Some determinants of social and environmental disclosures in New Zealand companies. Accounting, Auditing & Accountability Journal 9(1): 77–108.

Hilson, G. and Haselip, A. (2004). The environmental and socioeconomic performance of multinational mining companies in the developing world economy. Minerals and Energy 19(3): 25–47.

IIED. (2002). Breaking New Ground: The Report of the Mining, Minerals and Sustainable Development Project. http://www.iied.org/mmsd-final-report (accessed 22/11/2013).

IIED. (2012). MMSD+10: Reflecting on a Decade of Mining and Sustainable Development. http://www.iied.org/mining-minerals-sustainable-development-10-years-mmsd-10 (accessed 6/7/2013).

Kolk, A., Hong, P. and Dolen, W. (2010). Corporate social responsibility in China: an analysis of domestic and foreign retailers' sustainability dimensions. Business Strategy and the Environment 19: 289–303.

KPMG. (2006). The Global Mining Reporting Survey. http://www.kpmg.com.br/ publicacoes/industrial_markets/Global_Mining_survey.pdf (accessed 27/2/2012).

KPMG. (2011). International Survey of Corporate Responsibility Reporting. http://www. kpmg.com/global/en/issuesandinsights/articlespublications/pages/corporate sustainability.aspx (accessed 4/5/2011).

Krippendorff, K. (2004). Content Analysis: An Introduction to its Methodology. US: Sage.

Kuo, L., Yeh, C. and Yu, H. (2012). Disclosure of corporate social responsibility and environmental management: evidence from China. Corporate Social Responsibility and Environmental Management 19: 273–287.

Li, J. (2007). China's rising demand for minerals and emerging global norms and practices in the mining industry. Minerals & Energy 22(3-4): 105–126.

Li, Q., Luo, W., Wang, Y. and Wu, L. (2013). Firm performance, corporate ownership, and corporate social responsibility disclosure in China. Business Ethics: A European Review 22(2): 159–173.

Liu, X. and Anbumozhi, V. (2009). Determinant factors of corporate environmental information disclosure: An empirical study of chinese listed companies. Journal of Cleaner Production 17: 593–600.

Mitchell, R., Agle, B., Chrisman, J. and Spence, L. (2011). Toward a theory of stakeholder salience in family firms. Business Ethics Quarterly 21 (2): 235–255.

Mutti, D., DiegoVazquez-Brust, N. and Marco, M. (2012). Corporate social responsibility in the mining industry: Perspectives from stakeholder groups in Argentina. Resources Policy 37: 212–222.

Neuendorf, K. (2002). The Content Analysis Guidebook. UK: Sage.

Parmar, B., Freeman, R., Harrison, J., Wicks, A., Purnell, L. and Colle, S. (2010). Stakeholder theory: The state of the art. The Academy of Management Annals 1(6): 403–445.

Perez-Gladish, B., Benson, K. and Faff, R. (2013). Profiling socially responsible investors: Australian evidence. Australian Journal of Management 37(2): 189–209.

Qu, R. (2007). Effects of government regulations, market orientation and ownership structure on corporate social responsibility in China: An empirical study. International Journal of Management 24(3): 582–591.

Raar, J. (2002). Environmental initiatives: towards triple-bottom line reporting. Corporate Communications: An International Journal 7(3): 169–183.

Roberts Environment Centre. (2010). CSR Reporting of the World's Largest Mining, Crude-oil Production Companies. http://www.roberts.cmc.edu/psi/pdf/mining2010.pdf (Accessed on 8/9/2011).

Roca, L. and Searcy, C. (2012). An analysis of indicators disclosed in corporate sustainability reports. Journal of Cleaner Production 20: 103–118.

Situ, H. and Tilt, C. (2012). Chinese government as a determinant of corporate environmental reporting: A study of large Chinese listed companies. Journal of Asia Pacific Centre for Environmental Accountability 18(4): 251–286.

Skouloudis, A., Konstantinos, E. and Stavros, M. (2012). Accountability and stakeholder engagement in the airport industry: An assessment of airports' CSR Reports. Journal of Air Transport Management 18: 16–20.

Tu, J. (2007). Coal mining safety: China's Achilles' heel. China Security 3(2): 36–53.

Unerman, J. (2000). Methodological issues reflections on quantification in corporate social reporting content analysis. Accounting Auditing & Accountability Journal 13(5): 667–680.

United Nations. (2012). Report of the World Summit on Sustainable Development. http://www.un.org/jsummit/html/documents/summit_docs/131302_wssd_report_reissued.pdf (Accessed on 13/11/2011).

Wang, J. and Qin, S. (2010). Problems and prospects of CSR system development in China. International Journal of Business and Management 5(12): 128–134.

World Bank. (2008). Economically, Socially and Environmentally Sustainable Coal Mining Sector in China, Washington, DC.

Xinhua News. (2011). http://news.xinhuanet.com/energy/2011-11/25/c_122333691.htm (Accessed on 25/11/2011).

Zeng, S., Xu, X., Dong, Z. and Tam, V. (2010). Towards corporate environmental information disclosure: an empirical study in China. Journal of Cleaner Production 18: 1142–1148.

13

Political Connections, Ownership Structure and Performance in China's Mining Sector

Lei Xu,* Ron P. McIver, Shiao-Lan Chou and
Harjap Bassan

Introduction

As the world's largest emerging economy, China has, until recently, reported average annual growth in its GDP of around 10 per cent over three-and-a-half decades. This unparalleled growth has, to a large extent, been supported by its high consumption of natural resources, including mined resources, with China being the world's largest consumer of minerals and mineral commodities (Zhang et al. 2015). Thus, mining is recognised as a strategically important sector in sustaining China's economic and social development (Wang 2012).

As well as its role as a consumer, China is also a leading producer of many mineral commodities, coal being the dominant mineral, with mining contributing around 5 per cent of China's GDP. Mining is also seen as being particularly important in generating regional employment and in attracting regional infrastructure development in China (Zhang et al. 2015).

School of Commerce, University of South Australia, Adelaide, Australia.
* Corresponding author: lei.xu@unisa.edu.au

However, even though it is a major producer, high levels of tangible demand for natural resources generated by China's investment, domestic consumption and exports have been such that the outputs from its domestic mining firms have fallen short of its requirements. For example, in 2011, although China's mining sector increased its iron ore production by 23 per cent to 1.3 billion tons, it still faced a 0.7 billion ton shortage in supply. Thus, China's excess demand has boosted the prices of mineral resources worldwide.

Chinese mining firms may also be seen as having taken advantage of their favourable economic situation within China's economy during the last three-and-a-half decades of rapid growth. Chinalco's 2007 take-over bid for Rio Tinto marked the beginning of an era of Chinese offshore takeovers in the resources sector. Chinese mining firms have been acquiring their counterparts in many resource-abundant countries, such as Australia, Brazil and countries in Africa. Despite the slowdown in China's growth in late 2015, its mining firms remain highly active acquirers in the world, contributing to the One Belt One Road strategy (PWC 2016).

As well as having a global impact via trade and investment, the ownership structure and corporate governance of Chinese firms are significantly different from that of US, UK and European firms. Most listed firms in China are restructured state-owned enterprises (SOEs) and so state ownership is still a significant feature. This is despite the fact that, via partial privatisation, Chinese firms increasingly have involvement from more active foreign and private shareholders in their ownership structures. However, since mining firms play decisive roles in providing raw materials and fuel for the country's economic growth, they are heavily regulated by Chinese government policies. Thus, mining firms reveal higher average levels of state ownership than firms in other sectors, while government policy has also limited foreign ownership in this sector. Thus the mining sector may show unique features in terms of the impact of ownership factors compared to China's other sectors.

Political connectedness is also often a feature of firms with state ownership. However, local government connectedness is likely to have a greater impact on firm performance than Central Government connectedness. This reflects that the local governments (in China as elsewhere) have the potential to derive greater levels of benefit from SOEs than from other types of enterprises. Local officials may have power to appoint SOE senior management, including appointment of relatives, friends and political supporters, as well as the ability to divert financial resources from SOEs towards public works or personal uses. Given that mining is highly dependent on immobile mineral resources, and thus shows high level of regional concentration, local government rent-seeking has a higher likelihood of occurrence (Bai et al. 2004).

This chapter links literature on China's mining sector and the impact of ownership and political connectedness and performance. Academic literature has not, to our best of knowledge, explored such factors for this important sector. Our motivation in examining these issues reflects the mining sector's importance to the sustainability and development of China, differences in its ownership structure due to its role as a strategically important industry and likely local government politically connectedness, given the specifics of its domestic resource base and importance to regional economies.

In our pooled data analysis, we adopt Tobin's Q to capture firm financial performance. Through two-way and three-way interaction estimates of mining, ownership variables and political connectedness, we find that ownership concentration and proportion of state ownership appear to positively impact performance. Firm's size and gearing appear to negatively impact the performance. Institutional and foreign ownership and local government connectedness are not statistically significant. Differences are identified for mining firms. Both state and institutional ownership incrementally and positively impact performance. However, greater state and institutional ownership in the presence of local government connectedness negatively impact performance.

The remainder of this chapter is organised as follows: Section 2 presents a brief literature review; Section 3 describes the data and methodology; results are analysed in Section 4 and Section 5 concludes the chapter.

Literature and Hypotheses

With around 2,492 firms listed on the Shanghai and Shenzhen Stock Exchanges at the end of 2012, China's listed companies provide a unique data set for corporate governance and ownership studies. These studies include examination of the ineffectiveness of supervisory boards (Tam 2002; Dahya et al. 2003; Lin 2004; Wang 2007), the weakness of boards of directors (Tam 2002; Lin 2004; Feinerman 2007), and the impact of high ownership concentration on minority shareholders (Tam 2002; Lin 2004; Feinerman 2007).

Ownership Structure and Firm's Performance

The separation of ownership from control of the firm may induce principal-agent conflicts. A divergence of interests between owners (shareholders) and their agents (managers) may lead to a failure to maximise owners' benefits (Jensen and Meckling 1976). Conflict of interests may also extend to the firm's suppliers of capital, arising from the separation of risk-bearing, decision-making and control functions within the firm (Fama and Jensen

1983). In addition, Type II agency problems—in the form of principal–principal conflicts between majority and minority shareholders—may arise with China's listed firms (Shan and Xu 2012a; Shan and Round 2012; Shan 2013). This supports our focus on these matters in this chapter.

Under the (often implicit) assumption of widely dispersed ownership, the corporate governance literature focusses largely on conflict of interests between managers and shareholders. Traditionally it is asserted that the firm's owners identify corporate governance mechanisms that may prevent expropriation, or wasting of funds, by managers (Shleifer and Vishny 1997). However, ownership structure, either dispersed or concentrated, is also a determinant of control over the firm (Aoki 1995). In contrast to the traditional view (Berle and Means 1932), the separation of ownership and control may allow controlling shareholders, rather than professional managers, to effectively manage large firms (La Porta et al. 1999). The degree of ownership concentration determines the distribution of power within the firm. Therefore, both ownership structure and concentration in shareholdings are factors determining corporate control (Lannoo 1999).

China's planned economy history has bequeathed its firms with unique ownership structures, as compared to firms in developed countries. China's listed firms typically have five categories of shareholders: state, legal person (institutional investor), employee, foreign institutional and small domestic stock market investor (Sun and Tong 2003; Wei et al. 2005; Wei 2007). For many large listed firms, the Chinese state remains a significant shareholder, resulting in a highly concentrated ownership structure (Tam 2002). This reflects China's transition from full state ownership, through partial privatisation and towards a market-oriented economy.

Empirical studies have identified the significance of ownership structure for firm performance in China. Many studies identify that state ownership is negatively related to firm performance. This reflects reduced incentives to monitor managerial behaviour.

For example, Wei et al. (2005), Gunasekarage et al. (2007); Xiong et al. (2008) find concentrated state or institutional ownership to be negatively associated with firm performance, measured either by Tobins' Q or return on assets (ROA). Such findings are consistent with the perspective that high levels of ownership concentration allow controlling shareholders to exert pressure on the firm's managers, impact management incentives and corporate policy choices (Brickley et al. 1988; Pound 1988). However, Tian and Estrin (2008) identify that higher levels of government ownership may lead to better firm's performance, even where initial increases in concentration initially decrease it. The former reflects the ability of government to offer support (e.g., loans, subsidies, access to resources under state-controlled land) to companies in which its holdings are significant. Thus, a higher proportion of state ownership need not negatively impact firm performance. For example, the ability of the state, as a significant investor, to offer support to companies may be particularly important in the 2008–2013 period, as evidenced in the Chinese government's loan-based stimulus programme following the global financial crisis (GFC). This suggests a potentially positive impact of state ownership on the firm's performance.

Finally, Xu and Wang (1999) report a positive relationship between firm's profitability and ownership concentration. Sun and Tong (2003) argue that private ownership improves earnings, sales and productivity. Kato and Long (2006) argue that controlling shareholders and independent directors strengthen the relationship between the firm's performance and CEO turnover in China. Xu et al. (2005) and Zhang et al. (2001) identify that both private and foreign ownership are positively associated with the firm's performance.

Based on the empirical results of these studies, the first of the chapter's null hypotheses are:

$H0_{1A}$: *Ceteris paribus*, which increases in the levels of ownership concentration is positively associated with the performance of listed mining firms in China

$H0_{1B}$: *Ceteris paribus*, which increases in state ownership proportion is positively associated with the performance of listed mining firms in China

$H0_{1C}$: *Ceteris paribus*, which increases in institutional ownership proportion is positively associated with the performance of listed mining firms in China

Political Connectedness and Firm's Performance

Political intervention in business activities is likely to be more prevalent when institutional constraints are weak (Shleifer and Vishny 1994 and 1998). This has frequently been identified in China's governance regimes.

Political connections may provide preferential government intervention for connected firms (e.g., greater access to credit when in financial distress) and reduced investor fears of bankruptcy (Faccio et al. 2006; Faccio 2006). This would, potentially, increase the value of the firm. Alternatively, political affiliations of the firm's management may generate agency problems and weaken governance, increase management incentives to engage in rent-seeking activity and expropriation of firm resources. Thus, political affiliates may capture political benefits at the expense of other stakeholders (Wang 2015), reducing the efficiency of politically-connected firms. This is likely to reduce the firm's financial value, given its impact on expected cash flows.

In the case of China, distinctions also need to be drawn between political connections at the Central versus the local level. In the case of the latter, local SOEs are likely to be controlled by local governments, where local officials will emphasise regional economic outcomes in order to maximise their political and promotional prospects (Li and Zhou 2012). Given the nature and location of their ultimate resources, local factors are likely to dominate in the case of mining companies (Bai et al. 2004).

In the context of the above, Wu et al. (2012) and Wang (2015) find that the former result holds for China's listed firms. In the case of Wang (2015), whose focus is on firms listed on the Shanghai Stock Exchange over the 2003–2012 period, this is only for privately-controlled firms with a high proportion of politically-connected independent directors. This comes at the cost of increases in the amount of related party transactions with the controlling party. However, in the case of listed state-controlled firms, Wang (2015) finds that greater use of related-party transactions and more severe over-investment problems remove benefits derived from the presence of politically connected independent directors—a result more pronounced for firms controlled by local government. In contrast, Wu et al. (2012), using data for listed firms covering the 1999–2006 period, find a negative impact of state-ownership on firm performance largely due to the employment of surplus labour. This is particularly important in the case of local government connections. These latter discrepancies between studies suggest that further analysis on this area is justified.

Given the potential links between local government finances, regional employment and mining in China, the final null hypotheses are:

$H0_{2A}$: *Ceteris paribus*, local government connectedness is negatively associated with the performance of listed mining firms with higher levels of ownership concentration in China

$H0_{2B}$: *Ceteris paribus*, local government connectedness is negatively associated with the performance of listed mining firms with higher levels of state ownership in China

$H0_{2C}$: *Ceteris paribus*, local government connectedness is associated with differences in the performance of listed mining firms with higher levels of institutional ownership in China

Research Design

Data

This study utilises a pooled data set derived from an unbalanced panel of 8,105 firm-year observations for firms listed on the Shanghai Stock Exchange (SHSE) and the Shenzhen Stock Exchange (SZSE). The period under consideration is 2008 to 2013, which reflects the availability of data on political connectedness. This period also follows significant reforms to China's accounting standards (adoption of IFRS), strengthening of *the Company Law* and revisions to its corporate tax system. Data were collected from CSMAR.

Since few listed companies issue both A-shares and B-shares, or A-shares and H-shares, the sample focusses on A-share firms. Firms in the agriculture, forestry and fishing sector and firms in the banking and finance sector, are excluded. To reduce concerns regarding endogeneity, all independent variables, with the exception of industry dummies, are lagged. Additionally, modelling is based on a propensity score matched sub-sample of firms, matched against mining firms according to firm's size, debt-to-value ratio, ownership concentration and levels of state and legal person share ownership relative to total shares. This leaves 6,079 firm-year observations for regression analysis, including 200 firm-year observations for listed mining companies.

Dependent Variable

Tobin's Q (TOBINSQ) is the measure of firm performance. Although accounting performance proxies, such as ROA and ROE, provide alternative performance measures, TOBINSQ captures stock market investors' forward-looking expectations of the firm's future profitability. Therefore, it is regarded as a better indicator of financial market performance (Demsetz and Villalonga 2001; Hermalin and Weisbach 1991; McConnell and Servaes 1995; Wei et al. 2005; Gunasekarage et al. 2007; Gugler et al. 2008). Following Shan and McIver (2011), Shan and Xu (2012a) and Sing and Sirmans (2008), we measure TOBINSQ as the sum of the market value of equity and book value of debt relative to total assets.

Independent Variables

Independent variables (INDEPVAR) are defined as follows. Following Shan and Xu (2012a, 2012b) and Shan (2013), the level of concentration of state ownership (STATEOWN) is represented by the proportion of state shares in total shares, the level of institutional ownership is represented as the share of legal person shares in total shares and the level of concentration of foreign ownership (FOREIGNOWN) is measured by foreign investment relative to total shares. Ownership concentration (OWNCONC) is measured as the proportion of shares held by the top 10 shareholders. Local government political connectedness is captured via LGPCON. This takes a value of one where there is a local government political connection, and zero otherwise.

Control Variables

Control variables (CONTROLS) consist of firm's size (FIRMSIZE) and debt-to-value ratio (DEBTRATIO). FIRMSIZE is the natural logarithm of the book value of total assets. The DEBTRATIO captures the firm's leverage, given by total liabilities relative to total value (Cormier and Magnan 2003; Shan and Xu 2012a, 2013b; Shan 2013).

Sample Selection

As a robustness measure, a propensity score matching method, with five matches, was used to select the sample to be used in estimation. Matching was based on FIRMSIZE; DEBTRATIO; OWNCONC; STATEOWN; and LEGALOWN. FOREIGNOWN was not included as a matching variable due to zero foreign ownership in shares in the listed mining sector. The average treatment effect on TobinsQ for mining firms is positive and statistically significant, supporting further analysis of differences between the mining and other sectors (Table 1).

Table 1. Treatment effects analysis—average treatment effect (ATE) on Tobin's Q.

Treatment-effects estimation (no. of observations = 6079)				
TobinsQ	Coefficient	Standard Error	z	P > |z|
ATE MINING (1 vs 0)	0.7169	0.1409	5.09	0.0000
Observations	6079			

Notes:
- The definitions of the variables are firms designated as being in the mining sector (MINING) and Tobin's Q (TOBINSQ).
- The propensity score matching method, with five matches, was used. Matching was based on: the natural logarithm of the book value of total assets (FIRMSIZE); the debt-to-asset ratio is measured as total liabilities relative to total assets (DEBTRATIO); ownership concentration (OWNCONC) is the proportion of shares held by the top 10 shareholders; the proportion of state shares in total shares (STATEOWN); and the proportion of shares owned by institutional investors (legal shares) in total shares (LEGALOWN).
- The level of foreign investment relative to total shares (FOREIGNOWN) was not included due to zero foreign ownership in shares in the listed mining sector.

Multicollinearity Diagnostics

Collinearity diagnostics are used to examine the correlations between all independent and control variables in two ways. First is estimation of the Pearson correlation matrix (Table 2). None of the sample's pairwise correlation values is greater than the ('rule-of-thumb') critical value of 0.8.

Second, to determine whether the impact of multicollinearity is of concern, variance inflation factor (VIF) test results are examined (Table 2).

Table 2. Correlation matrix for dependent, independent and control variables.

	TobinsQ	FIRMSIZE	DEBTRATIO	LGPCON	OWNCONC	STATEOWN	LEGALOWN
FIRMSIZE	0.2426 ***	–					
DEBTRATIO	-0.1463***	0.4270***	–				
LGPCON	-0.0029	-0.0453***	-0.0605***	–			
OWNCONC	0.0049	0.1422***	-0.1369***	0.0963***	–		
STATEOWN	0.0022	0.1645***	0.0854***	-0.0086	0.2914***	–	
LEGALOWN	0.0363***	-0.1215***	-0.1060***	0.0656***	0.2695***	-0.1898***	–
FOREIGNOWN	-0.0020	-0.0362***	-0.1010***	0.0365**	0.1928***	-0.0474***	0.0549***

Notes: The definitions of the variables are Tobin's Q (TOBINSQ); the proportion of state shares in total shares (STATEOWN), the level of foreign investment relative to total shares (FOREIGNOWN); ultimate state control (STATECONT); ownership concentration (OWNCONC) is the proportion of shares held by the top ten shareholders; local government political connectedness (LGPCON); the number of members in the board of directors (BOARDSIZE); number of independent directors in the board of directors (INDEP); number of foreign board directors (FORDIR); number of members in the supervisory board size (SBSIZE); the natural logarithm of the book value of total assets (FIRMSIZE); the debt-to-equity ratio is measured as total liabilities relative to total equity (DERATIO), use of a Big-4 auditor (BIG4) and CEO duality (CEODUAL).

Table 3. Collinearity Diagnostics—Variance Inflation Factor (VIF).

Variable	VIF
FIRMSIZE	1.52
DEBTRATIO	1.57
LGPCON	0.96
OWNCONC	0.73
STATEOWN	0.79
LEGALOWN	0.81
FOREIGNOWN	0.92
Average	1.04

Notes: The definitions of the variables are the natural logarithm of the book value of total assets (FIRMSIZE); the debt-to-asset ratio is measured as total liabilities relative to total assets (DEBTRATIO); local government political connectedness (LGPCON); ownership concentration (OWNCONC) is the proportion of shares held by the top ten shareholders; the proportion of state shares in total shares (STATEOWN); the proportion of shares owned by institutional investors (legal shares) in total shares (LEGALOWN); and the level of foreign investment relative to total shares (FOREIGNOWN).

These indicate that the highest VIF values are 1.57 (DEBTRATIO) and 1.52 (FIRMSIZE), with the mean VIF value of all variables being 1.04, with most remaining VIFs being near or below this level. Gujarati (2003) suggests that the VIF value is less than the critical value of 10. Thus, significant multicollinearity is not apparent in the sample data.

3.6 Model Specification

The following empirical models are used to test the hypotheses discussed in this chapter:

$$TOBINSQ_{it} = \alpha + \sum_{j=1}^{5} \beta_j INDEPVAR_{it} + \sum_{k=1}^{2} \gamma_k CONTROLS_{it}$$
$$+ \sum_{t=1}^{5} \varphi_t YEAR_t + \sum_{n=1}^{7} \phi_n INDUSTRY_n + \varepsilon_{it}$$

Eqn. 1

$$TOBINSQ_{it} = \alpha + \sum_{j=1}^{5} \beta_j INDEPVAR_{it} + \sum_{k=1}^{2} \gamma_k CONTROLS_{it} + \sum_{j=1}^{4} \lambda_j INDEPVAR_{it} \times MINING_{it}$$
$$+ \psi_1 OWNCONC_{it} \times MINING \times LGPCON_{it} + \psi_2 STATEOWN_{it} \times MINING \times LGPCON_{it}$$
$$+ \psi_3 LEGALOWN_{it} \times MINING \times LGPCON_{it} + \sum_{t=1}^{5} \varphi_t YEAR_t + \sum_{n=1}^{7} \phi_n INDUSTRY_n + \varepsilon_{it}$$

Eqn. 2

Year and industry (mining, manufacturing, utilities, construction, retail, real estate, transportation, info. tech., leasing, public facilities, comprehensive) fixed effects are controlled via YEAR and INDUSTRY dummies. MINING is a dummy variable taking the value one for firms in the mining (MINING) sector and 0 otherwise.

Equation 1 is estimated prior to estimation of Equation 2 to assess the stability of coefficients as interactions are added within the model.

Results and Discussion

Descriptive Statistics

Table 4 provides the descriptive statistics on the main variables used in the study. Tobin's Q (TobinsQ) is higher on average and less variable for mining firms as compared to all sample firms. Top-10 ownership concentration (OWNCONC) and state ownership (STATEOWN) are slightly higher on an average in the mining sector. However, local government political connectedness (LGPCON) and institutional (LEGALOWN) are lower, while foreign ownership (FOREIGNOWN) is zero in the mining sector. Finally, gearing (DEBTRATIO) is slightly lower on the average for mining firms than for all sample firms.

Multivariate Analyses

Table 5 presents the random effects when panel regression results are used to test the hypotheses. Overall R^2 statistics are 0.2175 and 0.2258, respectively, for Equation 1 and Equation 2. Wald $\times^2$ statistics for each regression indicate that variation in the independent variables is statistically significant in explaining variations in TobinsQ. The Breusch and Pagan Lagrangian multiplier test for random effects confirms that use of the random effects model is an appropriate relative to use in a simple pooled regression (Table 6).

$H0_{1A}$ proposes that TobinsQ increases as ownership concentration rises. The sum of the coefficients on OWNCONC and OWNCONC#MINING should be positive. Both coefficients are positive and statistically significant. In the case of coefficient on OWNCONC, the result is consistent with McConnell and Servaes (1990) and Mudambi and Nicosia (1998). The net effect of concentrated ownership is positive for the mining sector and more so than for other sectors in general. $H0_{1A}$ is accepted. This may, for example, reflect that ownership concentration, by reducing Type 1 agency problems, benefits the firm's performance.

$H0_{1B}$ proposes that TobinsQ increases as the proportion of state ownership rises. The sum of the coefficients on STATEOWN and STATEOWN#MINING should be positive. Both coefficients are positive and statistically significant. The net effect of state ownership is positive for the mining sector and again more so than for all sectors on an average. $H0_{1B}$ is accepted. The results suggest that mining firms with a higher

Table 4. Descriptive Statistics for Treatment Effects Sample.

	Mean		Median		Min		Max		Std. Dev.	
	ALL	MINING	ALL	MINING	ALL	MINING	ALL	MINING	ALL	MINING
TobinsQ	2.363	2.859	1.808	2.168	0.683	0.880	232.708	15.101	4.169	2.275
FIRMSIZE	22.078	22.787	21.947	23.014	15.729	17.998	28.482	28.482	1.194	1.372
DEBTRATIO	0.482	0.463	0.497	0.491	0.000	0.046	2.186	0.916	0.206	0.177
LGPCON	0.109	0.085	0.000	0.000	0.000	0.000	1.000	1.000	0.312	0.280
OWNCONC	0.567	0.608	0.575	0.618	0.044	0.119	0.982	0.982	0.157	0.151
STATEOWN	0.105	0.192	0.000	0.000	0.000	0.000	0.862	0.847	0.193	0.258
LEGALOWN	0.082	0.050	0.000	0.000	0.000	0.000	0.917	0.769	0.169	0.131
FOREIGNOWN	0.012	0.000	0.000	0.000	0.000	0.000	0.885	0.000	0.069	0.000

Notes: The definitions of the variables are all firms in the sample data (ALL); firms designated as being in the mining sector (MINING); Tobin's Q (TOBINSQ); the natural logarithm of the book value of total assets (FIRMSIZE); the debt-to-asset ratio is measured as total liabilities relative to total assets (DEBTRATIO); local government political connectedness (LGPCON); ownership concentration (OWNCONC) is the proportion of shares held by the top ten shareholders; the proportion of state shares in total shares (STATEOWN); the proportion of shares owned by institutional investors (legal shares) in total shares (LEGALOWN) and the level of foreign investment relative to total shares (FOREIGNOWN).

Table 5. Random effects panel regression analysis–dependent variable Tobin's Q.

	Eqn. 1		Eqn. 2	
	Coefficient	P value	Coefficient	P value
FIRMSIZE	–0.5321	0.000	–0.5368	0.000
DEBTRATIO	–0.6109	0.001	–0.5799	0.002
LGPCON	–0.0255	0.796	0.0389	0.749
OWNCONC	0.8212	0.001	0.8174	0.001
STATEOWN	0.7881	0.000	0.7023	0.000
LEGALOWN	0.2084	0.165	0.2027	0.205
FOREIGNOWN	–0.2395	0.468	–0.1134	0.746
STATEOWN#LGPCON			–0.0974	0.851
LEGALOWN#LGPCON			–0.2164	0.517
FOREIGNOWN#LGPCON			–0.5565	0.553
LGPCON#MINING			–0.2385	0.514
OWNCONC#MINING			0.6480	0.011
STATEOWN#MINING			1.1384	0.021
LEGALOWN#MINING			2.5235	0.171
OWNCONC#LGPCON#MINING			0.2441	0.830
STATEOWN#LGPCON#MINING			–2.4508	0.020
LEGALOWN#LGPCON#MINING			–4.8598	0.017
Constant	13.5453	0.000	13.6178	0.000
Year Effects	Yes		Yes	
Industry Effects	Yes		Yes	
R-squared within	0.1621		0.1643	
R-squared between	0.2298		0.2441	
R-squared overall	0.2175		0.2253	
Wald χ^2	429.23		674.06	
Prob. > χ^2	0.0000		0.0000	
No. of observations	2,548		2,548	
No. of groups	1,187		1,187	

Notes:
- All regressors lagged one period, with the exception of the industry dummies.
- Results based on treatment effects sample.
- # indicates interaction between the variables.
- ***, **, and *, indicate significance at the one, 2 and 5 per cent levels (using 2-tailed p-values), respectively.
- The definitions of the variables are firms designated as being in the mining sector (MINING); Tobin's Q (TOBINSQ); the natural logarithm of the book value of total assets (FIRMSIZE); the debt-to-asset ratio is measured as total liabilities relative to total assets (DEBTRATIO); local government political connectedness (LGPCON); ownership concentration (OWNCONC) is the proportion of shares held by the top ten shareholders; the proportion of state shares in total shares (STATEOWN); the proportion of shares owned by institutional investors (legal shares) in total shares (LEGALOWN); and the level of foreign investment relative to total shares (FOREIGNOWN).

Table 6. Breusch and Pagan Lagrangian multiplier test for random effects.

| | Treatment Effects Estimation | | | |
	Variance	Standard Deviation	x^2	$P > x^2$
TobinsQ	1.8489	1.3597	860.77	0.0000
e	0.4946	0.7033		
u	0.9039	0.9507		

Note: Tobin's Q (TOBINSQ).

level of state ownership firms may have a competitive advantage over firms where other forms of control dominate. This is consistent with the presence of greater access to credit or credit on favourable terms and/or from government policies targeting this sector.

HO_{1C} proposes that a higher proportion of legal ownership will increase the TobinsQ of listed mining firms, suggesting a positive sum of the coefficients on LEGALOWN and LEGALOWN#MINING. While the coefficients on LEGALOWN and LEGALOWN#MINING are positive, each is statistically insignificant. HO_{1C} is rejected.

The final null hypotheses, HO_{2A}, HO_{2B} and HO_{2C}, propose that TobinsQ will be lower for firms with higher levels of ownership concentration as well as higher levels of state and institutional ownership, respectively, in China in the presence of local government connectedness. Thus, individually, each of the sums of the coefficients on the sets of regressors associated with ownership concentration and state and institutional ownership (OWNCONC, OWNCONC#MINING and OWNCONC#MINING#LGPCON; STATEOWN, STATEOWN#MINING and STATEOWN#MINING#LGPCON; and LEGALOWN, LEGALOWN# MINING and LEGALOWN#MINING#LGPCON) should be negative.

In the cases of state and institutional ownership, the absolute size of the coefficients on STATEOWN#MINING#LGPCON and LEGALOWN#MINING#LGPCON dominate the outcomes. HO_{2B} and HO_{2C} are accepted. However, HO_{2A} is rejected as the coefficient on OWNCONC#MINING#LGPCON is statistically insignificant (and positive). Thus, it is not ownership concentration in the presence of political connectedness that determines the impact of local government connectedness on financial performance; rather, it is the form that high levels of ownership takes. For state ownership, our results, although not fully comparable, differ slightly from those of Wang (2015), who finds no benefits from political connectedness in the case of listed state-controlled firms, with the result being more pronounced for firms under local government control. Our data does not allow for this latter distinction in terms of control. We posit that while local political connectedness may provide access to additional resources for firms with state ownership (e.g., greater access to local-government monopolised land supply), local political connectedness may be associated with a greater propensity for over-investment and expropriation via related-party transactions. However, further analysis of the precise nature of the controlling state entity (i.e., state, a governmental agency, government department, or local authority) is needed to examine this conjecture.

In addition to the above results for the eight hypotheses, we find that FIRMSIZE is negatively related to TobinsQ, including the mining-sector firms, suggesting that smaller firms may outperform larger firms in China. Finally, the impact of gearing (DEBTRATIO) on listed firms is negative.

Robustness Checks

Robustness of the primary results has been assessed in several ways. First, regressions involving interactions between each regressor and mining were performed following removal of the mining industry effect; the addition of data for agriculture, forestry and fishing, and the banking and finance sectors; addition of interaction terms between all regressors and LGPCON; and three-way interactions between all regressors, MINING and LGPCON. Additionally, regressions were performed with inclusion of the standard corporate governance variables (board size, number of independent directors, supervisory size, and CEO duality). The results (not reported in this chapter) indicate that there are no significant differences with the primary findings, with the qualitative and quantitative values of the coefficients in these regressions being consistent with those reported in Table 5.

Conclusion

This study has examined differences in the role of ownership factors in the financial performance of SHSE and SZSE-listed mining and other A-share firms. Firms in the mining sector are hypothesised to display the same characteristics with respect to a range of corporate governance factors and political connectedness as the listed firms in other sectors (the null hypotheses), based on established theory and/or previous empirical evidence for China's listed firms.

Analysis is based on 2008–2013 data comprising 6079 firm-year observations, of which 200 are for companies in the mining sector and include information on political connections and ultimate state control. Random effects regression modelling is used due to the time invariant nature of the mining classification, controlling year and industry effects.

Regressors (excepting a mining dummy) are lagged to limit endogeneity concerns, as well as the use of a propensity-matched sample derived from the treatment effects estimation controlling the natural logarithm of the book value of total assets (FIRMSIZE); the debt-to-asset ratio is measured as total liabilities relative to total assets (DEBTRATIO); ownership concentration (OWNCONC) is the proportion of shares held by the top 10 shareholders; the proportion of state shares in total shares (STATEOWN); and the proportion of shares owned by institutional investors (legal shares) in total shares (LEGALOWN).

Ownership concentration and proportion of state ownership are found to positively impact the performance (Tobin's Q) of China's listed firms. Firm's size and gearing negatively impact the performance. Higher levels of institutional ownership, local government connectedness and foreign ownership are not significant. Important differences are noted for listed mining firms. Ownership concentration and higher levels of each of state and institutional (legal person) ownership positively add to financial performance. Finally, in the presence of local government connectedness greater levels of each of state and institutional ownership negatively impact the financial performance of firms in the mining sector.

It is with respect to higher levels of state and institutional ownership rather than simply ownership concentration that the results for mining firms are, perhaps, most interesting. Firms with high levels of state and legal ownership appear to have financial performance advantages over firms where these forms of ownership are less dominant. However, these results are reversed for those firms that, in addition, have local government political connections. These findings warrant future research in this area, especially following the significant changes to the corporate-governance environment associated with China's legal and regulatory reforms throughout the 2000s.

This study has many limitations, but several of importance. The sample is confined to firms coded as mining firms under the CSRC industry code, suggesting future studies to extend the sample to other major mining players not coded as such by the CSRC. With respect to the impact of political connectedness, limitations associated with CSMAR data on political connectedness suggest the importance of the use of more detailed ownership data. Finally, the 2008–2013 focus, a period following significant regulatory and legal reform in China, limits comparability to studies based on earlier sample data (e.g., Wu et al. 2012). This suggests that studies based on more comprehensive sample panels may be productive in assessing the impact of China's recent ownership reforms and changes in the impact of political connectedness over time.

References

Aoki, M. (1995). Corporate Governance in Transitional Economies: Insider Control and the Role of Banks, The World Bank, Washington, D.C.

Bai, C.-E., Du, Y., Tao, Z. and Tong, S.Y. (2004). Local protectionism and regional specialisation: evidence from China's industries. Journal of International Economics 63: 397–417.

Berle, A. and Means, G. (1932). The Modern Corporation and Private Property, New Brunswick, NJ: Transaction Publishers.

Brickley, J., Lease, R.C. and Smith, C.W. (1988). Ownership structure and voting on antitakeover amendments. Journal of Financial Economics 20: 267–291.

Cormier, D. and Magnan, M. (2003). Environmental reporting management: A continental European perspective. Journal of Accounting and Public Policy 22: 43–62.

Dahya, J., Karbhari, Y., Xiao, J.Z. and Yang, M. (2003). The usefulness of the supervisory board report in China. Corporate Governance: An International Review 11: 308–321.

Demsetz, H. and Villalonga, B. (2001). Ownership structure and corporate performance. Journal of Corporate Finance 7: 209–233.

Faccio, M. (2006). Politically connected firms. American Economic Review 96: 369–386.

Faccio, M., Masulis, R.W., McConnell, J.J. and Offenberg, M.S. (2006). Political connections and corporate bailouts. Journal of Finance 61: 2597–2635.

Fama, E.F. and Jensen, M.C. (1983). The separation of ownership and control. Journal of Law and Economics 26: 301–325.

Feinerman, J.V. (2007). New hope for corporate governance in China? China Quarterly 191: 590–612.

Gugler, K., Mueller, D.C. and Yurtoglu, B.B. (2008). Insider ownership, ownership concentration and investment performance: an international comparison. Journal of Corporate Finance 14: 688–705.

Gujarati, D.N. (2003). Basic Econometrics, 4th edn. New York: McGraw-Hill.

Gunasekarage, A., Hess, K. and Hu, A.J. (2007). The influence of the degree of state ownership and the ownership concentration on the performance of listed Chinese companies. Research in International Business and Finance 21: 379–395.

Hermalin, B.E. and Weisbach, M.S. (1991). The effects of board composition and direct incentives on firm performance. Financial Management 20: 101–121.

Jensen, M.C. and Meckling, W.H. (1976). Theory of the firm: managerial behavior, agency costs, and ownership structure. Journal of Financial Economics 3: 305–360.

Kato, T. and Long, C. (2006). Executive turnover and firm performance and firm performance in China. American Economic Review 96: 363–367.

Lannoo, K. (1999). A European perspective on corporate governance. Journal of Common Market Studies 37: 269–294.

La Porta, R., Lopez-de-Silanes, F. and Shleifer, A. (1999). Corporate ownership around the world. Journal of Finance 54: 471–517.

Li, H. and Zhou, L. (2005). Political turnover and economic performance: the incentive role of personnel control in China. Journal of Public Economics 89: 1743–62.

Lin, T.W. (2004). Corporate governance in China: recent developments, key problems, and solutions. Journal of Accounting and Corporate Governance 1: 1–23.

McConnell, J.J. and Servaes, H. (1990). Additional evidence on equity ownership and corporate value. Journal of Financial Economics 27: 595–612.

McConnell, J.J. and Servaes, H. (1995). Equity ownership and the two faces of debt. Journal of Financial Economics 39: 131–157.

Mudambi, R. and Nicosia, C. (1998). Ownership structure and firm performance: evidence from the UK financial services industry. Applied Financial Economics 8: 175–180.

Pound, J. (1988). Proxy contests and the efficiency of shareholder oversight. Journal of Financial Economics 20: 237–265.

PWC (2016), M&A (2015). Review and 2016, available at: http://www.pwccn.com/home/eng/ma_press_briefing_jan2016.html (accessed 27 April 2016).

Shan, Y.G. (2013). Can internal governance mechanisms prevent asset appropriation? Examination of type I tunnelling in China. Corporate Governance: An International Review 21: 225–241.

Shan, Y.G. and McIver, R.P. (2011). Corporate governance mechanisms and financial performance in China: panel data evidence on listed non-financial companies. Asia Pacific Business Review 17: 301–324.

Shan, Y.G. and Round, D. (2012). China's corporate governance: emerging issues and problems. Modern Asian Studies 46: 1316–1344.

Shan, Y.G. and Xu, L. (2012a). Do internal governance mechanisms impact on firm performance? Empirical evidence from the financial sector in China. Journal of Asia-Pacific Business 13: 114–142.

Shan, Y.G. and Xu, L. (2012b). Bad debt provisions of financial institutions: Dilemma of China's corporate governance regime. International Journal of Managerial Finance 8: 344–364.

Shleifer, A. and Vishny, R. (1994). Politicians and firms. Quarterly Journal of Economics 109: 995–1025.

Shleifer, A. and Vishny, R.W. (1997). A survey of corporate governance. Journal of Finance 52: 737–782.

Shleifer, A. and Vishny, R. (1998). The Grabbing Hand: Government Pathologies and Their Cures. Harvard University Press, Cambridge, MA.

Sun, Q. and Tong, W.H.S. (2003). China share issue privatization: the extent of its success. Journal of Financial Economics 70: 183–222.

Tam, O.K. (2002). Ethical issues in the evolution of corporate governance in China. Journal of Business Ethics 37: 303–320.

Tian, L. and Estrin, S. (2008). Retained state shareholding in Chinese PLCs: does government ownership always reduce corporate value? Journal of Comparative Economics 36: 74–89.

Wang, J. (2007). The strange role of independent directors in a two-tier board structure of China's listed companies. Compliance and Regulatory Journal 3: 47–55.

Wang, J. (2012). Financing the mining industry in China. The Chinese Economy 45: 76–87.

Wang, L. (2015). Protection or expropriation: Politically connected independent directors in China. Journal of Banking and Finance 55: 92–106.

Wei, G. (2007). Ownership structure, corporate governance and company performance in China. Asia Pacific Business Review 13: 519–545.

Wei, Z., Xie, F. and Zhang, S. (2005). Ownership structure and firm value in China's privatized firms: 1991–2001. Journal of Financial and Quantitative Analysis 40: 87–108.

Wu, W., Wu, C. and Rui, O.M. (2012). Ownership and the value of political connections: Evidence from China. European Financial Management 18: 695–729.

Xiong, X., Li, J. and Wang, H. (2008). Stock ownership concentration and firm performance: an empirical study based on IPO companies in China. International Management Review 4: 37–47.

Xu, X. and Wang, Y. (1999). Ownership structure and corporate governance in Chinese stock companies. China Economic Review 10(1): 75–98.

Xu, L.C., Zhu, T. and Lin, Y.M. (2005). Politician control, agency problems and ownership reform: evidence from China. Economics of Transition 13: 1–24.

Zhang, A., Zhang, Y. and Zhao, R. (2001). Impact of ownership and competition on the productivity of Chinese enterprises. Journal of Comparative Economics 29: 327–346.

Zhang, A., Moffat, K., Boughen, N., Wang, J., Cui, L. and Dai, Y. (2015). Chinese attitudes toward mining: Citizen survey–2014 Results, CSIRO, Australia.

14

Corporate Income Tax Avoidance in China

Using Regulatory Change to Encourage Corporate Tax Sustainability

Guodong Yuan,[1] *Ron P. McIver,*[1] *Lei Xu*[1,]* and *Sang Hong Kang*[2]

Introduction

No government, whether simple or complex, of capitalist or socialist leaning, can operate or achieve its goals without tax revenue. Tax revenues, raised and then allocated to the benefit of society, underpin the functioning of all societies (Levi 1988; Martinez 1994; Mehrotra 2015). An effective and efficient corporate taxation system will impact both economic growth prospects, and the ability to fund expenditures promoting social inclusivity and social equity (European Commission 2016; Avi-Yonah 2008). Thus, tax avoidance behaviour by corporations, which deprive government of the resources to redress social problems, may be seen as both unethical and socially irresponsible (Dowling 2013), reflecting its negative impact on the sustainability of the social commons (Bird and Davis-Nozemack 2016).

Globally, concerns have been raised over corporate income tax avoidance, especially amongst large (including multinational) companies.

---

[1] School of Commerce, University of South Australia, Australia.
[2] Department of Business Administration, Pusan National University, Korea.
* Corresponding author: lei.xu@unisa.edu.au

This has led to calls for more transparent and simpler tax structures and stricter enforcement of these tax structures, to reduce the incentives and potential for such avoidance (e.g., European Commission 2016; The Economist 2016). However, while the calls for reform have been many, there is limited evidence of the extent to which tax avoidance behaviour, comprising taxpayer's utilisation of the tax regime to reduce the level of taxes paid, is actually impacted by changes in the tax regulatory environment. This chapter addresses this issue by examining one such set of changes, that for China.

In 2008 the taxation regulatory environment in China significantly changed with the implementation of the *Enterprise Income Tax Law*. Firstly, the income tax rate was reduced from 33 to 25 per cent and this rate was applied to all enterprises, including foreign enterprises and enterprises with foreign investments. Secondly, the taxation reform enhanced the taxation authority's scrutiny and enforcement activity to match the application of the 2007 *Accounting Standards for Business Enterprises No. 18.*

Corporate Income Tax Accounting

A novel feature of the study reported in this chapter is the 'natural experiment' opportunity provided by these tax regimes and accounting standard reforms in China to address two research questions. Firstly, have the changes to the tax regulatory environment affected the level of corporate tax avoidance of listed companies in China? Secondly, does the structure of ownership/control of these companies—state-controlled, private or foreign-invested, and implying different incentives to engage in tax aggressive behaviour—impact on the corporate tax avoidance response to these taxation regime changes?

This study contributes to the knowledge of the disciplines of accounting, governance, taxation and regulatory change. There is limited evidence of the extent to which tax avoidance behaviour, comprising the taxpayer's utilisation of the tax regime to reduce the level of taxes paid, is impacted by changes in the tax regulatory environment. Accordingly, a major contribution of this study is that it specifically addresses the effectiveness of a major tax regulatory reforms in limiting the tax avoidance behaviour of listed corporations. Secondly, a few studies have been conducted on whether the level of tax avoidance in transition economies displays different characteristics to that which has been shown in developed market-oriented economies. Most prior research to date has been conducted in the United States of America, with the tax avoidance behaviour in other countries rarely being documented. In China's case, the ability of its Central Government to raise revenues via taxation has historically been viewed as poor due to the devolvement of responsibility for collection to lower levels of government resulting in widespread tax avoidance/evasion and the provision of widespread tax relief (Deng and Smyth 2000). This suggests both significant differences to the U.S. case and the potential for significant revenue enhancement where major regulatory changes strengthen China's corporate taxation system.

Given this context and particularly as the examination of corporate tax avoidance in China has received little attention in the literature to date, the results from this study have a potential significance not only to China's Central Government but also to policy analysts, tax regulators, investors and corporations both within and outside China.

By drawing on effective tax planning, agency, tax avoidance and legitimacy theories to address the two research questions cited earlier, this study is consistent with other recent research that links tax avoidance behaviour to the book-tax gap representing the difference between the pre-tax income disclosed in financial reports and the taxable income reported to the tax authorities (Mills 1998; Desai and Dharmapala 2003, 2006, 2007, 2009; Moore 2007; Wilson 2007; Richardson and Lanis 2007; Jimenez-Angueira 2008; Rohaya et al. 2008; Hanlon and Slemrod 2009; Rego and Wilson 2012).

Accordingly, the book-tax gap is used to examine the responses of listed companies in China to changes in the country's corporate taxation regulatory environment. Data of the study comprised a balanced panel-data sample of 1,224 companies listed on the Shanghai and Shenzhen Stock Exchanges for the 2007–2010 period, with state-controlled, private or foreign-invested ownership characteristics, providing 4,896 firm-years of observations.

The remainder of this chapter is organised as follows: Section 2 provides a review of relevant literature and development of hypotheses; Section 3 describes the research design; Section 4 reports the empirical results and Section 5 presents conclusions.

Literature and Hypotheses

Business tax planning comprises activities to reduce the rate of tax paid on earnings and spans a spectrum that includes tax saving and tax avoidance (Jin and Lei 2011), with tax avoidance often used to describe outwardly legitimate but contrived arrangements (Woellner et al. 2010). To ensure clarity in the discussion and consistent with the related literature (e.g., that cited in Hanlon and Heitzman 2010), the term 'tax aggressiveness is used for tax avoidance behaviour that is at the end of the legal tax planning spectrum and may extend into illegal tax evasion activity.

Corporate tax aggressiveness has recently received increasing attention by researchers, including a focus on governance characteristics and implications for corporate value (Desai and Dharmapala 2009; Zheng and Han 2008) and the links between tax avoidance and corporate social responsibility (e.g., Hoi et al. 2013; Sari and Tjien 2016; Laguira et al. 2015). This research has found that perspectives of corporate tax aggressiveness vary by stakeholder groups. For example, a corporation that engages in aggressive tax avoidance may be favoured by investors where it results in the transfer of value from the government to the firm. However, given the inherent agency problems in publicly listed companies, there is the potential for tax avoidance behaviour to be intertwined with managerial efforts to divert value from shareholders (Desai and Dharmapala 2009). Furthermore, taxation authorities may attempt to enforce tax laws by introducing regulations and initiatives to encourage tax compliance, resulting in lower opportunity and marginal costs due to improved certainty about tax risk, clearer interpretations of the tax law and fewer tax audit interventions (OECD 2009). Additionally, many non-governmental organisations, such as the Global Reporting Initiative (GRI), have recently considered incorporating anti-tax avoidance implementation and corporate tax practice criteria into sustainability frameworks, such as reporting mechanisms. Leading market-based social benchmarks, such as the Dow Jones Sustainability Index (DJSI), also offer an affirmation for companies driven by sustainability with tax practices now being a part of the listing criteria (Urdangarin and VanderBeek 2015; Bird and Davis-Nozemack 2016). Given these factors, shareholders need an effective way to communicate to managers their preferences for the corporation's tax planning behaviour, especially under the circumstances of regulatory environment changes (Jimenez-Angueira 2008).

Existing literature laying the theoretical foundation for understanding the corporate tax planning behaviour within an agency framework argues that aggressive tax avoidance may result from managers' incentives to exploit the tax function to extract private rents and thereby increase their personal utility at the expense of shareholders' interests. To limit these rents and decrease agency costs requires corporate supervisory systems influencing corporate governance either internally, through effective corporate governance and/or externally, via outside stakeholders, such as external auditors, government regulatory bodies and the media (Jin and Lei 2011). As business behaviour in transition and emerging market economies is often significantly influenced by factors related to internal governance and the external regulatory environment, tax avoidance activity to maximise the firm's after-tax benefits will be affected by ownership patterns and regulatory scrutiny from the government.

Accordingly, although there is limited intersection between studies of regulatory environment, corporate control/governance and tax avoidance behaviour, the extant literature does provide both a theoretical link between the areas and an appropriate foundation for an empirical study on the interaction of regulatory change, ownership structure and tax avoidance in China. Therefore, the underlying theoretical framework is primarily located in the theory of effective tax planning and the theory of corporate tax avoidance, as outlined below.

Theory of Effective Tax Planning

Tax planning has received significant attention as an important factor in corporate strategic management linking tax-related behaviour and financial activity. For example, traditional tax planning theories focussed on minimising corporate taxpayers' explicit tax obligations through operational activities (Zheng and Han 2008). Although providing a simple set of ideas for implementation, this traditional approach does not consider the costs, legality and multiplicity of real constraints that may result in meeting this objective. To overcome such shortcomings, Scholes et al. (1990) introduced the 'theory of effective tax planning', which is based on the basic concepts and methods of modern contract theory.

In the presence of perfect markets, the objectives of the traditional and effective tax planning frameworks are almost identical. However, where uncertainty and information asymmetry exist, the objectives of the two frameworks will begin to differ. The core objective of effective tax planning theory is maximisation of total after-tax benefits, requiring consideration of the costs and constraints related to achieving this goal. Scholes et al. (1992) argue that the optimal scale for effective tax planning under conditions of uncertainty and information asymmetry in incomplete markets is based on three key considerations—the tax implications for all parties associated with the transaction; the implications of implicit taxes and the impact of non-tax costs on total costs of tax planning. As effective tax planning must consider the transactions of all parties, the appropriate goal should not be on tax minimisation *per se*, rather the optimisation of total tax burdens, including those passed on to/saved from other parties. Accordingly, in their choices of investment, financing, and compensation, corporations are encouraged to trade-off tax savings against non-tax costs with the following implications.

Firstly, all contracting parties to the transaction and their reactions should be taken into account during the tax planning process. From a contract perspective, these include employers, employees, customers and the tax authorities. Therefore, effective tax planning involves trade-offs of the benefits received by all transactional parties to achieve their long-term goals.

Secondly, when making investment and financing transactions, effective tax planning requires consideration of not just explicit taxes comprising the tax burden for the enterprise as regulated by the tax law and paid directly to the tax authorities, but also implicit taxes. Implicit taxes, although not paid to tax authorities under tax law, take the form of reduced rates of return associated with the firm's inability to capture explicit tax savings (Callihan and White 1999).

Thirdly, explicit tax savings do not necessarily provide the best (or the most feasible) solution in effective tax planning because this activity may lead to an increase in other non-tax costs. For example, a decrease in earnings per share associated with a tax planning decrease in profit reported in the financial statements may cause a fall in share prices and thus, in the firm's value, increasing the costs associated with capital market financing and increasing merger and acquisition risk.

A decline in reported profits may also affect managers' compensation and other entitlements, potentially causing inconsistencies between the managers' interests and those of shareholders and so increasing the agency costs. Also, under conditions of information asymmetry, various stakeholders may make decisions based on the company's external financial reports. This may result in management rejecting taking of substantial tax savings because of the impact on accounting profits, believing that while tax planning may increase cash flow, share prices are affected by accounting profit disclosures rather than cash flows. Therefore, the cost of financial reporting and the non-tax costs caused by asymmetric uncertainty are important constraints to be considered in effective tax planning.

Theory of Corporate Tax Avoidance

There are two major alternative perspectives derived from the theory of corporate tax avoidance that underpin the related empirical research. First is a commonly held view that corporate tax shelters are simply devices for achieving tax-savings but do not present other aspects of agency problems (Desai and Dharmapala 2009). This view mainly considers the direct costs of tax avoidance, such as managers' time and the possible risk of detection. Consequently, as managers conduct tax avoidance for the sole purpose of decreasing tax burdens and investors believe that this tax avoidance behaviour is a value-enhancing activity, managers should both be motivated to achieve and be compensated for tax avoidance activities (Kim et al. 2011). Other studies have identified the use of tax shelters being positively associated with firm characteristics, such as size and profitability (Graham and Tucker 2006), tax shelters may substitute for interest deductions in determining capital structure (Desai and Dharmapala 2009) and compensation for managers could motivate aggressive tax avoidance behaviour (Phillips 2003).

The second alternative perspective is that because of the separation of ownership and control, corporate tax avoidance may reflect agency problems, with shareholders and Board of Directors trying to find incentives and control mechanisms that reduce agency costs (Jensen and Meckling 1976). Therefore, the focus is on the interaction between tax avoidance and the agency tension between managers and investors inherent in publicly listed companies. This view of tax avoidance is underpinned by the theoretical foundations set by Slemrod (2004), Chen and Chu (2005), Crocker and Slemrod (2005) and Desai et al. (2007). For example, Chen and Chu (2005) use a 'standard principal-agent model' to examine corporate tax avoidance, finding that incentives to avoid tax are reduced by the costs associated with losses in internal controls that arise when management is compensated for engaging in risky tax avoidance behaviour. Similarly, Crocker and Slemrod (2005) examine the compensation of tax directors and the effectiveness of tax penalties and find that penalties applied to tax managers, rather than to shareholders, are more effective in reducing tax evasion, while Desai and Dharmapala (2006) and Desai et al. (2007) focus on the links between firms' governance arrangements and their responses to tax regulation. To summarise this view, corporate tax avoidance not only entails distinct costs, but these costs may outweigh the potential benefits to shareholders from the corporation engaging in aggressive tax avoidance behaviour.

The Trade-offs of Costs and Benefits of Tax Aggressive Behaviours: 'Profit-maximising Level of Tax Aggressiveness' (PMLTA)

Based on the agency, effective tax planning and tax avoidance theories, Jimenez-Angueira (2008) develops a theoretical framework to determine the optimal level of tax avoidance behaviour (tax aggressiveness) for the firm designated as the 'profit-maximising level of tax-aggressiveness' (PMLTA).

The traditional view of corporate tax avoidance argues that an increase in a firm's tax aggressiveness represents a wealth transfer from the government to the firm's shareholders. Thus, any increase in the firm's value comes at other taxpayers' expense (Jimenez-Angueira 2008). However, because of agency problems, shareholders must find an effective way to communicate their tax planning preferences to management. Jimenez-Angueira (2008) proposes that it is through the corporate governance system that shareholders must put in place incentives and controls that induce managers to take tax positions, that given the specific tax regime, result in a profit-maximising level of tax-aggressiveness (PMLTA). At this level, the marginal benefits of tax aggressive transactions are balanced against the marginal costs of those activities, with the costs of tax-aggressiveness not only including transaction, non-compliance and political costs, but also the related compensation and monitoring costs associated with the agency relationship. Consequently, tax regime changes that reduce the potential for mangers to extract rents through tax-related activities will reduce the level of tax aggressiveness undertaken by firms.

Related Empirical Studies

The established empirical research in identifying and measuring tax aggressiveness includes Desai and Dharmapala's (2009) study of the impact of tax avoidance on firm value, and Jimenez-Angueira's (2008) study of the effects of the interaction between tax environment changes and corporate governance on tax aggressiveness and market valuation. Previous research has also identified a set of characteristics that may provide a source of variation in measures of tax aggressiveness across firms. For example, Stickney and McGee (1982), Zimmerman (1983), Porcano (1986) and Rego (2003) provide evidence on the association between tax aggressiveness and firm size while Gupta and Newberry (1997) identify that tax aggressiveness is associated with lower profitability but higher leverage and capital intensity. Recent research (e.g., Graham and Tucker 2006; Wilson 2009; Lisowsky 2010) shows that firms accused of using tax shelters have larger book-tax differences, are more focussed on foreign operations with subsidiaries in tax havens, are more profitable, have more research and development (R&D) expenditures and have less leverage. Finally, research linking corporate social responsibility to tax avoidance behaviour (Hoi et al. 2013; Sari and Tjien 2016; Laguira et al. 2015) suggests that companies with excessive irresponsible CSR activities have a higher likelihood of engaging in tax-sheltering activities and greater discretionary/permanent book-tax differences.

With respect to the impact of ownership characteristics, a number of empirical studies have explored the impact of ownership structure on corporate tax aggressiveness (Rego and Wilson 2010). For example, Chen et al. (2010) provide evidence that family-owned firms have lower avoidance of income tax than non-family-owned firms because the dominant owner-managers of family-owned firms forego tax benefits to avoid concerns by minority shareholders that tax avoidance masks the presence of owner-manager rent extraction. Badertscher et al. (2010) suggest that public firms engage in more book-tax non-conforming tax avoidance behavior than private firms, while private firms engage in more book-tax conforming tax avoidance while Rego (2003) demonstrates that multinational corporations with more extensive foreign operations are more tax aggressive.

Limited empirical research has been conducted on tax aggressiveness in China Yanming (2002). To empirically test the impact of ownership structure on tax planning strategies, Zheng and Han (2008) used a sample of private and state-controlled listed companies in China over the period 2002–2005. Their results suggest that state-controlled listed companies tend to put in place conservative tax avoidance behaviours as compared to those of private listed companies.

As this previous research is based on data that predates recent major changes to China's accounting standard and corporate tax regulatory environment, the focus of the study detailed in this chapter is on the impact of these regulatory changes and ownership structure on corporate income tax avoidance behaviour in China.

Hypothesis Development

The regulatory change for this study of corporate income tax avoidance comprises China's introduction in 2008 of the *Enterprise Income Tax Law*, supported by China's 2007 implementation of *Accounting Standards for Business Enterprises No. 18—Corporate Income Tax Accounting*.

Accounting Standards for Business Enterprises No. 18—Corporate Income Tax Accounting specifies changes to the technical accounting standards required for the recognition and measurement of revenue, expenses and losses, and to the recorded differences between financial income-before-tax and taxable income and some of the changes introduced in the 2008 *Enterprise Income Tax Law*, include the income tax rate being lowered to 25 per cent and increased oversight and audit of taxpayers by China's taxation authority.

As the lowering of the tax rate and more stringent tax regulatory environment may reduce the incentives for tax avoidance behaviour, the following hypothesis is made:

Hypothesis 1: As a result of the 'Enterprise Income Tax Law' reforms of 2008, the tax aggressiveness of China's listed companies as measured by the book-tax gap has reduced.

The testing of Hypothesis 1 is achieved by considering changes in the average book-tax gap of China's listed companies between the pre-tax-environment-change period and the post-tax-environment-change period.

Regulatory environment and agency theories underpin this hypothesis consistent with the theoretical predictions of Desai et al. (2007), whereby the level of corporate tax aggressiveness would be affected directly, by the increased costs imposed by the greater scrutiny applied under the new tax regime and indirectly by the resolution of tax-related agency issues that would act to bring tax aggressiveness closer to its optimal level. These effects are expected to be larger for firms with greater pre-existing conflicts of interest related to the tax function that, by assumption, are firms with weak-governance ownership structures (Jimenez-Angueira 2008).

Two aspects of ownership structure are considered in this study. The first is who holds the company's shares, which references the quality of the ownership structure and second is the proportion of shares held by each kind of shareholder, which captures control of the ownership structure (Zheng and Han 2008).

Enterprise firms in China include state-controlled firms, family-owned firms, non-family-owned firms and foreign-invested companies. With reform of shareholder structures and the corporatisation of what were previously state sole proprietorships, both state-controlled and non-state-controlled companies can be publicly listed.

As differences in ownership structure may imply different non-tax costs and lead to different trade-offs in the perceived and actual benefits and costs of tax avoidance activities, the impact of regulatory reforms on the tax aggressiveness of listed companies with different ownership structures will potentially be different. This is particularly likely with the 2008 taxation reforms that unified the previous two systems applied to the taxation of domestic and foreign entities to a common 25 per cent tax rate for all entities.

Thus, the following two hypotheses, one directional and the other non-directional (Chen et al. 2010), are made to test the impact of different ownership structures in China on corporate tax aggressiveness:

Hypothesis 2a: Listed companies with a higher percentage of state-control exhibit a systematically lower level of tax aggressiveness.

Hypothesis 2b: Listed companies with a higher percentage of foreign shares exhibit a systematically different level of tax aggressiveness to companies with a lower percentage of foreign shares.

Consideration of legitimacy and political cost theories support Hypotheses 2a and 2b as state-controlled listed companies in China tend to receive more attention from their stakeholders and so have larger political costs than non-state-controlled listed companies. Accordingly, China's state-controlled and non-state-controlled companies differ in their tax incentives (Chen et al. 2011; Zheng and Han 2008). In particular, tax on a state-controlled company's profits simply reduces the amount of profits otherwise distributable to the government, and therefore, as the tax appears simply to move money from one arm of government's pocket to another, state-controlled companies may be less tax aggressive. Furthermore, sometimes the CEO of a state-controlled company may be given 'credit' for taxes paid, if the government chooses to use that as a measure of how much the state-controlled company contributes to society. The effect of each of these factors is to reduce incentives for the state-controlled company to engage in tax avoidance behaviour.

On the other hand, non-state-controlled companies are likely to be more tax aggressive because their focus is more on maximising (private) shareholders' value. Accordingly, privately-controlled listed companies may be expected to undertake more aggressive tax avoidance than state-controlled listed companies (Zheng and Han 2008).

For foreign-invested listed companies in China, the 2008-income-tax reform progressively removed the previous preferential tax treatment that applied to them. However, the direction of any impact on their tax aggressiveness is difficult to predict *a priori*. Given differences in corporate culture, business philosophy and other issues, it is not clear whether foreign-invested firms will be more or less tax aggressive than domestic firms. Although the benefits of tax aggressiveness could be expected to be higher for foreign-invested companies' owners than for owners in domestic firms, the political costs may also be higher given the need for official cooperation to ensure the success of many foreign-invested activities.

Sample and Research Design

Data Collection

Annual company financial reports and financial reporting information for the years 2007–2010 provide the data collected from OSIRIS (developed by Bureau van Dijk, a comprehensive database of listed companies, banks and insurance companies around the world), supplemented by data from CSMAR (developed by Shenzhen GuoTaiAn Information Technology Company Limited (GTA) in China) and from OneSource.

An audit of the collected data was undertaken. Where inconsistencies between the data presented in OSIRIS and original Chinese source material (e.g., annual reports) was determined, a manual collection of additional data was undertaken and the data set corrected. Inconsistencies mainly reflected the presence in the primary database of versions of annual reports that use Hong Kong accounting standards for companies listed both in Hong Kong and on one of the mainland China exchanges. In this situation, data from the mainland version of the annual report was used to ensure consistency with the remaining company data.

Additional information was derived from the following financial and economic websites: China Stock Markets (http://www.hkex.com.hk/eng/index.htm), Shanghai Stock Exchange (SHSE) (http://www.sse.com.cn), Shenzhen Stock Exchange (SZSE) (http://www.szse.cn), Chinese Listed Companies Information (http://www.cnlist.com), Juchao Information (http://cninfo.com.cn). China Infobank, a web-based online service providing Chinese news, business and legal information (Shan 2009).

Sample Selection

The choice of 2007–2010 as the sample period reflects requirements for China's listed companies to adopt in 2007 The *Accounting Standards for*

Business Enterprises No. 18—Corporate Income Tax Accounting, and from 2008 to operate under the new *Enterprise Income Tax Law*. Accordingly, to conduct comparable analysis, choose proxies and refer to previous international research findings, this study selects and defines the 2007 year as the pre-change tax regulatory environment period and the years 2008–2010 as the post-change tax regulatory environment period.

An original sample of 2,128 listed companies was derived from the current Shanghai Stock Exchange (SHSE) and Shenzhen Stock Exchange (SZSE) for the 2007–2010 period. From the 2,128 companies listed in the original sample, 28 financial service companies were excluded because of differences in the reporting basis and the characteristics of their financial reporting data. Similarly, 167 Special Treatment (ST) and Particular Transfer (PT) listed companies were excluded from the sample as they usually have poor profitability or no profits, so that their income-tax expense behaviour is unlikely to be consistent with that of profitable companies.

The resultant panel data sample set comprised matched company observations for the four years within the sample period. However it is unbalanced as some companies were listed after 2008 and data on some variables was missing in some of the periods.

In light of the objective of the study to test the impact of regulatory changes on the tax avoidance behaviour of an identifiable group of companies, it was determined that use of a balanced panel data set rather than the unbalanced panel data set would be appropriate. Thus, observations on firm-years with missing or insufficient data and abnormal values were deleted by removing 676 companies from the unbalanced panel sample.

As companies were classified by ownership structure reflecting the shareholders who have the largest proportion of equity (Jin and Lei 2011), a further 23 companies were excluded from the sample due to the identity of the ultimate controllers not being able to be determined. The remaining 1,224 companies comprised the balanced panel for this study.

Model

To test the hypotheses specified in Section 2.3, the following model has been constructed:

$$PBTD_{it} = + {}_1Postreg_t + {}_2State_t + {}_3Foreign_t + {}_4Postreg_t \times State_t$$
$$+ {}_5Postreg_t \times Foreign_t + {}_6PP\&E_{it} + {}_7INTA_{it} + {}_8Salesgr_{it}$$
$$+ {}_9OCF_{it} + {}_{10}R\&D_{it} + {}_{11}Leverage_{it} + {}_{12}TA_{it} + {}_{it} + {}_{it} \tag{1}$$

Dependent Variable (PBTD): Measurement of Tax Aggressiveness

Several measures of tax aggressiveness have been utilised in previous research. Considering the Chinese environment and based on previous research studies on China, this study uses the permanent book-tax difference/gap *(PBTD)* as the dependent variable.

Prior research (Rego and Wilson 2009; Shevlin 2001; Weisbach 2001) has shown that temporary book-tax differences reflect earnings management via pre-tax accruals (e.g., Hanlon 2005; Phillips et al. 2003) and that permanent book-tax differences are more reliable in measuring tax aggressiveness than total or overall book-tax differences (Khurana and Moser 2009). Therefore, consistent with Frank et al. (2008), Rego and Wilson (2009), and Khurana and Moser (2009) this study measures and calculates the permanent book-tax difference *(PBTD)* as follows:

$$PBTD_{it} = \frac{\left(BI_{it} - \dfrac{CTE_{it}}{STR} - \dfrac{DTE_{it}}{STR} \right)}{Assets_{it-1}} \tag{2}$$

The permanent book-tax difference *(PBTD)* is equal to the firm's pre-tax book income *(BI)* less an estimate of taxable income derived from current tax expense *(CTE)* grossed-up by the statutory corporate tax rate *(STR)* and deferred tax expense *(DTE)* grossed-up by the statutory corporate tax rate *(STR)*. The measure of permanent book-tax differences is scaled by beginning-period total assets *(Assets)*.

Independent Variables

The following independent variables identify characteristics of tax regulatory environment changes and ownership structure:

PostΔreg: To identify the impact of the 2008 changes of China's tax regulatory environment on corporate tax aggressiveness in light of the association with the accounting standards changes introduced in 2007, the sample was restricted to periods 2007–2010 divided into two parts, comprising the pre-tax-environment-change period (year 2007), and the post-tax-environment-change period (years 2008–2010).

As the new accounting standards and new income-tax law increased enforcement by China's taxation administration, by assumption, the pre-tax-environment-change period with lower tax regulation and enforcement is a period during which corporate tax aggressiveness is expected to be relatively high whereas the post-tax-environment-change period with high-tax regulation and enforcement is one where firms' incentives and intentions to engage in tax aggressive behaviour will be reduced. Accordingly, the empirical model uses the coefficient on 'PostΔreg', a dummy variable equal to one for the post-tax-environment-change period (years 2008–2010) and 0 otherwise, to capture the main effects of these tax environment changes.

State: It is arguably difficult to classify a state-controlled listed company in China. According to the *Corporation Law* in China, state-controlled listed companies are defined as those companies directly or indirectly owned or controlled by state asset-management bureaus or by other state-owned companies controlled by the Central Government or by local governments holding more than 50 per cent of shares, or by local governments holding less than 50 per cent of the shares but having real controlling rights or a significant impact on the Board of Directors.

On the other hand, listed non-state-owned companies are defined as those companies controlled by private investors, excluding township-village enterprises whose ultimate controlling shareholder cannot be identified (Zheng and Han 2008). Although La Porta et al. (1999) specify that an ultimate controlling shareholder can be identified via the pyramid shareholding structure, this is not easy, especially in the Chinese context (Liu and Sun 2003). Accordingly, following previous studies, the empirical model of this study specifies the type and level of state ownership control of the company by the variable '*State*' as the proportion of shares identified as held by the state.

Foreign: As with the definition of a state-controlled corporation, the classification of foreign-invested listed companies is also complicated. According to the classification by the State Administration of Industry and Commerce (SAIC), foreign direct investment in China is divided into four categories: Sino-foreign equity joint venture, Sino-foreign co-operative joint venture (set up with a contractual relationship where profits are distributed according to agreements rather than by proportion of shares); wholly foreign-owned enterprises; and foreign-funded companies limited by shares.

Generally speaking, listed companies in China are those corporations whose shares can be publicly circulated on stock exchanges after approval by the China Securities Regulatory Commission. In practice, wholly foreign-controlled enterprises are not permitted to be listed on China's stock exchanges, whereas joint ventures whose controlling shareholders are not foreign investors can be listed on China's two stock exchanges as foreign-invested listed companies.

China's foreign-invested listed companies are of two types—B-share corporations which are listed on China's stock exchanges and issue shares for foreign investors; and those listed on overseas stock exchanges in the form of H-share (Hong Kong) and N-share (New York) corporations. Unlike direct investments (such as Sino-foreign equity joint ventures, Sino-foreign co-operative joint ventures, wholly foreign-owned enterprises and foreign-funded companies limited by shares) these two types of listed companies are indirect foreign investments. Foreign investors who buy shares in these companies are only general subscribers to the issued tradable shares and are not permitted to appoint representatives to participate in company operations and management. Also, due to the high liquidity and free transferring of these issued shares, foreign shareholders change frequently even though the proportion of foreign shares in the registered capital of these enterprises remains stable. Accordingly, the empirical model in this study uses the variable *'Foreign'* to reflect the proportion of the company's shares held by foreign investors.

Other Measures and Control Variables

In Equation 1, the coefficient on *Post∆reg* indicates the average effect of the recent tax environment changes on the level of tax aggressiveness as measured by the book-tax difference (*PBTD*). A negative coefficient would suggest that, on an average, the regulatory changes have been effective in curbing tax aggressiveness in the post-tax-environment change period. On the other hand, a positive coefficient would indicate that, on an average, changes in the tax regulatory environment did not control the level of tax aggressiveness in the short period following the time at which the tax environment changes took place (Jimenez-Angueira 2008).

Furthermore, the coefficient on *State* is used to test for a significant relationship between the level of tax aggressiveness and the percentage of state-controlled shares and the coefficient on *Foreign* is used to test for a significant relationship between the level of tax aggressiveness and the percentage of foreign-invested shares.

Consistent with Jimenez-Angueira (2008), a set of control variables are included in the regression model of tax aggressiveness to isolate the effect of the tax regulatory environment changes from other confounding factors. Accordingly, Equation 1 includes the following variables to control for differences between accounting requirements and tax statutes:

PP&E (property, plant & equipment): To control for differences in depreciation schedules set by tax regulations and by managers' judgement based on accounting requirements (Jimenez-Angueira 2008). *PP&E* should be positively associated with *PBTD*.

INTA (intangible assets): To control differences in the tax and financial reporting treatment of intangibles, including goodwill, and is expected to be positively associated with *PBTD*.

Salesgr (sales growth): To control for revenue-recognition timing differences between the tax statute and accounting requirements and should exhibit a positive relationship with *PBTD*.

OCF (operating cash flow): To control the firms' profitability and should be positively associated with *PBTD* because more profitable firms potentially have a greater incentive to engage in tax avoidance activities.

R&D (research & development): To control the double impact that qualified R&D activities have on the firm's taxable income due to their deductibility and the availability of the R&D credit (Gupta and Newberry 1997; Hanlon et al. 2007) and should be positively associated with *PBTD*.

Leverage: To control the effect of the firm's financing decisions on tax avoidance. A positive association between leverage and *PBTD* would be consistent with highly leveraged firms benefiting from interest expense deductions relative to their counterparts. Alternatively, a negative association between leverage and *PBTD* would be consistent with firms using long-term debt as a substitute for other tax planning alternatives (Graham and Tucker 2006).

TA (total assets): Measured as the natural log of total assets is included to control the effect of firm size on tax aggressiveness. A positive coefficient on *TA* would indicate a positive association between tax aggressiveness and firm size, which would be consistent with the findings of Mills et al. (2002) that larger firms exhibit larger book-tax differences and with the argument that larger firms have greater economies of scale in terms of tax planning (Rego 2003). Alternatively, a negative coefficient on *TA* would be consistent with the political cost hypothesis, which suggests that larger and more successful firms are more visible and subject to greater public scrutiny (Watts and Zimmerman 1986).

Finally, interaction variables *PostΔreg×State* and *PostΔreg×Foreign* are included to assess whether there are differences between the pre-tax-environment-change period and post-tax-environment-change period results due to firm ownership characteristics.

Two measures of the correlation (Spearman and Pearson) between the independent variables were calculated and as no correlation coefficient between the independent variables is greater than 0.8, and the calculated Variance Inflation Factors (VIFs) are relatively low (smaller than 10), it can be concluded that serious multicollinearity problems are unlikely to be present in the regression model specified in Equation 1.

Results and Discussion

This study uses pooled OLS (Model 1) and panel fixed-effects (Model 2) panel data regression techniques. The results of the Hausman test with a p-value less than 0.05 indicate that a fixed-effects model (Model 2) is preferred over the alternative of a random effects model.

Regression Analysis

The regression results for the pooled OLS (Model 1) and the panel fixed-effects (Model 2) models are summarised in Table 1.

Table 1. Regression results for *PBTD* as dependent variable (N = 4,896).

Variables	Expected sign	Model (1): Panel OLS	Model (2): Panel fix-effects
PostDreg	–	–0.0140***	–0.0072**
		(–5.20)	(–3.03)
State	–	–0.0149*	–0.0113
		(–2.19)	(–1.57)
Foreign	+/–	0.0280*	0.0139
		(2.17)	(0.66)
State×PostΔreg		0.0049	0.0018
		(0.61)	(0.27)
Foreign×PostΔreg	–	–0.0337*	–0.0357**
		(-2.22)	(–2.78)
PP&E	+	0.0238***	0.0473***
		(8.21)	(11.47)
INTA	+	–0.0070	0.0028
		(–0.93)	(0.28)
Salesgr	+	0.0009**	0.0004
		(3.39)	(1.52)
OCF	+	0.0922***	0.0728***
		(14.73)	(11.09)
R&D	+	0.5381***	0.5686**
		(4.10)	(2.96)
Leverage	+/–	–0.0726***	–0.0984***
		(–15.92)	(–9.11)
TA	+/–	0.0049***	–0.0145***
		(4.42)	(–6.46)
Constant		–0.0188	0.3671***
		(–1.26)	(7.61)
F(12,4883)	69.49		
Prob > F	0.0000		
R-squared	0.1459		
Adj.-R-squared	0.1438		
		sigma_u	0.0447
		sigma_e	0.0447
		rho	0.5007
		F(123,3660) u_i = 0	2.87
		Prob > F	0.0000

t statistics in parentheses. $^*p < 0.05$, $^{**}p < 0.01$, $^{***}p < 0.001$

Both the Adjusted-R^2 and the F-statistics for each of the models suggest that the independent variables are able to provide statistically significant information about tax aggressiveness as captured in the chosen measure (*PBTD*). Furthermore, the significant *t*-statistics with a negative sign for *Post∆reg* for both Model 1 and Model 2 suggest a significant negative relationship between tax aggressiveness and the post-tax-environment-change period (*Post∆reg*).

Accordingly, Hypothesis 1: *As a result of the 'Enterprise Income Tax Law' reforms of 2008, the tax aggressiveness of China's listed companies as measured by the book-tax gap measure has reduced* is supported.

This result is consistent with the regulatory environment and agency theories that in the post-tax-environment-change period the level of tax aggressiveness would be reduced directly through the increased costs imposed on companies by the new tax regime, and indirectly by the resolution of tax-related agency issues bringing tax aggressiveness closer to its optimal level.

In relation to Hypothesis 2a: *Listed companies with a higher percentage of state-control exhibit a systematically lower level of tax aggressiveness* and Hypothesis 2b: *Listed companies with a higher percentage of foreign shares exhibit a systematically different level of tax aggressiveness to companies with a lower percentage of foreign shares*, the results of Model 1 provide a statistically significant difference in the level of tax avoidance for firms with higher levels of state-control (*State*) and for firms with foreign-invested ownership (*Foreign*). However, as the coefficients on the *State* and *Foreign* variables in Model 2 are not statistically significant, both Hypothesis 2a and Hypothesis 2b are rejected.

Even though there was a lack of statistically significant differences in the tax aggressiveness of firms with different ownership structures, the negative sign of the coefficients on *State* in both Model 1 and Model 2 indicate that the tax aggressiveness of firms with a higher percentage of state control is less than for firms with a lower percentage of stage control. This is consistent with the findings of other studies using data from an earlier period and under different accounting standards and tax regime requirements (Chen et al. 2011; Zheng and Han 2008). Additionally, the statistically insignificant coefficient on the interaction variable *Post∆reg×State* supports the view that the relationship between these firms and the state minimises the incentives for the firms' management to engage in aggressive tax avoidance behaviour.

In the case of Hypothesis 2b, the 2008 enterprise income-tax law removal of preferential tax structures for foreign-invested listed companies was expected to have a significant impact on their tax avoidance behaviour in the post-tax-environment-change period. While the coefficient on *Foreign* is not statistically significant, the coefficient on the interaction variable *PostΔreg×Foreign* is statistically significant. This suggests that foreign-invested listed companies did reduce their level of tax avoidance behaviour in the post-tax-environment-change period.

Robustness Check

To provide a robustness test of the *PBTD* measure of tax aggressiveness detailed above, the Desai-Dharmapala Book-tax difference (gap) *(DDBTD)* measure of tax aggressiveness was used with the following model.

$$DDBTD_{it} = + {}_1Postreg_t + {}_2State_t + {}_3Foreign_t + {}_4Postreg_t{\times}State_t$$
$$+ {}_5Postreg_t{\times}Foreign_t + {}_6PP\&E_{it} + {}_7INTA_{it} + {}_8Salesgr_{it}$$
$$+ {}_9OCF_{it} + {}_{10}R\&D_{it} + {}_{11}Leverage_{it} + {}_{12}TA_{it} + {}_{it} + {}_{it} \tag{3}$$

The Desai-Dharmapala Book-tax difference (gap) *(DDBTD)* is the residual from a regression of the Manzon-Plesko book-tax difference on total accruals. As the book-tax difference can be a result of both earnings management and tax planning, the Desai-Dharmapala measure removes, at least partially, the book-tax difference caused by earnings management activities (Chen et al. 2010). To quantify the degree to which earnings management is responsible for the gap, Desai and Dharmapala's (2006) approach was adopted to isolate the component of total book-tax difference (BT_{it}) that is attributable to earnings management by using data on accruals by the following ordinary least squares (OLS) regression.

$$BT_{it} = {}_1TACC + {}_{it} + {}_{it} \tag{4}$$

Where, BT_{it} is book–tax gap for firm i in year t, scaled by the lagged value of assets; $TACC_{it}$ is total accruals for firm *i* in year *t*, scaled by the lagged value of assets. The residual from this regression (the component of BT_{it} that cannot be explained by variations in total accruals, and hence by earnings management) can be interpreted as a measure of tax aggressive activity. This study denotes this residual book-tax gap by $DDBTD_{it}$, where:

$$DDBTD_{it} = {}_{it} + {}_{it} \tag{5}$$

The results of regressions in the robustness check using *DDBTD* are consistent with the results reported in Table 1 using *PBTD* as the dependent variable.

Conclusions

Existing research has often examined corporate tax avoidance behaviour from an agency perspective focussing on manager incentives and the impact of internal governance mechanisms. Much of this previous research has a US focus and to date, studies of tax avoidance in countries in transition to a market-oriented economy are limited. It is in this context that this study, by examining a significant tax regulatory change in China, contributes to research and literature on corporate tax avoidance behaviour in major transition economies.

Guided by agency, effective tax planning and tax avoidance theories, this study uses a balanced panel data sample derived from 1,224 companies listed from 2007–2010 on China's Shanghai and Shenzhen Stock Exchanges to examine the impact of a major change in 2008 of China's tax regime on corporate tax avoidance behaviour. The period 2007–2010 was chosen for the study as it provided a 'natural experiment platform' comprising consistent accounting regulation following the introduction in 2007 of the *Accounting Standards for Business Enterprises No. 18—Corporate Income Tax Accounting* and a major tax regulatory change following the implementation in 2008 of the new *Enterprise Income Tax Law*. The impact on tax avoidance behaviour from different ownership structures (state-controlled, private and foreign-invested) of the sampled companies was also examined.

An important implication can be drawn from the results of this study. The reduction in the level of tax aggressiveness of listed companies in China after the introduction of the 2008 *Enterprise Income Tax Law* reforms indicates the potential for transition economy (and other) governments to significantly reduce the level of corporate tax avoidance by the implementation of appropriate changes to tax law, accounting and enforcement regulations. By encouraging greater compliance with the corporate taxation system, reductions in avoidance improve the sustainability of the government's revenue base. The study also found some support for different ownership structures and therefore, potentially, differences in governance and group incentives influencing the level of tax avoidance behaviour. Although consistent with Zheng and Han (2008) who used data from a period before the 2007 accounting and 2008 tax regime changes in China, this support must be treated with some caution as the coefficients on a majority of the ownership structure variables were not statistically significant. This leads to the final implication of the study that further research of the impact of corporate ownership structure and tax avoidance behaviour in transition economies like China is warranted.

References

Avi-Yonah, R.S. (2008). Corporate social responsibility and strategic tax behaviour. pp. 183–198. *In*: Schön, W. (ed.). Tax and Corporate Governance. Vol. 3, Springer: Berlin Heidelberg.

Badertscher, B., Katz, S.P. and Rego, S.O. (2010). The impact of private equity ownership on portfolio firms corporate tax planning. Working Paper, Harvard Business School.

Bird, R. and Davis-Nozemack, K. (2016). Tax avoidance as a sustainability problem. Journal of Business Ethics, DOI: 10.1007/s10551-016-3162-2.

Chen, H., Chen, J.Z., Lobo, G.J. and Wang, Y. (2011). Effects of audit quality on earnings management and cost of equity capital: evidence from China. Contemporary Accounting Research 28: 892–925.

Chen, K.P. and Chu, C.Y.C. (2005). Internal control versus external manipulation: a model of corporate income tax evasion. RAND Journal of Economics 36: 151–164.

Chen, S., Chen, X., Cheng, Q. and Shevlin, T. (2010). Are family firms more tax aggressive than non-family firms? Journal of Financial Economics 95: 41–61.

Crocker, K.J. and Slemrod, J. (2005). Corporate tax evasion with agency costs. Journal of Public Economics 89: 1593–1610.

Desai, M.A. (2003). The divergence between book and tax income. Tax Policy and the Economy 17: 169–206.

Desai, M.A. and Dharmapala, D. (2006). Corporate tax avoidance and high-powered incentives. Journal of Financial Economics 79: 145–179.

Desai, M.A. and Dharmapala, D. (2009). Corporate tax avoidance and firm value. The Review of Economics and Statistics 91: 537–546.

Desai, M.A., Dyck, A. and Zingales, L. (2007). Theft and taxation. Journal of Financial Economics 84: 591–623.

Dowling, G.R. (2013). The curious case of corporate tax avoidance: is it socially irresponsible? Journal of Business Ethics 124(1): 1–12.

European Commission. (2016). Commission proposes major corporate tax reform for the EU, Press release, Strasbourg, 25 October 2016, accessed 25 May 2017, http://europa.eu/rapid/press-release_IP-16-3471_en.htm.

Frank, M., Lynch, L. and Rego, S. (2008). Does aggressive financial reporting accompany aggressive tax reporting (and vice versa). Working Paper, University of Virginia.

Graham, J.R. and Tucker, A.L. (2006). Tax shelters and corporate debt policy. Journal of Financial Economics 81: 563–594.

Hanlon, M. (2005). The persistence and pricing of earnings, accruals, and cash flows when firms have large book-tax differences. The Accounting Review 80: 137–166.

Hanlon, M. and Heitzman, S. (2010). A review of tax research. Journal of Accounting and Economics 50(2): 127–178.

Hanlon, M., Mills, L.F. and Slemrod, J. (2007). An empirical examination of corporate tax compliance. In: Averbach, A., Hines, J. Jnr. and Slemrod, J. (eds.). Taxing Corporate Income in the 21st Century. Cambridge, Cambridge University Press.

Hanlon, M. and Slemrod, J. (2009). What does tax aggressiveness signal? Evidence from stock price reactions to news about tax shelter involvement. Journal of Public Economics 93: 126–141.

Chun Keung Hoi, C.K., Wu, Q. and Zhang, H. (2013). Is Corporate Social Responsibility (CSR) associated with tax avoidance? Evidence from irresponsible CSR activities. The Accounting Review 88(6): 2025–2059.

Jensen, M.C. and Meckling, W.H. (1976). Theory of the firm: managerial behavior, agency costs and ownership structure. Journal of Financial Economics 3: 305–360.

Jimenez-Angueira, C.E. (2008). Tax aggressiveness, tax environment changes, and corporate governance. Doctoral dissertation, University of Florida.

Jin, X. and Lei, G.Y. (2011). Audit supervision, property of ultimate controller and tax aggressiveness. Auditing Research 5: 98–105.

Khurana, I.K. and Moser, W.J. (2009). Shareholder investment horizons and tax aggressiveness. Working paper, University of Missouri.

Kim, J.-B., Li, Y. and Zhang, L. (2011). Corporate tax avoidance and stock price crash risk: firm-level analysis. Journal of Financial Economics 100: 639–662.

Laguira, I., Stagliano, R. and Elbaz, J. (2015). Does corporate social responsibility affect corporate tax aggressiveness? Journal of Cleaner Production 107: 662–675.

Levi, M. (1988). Of rule and revenue. Los Angeles: University of California Press.

Liu, G.S. and Sun, P. (2003). Identifying ultimate controlling shareholders in Chinese public corporations: an empirical survey. Working Paper 2, Royal Institute of International Affairs, United Kingdom.

Martinez, L.P. (1994). Taxes, morals, and legitimacy. Brigham Young University Law Review 1994(3): 541–569.

Mehrotra, A.K. (2015). Reviving fiscal citizenship. Michigan Law Review 113: 943–971.

Mills, L.F. (1998). Book-tax differences and Internal Revenue Service adjustments. Journal of Accounting Research 36: 343–356.

Moore, J. (2007). Do board and/or audit committee independence affect tax reporting aggressiveness? Working Paper, Arizona State University.

Phillips, J., Pincus, M. and Rego, S.O. (2003). Earnings management: new evidence based on deferred tax expense. Accounting Review 78: 491–521.

Phillips, J.D. (2003). Corporate tax-planning effectiveness: the role of compensation-based incentives. Accounting Review 78: 847–874.

Rego, S.O. (2003). Tax-avoidance activities of U.S. multinational corporations. Contemporary Accounting Research 20: 805–833.

Rego, S. and Wilson, R. (2009). Executive compensation, tax reporting aggressiveness, and future firm performance. Working paper, University of Iowa.

Rego, S. and Wilson, R. (2010). Executive compensation, equity risk incentives, and corporate tax aggressiveness. Unpublished paper, University of Iowa.

Rego, S.O. and Wilson, R. (2012). Equity risk incentives and corporate tax aggressiveness. Journal of Accounting Research 50: 775–810.

Richardson, G. and Lanis, R. (2007). Determinants of the variability in corporate effective tax rates and tax reform: evidence from Australia. Journal of Accounting and Public Policy 26: 689–704.

Rohaya, M.N., NorAzam, M. and Barjoyai, B. (2008). Corporate effective tax rates: a study on Malaysian public listed companies. Malaysian Accounting Review 7: 1–20.

Sari, D. and Tjen, C. (2016). Corporate social responsibility disclosure, environmental performance, and tax aggressiveness. International Research Journal of Business Studies 9(2): 93–104.

Scholes, M., Wolfson, M.A., Erikson, M., Maydew, E. and Sehvlin, T. (1992). Taxes and Business Strategy. Englewood Cliffs, NJ: Prentice-Hall.

Scholes, M.S., Wilson, G.P. and Wolfson, M.A. (1990). Tax planning, regulatory capital planning, and financial reporting strategy for commercial banks. Review of Financial Studies 3: 625–650.

Shan, Y.G. (2009). Corporate Disclosures of Related-party Relationships and Transactions in China: Agency, Governance, Legitimacy and Signalling Influences. Doctoral dissertation. University of South Australia.

Shevlin, T. (2001). Corporate tax shelters and book-tax differences. Tax Law Review 55: 427.

Slemrod, J.B. (2004). The Economics of Corporate Tax Selfishness. Cambridge, Mass., USA: National Bureau of Economic Research.

The Economist. (2016). Simple, independent and multinational; another trilemma: International tax avoidance, April 6, 2016.

Urdangarin, J. and Vanderbeek, B. (2015). 6 Reasons to respond to the Dow Jones sustainability index survey. GreenBiz. Accessed 25 May 2017, http://www.greenbiz.com/article/six-reasons-respond-dow-jones-sustainability-index-survey.

Wang, Y. (2002). The sensitivity analysis of the changes of Chinas corporate income tax rate for listed companies. Economy Research 009: 74–80.

Weisbach, D.A. (2001). Ten truths about tax shelters. Tax Law Review 55: 215.

Wilson, R.J. (2007). An Examination of Corporate Tax Shelter Participants. Doctoral dissertation, University of Washington.

Woellner, R.H., Barkoczy, S., Murphy, S., Evans, C. and Pinto, D. (2010). Australasian Taxation Law. 17th edition. Sydney: CCH.

Wu, L. and Li, C. (2007). Tax return policy for the corporate income tax and the effectiveness of tax policy. China Social Science 4: 61–73.

Yanming, W. (2002). A sensitivity analysis of income tax rate changes on listed companies. Economic Research Journal 9: 74–80.

Zheng, H.X. and Han, M.F. (2008). Different tax planning behaviour based on ownership structure of listed companies—the empirical evidence from Chinese state-owned listed companies and private listed companies. China Soft Science 9: 122–131.

Index